The first and second editions of *The Dead Sea Scriptures* have been praised as classics in their field:

"Dr. Gaster's book is excellent: there is nothing available in book form which covers the ground so thoroughly and with such restraint. Both his comments and the translation of the Hebrew documents are written in superb English, which is a pleasure to read . . . a masterly production, which can safely be put into the hands of laymen in the field."

> W. F. ALBRIGHT
> Johns Hopkins University

"It furnishes the most complete translations yet to be published together with Gaster's introductions and notes. The book is addressed to the intelligent general reader. Actually, as all who know Prof. Gaster could predict, it contains a wealth of original insights drawn from his wide knowledge of Judaism and comparative religion so that the book will prove very useful to the scholar as well."

> FRANK M. CROSS, JR.
> *The Biblical Archaeologist*

"I am tremendously impressed with the quality of the scholarship which it demonstrates. I have read your introduction very carefully and find myself in practically complete agreement . . . in almost every detail."

> JULIAN MORGENSTERN
> Hebrew Union College

"It is a book which I will always have on hand in order to refer to [its] translations. I am very pleased by [his] Introduction, which gives reasonable solutions and rejects the absurd interpretations which have recently been given."

> R. P. DE VAUX
> Director of Excavations, Jerusalem

THEODOR H. GASTER is one of the world's most eminent Hebraists and an expert on the period during which the scrolls were written. Working in twenty-nine languages and dialects, Professor Gaster is the author of many distinguished articles and books on the religions and civilizations of the Ancient Near East. His major work *Thespis* (1950) is a study of the ritual origins of the drama. He is also the author of the standard work *Myth, Legend and Custom in the Old Testament* (1969). Emeritus Professor of Religion at Barnard College—Columbia University, he is currently a member of the faculty and Chairman of the Ancient Near Eastern Study Program at Dropsie University in Philadelphia. He has served as Fulbright professor, History of Religions, at the University of Rome as well as Fulbright professor, Biblical Studies, at the University of Melbourne, Australia. He has been the recipient of two Guggenheim awards. Professor Gaster is also the editor of *The New Golden Bough.*

THE DEAD SEA
SCRIPTURES

In English Translation
With Introduction and Notes by
THEODOR H. GASTER

THIRD EDITION
REVISED AND ENLARGED

Anchor Books
DOUBLEDAY

NEW YORK LONDON TORONTO SYDNEY AUCKLAND

To the Memory of
the Men of Qumran

Ye that did cleave unto the Lord your God
are alive every one of you this day.

DEUTERONOMY 4.4

AN ANCHOR BOOK

PUBLISHED BY DOUBLEDAY

a division of Bantam Doubleday Dell Publishing Group, Inc.
666 Fifth Avenue, New York, New York 10103

ANCHOR BOOKS, DOUBLEDAY, and the portrayal of an anchor
are trademarks of Doubleday, a division of Bantam Doubleday
Dell Publishing Group, Inc.

Library of Congress Cataloging-in-Publication Data
Dead Sea scrolls, English
    The Dead Sea scriptures, in English translation.
    Includes bibliographical references and index.
    I. Gaster, Theodor Herzl, 1906–   II. Title.
BM487.A3G3   1976   221.4   76-2840
ISBN 0-385-08859-0

BVG 01

CONTENTS

PREFACE

The purpose of this book is to provide a complete and reliable translation of the celebrated Dead Sea Scrolls, insofar as the original Hebrew texts have yet been published. Everything that is sufficiently well preserved to make connected sense has been included. Mere fragments, however, have been left out, because there is no point in rendering disjointed (and often incomplete) sentences wrested from their contexts. Furthermore, no translation is offered of the Dead Sea Scroll of Isaiah or of the other more fragmentarily preserved Biblical manuscripts. The contents of the Bible are readily available in English, and the special contribution of the Dead Sea Scrolls in this field is of interest only to scholars.*

This book is addressed to laymen. It is not intended as an independent scholarly contribution to the problem (or problems) of the Scrolls, nor as a survey of, or introduction to, the current controversy about them. It is concerned only with what the Scrolls themselves have to say, not with what has been or is being said about them. The Introduction therefore confines itself to providing background material for an understanding of the documents, but does not venture into any detailed discussion of the various theories that have been advanced concerning their date, the possibility of recognizing historical allusions, and the like.

The present writer holds the view that:

(a) The texts here presented were composed at various dates between about 250 B.C. and 68 A.D.

---

* For the same reason no translation is offered of fragments from known apocryphal and pseudepigraphic works.

(b) They formed part of the library of a religious brotherhood located at Qumran, but not all of them were necessarily composed in the first place by or for members of that community. The latter may simply have adopted them out of a body of traditional literature dealing with that future regenerated House of Israel which they were seeking to create.

(c) The Dead Sea Scrolls and the religious movement which they depict help us to reconstruct the spiritual climate of early Christianity and throw light especially on the mission of John the Baptist and on the constitution of the primitive Church. But the Scrolls contain no anticipation of, or parallel to distinctive Christian doctrines, e.g., Incarnation, Vicarious Atonement or Communion.

(d) The religious brotherhood represented by the Scrolls did *not* believe, as has been supposed, in a martyred Messianic 'Teacher of Righteousness' who reappeared posthumously to his disciples and whose Second Coming was awaited. The title 'Teacher of Righteousness' (more correctly, 'true exponent of the Law') designates an office, not a particular person. The passage of the texts on which the sensational theory has been based has been misunderstood. The writers of the Scrolls indeed looked forward to the advent of a prophetic and priestly Teacher before the Final Era, but this was not the Second Coming of a martyred Christ.

(e) It is unsafe at present to draw historical conclusions from the texts or to speculate about historical allusions in them. Indeed, the latter need not necessarily refer to the vicissitudes of the particular Qumran community.

More than to all the foregoing, however, the writer adheres to the view that the Dead Sea Scrolls should be regarded as something more than the subject matter of a scholarly controversy. For those who will read them sympathetically, they possess value in their own right as conveying the religious message of men who gave up the world and were able to find God in a wilderness, simply because they preferred nakedness to motley and because they realized that, in the larger analysis, crucifixion can itself be resurrection.

The translation of the non-literary documents (e.g., *The Manual of Discipline*) aims to reproduce the original in idiomatic English. The same liberties have been taken in breaking up the sequences of the Hebrew sentences, rendering copulas by punctuation-marks, and the like as would readily be permitted—even expected—in any version of a modern work. These renderings, therefore, while they are not to be regarded as slavish 'ponies', are not mere paraphrases. They stick strictly to the letter of the text, and every word of the original is covered.

The hymns and prayers present a special problem. These are written, by and large, in the style of the Biblical Psalms; but to the composer this style was a conscious archaism, while it fell on the ears of the reciters with the same effect as does the language of the Anglican Prayer-book or the King James Version upon the modern church-goer. The only feasible way of reproducing this effect is to fall back on 'Biblical English'. Readers who may be irritated or impeded by the 'howbeits' and 'whiloms' and the like need only to be reminded that the original reciters were, in all probability, just as much put out by the plethora of rare and recondite words and by the artificial manipulation of Biblical 'tags' in which the authors indulged. But to smooth this out would be to lose the flavor; it would be like trying to make Lyly talk the language of Housman.

As for the other literary texts, my aim has been to bring out not only the overt meanings of words and phrases, as these might be determined in a dictionary, but also their subliminal suggestions and associations. For it scarcely needs pointing out that it is precisely in the conveyance or evocation of these latter that the art of any creative writer really lies. A translator therefore short-changes both author and reader if he does not at least try his best to reproduce tone as well as text. In the present case, this applies especially to the rendering of the commentaries and discourses on passages of Scripture, where at least half of the sense depends on what is read *into* the text, as the complement

of what is read *out of* it. Obviously, this involves a subjective element, but so does all intelligent reading, for
meaning is, in the final analysis, the junction of an author's
statement with a reader's experience and perception. The
translator is, in fact, in much the same position as is a concert artist playing a score; he has to use his ear and heart
as well as his hands; and no two performers will play the
same piece alike. In other words, this book represents my
own understanding of the Scrolls. No one can honestly
produce any other kind of translation of anything.

For the benefit of those who may wish to use this book
alongside of the original texts, I should like to point out
that the translations have been made in all cases from the
facsimile plates, not from the editors' transcriptions. This
means that in a few instances I have read faint traces or
ambiguous spellings somewhat differently.

Then, too, it should be pointed out that in rendering
the innumerable Biblical 'tags' that are interwoven in all
the texts, I have not simply fallen back on the standard
English versions. The original authors often understood
the Scriptural passages in a way quite different from ours,
and more often they deliberately manipulated them to produce effective phrases and tropes. In all cases I have carefully consulted the Ancient Versions (especially the
Aramaic Targum and the Syriac Peshitta) in order, if possible, to recover from those sources traces of the tradition
that the authors may have followed. Not infrequently, this
has provided the clue to expressions that would otherwise
be obscure; but it means that in translating the 'tags' I have
had perforce to render them somewhat unrecognizable to
those brought up on the English Bible. This is especially so
in the case of the Hymns, where the impression that is
made on a reader familiar with the Hebrew Scriptures can
scarcely be reproduced. For even measure, however, I
have cited in the notes all the main Scriptural passages
from which the writers borrowed. The reader must be
warned, nonetheless, that these will have to be turned up
in the Hebrew Bible. (It is for that reason that they are
cited according to the Hebrew rather than the English
numeration.)

Finally, the reader is asked to bear in mind that only a fraction of the material recovered from Qumran has yet been published. All work on these documents is therefore in large measure provisional. Many of us who stand outside the charmed circle of the 'Scrolls team' in Jerusalem deplore the fact that, after nearly twenty years, so relatively little has been made generally available to us, and even more the tendency of those in charge of the texts to publish tantalizing snippets and excerpts, the proposed interpretations of which other scholars cannot control because so much of the context has not yet been revealed to them. One cannot but contrast this with the promptness and rapidity with which the important cuneiform tablets from Ras Shamra or the Hittite texts from Boghazköy are being made available, and regret wistfully that the prevailing policy will, by the hazards of mortality, prevent a whole generation of older scholars from making their contribution. Meanwhile, we can try only to do by our strength whatsoever our hand attaineth to do.

NOTE TO THE THIRD EDITION

Twenty-four more texts, published since the last edition of this book (1964), have now been added,† the renderings of the others further revised, the notes and General Introduction amplified, and the indices enlarged.

The scholarly literature on the Scrolls increases from day to day, and much that was at first obscure is gradually becoming clear. On the other hand, varying theories and 'reconstructions', often premature and fantastic, still abound, and there is a crying need for the interpretation of the texts to be both 'de-mythologized' and de-sensation-

† They are: *The Letter of the Law* (*'Ordinances'*); five fragments from *The Book of Hymns;* six *Poems from a Qumran Hymnal* (i.e., the so-called *Apocryphal Psalms*); *Lament for Zion;* two short compositions here entitled *Hymns of Triumph; Commentary on Psalm 45; The Rout of Belial; Weal and Woe; The Last Jubilee; The Wondrous Child; The Wooing of Wisdom; The Wiles of the Harlot; The Last Words of Amram;* and *The Epochs of Time.* For details concerning these texts (here largely renamed) see the Index of Sources, pp. 541ff.

alized. Nevertheless, I have kept this book to its original purpose, which is to provide a reasonably reliable and literary translation, with only such comment and explication as is minimally necessary to give background and render allusions intelligible to the general reader.‡ This avoids the encumbrance (if also the spice) of technical controversy.

T.H.G.

New York
July 1975

‡ This 'minimum' includes, in some cases, brief explanations of how I have attempted to restore incomplete passages. Such explanations are addressed more especially to readers who are able to follow the original texts and who might otherwise wonder how on earth I 'get it'.

INTRODUCTION

Almost everyone has heard by now of the ancient Hebrew writings that have been found during recent years in caves near the Dead Sea. Almost everyone has been moved by the assertion of scholars that they come from the very community in which 'John the Baptist taught and Jesus learned'. And almost everyone has been intrigued by the much-publicized claim that they reveal to us a long-lost forerunner of Christianity—a sect which believed in a martyred 'Teacher of Righteousness' who would eventually reappear to the faithful. It is, however, one thing to read *about* the Scrolls; quite another to read the texts themselves. This book offers renderings of all the principal and intelligibly preserved documents thus far published, and of a related text (the so-called *'Zadokite' Document*) which was discovered, nearly fifty years ago, in an old synagogue at Cairo and earlier fragmentary copies of which have now turned up in the Dead Sea caves. Moreover, it does not gear these renderings to any particular theory, but allows the documents to raise their own voice and give their own testimony amid the din and hubbub of current controversy about them.

I

We do not yet know for certain who wrote the Dead Sea Scrolls, when and where. Attempts have been made to date them by palaeography—that is, by the form (or forms) of script which they employ—and by detecting in them allusions to known persons or events. Neither method, however, has thus far yielded conclusive results. Palaeography could determine, at best, the time when our actual manuscripts were penned, but not when their contents were originally composed. Moreover, as things are, most of the ancient documents used for purposes of comparison or contrast are themselves of uncertain date, are executed in a wide variety of media (stone, sherds and papyrus) and are the products of widely different environments, so that they scarcely represent a single linear development of Hebrew script. And as to the alleged historical allusions, the difficulty here is that even if the passages in question do indeed possess specific reference, most of them are so vague and ambiguous that they can be pegged with equal plausibility to any number of different persons and events all the way from the third to the first century B.C., if not also slightly later.[1]

To be sure, a useful clue might be afforded by matching special expressions and phrases used in the Scrolls with those found in various pseudepigraphical writings, e.g., the *Book of Enoch* or the *Testaments of the Twelve Patriarchs*. Indeed, in the course of his work the present writer has compiled a virtual concordance of such parallels. Here too, however, great caution must be exercised, for the dates of those works (or of their constituent parts) are, as often as not, themselves disputed.

In these circumstances, it seems best at present to leave in abeyance the question of ultimate origin and to start from the situation that existed at the time the documents were cached in the caves. That situation is that, whenever, wherever and by whomever they may have been composed, they had come to be accepted as the literature or religious repertoire of an ascetic, 'protestant' and 'puritan' Jewish community that lived in the Desert of Judah—more precisely, on the western shore of the Dead Sea—during the early years of the Common Era; that is, in the very area and at the very time in which John the Baptist 'came for witness, that he might bear witness of the light'. It is this fact that gives them today their main interest and importance. They recover for us what may best be de-

scribed as the backdrop of the stage on which the first act
of the Christian drama was performed.

The community of which we have been speaking was
situated in the forbidding ravine of Qumran, at the northern end of the Dead Sea. It was clustered around a central building located about a kilometer away from the cave
in which the principal scrolls were discovered by an Arab
boy in 1947. This building has now been excavated, and
on the evidence of coins found within it, it has been established that it was occupied continuously (except for a
break, due to earthquake, between about 31 B.C. and 5
B.C.) from, approximately, 125 B.C. until 68 A.D. Now this
latter date coincides with the entry into the area of the
Tenth Roman Legion which had been despatched thither
to suppress the First Jewish Revolt. It is therefore a plausible conjecture that the building was abandoned when
the troops drew near, and that the manuscripts of its
library were then cached for safekeeping in the surrounding caves.

The prevailing view of scholars (though there are some
dissident voices) is that the men of Qumran were Essenes
—that is, members of a pietistic brotherhood whose tenets
and practices, as described by the first-century writers
Philo and Josephus, bear a striking resemblance to those
outlined in the Scrolls and who are indeed said by Pliny
the Elder (23–79 A.D.) to have lived in the area at the
period in question.

Here, however, a word of caution is in order. It by no
means follows, because the Scrolls were read and cherished
by the Essenes, that they were all necessarily composed
by them. While this may well be true of the *Hymns of
Thanksgiving* and other liturgical pieces—expressing as they
do the moods and feeling of a living congregation—we
should not immediately jump to the conclusion (as most
scholars have done) that the community whose constitution and doctrines are portrayed in such works as the
Manual of Discipline or the *'Zadokite' Document* was necessarily that of the Essenes or the men of Qumran. In the

present writer's opinion, it is just as possible that the community which is there depicted is an *ideal* one—the ideal regenerated House of Israel which the men of Qumran believed themselves to be or which they at least sought to emulate, these traditional writings serving them at once as authority and model. (References in those works to such characters as the Teacher of Righteousness, the Wicked Priest, and the like would then allude to figures in the history not of the specific Qumran community but of Israel as a whole.) This hypothesis has the added advantage that it enables us to account for the discrepancies as well as the similarities between the beliefs and institutions described in the Scrolls and those associated with the Essenes by Philo and Josephus, for it is not difficult to conceive that the Essenes, constituted under particular conditions and possibly influenced also by other considerations, may sometimes have failed to realize, or been constrained to modify, the archetypal pattern.

Ideal or real as the community of the Scrolls may have been, our prime source of information concerning its basic principles, constitution and practices are the so-called *Book of the Order* (or *Manual of Discipline*) and the complementary *'Zadokite' Document;* while for the beliefs and religious concepts—as evinced by the living congregation at Qumran—we may draw mainly on the more personal and less academic *Book of Hymns* (or *Psalms of Thanksgiving*).

II

We are introduced by these writings to a community which is conceived as the true and ideal Congregation of Israel, the small remnant that has stayed faithful to the traditional Covenant and that is thereby ensuring the continuance of God's people and the eventual cleansing of His land from the stain of guilt. The Covenant, it is held, has been maintained and preserved throughout history only by a succession of such pious 'remnants'.

The members of the community conceive of themselves as repeating in a later age the experience of their remote forefathers in the days of Moses. When they leave the cities and villages and repair to the desert, they picture themselves as going out into the wilderness to receive a new Covenant. What is envisaged, however, is no 'New Testament' in the Christian sense of the term, no abrogation or substitution of the old Covenant, but simply a new affirmation of it. This is in accordance with the traditional Jewish view that the eternal Covenant is periodically reaffirmed and that the Pact concluded at Sinai was itself but a re-articulation of that which God had previously made, in their several generations, with Abraham, Isaac and Jacob.

To emphasize this basic idea and to bring out more clearly its sense of continuity with previous 'remnants', the community is designated in the Scrolls by a series of titles, styles and epithets charged with significant historical associations. It is described, for instance, as 'the elect' or 'rightfully chosen', in reference especially to the election of Israel at Mount Sinai. Its priests are called 'the sons of Zadok', in reference to the foremost priestly family in the time of David (cf. II Sam. 8.17) and to those whom the prophet Ezekiel had designated, in his visions of the future restored Temple, as the only legitimate priests (Ezek. 40.46; 43.19; 44.15; 48.11). Its sojourn in the forbidding desert is portrayed as exile in 'the wilderness of Damascus', thereby dramatizing it as the fulfillment of the prophet Amos' prediction that God would cause His people to 'go into exile beyond Damascus' (Amos 5.27). And it regards itself as the militia of God—a kind of Salvation Army— ready, like its ancestors under Moses and Joshua, to do battle for His name and to drive out the heathen from His land—in this case, from the whole earth. (Indeed, it sometimes calls its adherents 'the volunteers'—a name with distinctly military overtones; and it even drew up an elaborate plan of campaign for 'Armageddon'!)

There is, however, one crucial difference between this community and its remote prototype: it is not waiting to receive the Law; it already possesses it. Its aim is simply to assert that Law, to deliver it from the realm of darkness in which it had become engulfed. The Torah—that is, the Divine Teaching (or Guidance) as revealed to Moses—has, it is held, been successively garbled and perverted by 'false expositors'. The community's main purpose is to exemplify and promulgate the true interpretation. It bases that interpretation on a kind of 'apostolic succession', begun by the prophets and continued by a series of inspired leaders each of whom is known as 'the correct expositor' or 'right-teacher' (*not* 'Teacher of Righteousness', as many scholars have rendered it)—that is, the *orthodox* expounder of the Word.[2] The 'right-teacher' was probably in every case a *priest*,[3] his title being derived from Moses' farewell blessing upon the priestly tribe of Levi: 'They have observed Thy word and kept Thy covenant. They shall *teach* Jacob Thine ordinances, and Israel Thy Law' (Deut. 33.9–10).

Just as Israel has been led of old by these prophets and teachers, so, it is held, a new Prophet and a new Teacher (perhaps, indeed, one and the same person) will arise at the end of the present era to usher in the Golden Age, when the scattered hosts of Israel will be gathered in, a duly anointed high priest and a duly anointed king ('the Messiahs [anointed] of Aaron and Israel') installed, and 'the earth filled with the knowledge of the Lord like the waters which cover the sea'. The concept is derived directly from the words of Moses in Deuteronomy 18.15–18: 'The Lord thy God will raise up unto thee a prophet from the midst of thee, of thy brethren, like unto me; unto him ye shall hearken. . . . The Lord hath said unto me . . . "I will raise them up a prophet from among their brethren, like unto thee; and I will put My words in his mouth, and he shall speak unto them all that I shall command him" '. Indeed, it is significant that on a small fragment found in one of the caves, that very passage heads a list of Scriptural quotations justifying the Messianic ideas of the community, and that it is there associated with the words of Moses' final Blessing which we have just seen to be the source of the technical term, 'teacher'!

III

But even if the Torah be correctly expounded by prophet and teacher, men, it is held, can and will receive it only if they be correctly attuned. And that attunement comes— if we may mix the metaphor—through inner 'enlightenment'. The community considers itself, therefore, not only the remnant of Israel but also the specially 'enlightened'. Over and over again in the *Book of Hymns* thanks are rendered to God for 'illumining the face' of His servant or for shining His light in His servant's heart. The acquisition of that light, however, is not attributed to any sudden, spontaneous act of grace. Rather is it the result of man's own voluntary exercise of that power of discernment which God placed in every creature at the moment of its creation. All things, it is affirmed—even the sun and moon and stars —have been endowed by God with sensate knowledge, though the choice of using it or ignoring it has been left, in the case of man, to his individual will. If he heeds the gift, he achieves harmony with the eternal cosmic scheme and breaks the trammels of his mortality. Automatically, he is embraced in the communion of eternal things; he becomes one with the non-mortal beings of the celestial realm—the 'holy ones' who stand for ever in direct converse with God.

It is this state that the members of the Qumran community claim for themselves. This is the ultimate goal of their entire spiritual adventure; the aim and *raison d'être* of the Torah and of the disciplined life which it enjoins. They hold that by virtue of their 'enlightenment' they are members not only of the consecrated earthly brotherhood but *eo ipso* also of the Eternal Communion. As one of their psalmists puts it, they walk for ever 'in uplands unbounded' and know that 'there is hope for that which is molded of clay to have converse with things everlasting'. This is not, as all too many scholars have supposed, a mere belief in bodily resurrection or a mere hope for the survival of the soul in some cloudland of bliss. Rather is it the sound mystic sense that, given the right spiritual posture, given the victory over that darkness which is set before him along with the light, man may live even on earth in a dimension of eternity.

IV

It would be a mistake to suppose that the writers of the Scrolls and the men of Qumran were inspired only by recollection of things past or that they chose their way of life simply because they were unsettled by political turbulence or disgusted by the venality of the Jerusalemitan priests. They were swept also by other winds. One of these was a widespread and well-attested contemporary belief that the great cycle of the ages was about to complete its revolution. This belief was based on a conception, which can in fact be traced to remote Indian antiquity, that existence consists not in linear progressive development—that is, in 'history'—but in a constant cyclic repetition of primordial and archetypal events. When major upheavals occurred, it was promptly supposed that the cycle was nearing its end, that the Great Year was at hand, and that cosmos was about to revert to chaos. The primal elements, restrained and regulated at the beginning of the world, would again be unleashed; all things would dissolve in an overwhelming deluge or be burned in that everlasting fire which rages in the depths of the earth. Then the cycle would begin again; a new world would be brought to birth.

For men, this theory posed the immediate problem of escape, and Religion answered that problem by the postulate that 'righteousness delivereth from death' and that 'the just shall live by his faith'. There was a sense in which, if he could not be delivered from the body of this death, man could at least be released from the trammels of this life. He could immerse himself in eternal things, divorce himself from the temporal and the mundane and, reversing the old adage, find that in the midst of death he was in fact in life.

The authors of the Scrolls and the men of Qumran lived at a time of such 'cyclic crisis'. It is writ large in the pseudepigraphic literature of the two centuries immediately preceding the Common Era, and its fading echo may be heard in John the Baptist's cry that 'the Kingdom of Heaven is at hand'. It was escape from the inexorable cycle, release not from sin but from mortality, that these men were seeking. The desert to which the Dead Sea brotherhood repaired was not simply the Desert of Judah; it was also the mystic's Desert of Quietude—what John Tauler called 'the Wilderness of Godhead, into which He leads all who are to receive this inspiration of God, now or in eternity'. In that wilderness, they would not merely receive a renewal of the Covenant; they would also have the vision of the Burning Bush. Removed from men, they would acquire an unobstructed view of the divine. Thirsting in an inhospitable wild, they would drink the unfailing waters of God's grace. Shorn of earthly possessions, theirs would be the poverty of the mystics—that poverty which Evelyn Underhill has described as 'complete detachment from all finite things'. Burned by the scorching sun, they would see the *semplice lume* of Dante, the 'infused brightness' of Saint Teresa, and by that light they would not be dazzled. They would achieve an intimacy, a communion with the eternal, unchanging things, such as one can achieve only in a desert or on a sea. And in this experience they would reproduce and concentrate within themselves the drama of the cosmic cycle, the dissolving of the old order and the birth of the new.

It is impossible for anyone who reads the *Book of Hymns* sensitively and sympathetically not to apprehend, behind the cliché-ridden language, the tortuous and barely grammatical sentences, the incessant filching of Scriptural 'tags', the movement of these deep mystic currents; and they too must be taken into account.

In strange juxtaposition with such rarefied speculations, however, these men also take a severely practical view of what is going to happen when the time for the world's renewal falls due. Even if individual men escape the impending doom, general doom there still will be, and a good deal of evil will still remain to be destroyed. The destruction will come by means of a forty years' war waged by 'the sons of light',[4] aided by the celestial hosts,[5] against 'the sons of darkness'. In three campaigns they will win; in three, lose. At last, at the seventh encounter, God will triumph over Belial. This will be the Day of Vengeance. Thereafter all things will be renewed.[6] The Era of Divine Favor[7] (in contrast to the Era of Wrath)[8] will be ushered in. God's light will shine sevenfold strong.[9] He will reaffirm the Covenant with the faithful, and engrave His Law on their hearts.

V

Concerning the practical organization of the community, we are particularly well-informed both by the *Manual of Discipline* and by the so-called *'Zadokite' Document*.

Children are to undergo a ten-year period of study in the provisions and institutions of the Covenant and in a manual known as the *Book of Study*. At twenty years of age, they become eligible for membership. Every candidate is to be examined publicly regarding his intellectual capacity and his moral character. If he passes the test, he undergoes a year's probation, but is permitted no share in the community's resources nor is he admitted to the common table. At the end of the probationary year, he comes up again for review. If his conduct be deemed satisfactory, he then serves a further probation of one year within the community itself. He has to place all his property in trust with an 'overseer', but he himself is not yet permitted to enjoy the resources of the group or to dine with them. Only after this second year can he become fully enrolled, and then only by general vote, and after swearing an oath of allegiance.

No one under twenty-five may occupy a communal office, and no one under thirty can be reckoned as head of a family or hold rank in the community's military establishment.

The supreme authority in all doctrinal and economic matters is vested in the priests, assisted by the levites. In any group of ten men, if one of them happens to be a priest, he is not to move to another place, and every such group is to have an 'expounder of the law' to whom reference can be made at any time of day or night.

There is a general 'council' to which any member of the community may be elected. This serves as a kind of parliament for purposes of deliberation, but it does not determine matters of doctrine, which are left to the priests.

For administrative purposes, there is also a kind of presbytery, consisting of three priests and twelve especially qualified laymen—an imitation, no doubt, of the priestly triumvirate of Aaron, Eleazar and Ithamar (Num. 3.4) and of the twelve leaders of the tribes associated with Moses (Num. 1.4–16; Deut. 1.13–15). These 'presbyters' are known as 'the men of (special) holiness', and they have to undergo a two-year period of training before appointment.

Every member of the community is assigned a special rank, which is reviewed from year to year, promotions or demotions being determined by general vote. It may be questioned, however, whether such rank is really a matter of individual status rather than of class. At all events, we hear in the documents of clear distinctions between priests, 'men of (special) holiness', 'dignitaries' (literally, 'men of repute'), 'men eligible for summons to the assembly', and 'heads of families'. Moreover, there is frequent reference to admission to, or rejection from, 'the purity', and this would seem, in the various contexts, to refer most naturally to the different degrees or levels of purity credited to various strata within the total group. Josephus, it may be observed, speaks of four such degrees as having been recognized among the Essenes.

All goods and wages are placed in a common pool, administered by an 'overseer' or 'superintendent'. A similar officer presides over the allocation of communal tasks and duties.

Members of the community dine together, the food being first blessed by the priest. Everyone sits in order of rank or class, the priest occupying first place. They also meet together regularly for prayer and study, and are obliged to spend one third of all the nights of the year in such spiritual exercise.

Breaches of the rules are punished by temporary ostracism and exclusion from normal rations of food. Repeated offenses, or acts amounting to repudiation of the basic Covenant, entail irrevocable expulsion.

A quorum of ten appears to be required, in accordance with normal Jewish practice, in order to constitute a 'congregation' or conventicle. Members of the community are encouraged to discuss matters of law and doctrine for their mutual instruction and edification, but they are forbidden to indulge in theological disputation with 'disreputable persons' (literally, 'men of corruption')—that is, to all intents and purposes, with outsiders.

To form an idea of the temper and complexion of this strange community, as it was evidently exemplified at Qumran, one could scarcely do better than to compare it with the Waldensian Brotherhood as described (albeit with an overtone of polemic) by Bernard Gui in the early fourteenth century. From the viewpoint of religious psychology, the comparison is, indeed, both arresting and illuminating.

In both cases we have a group in revolt against the doctrinal degeneration and material venality of the established 'church', and in both cases the dissent takes the form not of innovation or reformulation but of a return to the true but corrupted 'apostolic' tradition.

In both cases, the dissenters constitute not merely a spiritual fellowship of faith, but a concrete social organism. The Waldenses, like the Dead Sea Covenanters, 'eat and drink at common meals'. They do not own private property, but, on admission to the sect, 'sell all they possess and give the price to the common fund'.

They hold annual conventions for the transaction of communal affairs, just as the *Manual of Discipline* prescribes annual 'reviews'. The more advanced members of the sect are called 'the perfect'—exactly like 'the men of perfect conduct' of the *Manual*, and, like them, they serve as guides, preachers and 'apostles' of the sect.

Members of the brotherhood are forbidden to lie or to swear oaths. They call themselves 'the poor', a name which recalls the fact that in the Aramaic dialect of the early Palestinian Christians—that is, the same dialect as would have been spoken at Qumran—the word for 'poor' also bore the specific sense of 'ascetic'.

Finally, the Waldenses claimed to be the most ancient of all Christian sects, 'going back to the time of the early Fathers'; and to this we may find a telling parallel in Philo's statement that 'our lawgiver Moses formed countless disciples into a fellowship called Essenes'.

VI

Having now reviewed the basic ideas of the Scrolls, and the beliefs and institutions of the Qumran brotherhood, we are ready to answer the burning question: *Do these documents restore to us a long-lost forerunner of Christianity?*

The answer is, Yes and No.

Yes, in the sense that they furnish a picture of the religious and cultural climate in which John the Baptist conducted his mission and in which Jesus was initially reared. They portray for us, in vivid but authentic colors, the environment whose spiritual idiom John and Jesus spoke, whose concepts they developed and transmuted and whose religious ideas served largely as the seedbed of the New Testament. They also mirror a form of religious organization many elements of which were adopted by the primitive Church.

No, in the sense that what we have in these documents and in the Qumran community is, as it were, but the rude clay as yet unmolded by Christian hands. The Scrolls contain no trace of any of the cardinal theological concepts—the incarnate Godhead, Original Sin, redemption through the Cross, and the like—which make Christianity a distinctive faith.

The affinities between the thought and language of these writings and that of the New Testament may best be gauged by a representative list of examples:

1. The members of the community style themselves 'the elect' or 'the elect of God'. Compare Titus 1.1: 'Paul, a servant of God, and an apostle of Jesus Christ, according to the faith of God's elect'; or I Peter 1.1: 'Peter, an apostle of Jesus Christ to the elect who are sojourners of the Dispersion'.

2. The truth of God, as revealed in His law, is constantly called the Light. Compare John 1.7–9: '[John] came for witness, that he might bear witness of the light . . . There was the true light, which lighteth every man, coming into the world'; John 8.12: 'I am the light of the world'.

3. The 'enlightened' members of the community describe themselves as 'Sons of Light'. Compare John 12.36: 'While ye have the light, believe on the light, that ye may become sons of light'; Ephesians 5.8: 'Walk as children of light'.

4. In the *Book of Hymns*, the faithful frequently declare that they stand in the eternal congregation of God, hold direct converse with Him, and 'share the lot of the holy beings'. Compare Ephesians 2.19: 'Ye are no more strangers and sojourners, but ye are fellow-citizens with the holy ones (E.V. saints), and of the household of God'.

5. A basic tenet is the doctrine of the 'remnant'—the belief that the community constitutes the true 'relic' of Israel, faithful to the Covenant. Compare Romans 11.3–5: 'Lord, they have killed Thy prophets, they have digged down thine altars: and I am left alone, and they seek my life. But what saith the answer of God . . . ? Once I left for myself seven thousand men that bowed not the knee to Baal. Even so then at this present time also there is a remnant by the election of grace'.

6. The spiritual leader of the community is called 'teacher' or 'right-teacher'. In John 3.2, Jesus is hailed as the teacher sent by God—that is, as the teacher who, it was held, would arise in the last days. So, too, in John 16.13, the incarnate Spirit of Truth is described as one 'who shall guide you unto all the truth', and these words

are an almost perfect translation of the term rendered 'right-teacher', for Hebrew has only one expression for 'teacher' and 'guide'.

7. In the *Manual of Discipline*, it is said that, if the community abide by the prescribed rules, it will be a veritable 'temple of God, a true holy of holies'. Compare I Corinthians 3.16–17: 'Know ye not that ye are a temple of God, and that the Spirit of God dwelleth in you? If any man destroy the temple of God, him shall God destroy, for the temple of God is holy, which temple ye are'. (A similar sentiment may be found also in Eph. 2.20–22.)

8. In the same *Manual of Discipline* there is a long passage describing the Two Ways, viz. of good and evil, light and darkness, which God sets before every man. The idea is indeed a commonplace of ancient Iranian and later Jewish thought, but it is interesting to note the development of the same basic imagery in the familiar picture of the wide and straight gates in Matthew 7.13f. and Luke 13.23f.

9. The Prophet that is to arise at the end of days, in accordance with the promise in Deuteronomy 18.18, was, as we have seen, a key figure in the religious doctrine of the Dead Sea Scrolls. Compare, then, Matthew 17.10f. and Mark 9.11f., where Jesus is asked whether Elijah should not have preceded his coming. Compare also John 6.14: 'Then those men, when they had seen the miracle that Jesus did, said, This is of a truth that prophet that should come into the world'. And note that Stephen, when arraigned before the council, quotes the very passage of Deuteronomy in evidence of the true character of Jesus (Acts 7.37).

10. The *Manual of Discipline* quotes the famous words of Isaiah (40.3), 'Prepare in the desert a highway', in token of the fact that the final apocalyptic age is at hand. In John 1.23, the Baptist quotes exactly the same passage in exactly the same context.

11. The community is often styled 'God's plantation' (after Isa. 60.21). So, in I Timothy 3.6, a novice is called a 'neophyte'—literally, one 'newly planted'.

12. The river (or lake) of fire graphically portrayed in one of the *Hymns* as destined to burn up the wicked (cf. Dan. 7.10f.), finds its counterpart in Revelation 19.20;

20.10, 14f.; 21.8, suggesting that this was a standard element of the current eschatological 'nightmare'.

These, it must be emphasized, are but a few of the many parallels that could be quoted. One might refer also to the use of the same literary devices both in the Scrolls and in the New Testament, e.g., the stereotyped catalog of vices in the *Manual of Discipline* (col. iv) on the one hand and in such passages as Galatians 5.19f.; Romans 1.29f.; 13.13; Colossians 3.5, 8 on the other. Or one might adduce some striking *verbal* analogues, as when the Fourth Gospel speaks of 'men from beneath' (8.23) or of a 'son of perdition' (17.12), both of which curious expressions occur in the *Hymns;* or when John 1.3 is found in virtually the same words at the end of one of those same compositions! Similarly too, when the Epistle of James speaks (1.14) of men 'hooked and trapped by their lusts' (for that is what the Greek words really mean), we cannot but recall the passages in the *Hymns* (iii, 26; v, 8) where exactly the same metaphor is used to describe the enticement of the unwary. And when James declares (1.17) that 'every good endowment and every perfect gift is from above, coming down from the Father of Lights', his words find a striking counterpart in that curious compound expression 'Light-Perfection' which the Qumran documents employ (e.g., *Hymns* iv, 6; xviii, 29) to describe the special endowment of the faithful. Nor, further, can we fail to recall that, according to the *Manual of Discipline* (iii, 20), control over the 'sons of righteousness' is 'in the hand of the Prince of Lights'. Indeed, we may perhaps not unreasonably conclude that the Dead Sea Scrolls actually open a window upon the little community of Jewish Christians clustered around James in Jerusalem. These men may have been originally the urban brethren of the hardier souls that betook themselves to Qumran and to other camp-settlements in the Desert of Judah. For the *'Zadokite' Document* provides expressly for urban as well as camp communities; while of the Essenes, with whom they may be identical, Josephus states (*War,* II, viii, 4) that they also lived in the cities.

The possibility is increased by a number of significant

statements made about James by Hegesippus, an early Christian writer who wrote during the latter half of the second century C.E. 'Because of his exceeding righteousness', we are informed, 'James was named the Righteous'; and once, when the scribes urged him to preach against Jesus, they addressed him pointedly as 'Thou Righteous One, to whom we are all bound to listen'. Does not this sound uncommonly like a reflection of the title 'Teacher of Righteousness' (or, True Expounder of the Law) which occurs so frequently in the Scrolls and in the 'Zadokite' Document as that of the spiritual instructor of the Brotherhood? And is it not equally significant that, according to this same Hegesippus, James habitually eschewed the use of oil and wore linen garments only—two of the characteristic traits which Josephus (*War*, II, viii, 3, 5) attributes to the Essenes?

Nor is it only in the realm of ideas and doctrines that the Dead Sea Scrolls present affinities to early Christianity. No less arresting are certain parallels between the organization of the community and that of the primitive Church. It is significant, for instance, that some of the terms used to define its several constituent elements, though themselves derived ultimately from the Old Testament, possess in the Palestinian Aramaic dialect of the early Christians exactly the same quasi-technical sense as denoting parts of the ecclesiastical organization. A case in point is the term employed to denote the deliberative assembly (viz. *'eṣah*); in Palestinian Aramaic (where, significantly, it is a loanword) this means specifically the council of the church or synagogue: it is used in the Scriptures as the rendering of the Greek *synhedrion*, more familiar to us in the Hebraized form, *sanhedrin*. Similarly, the word used to denote the total congregation (viz. *'edah*), though borrowed from the Old Testament, was likewise adopted in Syriac as the regular term for 'church'. In other words, the technical vocabulary of the early Palestinian Church seems to reproduce that used by the Dead Sea Covenanters to describe their own organization.

Again, the Dead Sea Scrolls might at last clear up the vexed problem of the distinction between bishops and presbyters in the primitive Church, for in these documents the administrative officers of the community consist not only of *mebaqqerim*, or 'overseers'—the exact equivalent of the Greek *episkopos*, whence our 'bishop'—but also of the twelve good laymen and true who assisted the three priests and in whom we may very well see the counterpart of the Christian 'presbyters'.

Then, too, it is worth pointing out that the rule requiring all 'who perform communal service' to be at least twenty-five years old, and all 'heads of families' and military officers to be at least thirty survived in the Church in the statement of the Council of Hippo (393 A.D.) that no one is to be ordained under twenty-five, and in the Neo-Caesarean and Maronite rules that no presbyter may be under thirty.

VII

On the other hand, it must be stated emphatically—particularly in view of recent exaggerated claims—that the community envisaged by the Dead Sea Scrolls and translated into reality at Qumran is in no sense Christian and holds none of the fundamental theological doctrines of the Christian faith.

It has been asserted, for instance, that the several references in the Scrolls to the 'right-teacher' all refer to a single historical Teacher of Righteousness—a prototype of Jesus—and that a passage in one of them which speaks of his having been 'persecuted' but having subsequently 'appeared' to the community on the Day of Atonement foreshadows the Christian doctrine of the suffering and resurrected Saviour. Even, however, if the interpretation were correct (which is very doubtful), this would still be poles apart from the Christian belief that the crucified Master was God incarnate Who by His passion removed a sinfulness inherent in man through a pristine fall from grace. Of this basic doctrine of Christianity there is not a shred or trace in the Dead Sea Scrolls.

Other essential doctrines also are missing. There is, here,

for instance, no vestige of the idea of Original Sin. On the contrary, the idea is affirmed constantly in the *Book of Hymns* that every man is endowed at birth with the charisma of knowledge and discernment and that any sinfulness which he incurs is due only to his individual neglect of these gifts and to his individual submission to, or entrapment by, the domination of the evil impulse (Belial). Moreover, because sin is individual and not the inherited lot of man, and because it is incurred by his own personal disposition, it can be removed also by his own individual experience. Once he 'sees the light' by the exercise of his own God-given powers, he is out of darkness. In such a system, since there is no concept of original, universal sin, there is obviously no place for universal vicarious atonement. Men suffer their individual crucifixions and resurrections; there is no Calvary.

Again, there is no Communion. Certain scholars, to be sure, have tried to find a prototype of the Eucharist in the description given, in a fragment of the *Manual of Discipline* (or an analogous document), of a banquet attended by 'the Messiah'. But this interpretation is untenable for several reasons. First, the 'Messiah' in question is no divine eschatological figure. He is simply the duly anointed king of Israel *at any future epoch*. The aim of the passage—which the reader can examine for himself on p. 441—is simply to indicate that, as in normative Jewish law, the sacred seed of Aaron has precedence over all laymen. Accordingly, it is affirmed, even if the anointed king—what we should call 'a crowned head'—should happen to be present at a meal, he and his retinue are not to take their seats until the high priest and *his* priestly retinue have done so, and it is still to be left to the priest to pronounce the customary benediction over the food.

Second, it is to be observed that the rule in question forms part of a code promulgated for 'the whole Congregation of Israel *in future times*'. Accordingly, on any showing, it affords no testimony to the current beliefs or practices of the men of Qumran.

Third, this document does not refer to any banquet 'at the end of days', as some scholars have supposed, the Hebrew words so rendered being a common idiom for 'the future, hereafter'.

Fourth—and, perhaps, most important—even if, for argument's sake, this document *did* refer to a divine eschatological Messiah attending a banquet with his disciples, it would still not be a eucharist in the Christian sense, for there is not the slightest suggestion that the bread and wine were regarded as his flesh and blood or that consumption of them had any redemptive power. At most, it would be an *agape,* or 'love-feast'.[10]

VIII

In order to get this whole question into the right perspective, it should be observed that just as many ideas and phrases in the Dead Sea Scrolls as can be paralleled from the New Testament can be paralleled equally well from the Apocrypha and Pseudepigrapha of the Old Testament —that is, from the non-canonical Jewish 'scriptures' that were circulating between 200 B.C. and 100 A.D.—and from the earlier strata of the Talmud. Moreover, many of them find place also in the ancient doctrines of such sects as the Mandaeans of Iraq and Iran and the Samaritans, so that even if they have not come down to us through *Jewish* channels, we can still recognize in them part of the common Palestinian thought and folklore of the time. Accordingly, to draw from the New Testament parallels any inference of special relationship is misleading.

The point can best be illustrated by a few pertinent examples.

1. The Brethren called themselves 'the sons of light'. The title is familiar from the New Testament (Luke 16.8; John 12.36; I Thess. 5.5). But it is common also among the Mandaeans of Iraq and Iran as a name for those celestial beings with whom, indeed, the men of the Brotherhood claimed to stand in a single communion.

2. The Brethren also affected the name of 'the Elect'. This, too, is especially familiar to us from the New Testa-

ment. But it is also a common style among the Mandaeans; while the Manichaeans (who share many of their ideas) likewise call themselves 'the chosen' (vičidagan).

3. Another common title of the Brethren was 'God's plantation' (cf. *Hymns* vi, 15; viii, 6.10). This, of course, was derived from the Bible (Isa. 60.21). But it is likewise a common image in pseudepigraphic literature (e.g., *Psalms of Solomon* 14.3–4; *Odes of Solomon* 38.18–21), and it is also very frequent among the Mandaeans (e.g., Lidzbarski, *Mandäische Liturgien*, 149, 190, 194ff.; *Right Ginza* II, iv, *init.*).

4. The Brethren claimed that they were especially 'enlightened' or 'endowed with insight'. Exactly the same claim—expressed by exactly the same Semitic word—is made by the Mandaeans; while among the Manichaeans, the lay member of the community (nigōšag) was known as 'the man with insight'. Moreover, the Brethren sometimes described this special illumination by the strange compound word Ôr-Tôm—literally, 'Light-Perfection', and this was simply a play on the Biblical Urim and Thummim of the high priest. The light in question, it may be added, seems often to be identified with the Law (*Torah*), and this idea, too, is found in pseudepigraphic literature (e.g., in the *Testament of Levi*, written between 109 and 106 B.C.) and in the Talmud (e.g., Berachôth 17a).

5. The Brethren held that the deeds of men are divided between the dominion of God, which is light, and that of Belial, which is darkness (*Manual*, iv). Here again we have a concept familiar enough from the New Testament and one which, at a far earlier date, dominated Iranian religion. But the fact is that by the second century B.C. it had already percolated into Jewish thought. The *Testament of Levi* says explicitly (19.1): 'Choose either the light or the darkness, either the Law of the Lord or the works of Beliar (i.e., Belial)'; while in the *Testament of Joseph*, Belial is called 'the spirit of darkness'.

6. The *Manual of Discipline* says that the faithful will receive a crown of glory (kelîl kabôd; iv, 7). Peter and James, it is true, use a similar image; but in Mandaean thought the 'lustrous crown' plays an extremely important

role and is frequently mentioned in the hymns of the sect (e.g., Lidzbarski, *Mandäische Liturgien*, 4f., 29, 108, 177, 243); and in the pseudepigraphic *Odes of Solomon*, there is a reference (9.11) to the 'crown of truth'.

The correspondence between the ideas of the Brotherhood and those that obtained generally in Palestine during the Graeco-Roman age and that survive sporadically among the more 'exotic' sects is especially striking in the field of eschatology—that is, the lore about the Last Things.

1. The concept of a 'final conflagration', to which we have already alluded (above, p. 8), occurs frequently in the Third Book of the *Sibylline Oracles*, a basically Jewish compilation dating about 140 B.C. The Jews appear to have adopted it from Gentile sources (although there is a foregleam of it in Isa. 34.9–10), for it was held by Zeno and the Stoics and dominated the Roman-Oriental world from the first century B.C. until the third century C.E.

2. The idea, articulated especially in the Qumran text called *The War of the Sons of Light and the Sons of Darkness*, that the world is at present in the clutches of Belial, but that he will ultimately be defeated, occurs again, not only in the New Testament (Mat. 24.5–12), but even more explicitly in the *Testament of Levi* (5.27) and in the *Sibylline Oracles* (ii, 165f.). The apocalyptic war (mentioned also in *Hymns* iii.29ff.; 35–36; 34–35)—an idea derived ultimately from the Biblical prophets (Isa. 13.9; Zech. 14.3)—is likewise commonplace in pseudepigraphic writings (e.g., *Syriac Apocalypse of Baruch*, 70.7–10) and in the Talmud; while the notion that angels too will fight finds an echo in the *Slavonic Book of Enoch* 17.1, where they are described as 'the armed troops of heaven'—a play, of course, on the expression 'heavenly host'.

3. The picture which is painted in Hymn No. 5 of the world travailing in the throes of new birth is admirably illustrated by the fact that the Messianic turmoil preceding the final Golden Age is called in the Talmud (Shab. 118a; Sanh. 98b) 'the birth-pangs of the Messiah' (cp. Mat. 24.8; Mark 13.8–9; I Thess. 5.3).

4. The doctrine that all things will be renewed (*Hymns* xi.13f.; xiii.11–12) is again part and parcel of Oriental thought at the time, and cannot be compared exclusively with Matthew's well-known reference (19.28) to the eventual 'regeneration'. The pseudepigraphic *Testament of Abraham*, and likewise *The Book of Jubilees* (1.29) speak of a renewal of the world after seven millennia; while the concept of a periodic renewal was also a favorite doctrine of Neo-Pythagoreanism, which enjoyed a great vogue in Roman society in the second and first centuries B.C. An allusion to this idea, it may be added, occurs in the very ancient form of the Jewish doxology (*Kaddish*) which is recited after a funeral, for God is there extolled as 'He who will hereafter renew the world and quicken the dead'.

5. One of the *Hymns* states (vii.24) that God's light will eventually shine sevenfold strong. The basic idea has, of course, good Old Testament authority (Isa. 60.19), but it is interesting to observe that, according to the Talmud (Sanh. 91b), the light of the Messianic sun will be seven times as powerful as usual.

6. Finally, the important concept of the New Covenant to be concluded with the faithful at the end of the present era is admirably illustrated by the standard Samaritan tenet that God's bond with Israel has already been concluded on no less than seven occasions, viz. with Noah in the rainbow; with Abraham in circumcision; with Moses in the Sabbath; with the Two Tablets of the Ten Commandments; with the Passover; with the Covenant of Salt (Num. 18.19); and with the Covenant of Priesthood with Phinehas (Num. 25.12f.).

IX

Significant also in this connection are the parallels which exist between the doctrines and concepts of the Scrolls and those which appear in *Iranian* lore. To be sure, these affinities present a thorny problem, because, while some of them indeed occur in the really ancient portion of the Iranian scriptures—the Gathas—others are to be found only in writings of relatively late date, and these may themselves be derived (directly or indirectly) from Jewish sources. Either way, however, the parallels are worthy of attention. If, on the one hand, they are all genuinely ancient (even though some may be attested only in late sources), they will lend added support to the view which is still maintained by a respectable body of scholarship (or a body of respectable scholarship) that the elaborate angelology, demonology, and eschatology which developed in Judaism during the intertestamental period owed much to earlier contacts with Iranian thought. Indeed, it is not difficult to conceive how, in the dark days of national eclipse, some at least of the Jews may have sought in Iranian dualism a more comforting explanation of the fate which had befallen them than that afforded by their own traditional doctrines. For, instead of having to believe that an outraged God had revoked His covenant with them, they could thus find hope and solace in the notion that what they were suffering was, after all, no more than a momentary triumph of Evil in its continuous struggle with Good—a purely temporary setback which would be followed inevitably by the final discomfiture of Falsehood (*Druj*), the condign punishment of all who had espoused it, the reward of the partisans of Truth or Right (*Asha*), the dissolution of a corrupt world in fire and brimstone (*ayah khshusta*), and the eventual emergence of that new world which is continually a-borning (*frashokereti*). If, on the other hand, many of the Iranian parallels are themselves derived from Jewish lore, they will nevertheless provide valuable testimony, from an independent source, of the new direction which Jewish thought was taking—especially in 'non-normative' circles—and which leaves its traces also in pseudepigraphic and rabbinic literature and in the doctrines of such 'off-beat' sects as the Mandaeans.

The principal parallels which come into question are the following:

If the Scrolls say that the God of Knowledge has appointed for man the two equal but rival spirits of Truth and Perverseness,[11] the Avesta says that Ahura Mazda, the Lord of Wisdom, has set in the world the twin but rival powers of Truth, or Right (Asha) and of Perverseness, or Falsehood (Druj).[12] If the Scrolls say that the one comes from the source of light, and the other from that of darkness,[13] Plutarch records the same belief among the Iranians.[14] If the Scrolls call the human partisans of the one 'sons of righteousness', and of the other, 'sons of perverseness', precisely the same designations (*ashovanō* and *dregvatō*) are given to them in the Avesta. If the Scrolls declare that at the end of the present era, God, with his human and celestial partisans, will do battle against the forces of Belial,[15] the Iranian scriptures aver in the same way that Ahura Mazda with his earthly and heavenly supporters will ultimately engage the forces of evil (Angra Mainyu, Druj).[16] If the Scrolls say that God will be victorious only after six previous campaigns,[17] exactly the same belief is attributed to the Iranians by the Greek writer Theopompus, and is repeated by the church father Lactantius.[18] If the Scrolls speak of the eventual dissolution of this world in fire and brimstone, when even granite rocks will be turned to streams of pitch,[19] the Iranian scriptures likewise foretell a final 'ordeal of molten metal' when even the metals in the mountains will melt.[20] If the Scrolls foretell for the wicked an endless torment in fire and darkness,[21] the Avesta dooms them to the unquenchable flame and the eternal agony of gloom (*anaghra temah*).[22] And if, conversely, the Scrolls hold out to the faithful the promise of a 'crown of glory' and a 'robe of honor',[23] and the prospect of joining the celestial choir after death,[24] the Iranian doctrine envisages the bestowal of a similar crown and robe,[25] the enjoyment of celestial radiance (*khvarenah*), and a similar translation to the heavenly 'mansion of song' (*garo demāna*).[26] If, in the teaching of the Scrolls, God will test mankind in fire and spirit,[27] the Avesta says precisely the same of Ahura Mazda.[28] And if the Scrolls affirm that at the end of the present 'Era of Wrath', there will eventually arise a new Teacher to usher in that Golden Age when God's truth will be made manifest[29] and all things be renewed,[30] so, in Iranian doctrine, after the ravages of Aeshma, the demon of wrath and fury,[31] a new teacher will appear,[32] Asha (Truth, Right) will emerge triumphant,[33] and the world will achieve the culmination of the constant process of renewal (*frashokereti*).[34]

Indeed, in one of our texts (below, pp. 390ff.) the future Messianic king is identified with Melchizedek, king of Shalem, mentioned in Genesis 14.18–20, simply because the name of that monarch lends itself readily to the interpretation, 'king of righteousness' (*melech zedek*) and that of his city suggests the Hebrew words, *shālôm*, 'peace', and *shallem*, 'requite', thus identifying him as a prefiguration of the future king who will bring both peace to the faithful and requital to the wicked.

It is not to be supposed, of course, that the writers of the Scrolls had any direct knowledge of the Iranian scriptures. These ideas came to them only, at one or more removes, as part of an inherited folklore or of the general ideological climate of the day; as we have seen, they are writ large both in contemporary pseudepigraphic literature and in the New Testament, and they are present also in the Talmud and in later rabbinic writings. Moreover, wherever possible, they were deftly Judaized—'made kosher', as it were—by being coated with the veneer of Biblical language. Thus, Ahura Mazda, the Lord of Wisdom, is cleverly translated into the 'God of Knowledge' of Hannah's prayer (I Sam. 2.3); Angra Mainyu, the incarnation of evil, becomes Belial; Druj, the female personification of perverseness, becomes 'avlah, 'crookedness', or even Maṣṭemah, a feminine cognate of the word Satan. The fravashis who aid Ahura Mazda in the final combat become the 'holy ones' associated in Zechariah 14.5 with God's own eventual battle. The final conflagration is portrayed in terms borrowed directly from the farewell song of Moses (Deut. 32.22) and from Isaiah (34.9), and the Restorer (Saoshyant) is identified with the Star foretold in the prophecies of Balaam (Num. 24.17). Indeed, not the least fascinating feature of the Scrolls is precisely this blend of the Iranian with the Hebraic.

X

Just as unfortunate as the attempts to 'Christianize' the Scrolls are the attempts unduly to 'historicize' them—that is, to detect in them precise and specific historical allusions.

In order to emphasize that what was happening or about to happen both to Israel and to the world at large was but the fulfillment of Biblical prophecy, the Scrolls make use of a kind of figurative geography, based on the Scriptures. Thus, they speak of the voluntary withdrawal of the elect from the normative forms of Jewish life as 'exile in the desert of Damascus', in allusion to the words of God in the Book of Amos (5.27): 'I will cause you to go into exile beyond Damascus'. Conversely, the future regeneration of Israel is depicted as a return from 'the wilderness of the peoples' (cp. Ezek. 20.35) to the 'Desert of Judah'. The prime enemy—the representative of Belial or the Evil One—is styled Gog, originally the name of a northern power whose doom had been foretold by the prophet Ezekiel (chaps. 38–39). Alternatively, and more often, the hostile forces are described as Kittians (or Kittaeans), a term which originally denoted the inhabitants of Kition, in Cyprus (cp. Gen. 10.4), but which came later to be used in an extended sense—rather like 'Huns' or 'Tartars'—of 'barbarians' in general and was applied in the Hellenistic age to the 'Macedonians' of the Alexandrian Empire, and in the Roman age to the Romans themselves. *The War of the Sons of Light and the Sons of Darkness*, a text which describes the final apocalyptic conflict, refers to 'Kittians of Assyria' and 'Kittians of Egypt', where nothing more is meant than the heathen population of either land, the doom of which had long since been foretold (cp. Zech. 10.10–11, etc.).

There is no need to take such references literally and consequently to set off on a wild-goose chase after historical identifications. The figurative use of names, always designed to evoke traditional associations, is commonplace in most cultures; we need think only of such terms as

'Parnassus', 'Mecca', 'Babylon', or 'Waterloo' in current English parlance.

There is likewise a figurative use of *personal* names. Wicked priests who once opposed the 'teacher of righteousness'—himself a priest—are described as a 'house of Absalom', in reference to the Biblical Absalom's treason against his own father, David. Schismatics are referred to fancifully as 'the house of Peleg' (cp. Gen. 10.25), simply because the Hebrew word *p-l-g* means 'divide'. Such designations should deceive no one; it is quite futile to go casting around among the records of the Hellenistic or Roman periods of Jewish history for a particular villain called Absalom. The name must be treated simply like 'Attila', 'Machiavelli', 'Benedict Arnold', or 'Quisling' in modern speech.

Unfortunately, however, the true understanding of the Scrolls has been compromised (or, at least, embarrassed) by the understandable eagerness of scholars to peg them to a definite date, and under this impulse there has arisen an almost frenetic tendency to read specific historical reference into these purely figurative names. Consequently, the literature on the subject is cluttered up with all kinds of ingenious, but usually very forced, attempts to give them specific setting in the Hellenistic or Roman periods. It has been assumed, for instance, that the 'Kittians of Assyria' and the 'Kittians of Egypt' are necessarily the Seleucid and Ptolemaic empires; that the sect really migrated, allegedly in the face of the Roman troops, from the western shores of the Dead Sea to the region of Damascus; and that 'the house of Absalom' may have been that of an Absalom mentioned casually in the First Book of the Maccabees (11.70; 13.11) or of the son of John Hyrcanus I who bore that name (Josephus, *Ant.*, XIV, 4.4)!

Nowhere has this 'historicizing' tendency (or aberration) played more havoc than in the attempts which have been made to weld the several references to 'the teacher of righteousness' into a single consistent biography, and to reconstruct from the collateral allusions to a 'wicked priest' and a 'man of lies' who persecuted him a specific historical situation. All sorts of characters (Onias, Menelaus, Antiochus Epiphanes, Alexander Jannaeus, John Hyrcanus, Mattathias, the father of Judas Maccabaeus—even Jesus, John the Baptist, and Paul) have been proposed to fill these several roles. If, however, we look at the data without prejudice or preconception, it is pretty apparent that the 'teacher of righteousness' denotes a continuing office rather than a particular individual, and that the various allusions to him are not in fact to one and the same person.

In the 'Zadokite' Document, for example, we are told that God raised up a 'teacher of righteousness' some twenty years after the beginning of a 390-year period of His displeasure, calculated from the capture of Jerusalem by Nebuchadnezzar. This evidently refers to Nehemiah or—perhaps more probably, seeing that he was a priest—to Ezra. On the other hand, we are told in the same document (ix.29ff.) that 'about forty years will elapse from the death of the teacher of righteousness until all who have taken up arms and relapsed in the company of the Man of Falsehood are finally destroyed'. Here, obviously, the reference is to a *future* teacher, one who will arise to occupy the traditional office in advance of that forty-year period of 'Messianic woes' of which we indeed read in Talmudic and later rabbinic literature. This figure is, in fact, a prototype of the Arabic *Mahdi*.

Similarly, if we go soberly through the several references to the 'teacher of righteousness' in the *Commentary on Habakkuk*, it soon becomes apparent that the author is simply citing a number of historical incidents which might illustrate the prophet's words. There is no compelling reason why they should be taken to constitute a connected biographical narrative. Thus, when he interprets the verse (1.13), 'Why do ye look on, ye traitors, and keep silent when the wicked confounds one more righteous than he?' as referring to 'the "house of Absalom" and the men of their company who kept silent when charges were brought against the teacher of righteousness, and who did not come to his aid against the man of lies', he may be referring to an historical incident which involved one particular 'teacher of righteousness'; while when he speaks (in the comment on 2.15) of such a teacher's having once been vexed by a wicked priest who attempted (apparently) to usurp his office, he may be referring to quite a different person living at quite a different period. Indeed, it is significant in this respect that the fragmentary *Commentary on Micah* (1.5) actually speaks of 'teachers of righteousness', and that this is not simply a scribal error (as some scholars have all too rashly supposed) is shown by the fact that the expression serves to explain a word in the Scriptural text which is itself *in the plural*.

Similarly, too, the allusion (in *The Manual of Discipline for the Future Congregation of Israel*) to the presence of a 'messiah' at a communal banquet is no evidence, as has been somewhat sensationally supposed, that the Brotherhood believed in a single Christlike Teacher of Righteousness who had suffered martyrdom but whose Second Coming was expected. For the plain fact is that the term 'messiah' there means simply 'anointed king'. The text in question gives the protocol which is to be observed in the future dispensation, and its whole point is to emphasize that even an anointed king will then have to yield place to an anointed priest at public gatherings!

This is not to say, of course, that specific and identifiable allusions are not of crucial importance in determining upward and downward limits for the dates to which our texts are to be assigned. It is simply to warn against the tendency to string such allusions together into a consistent narrative and then to draw from that synthetic narrative far-reaching historical and doctrinal conclusions. What we have to realize is that the commentators are merely fitting a stock set of masks ('the righteous man', 'the wicked man', 'the foreign invader') upon a stock set of characters ('the teacher of righteousness', 'the wicked priest', 'the Kittians'), differently identified at different epochs. We should be alive also to the danger that the frenzied scramble for historical identification may trample the flowerbeds. An obsessive preoccupation with the historical context of a piece of literature can all too easily obscure its wider significance; for real understanding it is necessary not only to know 'all about it', but also to be sensitive to what it is all about.

*   *   *

The archaeologists tell us that the Dead Sea caves are hot and dark. The same might be said of the controversy which has raged around their contents. At this point, however, it might be healthy to stand back a little from the din and furor and clouds of dust and try to appreciate the scriptures and the life of the Qumran Brotherhood simply from the point of view of what they offer to religious thought and insight. They bespeak an experience which has been repeated often enough in history—the experience of the typical nonconformist who combines, by a strange and wonderful alchemy, an inner quietude with an outer fanaticism, and whose sense of God is a sense of burning fire as well as of radiant light. It may be true that the documents which have come down to us are not great literary masterpieces. Nevertheless they are the testimonies of men who, like their greater forebear, stood in the cleft of a rock and saw the glory of God passing by.

NOTES

Introduction

1. These efforts turn mainly on two assumptions, viz. (a) that various characters described respectively as 'the Teacher of Righteousness', 'the Wicked Priest', and 'the Man of Lies' are particular individuals that can be identified; and (b) that a people called the Kittians may be identified as either the Macedonian Greeks of the Alexandrian Empire or as the Romans. Details of the various theories are set forth in Millar Burrows' two useful volumes: *The Dead Sea Scrolls* (1956) and *More Light on the Dead Sea Scrolls* (1958), and in A. Dupont-Sommer's exciting work, *The Essene Writings from Qumran* (1962); while a useful survey of more recent studies is provided by James A. Sanders in *The Biblical Archaeologist* 36 (1973), 110–48. At the moment, it may be said, the darkness of the Dead Sea caves has not yet been dissipated, and scholars are really in the position of eager readers guessing the solution of a serialized 'whodunit' before the final installment has been published!

2. It may be observed that the Hebrew word for 'teacher' derives from the same verbal root as the word 'Torah'. The 'right-teacher' is therefore, in this context, 'the man who expounds the Torah aright'.

3. First: only a priest would have had uncontested authority so to lay down the law. Second, our documents say specifically, over and over again, that the rules and standards of the community were determined of old by 'the sons of Zadok, *the priests*'. Third: the *Manual of Discipline* affirms expressly that '*the priests* alone are to have authority in all judicial and economic matters'. Fourth: the Prophetic Teacher who will arise

at the end of the present era and usher in the Messianic Age is invariably associated in Jewish tradition with either Elijah or Phinehas or even Melchizedek, *all of whom were priests.*

4. See pp. 14, 20f.
5. *Hymns* iii.35–36; vi.29; x.34–35.
6. *Lymns* xi.13f.; xiii.11–12.
7. *Hymns* xv.15; frag. 9.8.
8. *'Zadokite' Document,* i.5.
9. *Hymns* vii.24.
10. We may safely leave out of serious consideration the alleged occurrence in this text of a phrase reading, 'If [God] begets the Messiah'. This bizarre statement rests on nothing more substantial than an arbitrary reading of a faded word and an even more capricious restoration of a lacuna. Such a statement, it need scarcely be observed, would be utterly preposterous to a community of Jews committed to belief in the Torah and in the traditional doctrines of their faith. This whole document, in fact, has been egregiously misunderstood; see below, pp. 392ff.
11. *Manual,* iii.15–25; iv.16.
12. Yasna 30.2–4; 45.2.
13. *Manual,* iii.19.
14. *De Iside et Osiride,* 46–47.
15. *War,* xiv.14; xix.1; *Hymns* xii.36.
16. Yasht 30.3; Yasna 44.15; 19.11, 45.
17. *War,* i.14–15.
18. Quoted by Plutarch, *De Iside et Osiride,* 47. Re Lactantius, see F. Cumont, in *Revue de l'histoire des religions,* 1931. 88f.
19. *Manual,* ii.8; *Hymns* iii.28–29; *War,* xiv.7.
20. Yasna 31.3; 43.4; 47.6; 51.9; Bundahesh 30.19ff.
21. *Manual,* iv.13.
22. Yasht 22.33.
23. *Manual,* iv.7–8; *Hymns* ix.24.
24. *Hymns* iii.23; xi.14, 22.
25. Yasna 55.22; Bundahesh 30.28.
26. Yasna 22.15; 24.6; 45.8; 50.4; cp. Bundahesh 31.
27. *Manual,* iv.20–21.

28. Yasna 31.3; cp. also 51.9.
29. *Manual,* iv.19–20; *Hymns* iii.34.
30. *Manual,* iv.25; *Hymns* xi.13–14; xii.11–13.
31. Cp. Yasna 29.1; 30.6; 48.12.
32. Bundahesh 30.17; 32.8.
33. Yasna 43.10; cp. also 29.10; 31.8.
34. Yasht 19.11ff.; Yasna 30.9; 44.2. Cp. also Diogenes Laertius, *Proaem.* 9; Plutarch, *De Iside et Osiride,* 47.

THE SERVICE OF GOD

Rules and Admonitions for the Elect

*They that loved the synagogues of the pious
fled from them, as sparrows that fly from their
nest.*

*They wandered in deserts that their lives
might be saved from harm.*

PSALMS OF SOLOMON 17.15–16.

INTRODUCTION

Because the Brotherhood at Qumran regarded itself as the true Congregation of Israel, charged with the specific task of maintaining the Law and Covenant of God in an age of apostasy and confusion, of bringing men back to the True Way before the Final Judgment overtook them, and of fighting the ultimate battle against the heathen, it organized itself into what may fairly be described as a 'church'. Such an organization requires a formal set of principles and a constitution, and these are set forth in the two documents known respectively as *The Manual of Discipline* and *The 'Zadokite' Document.**

The former is contained in one of the scrolls discovered at Qumran in 1947 and in fragmentary copies subsequently brought to light. The latter, on the other hand, has been known for several years from two twelfth-century copies found by the late Solomon Schechter, in 1896–97, and the Ezra synagogue at Old Cairo (Fostat), where they formed part of the *genizah*, or repository of discarded manuscripts. Although published as far back as 1910, it

---

* The title, *'Zadokite' Document,* here retained purely for convenience, is in fact a misnomer, based on the false assumption that the expression, 'sons of Zadok' which occurs in sundry passages designates the Brotherhood as a whole (so named for its putative founder), whereas it really denotes only the priests. Similarly, because of its references to a 'new covenant' contracted in 'the land of Damascus', some scholars have assumed that it is the manual of discipline of the Brotherhood as reconstituted in that city after the Romans had stormed Qumran. But, in my opinion, the references in question are all purely figurative and typological and afford no evidence of an actual migration (see above, p. 27).

was not until the Qumran texts came to light that the true character of this document and its relation to the Dead Sea Brotherhood were made manifest. That relation is immediately apparent as soon as it is read alongside of the *Manual;* and it has been confirmed by the fact that fragments of earlier copies have actually been found in one of the caves at Qumran.

Both documents are in the nature of compilations. They are, so to speak, communal 'commonplace books' in which several different formulations of the Code and Principles have been bound up together. This is especially apparent in the case of the *Manual* from a long interpolation reciting the doctrine of the Two Instincts of Man (cols. iii–iv) and headed explicitly 'For the use of the Instructor' (literally, 'him who would bring others to the inner vision'), shewing that this section was originally the 'prompt-book' for a sermon. In the case of the *'Zadokite' Document,* a clear distinction can be recognized between the initial portion, which is in the nature of a homiletical discourse about the history of Israel and the doctrine of the Remnant, and the subsequent sections which recite the actual rules of the community.

As we have previously pointed out,† there is no proof that either document was composed originally by or for the men of Qumran. They may well represent pieces of traditional literature which nonconformist groups like the Qumran brotherhood came readily to adopt as their models. On that very natural assumption, it need not surprise us to find that several of the practises and institutions prescribed in these texts in fact bear a striking similarity to those which the first-century writers Josephus and Philo associate with the ascetic sect known as the Essenes—a sect many of whose members were, according to Pliny the Elder, likewise settled at that time on the western shore of the Dead Sea. There is, for instance, basically the same system of probation and initiation; the same order of 'de-

† See above, pp. 3ff.

grees of purity'; the same communal ownership of property; the same communal meals; the same system of 'overseers'; the same provision against blasphemy and the like; and the same rule about speaking in public sessions; and there was also among the Essenes the same distribution over urban and camp settlements as is envisaged in the *Zadokite' Document.*

Nor should it surprise us any the more that there are also significant differences, for the Essenes (like the men of Qumran themselves) may well have accommodated the provisions of these traditional 'scriptures' to their own special needs.

There is, in short, no need to deduce from these affinities that the writers of the Scrolls and the covenanters at Qumran were actually Essenes, and on this hypothesis to explain away the discrepancies on the facile assumption that, after all, Philo and Josephus were describing conditions as they obtained in the first century c.e., whereas our texts may refer to an earlier stage in the history of the Essenes or even ascend to their putative forerunners, the Hasidim (Pious Ones) of Maccabean times!

No less interesting, and perhaps more exciting, than their connection with the Essenes are the many parallels which these texts afford with the organization of the primitive Christian Church. The community calls itself by the same name (*'edah*) as was used by the early Christians of Palestine to denote the Church. The same term is employed to designate its legislative assembly as was used by that community to denote the council of the Church. There are twelve 'men of holiness' who act as general guides of the community—a remarkable correspondence with the Twelve Apostles. These men have three superiors, answering to the designation of John, Peter and James as the three pillars of the Church (Gal. 2.9f.). There is a regular system of *mebaqqerîm* or 'overseers'—an exact equivalent of the Greek *episkopoi*, or 'bishops' (before they had acquired *sacerdotal* functions). And the Brotherhood describes itself as 'preparing the way in the desert'—words which John the Baptist likewise quoted from the Old Testament in defining his mission (John 1.23).

The *Manual of Discipline* and the '*Zadokite*' *Document* may be compared, in fact, with the *Didachē*, the *Didascalia Apostolorum* and the *Apostolic Constitutions*—the primary documents relating to the organization of the primitive Church. Indeed, if we get away from the Greek terminology in which the details of that organization have mostly come down to us, and if we translate it back into Hebrew or Aramaic, we shall find that it bears a quite remarkable correspondence to that found in the Qumran texts, showing that the latter reflect a type of religious organization upon which the early Christian Church was largely patterned.

A supplement to these two major documents is the fragmentary text usually known as *Ordinances* but here entitled *The Letter of the Law*. This is part of a systematic guide (somewhat in the style of the Mishnah) to the practical application of the Mosaic Law. Whether it was intended as a regulatory code for the existent Brotherhood or for the future regenerated House of Israel cannot be determined, nor whether it is really part of *The Book of Study* [*H-g-û/y*] prescribed elsewhere in the Scrolls as 'required reading'.

A pendant to these documents is the fragmentary *Formulary of Blessings*.

This little document gives the protocol for the exchange of greetings ('blessings') between members of the community. These greetings are based on the Priestly Benediction in the Biblical Book of Numbers (6.24–26), the ancient words being so interpreted and elaborated in each case as to bear special application to the person addressed. The interpretations rest on the device, familiar from rabbinic literature, of reading further meaning into a Scriptural text by mentally correlating it with other passages in which the same words are used in different contexts.

Thus, the phrase, 'The Lord bless thee' is tacitly associated with such a passage as Psalm 68.26, where the word 'bless' occurs beside the expression, 'fountain of Israel'. This at once suggests the thought that the blessing is to consist in draughts from the Divine Fountain.

Similarly, the phrase, 'and keep thee' at once recalls such passages as Deuteronomy 7.12: 'The Lord shall keep with thee the covenant', or Psalm 121.7: 'The Lord shall keep thee from all evil'. Accordingly, it evokes the idea that the blessing is to consist in maintenance of the Covenant and in protection from satanic influences.

Again, the words, 'The Lord lift up His countenance' are interpreted in the light of the various senses of the word 'lift', e.g., of lifting the soul from the pit, the sword and standard in battle, obstacles from the path.

This method of interpreting the Priestly Benediction may be admirably illustrated from the way in which it is in fact expounded in the rabbinic classic, *Sifrê*, a compilation made from earlier sources in the third century C.E.:

And keep thee: Rabbi Isaac says: This means, keep thee from the evil inclination, even as the Scripture declares, 'The Lord will be thy confidence, and will keep thy foot from being caught' (Prov. 3.26). Another explanation is that the words mean, keep thee from the demons, even as the Scripture says, 'He giveth His angels charge over thee, to keep thee from all evil' (Ps. 91.11). Yet another explanation is that they mean that God will keep unto thee the covenant made with thy fathers, as it is said, 'The Lord thy God will keep for thee the covenant and the mercy which He swore unto thy fathers' (Deut. 7.12). Or again, the words may be taken to mean that God will keep (in mind) for thee the appointed consummation, as the Scripture says: 'Watchman (Heb. Keeper), what of the night? Watchman, what of the night? Saith the Watchman (i.e., He who keeps the time in mind), 'Morning cometh, though now it be night' (Isa. 21.11–12). Lastly, the words may be referred to God's keeping thy soul at the hour of death, even as the Scripture says, 'The soul of my lord shall be bound up (i.e., kept tight) in the bond of life' (I Sam. 25.29); or of His keeping thy feet from hell, as it is said, 'He will keep the feet of His pious ones' (I Sam. 2.9).

The same compilation, it may be added, also records interpretations of the words, 'The Lord make His face to shine upon thee and be gracious unto thee', which are in perfect agreement with those given in our little document:

Be gracious unto thee: This means, give thee grace in the sight of all creatures . . . or, give thee the grace of knowledge and understanding and intelligence and instruction and wisdom . . . or, again, grace thee with study of the Torah.

In prescribing the greetings ('blessings') of the priests in general and of the high priest in particular, our document adopts yet another device. It plays on the various outward symbols of the priestly office. Thus, since the priest ministered in the 'holy place', the blessing is invoked upon him that he may minister hereafter in the celestial 'holy place'; since the high priest wore a crown or mitre, it is invoked upon him that he be crowned by God with the diadem of eternal honor. Since the priest normally received the first portion of the offerings, he is saluted with the hope that he may enjoy 'the first portion of delights'; and since he is a ministrant at the altar, that he may 'share the lot of the ministering angels'. (This last, it may be observed, likewise has a remarkable parallel in *Sifrê.* 'When Torah issues from the priests' mouths', we read, 'God speaks of them as if they were ministering angels' [*Korah,* §119]).

Our text bears the title 'For the *Maskil'.* The same title recurs in the *Manual of Discipline* in the passage dealing with the two spirits which God has placed in every man (cols. iii–iv). It is not quite certain what the Hebrew word *Maskil* means in these contexts. Formally, it can denote either (a) one endowed with inner vision, or (b) one who seeks to impart such vision to others.‡ If it bears the latter sense, it is possible that both our present text and the passage in the *Manual* were originally designed as 'model sermons' for the religious instructors of the community. Indeed, we may even venture the conjecture that they were expository discourses designed to accompany readings from the Law; our present document being geared to that section of the Book of Numbers which includes the Priestly Benediction, and the passage in the *Manual* to some such 'lesson' as Deuteronomy 11.26ff. ('Behold I set before you this day a blessing and a curse'). Josephus tells us explicitly that among the Essenes such expositions were a regular feature of the sabbath services.

The text of this document is very fragmentary, and in some cases the rubrics indicating to whom a particular blessing is addressed are missing. But the tenor of the blessing itself usually indicates who is intended. In this matter I have followed the suggestions of the original editors. For the rest, my restorations (indicated by brackets) are based on a recognition of that underlying method of Scriptural exegesis which has been outlined above.

‡ The word occurs in this latter sense in Dan. 12.3 where, however, it is commonly rendered 'they that are wise'.

THE MANUAL OF DISCIPLINE

Of the Commitment (i, 1–15)

Everyone who wishes to join the community must pledge himself to respect God and man; to live according to the communal rule; to seek God [   ]; to do what is good and upright in His sight, in accordance with what He has commanded through Moses and through His servants the prophets; to love all that He has chosen and hate all that He has rejected; to keep far from all evil and to cling to all good works; to act truthfully and righteously and justly on earth and to walk no more in the stubbornness of a guilty heart[1] and of lustful eyes,[2] doing all manner of evil; to bring into a bond of mutual love all who have declared their willingness to carry out the statutes of God; to join the formal community of God; to walk blamelessly before Him in conformity with all that has been revealed as relevant to the several periods during which they are to bear witness (to Him); to love all the children of light,[3] each according to his stake in the formal community of God; and to hate all the children of darkness, each according to the measure of his guilt, which God will ultimately requite.

All who declare their willingness to serve God's truth must bring all of their mind, all of their strength, and all of their wealth into the community of God,[4] so that their minds may be purified by the truth of His precepts, their strength controlled by His perfect ways, and their wealth disposed in accordance with His just design. They must not deviate by a single step from carrying out the orders of God at the times appointed for them; they must neither advance the statutory times nor postpone the prescribed seasons.[5] They must not turn aside from the ordinances of God's truth[6] either to the right or to the left.

Of initiation (i, 16–ii, 18)

Moreover, all who would join the ranks of the community must enter into a covenant in the presence of God to do according to all that He has commanded and not to turn away from Him through any fear or terror[7] or through any trial to which they may be subjected through the domination of Belial.[8]

When they enter into that covenant, the priests and the levites are to pronounce a blessing upon the God of salvation and upon all that He does to make known His truth; and all that enter the covenant are to say after them, Amen, amen.[9]

Then the priests are to rehearse the bounteous acts of God as revealed in all His deeds of power, and they are to recite all His tender mercies towards Israel; while the levites are to rehearse the iniquities of the children of Israel and all the guilty transgressions and sins that they have committed through the domination of Belial. And all who enter the covenant are to make confession after them, saying, We have acted perversely, we have transgressed, we have sinned, we have done wickedly, ourselves and our fathers before us, in that we have gone counter to the truth. God has been right to bring His judgment upon us and upon our fathers.[10] Howbeit, always from ancient times He has also bestowed His mercies upon us, and so will He do for all time to come.

Then the priests are to invoke a blessing on all that have cast their lot with God,[11] that walk blamelessly in all their ways; and they are to say: MAY HE BLESS THEE with all good and KEEP THEE from all evil, and ILLUMINE thy heart with insight into the things of life, and GRACE THEE with knowledge of things eternal, and LIFT UP HIS gracious COUNTENANCE TOWARDS THEE to grant thee peace everlasting.[12]

The levites, on the other hand, are to invoke a curse on all that have cast their lot with Belial, and to say in response: Cursed art thou for all thy wicked guilty works. May God make thee a thing of abhorrence at the hands of all who would wreak vengeance, and visit thine offspring with destruction at the hands of all who would mete out retribution. Cursed art thou, beyond hope of mercy. Even as thy works are wrought in darkness, so mayest thou be damned in the gloom of the fire eternal.[13] May God show thee no favor when thou callest, neither pardon to forgive thine iniquities. May He lift up an angry countenance towards thee, to wreak vengeance upon thee. May no man wish thee peace of all that truly claim their patrimony.[14]

And all that enter the covenant shall say alike after them that bless and after them that curse, Amen, amen.

Thereupon the priests and the levites shall continue and say: Cursed be every one that hath come to enter this covenant[15] with the taint of idolatry in his heart and who hath set his iniquity as a stumblingblock before him[16] so that thereby he may defect, and who, when he hears the terms of this covenant, blesses himself in his heart, saying, May it go well with me, for I shall go on walking in the stubbornness of my heart! Whether he satisfy his passions or whether he still thirst for their fulfillment,[17] may his spirit be swept away and receive no pardon. May the anger of God and the fury of His judgments consume him as by fire unto his eternal extinction, and may there cleave unto him all the curses threatened in this covenant. May God set him apart for misfortune, and may he be cut off from the midst of all the children of light in that through the taint of his idolatry[18] and through the stumblingblock of his iniquity he has defected from God. May God set his lot among those that are accursed for ever! And all who have been admitted to the covenant shall say after them in response, Amen, amen.

Of the annual review   (ii, 19–25)

The following procedure is to be followed year by year so long as Belial continues to hold sway.

The priests are first to be reviewed in due order, one after another, in respect of the state of their spirits. After them, the levites shall be similarly reviewed, and in the third place all the laity[19] one after another, in their thousands, hundreds, fifties and tens. The object is that every man in Israel may be made aware of his status in the community of God in the sense of the ideal, eternal society,[20] and that none may be abased below his status nor exalted above his allotted place. All of them will thus be members of a community founded at once upon true values and upon a becoming sense of humility, upon charity and mutual fairness—members of a society truly hallowed, partners in an everlasting communion.[21]

Of those who are   (ii, 25–iii, 12)
to be excluded

Anyone who refuses to enter the (ideal) society of God and persists in walking in the stubbornness of his heart shall not be admitted to this community of God's truth. For inasmuch as his soul has revolted at the discipline entailed in a knowledge of God's righteous judgments, he has shown no real strength in amending his way of life, and therefore cannot be reckoned with the upright. The mental, physical and material resources of such a man are not to be introduced into the stock of the community, for such a man 'plows in the slime of wickedness'[22] and 'there are stains on his repentance'. He is not honest in resolving the stubbornness of his heart. On paths of light he sees but darkness. Such a man cannot be reckoned as among those essentially blameless. He cannot be cleared by mere ceremonies of atonement, nor cleansed by any waters of ablution, nor sanctified by immersion in lakes or rivers, nor purified by any bath. Unclean, unclean he remains so long as he rejects the government of God and refuses the discipline of communion with Him. For it is only through the spiritual apprehension of God's truth that man's ways can be properly directed. Only thus can all his iniquities be shriven so that he can gaze upon the true light of life. Only through the holy spirit can he achieve union with God's truth and be purged of all his iniquities.[23] Only by a spirit of uprightness and humility can his sin be atoned.

Only by the submission of his soul to all the ordinances of God can his flesh be made clean. Only thus can it really be sprinkled with waters of ablution. Only thus can it really be sanctified by waters of purification. And only thus can he really direct his steps to walk blamelessly through all the vicissitudes of his destiny in all the ways of God in the manner which He has commanded, without turning either to the right or to the left and without overstepping any of God's words. Then indeed will he be acceptable before God like an atonement-offering which meets with His pleasure, and then indeed will he be admitted to the covenant of the community for ever.

Of the two spirits in man (iii, 13–iv, 26)

This is for the man who would bring others to the inner vision,[24] so that he may understand and teach to all the children of light the real nature of men, touching the different varieties of their temperaments with the distinguishing traits thereof, touching their actions throughout their generations, and touching the reason why they are now visited with afflictions and now enjoy periods of well-being.

All that is and ever was comes from a God of knowledge.[25] Before things came into existence He determined the plan of them; and when they fill their appointed roles, it is in accordance with His glorious design that they discharge their functions. Nothing can be changed. In His hand lies the government of all things. God it is that sustains them in their needs.

Now, this God created man to rule the world, and appointed for him two spirits after whose direction he was to walk until the final Inquisition.[26] They are the spirits of truth and of perversity.

The origin of truth lies in the Fountain of Light, and that of perversity in the Wellspring of Darkness. All who practice righteousness are under the domination of the Prince of Lights,[27] and walk in ways of light; whereas all who practice perversity are under the domination of the Angel of Darkness and walk in ways of darkness. Through the Angel of Darkness,[28] however, even those who practice righteousness are made liable to error. All their sin and their iniquities, all their guilt and their deeds of transgression are the result of his domination; and this, by God's inscrutable design, will continue until the time appointed by Him. Moreover, all men's afflictions and all their moments of tribulation are due to this being's malevolent sway.[29] All of the spirits that attend upon him are bent on causing the sons of light to stumble. Howbeit, the God of Israel and the Angel of His truth[30] are always there to help the sons of light. It is God that created these spirits of light and darkness and made them the basis of every act, the [instigators] of every deed and the directors of every thought. The one He loves to all eternity, and is ever pleased with its deeds; but any association with the other He abhors, and He hates all its ways to the end of time.

This is the way those spirits operate in the world. The enlightenment of man's heart, the making straight before him all the ways of righteousness and truth, the implanting in his heart of fear for the judgments of God, of a spirit of humility, of patience, of abundant compassion, of perpetual goodness, of insight, of perception, of that sense of the Divine Power that is based at once on an apprehension of God's works and a reliance on His plenteous mercy, of a spirit of knowledge informing every plan of action, of a zeal for righteous government, of a hallowed mind in a controlled nature, of abounding love for all who follow the truth, of a self-respecting purity which abhors all the taint of filth, of a modesty of behavior coupled with a general prudence and an ability to hide within oneself the secrets of what one knows[31]—these are the things that come to men in this world through communion with the spirit of truth.[32] And the guerdon of all that walk in its ways is health and abundant well-being, with long life and fruition of seed along with eternal blessings and everlasting joy in the life everlasting, and a crown of glory[33] and a robe of honor,[34] amid light perpetual.

But to the spirit of perversity belong greed, remissness in right-doing, wickedness and falsehood, pride and presumption, ruthless deception and guile, abundant insolence, shortness of temper and profusion of folly, arrogant pas-

sion, abominable acts in a spirit of lewdness, filthy ways
in the thralldom of unchastity, a blasphemous tongue,
blindness of eyes, dullness of ears, stiffness of neck and
hardness of heart, to the end that a man walks entirely
in ways of darkness and of evil cunning.[85] The guerdon
of all who walk in such ways is multitude of afflictions
at the hands of all the angels of destruction,[36] everlasting
perdition through the angry wrath of an avenging God,
eternal horror and perpetual reproach, the disgrace of final
annihilation in the Fire, darkness throughout the vicissitudes of life in every generation, doleful sorrow, bitter misfortune and darkling ruin—ending in extinction without
remnant or survival.

It is to these things that all men are born, and it is to
these that all the host of them are heirs throughout their
generations. It is in these ways that men needs must walk
and it is in these two divisions, according as a man inherits
something of each, that all human acts are divided throughout all the ages of eternity. For God has appointed these
two things to obtain in equal measure until the final age.

Between the two categories He has set an eternal enmity.
Deeds of perversity are an abomination to Truth, while
all the ways of Truth are an abomination to perversity;
and there is a constant jealous rivalry between their two
regimes, for they do not march in accord. Howbeit, God
in His inscrutable wisdom has appointed a term for the
existence of perversity, and when the time of Inquisition
comes, He will destroy it for ever. Then truth will emerge
triumphant for the world, albeit now and until the time
of the final judgment it go sullying itself in the ways of
wickedness owing to the domination of perversity. Then,
too, God will purge all the acts of man in the crucible
of His truth, and refine for Himself all the fabric of man,
destroying every spirit of perversity from within his flesh
and cleansing him by the holy spirit from all the effects
of wickedness. Like waters of purification He will sprinkle
upon him the spirit of truth,[87] to cleanse him of all the
abominations of falsehood and of all pollution through the
spirit of filth; to the end that, being made upright, men
may have understanding of transcendental knowledge and

of the lore of the sons of heaven,[38] and that, being made blameless in their ways, they may be endowed with inner vision. For them has God chosen to be the partners of His eternal covenant, and theirs shall be all mortal glory.[39] Perversity shall be no more, and all works of deceit shall be put to shame.

Thus far, the spirits of truth and perversity have been struggling in the heart of man. Men have walked both in wisdom and in folly. If a man casts his portion with truth, he does righteously and hates perversity; if he casts it with perversity, he does wickedly and abominates truth. For God has apportioned them in equal measure until the final age, until 'He makes all things new'.[40] He foreknows the effect of their works in every epoch of the world, and He has made men heirs to them that they might know good and evil. But [when the time] of Inquisition [comes], He will determine the fate of every living being in accordance with which of the [two spirits he has chosen to follow].

Of social relations (v, 1–7)

This is the rule for all the members of the community— that is, for such as have declared their readiness to turn away from all evil and to adhere to all that God in His good pleasure has commanded.

They are to keep apart from the company of the froward.

They are to belong to the community in both a doctrinal and an economic sense.

They are to abide by the decisions of the sons of Zadok,[41] the same being priests that still keep the Covenant, and of the majority of the community that stand firm in it. It is by the vote of such that all matters doctrinal, economic and judicial are to be determined.

They are concertedly and in all their pursuits to practise truth, humility, righteousness, justice, charity and decency, with no one walking in the stubbornness of his own heart or going astray after his heart or his eyes or his fallible human mind.

Furthermore, they are concertedly to remove the impurity of their human mold, and likewise all stiffneckedness.

They are to establish in Israel a solid basis of truth.

They are to unite in a bond indissoluble for ever.

They are to extend forgiveness to all among the priesthood that have freely enlisted in the cause of holiness, and to all among the laity that have done so in the cause of truth, and likewise to all that have associated themselves with them.[42]

They are to make common cause both in the struggle and in the upshot of it.

They are to regard as felons all that transgress the law.

Of the obligation of holiness   (v, 7–20)

And this is the way in which all those ordinances are to be applied on a collective basis.

Everyone who is admitted to the formal organization* of the community is to enter into a covenant of God in the presence of all fellow-volunteers in the cause and to commit himself by a binding oath[43] to return with all his heart and soul to the commandments of the Law of Moses, as that Law is revealed to the sons of Zadok—that is, to the priests who still keep the Covenant and seek God's will —and to a majority of their co-covenanters who have volunteered together to adhere to the truth of God and to walk according to His pleasure.

He that so commits himself is to keep apart from all froward men that walk in the path of wickedness; for such men are not to be reckoned in the Covenant inasmuch as they have never sought nor studied God's ordinances in order to find out on what more arcane points they may guiltily have gone astray, while in regard to the things which stand patently revealed they have acted highhandedly. They have thus incurred God's angry judgment and caused Him to take vengeance upon them with all the curses threatened in the Covenant[44] and to wreak great

* Heb. 'council'.

judgments upon them that they be finally destroyed without remnant.

No one is to go into water in order to attain the purity of holy men.[45] For men cannot be purified except they repent their evil. God regards as impure all that transgress His word. No one is to have any association with such a man either in work or in goods, lest he incur the penalty of prosecution. Rather is he to keep away from such a man in every respect, for the Scripture says: 'Keep away from every false thing' [Ex. 23.7].[46] No member of the community is to abide by the decision of such men in any matter of doctrine or law. He is not to eat or drink of anything that belongs to them nor to receive anything from them except for cash, even as it is written: 'Desist from man whose breath is in his nostrils, for as what is he reckoned?' [Isa. 2.22].[47] All that are not reckoned in the Covenant must be put aside, and likewise all that they possess. A holy man must not rely on works of vanity, and vanity is what all of them are that have not recognized God's Covenant. All that spurn His word will God blast out of the world. All their actions are as filth before Him, and He regards all their possessions as unclean.

Of the examination   (v, 20–24)
of initiants

When a man enters the covenant, minded to act in accordance with all the foregoing ordinances and formally to ally himself to the holy congregation, inquiry is to be made concerning his temper in human relations and his understanding and performance in matters of doctrine. This inquiry is to be conducted jointly by the priests who have undertaken concertedly to uphold God's Covenant and to supervise the execution of all the ordinances which He has commanded, and by a majority of the laity who have likewise undertaken concertedly to return to that Covenant. Every man is then to be registered in a particular rank, one after the other, by the standard of his understanding and performance. The object is that each person will be rendered subject to his superior. Their spiritual attitudes and their performance are to be reviewed, however, year by year, some being then promoted by virtue of their (improved) understanding and the integrity of their conduct, and others demoted for their waywardness.

Of accusations and grudges (v, 24–vi, 1)

When anyone has a charge against his neighbor, he is to prosecute it truthfully, humbly and humanely. He is not to speak to him angrily or querulously or arrogantly or in any wicked mood.[48] He is not to bear hatred [towards him in the inner recesses] of his heart. When he has a charge against him, he is to proffer it then and there† and not to render himself liable to penalty by nursing a grudge. Furthermore, no man is to bring a charge publicly against his neighbor except he prove it by witnesses.

Of communal duties   (vi, 1–8)

This is the procedure which all members of the community are to follow in all dealings with one another, wherever they dwell.

Everyone is to obey his superior in rank[49] in all matters of work or money. But all are to dine together, worship together and take counsel together.[50]

Wherever there be ten men[51] who have been formally enrolled in the community, one who is a priest is not to depart from them. When they sit in his presence, they are to take their places according to their respective ranks; and the same order is to obtain when they meet for common counsel.

When they set the table for a meal or prepare wine to drink, the priest is first to put forth his hand to invoke a blessing on the first portion of the bread or wine.[52]

In any place where there happen to be ten such men, there is not to be absent from them one who will be available at all times, day and night, to interpret the Law (*Torah*),[53] each of them doing so in turn.

† Heb. 'on the selfsame day'.

The general members of the community are to keep awake for a third of all the nights of the year reading book(s),‡ studying the Law and worshiping together.[54]

Of the General Council   (vi, 8–13)

This is the rule covering public sessions.

The priests are to occupy the first place. The elders are to come second; and the rest of the people are to take their places according to their respective ranks. This order is to obtain alike when they seek a judicial ruling, when they meet for common counsel, or when any matter arises of general concern.

Everyone is to have an opportunity of rendering his opinion in the common council. No one, however, is to interrupt while his neighbor is speaking, or to speak until the latter has finished.[55] Furthermore, no one is to speak in advance of his prescribed rank. Everyone is to speak in turn, as he is called upon.

In public sessions, no one is to speak on any subject that is not of concern to§ the company as a whole.[56] If the superintendent[57] of the general membership or anyone who is not of the same rank as the person who happens to be raising a question for the consideration of the community, has something to say to the company, he is to stand up and declare: I have something to say to the company; and only if they so bid him, is he to speak.

Of postulants and novices   (vi, 13–23)

If any man in Israel wish to be affiliated to the formal congregation of the community, the superintendent of the general membership is to examine him as to his intelligence and his actions and, if he then embark on a course of training, he is to have him enter into a covenant to return to the truth and turn away from all perversity. Then he is to apprise him of all the rules of the community.

‡ Or, 'the Book (of the Law)'.
§ Or, 'to the liking of'.

Subsequently, when that man comes to present himself to the general membership, everyone is to be asked his opinion about him, and his admission to or rejection from the formal congregation of the community is to be determined by general vote.

No candidate, however, is to be admitted to the formal state of purity enjoyed by the general membership of the community[58] until, at the completion of a full year, his spiritual attitude and his performance have been duly reviewed. Meanwhile he is to have no stake in the common funds.[59]

After he has spent a full year in the midst of the community, the members are jointly to review his case, as to his understanding and performance in matters of doctrine. If it then be voted by the opinion of the priests and of a majority of their co-covenanters to admit him to the sodality, they are to have him bring with him all his property and the tools of his profession. These are to be committed to the custody of the community's 'minister of works'. They are to be entered by that officer into an account, but he is not to disburse them for the general benefit.

Not until the completion of a second year among the members of the community is the candidate to be admitted to the common board.**[60] When, however, that second year has been completed, he is to be subjected to a further review by the general membership,[61] and if it then be voted to admit him to the community, he is to be registered in the due order of rank which he is to occupy among his brethren in all matters pertaining to doctrine, judicial procedure, degree of purity and share in the common funds. Thenceforth his counsel and his judgment are to be at the disposal of the community.

Of false, impudent   (vi, 23–vii, 5)
and blasphemous speech

And these are the rules to be followed in the interpretation of the law regarding forms of speech.

** Heb. 'drink'.

If there be found in the community a man who consciously lies in the matter of (his) wealth, he is to be regarded as outside the state of purity entailed by membership, and he is to be mulcted of one fourth of his food ration.

If a man answer his neighbor defiantly or speak brusquely so as to undermine the composure†† of his fellow, and in so doing flout the orders of one who is registered as his superior [   ],‡‡ he is to be mulcted for one year.

If a man, in speaking about anything, mention that Name which is honored above all [names],§§[62] or if, in a moment of sudden stress or for some other personal reason, he curse the   (i.e., the man who reads the Book of the Law or leads worship),*[63] he is to be put out and never to return to formal membership in the community.

If a man speak in anger against one of the registered priests, he is to be mulcted for one year, placed in isolation, and regarded as outside the state of purity entailed in membership of the community. If, however, he spoke unintentionally, he is to be mulcted only for six months.

If a man dissemble about what he really knows, he is to be mulcted for six months.

If a man defames his neighbor unjustly, and does so deliberately, he is to be mulcted for one year and regarded as 'outside'.

†† Heb. 'shake (or, disturb) the foundation'.

‡‡ An imperfectly preserved phrase follows in the text. Possibly, it means, 'And if his hand act wickedly against him', i.e., if he bodily assaults him.

§§ I.e., the name of God.

* This, gap and all, is how the text reads in the original. It is apparent that the scribe found in the archetype (or heard from dictation?) a rare word which he did not understand fully. He therefore left a blank, but added a gloss giving the approximate sense. The word must have been a technical term for something like 'precentor' or 'deacon'.

Of fraud   (vii, 5-8)

If a man speak with his neighbor in guile or consciously practice deceit upon him, he is to be mulcted for six months. If, however, he practices the deceit [unintentionally],† he is to be mulcted only for three months.

If a man defraud the community, causing a deficit in its funds, he is to make good that deficit. If he lack means to do so, he is to be mulcted for sixty days.

Of vindictiveness   (vii, 8-9)

If he harbor a grudge against his neighbor without legitimate cause, he is to be mulcted for six months [supralinear correction: 'one year']. The same is to apply also to anyone who takes personal revenge on his neighbor in any respect.

Of improper speech   (vii, 9)

Anyone who indulges in indecent talk is to be mulcted for three months.

Of misconduct   (vii, 9-12)
at public sessions

Anyone who interrupts his neighbor in a public session is to be mulcted for ten days.

Anyone who lies down and goes to sleep at a public session is to be mulcted for thirty days.

Anyone who leaves a public session gratuitously and without reason for as many as three times during one sit-

† There is again a blank in the original. The scribe evidently could not decipher the word in his archetype, but the sense is clear.

ting is to be mulcted for ten days. If he leaves while everyone else is standing(?),‡ he is to be mulcted for thirty days.

Of indecorous acts   (vii, 12–15)

If, except he be under duress (?)§, a man walk naked before his neighbor, he shall be mulcted for six months.

If a man spit into the midst of a public session, he shall be mulcted for thirty days.

If a man bring out his hand from under his cloak, and so expose himself that his private parts become visible, he shall be mulcted for thirty days.

If a man indulge in raucous, inane laughter, he shall be mulcted for thirty days.

If a man put forth his left hand[64] to gesticulate with it in conversation, he shall be mulcted for ten days.

Of slander   (vii, 15–18)
and incrimination

If a man slander his neighbor, he shall be regarded as outside the communal state of purity for one year, and he shall also be mulcted. But if he slander the entire group, he is to be expelled and never to return.

If a man complain against the whole basis of the community, he is to be expelled irrevocably.

If he complain against his neighbor without legitimate cause, he is to be mulcted for six months.

Of defection   (vii, 18–25)

If a man's spirit waver so far from the basis of the community that he betray the truth and walk in the stubbornness of his own heart, but if he subsequently repent, he shall be mulcted for two years. During the first, he shall

‡ This word is partly obliterated. The sense is therefore obscure.

§ Heb. uncertain.

be regarded as outside the communal state of purity altogether. During the second, he shall be excluded only from the communal board** and occupy a place behind all the other members. At the completion of the two years, the membership in general shall hold an enquiry about him. If it then be decided to readmit him, he shall again be registered with duly assigned rank and thereafter he too shall be called upon to render his opinion in deliberations concerning the rules.

If a man has been a formal member of the community for a full ten years, but then, through a spiritual relapse, betray the principles of the community and quit the general body in order to walk in the stubbornness of his own heart, he is never to return to formal membership in the community. No member of the community is to associate with him either by recognizing him as of the same state of purity or by sharing property with him. Any of the members who does so shall be liable to the same sentence: he too shall be expelled.[65]

Of the appointment   (viii, 1–19)
of 'presbyters'

In the deliberative council of the community there shall be twelve laymen and three priests schooled to perfection in all that has been revealed of the entire Law.[66] Their duty shall be to set the standard for the practice of truth, righteousness and justice, and for the exercise of charity and humility in human relations; and to show how, by control of impulse and contrition of spirit, faithfulness may be maintained on earth; how, by active performance of justice and passive submission to the trials of chastisement, iniquity may be cleared, and how one can walk with all men with the quality of truth and in conduct appropriate to every occasion.

So long as these men exist in Israel, the deliberative council of the community will rest securely on a basis of truth. It will become a plant evergreen. Insofar as the lay-

** Heb. 'drink'.

men are concerned, it will be indeed a sanctuary; and insofar as the priesthood is concerned, it will indeed constitute
the basis for a true 'holy of holies'. The members of the
community will be in all justice the witnesses of God's
truth and the elect of His favor,[67] effecting atonement for
the earth and ensuring the requital of the wicked. They
will be, indeed, a 'tested bulwark' and 'a precious corner-
stone' [cf. Isa. 28.16],[68] which shall never be shaken or
moved from their place. As for the priesthood, they shall
be a seat for the holy of holies, inasmuch as all of them
will then have knowledge of the Covenant of justice and
all of them be qualified to offer what will be indeed 'a
pleasant savor' to the Lord. And as for the laity, they will
constitute a household of integrity and truth, qualified to
maintain the Covenant as an everlasting pact. They shall
prove acceptable to God, so that He will shrive the earth
of its guilt, bring final judgment upon wickedness, and
perversity shall be no more.

When these men have undergone, with blamelessness of
conduct, a two-year preparation in the fundamentals of the
community, they shall be segregated as especially sacred
among the formal members of the community. Any knowledge which the expositor of the law may possess but which
may have to remain arcane to the ordinary layman, he shall
not keep hidden from them; for in their case there need
be no fear that it might induce apostasy.[69]

When these men exist in Israel, these are the provisions
whereby they are to be kept apart from any consort with
froward men, to the end that they may indeed 'go into
the wilderness to prepare the way', i.e., do what Scripture
enjoins when it says, 'Prepare in the wilderness the way
. . . make straight in the desert a highway for our God'
[Isa. 40.3].[70] (The reference is to the study of the Law
which God commanded through Moses to the end that,
as occasion arises, all things may be done in accordance
with what is revealed therein and with what the prophets
also have revealed through God's holy spirit.)

No member of the community—that is, no duly covenanted member—who blatantly deviates in any particular

from the total body of commandments is to be permitted
to come into contact with the purity enjoyed by these specially holy men or to benefit by†† their counsel until his
actions be free of all perversity and he has been readmitted
to the common council by decision of the general membership and thereupon reinstated in his rank.

The same rule is to apply also to novices.

Of the conduct   (viii, 20–ix, 6)
of 'presbyters'

These are the rules of conduct for the 'men of perfect
holiness' in their dealings with one another.

If any of those that have been admitted to the degree
of special sanctity—that is, to the degree of 'those that walk
blamelessly in the way as God has commanded'—transgress
a single word of the Law of Moses either blatantly or devi-
ously, he is to be excommunicated and never to return.
No other person in the degree of the specially holy is to
have anything to do with him in the sharing either of property or of counsel.

If, however, he erred unintentionally, he is to be de-
barred only from that particular degree of purity and from
participation in the common council. This is to be interpreted to mean that he is not to render any judgment nor
is his counsel to be invited in any matter for a full two
years. This holds good, however, only if, after the expiration of the full two years, his conduct be considered, in
the judgment of the general membership, to be perfect alike
in attendance at general assemblies, in study and in frame
of mind, and if he has not meanwhile committed any further act of inadvertence. In other words, this two-year penalty is to apply only in the case of a single inadvertent
error, whereas if a man acts blatantly, he is nevermore to
be readmitted. In sum, it is only the man who acts by
inadvertence that is to be placed on probation for two years
to see whether, in the opinion of the general membership,
his conduct and frame of mind have meanwhile again be-

†† Heb. 'know'.

come blameless. If so, he may be reinstated in the body of the especially holy.

When these things obtain in Israel, as defined by these provisions, the Holy Spirit will indeed rest on a sound foundation; truth will be evinced perpetually; the guilt of transgression and the perfidy of sin will be shriven; and atonement will be made for the earth more effectively than by any flesh of burnt-offerings or fat of sacrifices. The 'oblation of the lips' will be in all justice like the erstwhile 'pleasant savor' on the altar; righteousness and integrity like that free-will offering which God deigns to accept. At that time, the men of the community will constitute a true and distinctive temple—a veritable holy of holies—wherein the priesthood may fitly foregather, and a true and distinctive synagogue made up of laymen who walk in integrity.

Of the authority of the priests (ix, 7)

The priests alone are to have authority in all judicial and economic matters, and it is by their vote that the ranks of the various members of the community are to be determined.

Of the property of 'presbyters' (ix, 8–11)

The property of the 'specially holy men'—that is, of 'the men that walk blamelessly'—is not to be put into a common pool with that of men who may still be addicted to deceit‡‡ and may not yet have achieved that purity of conduct which leads them to keep apart from perversity and to walk in integrity.

Until the coming of the Prophet§§ and of both the priestly and the lay Messiah,[71] these men are not to depart

‡‡ Heb. simply, 'men of deceit'.

§§ That is, the prophet foretold in Deut. 18:18, 'I will raise them up a prophet from among their brethren, like unto thee [Moses]; and I will put My words in his mouth, and he shall speak unto them all that I shall command him'. See Introduction, p. 6.

from the clear intent of the Law to walk in any way in the stubbornness of their own hearts. They shall judge by the original laws in which the members of the community were schooled from the beginning.

Of the daily conduct   (ix, 12–16)
of the faithful

These are the ordinances for the conduct of any man that seeks after inner vision, in regard alike to human relations, the regulation of affairs on specific occasions, and the balanced appraisal of his fellow men, to the end that he may perform at all times the will of God which has been revealed as pertinent to this or that occasion; that he may at all times accommodate theory to circumstance; and that he may come to make the proper distinctions and evaluate the sons of Zadok (i.e., the priests) and the elect of any particular epoch by the standard of their spiritual attitudes, and appraise them by that criterion, thus conforming to the will of God, as He has commanded.

Everyone is to be judged by the standard of his spirituality. Intercourse with him is to be determined by the purity of his deeds,* and consort with him by the degree of his intelligence. This alone is to determine the degree to which a man is to be loved or hated.

Of religious discussion   (ix, 16–21)

No one is to engage in discussion or disputation with men of ill repute; and in the company of froward men everyone is to abstain from talk about† the meaning of the Law [Torah].

With those, however, that have chosen the right path everyone is indeed to discuss matters pertaining to the apprehension‡ of God's truth and of His righteous judgments. The purpose of such discussions is to guide the minds of

---

* Heb. 'hands (palms)'.
† Heb. 'keep hidden'.
‡ Heb. 'knowledge'.

the members of the community, to give them insight into God's inscrutable wonders and truth, and to bring them to walk blamelessly each with his neighbor in harmony with all that has been revealed to them. For this is the time when 'the way is being prepared in the wilderness', and it behooves them to understand all that is happening. It is also the time when they must needs keep apart from all other men and not turn aside from the way through any form of perversity.

Of loving and hating fellow- (ix, 21–26)
men; and of duty to God

And these are the regulations of conduct for every man that would seek the inner vision in these times, touching what he is to love and what he is to hate.

He is to bear unremitting hatred towards all men of ill repute, and to be minded to keep ⋮ ﹀ clusion from them. He is to leave it to them to pursᵤ ;alth and mercenary gain, like servants at the mercy of ι ir masters or wretches truckling to a despot.

He is to be zealous to carry out every ordinance punctiliously, against the Day of Requital.[72]

In all his emprises and in all things over which he has control he is to act in a manner acceptable to God, in accordance with what God has commanded.

He is to accept willingly whatever befalls him and to take pleasure in nothing but the will of God.

He is to make [all] the words of his mouth acceptable, and not to lust after anything that God has not commanded.

He is to watch ever for the judgment of God, and [in every vicissitude of his existence] he is to bless his Maker. Whatever befalls, he is to [recount God's glory] and to bless him [with 'the oblation of] the lips'.

THE 'ZADOKITE' DOCUMENT*

[I]

*   *   *

I [II]

Of God's vengeance   (i, 1–ii, 12)
and providence

Now listen, all right-minded men, and take note how God
acts: He has a case against all flesh and exacts satisfaction
from all who spurn Him.

Whenever Israel broke faith and renounced Him, He hid
His face both from it and from His sanctuary and con-
signed them to the sword. But whenever He called to mind
the covenant which He had made with their forbears, He
spared them a remnant and did not consign them to utter
extinction.

So, in the Era of Anger, that era of the three hundred
and ninety years,[1] when He delivered them into the hand
of Nebuchadnezzar, king of Babylon, He took care of them
and brought to blossom alike out of the priesthood and
out of the laity that root which had been planted of old,
allowing it once more to possess the land and to grow fat
in the richness of its soil. Then they realized their iniquity

* From earlier copies found at Qumran it is now known that
when this document was first published, in 1910, from medieval
copies discovered in the Cairo Genizah, the pages were arranged
in the wrong order. The correct sequence is here added in
square brackets after the numeration of each major part. Parts
I, III and V of the original text are missing from the Cairo
manuscripts, but are preserved in fragments from Qumran.
These, however, have not yet been fully published.

and knew that they had been at fault. For twenty years, however, they remained like blind men groping their way,[2] until at last God took note of their deeds, how that they were seeking Him sincerely, and He raised up for them one who would teach the Law correctly,[3] to guide them in the way of His heart and to demonstrate to future ages what He does to a generation that incurs His anger, that is, to the congregation of those that betray Him and turn aside from His way.

The period in question was that whereof it is written, 'Like a stubborn heifer, Israel was stubborn' [Hos. 4.16]. It was the time when a certain scoffer arose to distil upon Israel the waters deceptive[4] and to lead them astray in a trackless waste, bringing low whatsoever had once been high, diverting them from the proper paths and removing the landmarks which their forbears had set up, to the end that through his efforts those curses cleaved to them which had been prescribed when the Covenant was concluded, and they were delivered to the sword. Thus was avenged that breach of the Covenant which they had committed in seeking smooth things and in preferring delusion and in being constantly on the watch to breach the faith and in choosing to walk proudly and in justifying the wicked and condemning the righteous, and in abrogating the Covenant and annulling the pact, and in assailing the life of the righteous and abhorring all whose conduct was blameless, and in pursuing them with the sword, and in raising a general clamor against them. God then grew angry with their horde and utterly destroyed all their throng and treated all their works as an abominable thing unclean.

Of God's judgment on the wicked (ii, 2–13) and His clemency to the righteous

And now, listen to me, all who have entered the Covenant, and I will open your ears to the fate which attends the wicked.

God loves knowledge. Wisdom and sound sense has He posted before Him. Prudence and knowledge minister to Him.[5] Patience attends on him and abundant forgiveness, so that He may shrive the repentant. But also with Him are might and power and great wrath, along with flames of fire and all the angels of destruction[6]—appointed for them that turn aside from His way and treat His ordinance as a thing to be shunned, to the end that they shall be left without remnant or survival.

Never, from the very beginning of the world, has God approved such men. He has always known what their actions would be, even before the foundations of them were laid. He has anathematized whole generations on account of bloodshed, hiding His face from the land. Their end has always been pre-determined. He has always foreknown how long they would endure and the exact and precise extent of their continuance; yea, all that has happened in their several epochs throughout history, and likewise all that was to befall them.

Nevertheless, in all of their generations He has ever raised up for Himself duly designated men, so that He might provide survival for the earth and fill the face of the world with their seed. And to these has He ever revealed His holy spirit at the hands of His anointed[7] and has ever disclosed the truth; and He has clearly specified who they were. But those whom He hated He has always left to wander astray.

Of ancient sinners   (ii, 14–iii, 12)

And now, children, listen to me, and I will open your eyes to see and understand how God acts, so that you may choose what He has desired and reject what He has hated, walking blamelessly in all His ways and not straying after thoughts of guilty lust or after whoring eyes. For many there be that have strayed thereby from olden times until now, and even strong heroes have stumbled thereby.

Because they walked in the stubbornness of their hearts, the Watchers of heaven fell;[8] yea, they were caught thereby because they kept not the commandments of God.

So too their sons, whose height was like the lofty cedars and whose bodies were as mountains.[9] They also fell.

So too 'all flesh that was upon the dry land'.[10] They

also perished. These became as though they had never been, because they did their own pleasure and kept not the commandments of their Maker. In the end His anger was kindled against them.

In the same way, too, the sons of Noah went astray,[11] and thereby they and their families were cut off.

Abraham, however, did not walk in this way. Therefore, because he kept the commandments of God and did not prefer the desires of his own spirit, he was accounted the Friend of God[12] and transmitted this status in turn to Isaac and Jacob. They too kept the commandments, and they too were recorded as Friends of God and as partners in His everlasting Covenant.

But the sons of Jacob strayed in that way and they were punished for their aberration.

Their sons, too, when they were in Egypt, walked in the stubbornness of their hearts, plotting against the commandments of God and doing each what was right in his own eyes. Because they ate blood all their males were cut off in the wilderness. God said to them at Kadesh: 'Go up and possess the land' [Deut. 9.23], [but they followed the desire of] their own spirits and hearkened not to the voice of their Maker neither to the orders of their leader, but kept murmuring in their tents. So the anger of God was kindled against their horde.[13]

Their sons too perished by such conduct. Their kings were cut off through it, and their heroes perished through it, and their land was laid waste through it.

Thus, whenever in ancient times those who had entered the Covenant became guilty on this account, forsaking that Covenant of God, preferring their own pleasure and going astray after the stubbornness of their hearts, doing each man as he pleased, they were invariably delivered to the sword.

Of the righteous remnant (iii, 12–iv, 6)

Howbeit, with the rest of them—that is, with those that held fast to His commandments—God ever made good His everlasting Covenant with Israel, revealing to them the hidden things concerning which Israel in general had gone astray—even His holy sabbaths and His glorious festivals, His righteous ordinances, the ways of His truth and the purposes of His will, 'the which, if a man do, he shall live' [Lev. 18.5]. He opened for them a well with water abounding,[14] which they might dig. But them that spurned those waters He did not permit to live. And though they kept sullying themselves with human transgression and with filthy ways, and kept saying, ''Tis our own concern', yet did God with His mysterious power shrive their iniquity and forgive their transgression and build for them in Israel a firmly established House the like of which has not existed from ancient times until this day.

They that hold fast unto Him are destined for life eternal, and theirs is all mortal glory, even as God has sworn unto them by the hand of the prophet Ezekiel, saying: 'The priests and the levites and the sons of Zadok that kept the charge of My sanctuary when the children of Israel went astray from Me, these it is that shall offer unto Me the fat and the blood' [Ezek. 44.15]. By 'priests' is meant those in Israel that repented and departed from the land of Judah. [By 'levites'] is meant those that associated themselves[15] with them. By 'sons of Zadok' is meant those elect of Israel that have been designated by name and that shall go on functioning in the last days. Behold, their names have been specified, the families into which they are to be born, the epochs in which they are to function, the full tale of their tribulations, the length of their sojourn in exile, and the precise nature of their deeds.

Of the reward of the faithful   (iv, 6–12)

These were the 'holy men'[16] of former times—the men whose sins God pardoned, who knew right for right and wrong for wrong. But all who up to the present time have succeeded them in carrying out explicitly the Law from which those ancients drew their lessons, them too will God forgive, in accordance with the Covenant which He made with those ancients to forgive their iniquities. And when the present era is completed, there will be no more express affiliation with the house of Judah; every man will 'mount guard' for himself. 'The fence will be rebuilt, and the bounds be far-flung' [cf. Mic. 7.11].[17]

Of the works of Belial   (iv, 12–v, 17)

Meanwhile, however, Belial will be rampant in Israel, even as God has said through the prophet Isaiah, the son of Amoz: 'Terror and the pit and the trap shall be upon thee, O inhabitant of the land!' [Isa. 24.17]. The reference is to those three snares, viz. (a) whoredom, (b) lucre, and (c) desecration, concerning which Levi the son of Jacob said[18] that by making them look like three kinds of righteousness Belial ensnares Israel in them. He who escapes the one gets caught in the other, and he who escapes the other gets caught in the third.

Such men may be described as 'builders of a rickety wall' [Ezek. 13.10], or as persons that have 'walked after filth' [Hos. 5.11]. The 'filth' in question is the babbling preacher of whom God said, 'Babble-babble shall they preach' [Mic. 2.6]; while the fact that *two* words [viz. 'pit' and 'trap'] are used to describe the net in which they will be caught alludes to the whorish practice of taking *two* wives at the same time, the true basis of nature being the pairing of one male with one female, even as it is said (of Adam and Eve), 'A male and a female created He them' [Gen. 1.27], and of those that went into the ark, 'In pairs they entered' [Gen. 7.9]. Similarly, too, it is said concerning a prince: 'He shall not take more than one wife' [Deut. 17.17].†[19]

† David, however, had never read the Book of Law, for it was sealed up in the ark and remained unopened in Israel from the day when Eleazar and Joshua and the Elders were gathered to their rest. The people worshiped Ashtoreth, while the ark remained hidden and unopened until indeed a Zadokite entered into office [in the person of Hilkiah the priest]. Accordingly, David's actions were not punished, save the spilling of the blood of Uriah, but God remitted the penalty for them.

This is part of the original text, but is here relegated to a footnote, as it would have been in a modern work, in order not to interrupt the sequence of thought.

Such persons commit [desecration] inasmuch as they lie with women in their periods and do not put them aside, as enjoined in the Law.[20] Moreover, they marry the daughters of their brothers and sisters, whereas Moses has said: 'Thou shalt not enter into intimate relations with the sister of thy mother; she is thy mother's kin' [cf. Lev. 18.13]. (The laws of forbidden degrees are written, to be sure, with reference to males, but they hold good equally for females. A niece, for instance, who indulges in carnal intercourse with her paternal uncle is equally to be regarded as his kin.)

Furthermore, such men have desecrated the holy spirit within them, and with mocking tongue have opened their mouths against the statutes of God's Covenant, declaring, 'They have no foundation'. They have spoken disgracefully about them.

All such men may be described as persons that 'kindle a fire and set firebrands alight' [Isa. 50.11]. Of them it may be said that 'their webs are spiders' webs and their eggs basilisks' eggs' [Isa. 59.5]. None that have contact with them shall go unscathed; the more one does so, the more guilty he becomes—unless, of course, he does so under compulsion.

Throughout antiquity, however, God has always taken note of the deeds of such men, and His anger has always been kindled against their acts. Always, in fact, they have proved to be 'a witless folk' [Isa. 27.11], 'a nation void of sense' [Deut. 32.28] in that they lacked discernment.

Of the Remnant   (v, 17–vi, 11)

When, in antiquity, Israel was first delivered, Moses and Aaron still continued in their charge, through the help of the Angel of Lights,‡ even though Belial in his cunning had set up Jannes and his brother in opposition to them.[21]

Similarly, at the time when the land was destroyed, men arose who removed the ancient landmarks and led Israel

‡ Heb. *Urim*. See *Manual of Discipline*, iii.20.

astray; and it was, indeed, because they uttered sedition against the commandments of God which He had given through Moses and through His holy anointed priest Aaron, and because they gave forth false prophecies in order to subvert Israel from God, that the land was laid utterly waste. Nevertheless, God still remembered the Covenant which He had made with their forbears and raised from the priesthood men of discernment and from the laity men of wisdom, and He made them hearken to Him. And these men 'dug the well'—that well whereof it is written, 'Princes digged it, nobles of the people delved it, with the aid of a meḥôqeq' [Num. 21.18]. The 'well' in question is the Law. They that 'digged' are those of Israel who repented and departed from the land of Judah to sojourn in 'the land of Damascus'.§ God called them all 'princes' because they went in search of Him, and their glory was never gainsaid (?) by any man's mouth.[22] The term meḥôqeq [which can mean 'lawgiver' as well as 'stave'] refers to the man who expounds the Law. Isaiah has employed an analogous piece of imagery when in allusion to the Law he has spoken of God's 'producing a tool for His work' [cf. Isa. 54.16]. As for the 'nobles of the people', these are the men that come, throughout the Era of Wickedness, to delve the well, using as their staves [Heb. me-ḥôq-eq] the statutes [Heb. ḥuq-îm] which the Lawgiver prescribed [Heb. ḥaqaq ha-meḥôqeq] for them to walk in. Without such 'implements', they would, indeed, never achieve their goal until such time as the true Expositor arises at the end of days.

Of the obligation   (vi, 11–vii, 6a)
of the Covenant

All that enter the covenant with no intention of going into the sanctuary to keep the flame alive on the altar do so in vain. They have as good as shut the door. Of them God has said: 'Who is there among you that would shut

§ Scarcely to be taken literally. See above, pp. 5, 27.

the door, and who of you would not keep alive the flame upon Mine altar?' In vain [Mal. 1.10] [are all their deeds] if, in an era of wickedness, they do not take heed

to act in accordance with the explicit injunctions of the Law;

to keep away from men of ill-repute;

to hold themselves aloof from ill-gotten gain;

not to defile themselves by laying hands on that which has been vowed or devoted to God or on the property of the sanctuary;

not to rob the poor of God's people;

not to make widows their prey or murder the fatherless;

to distinguish between unclean and clean and to recognize holy from profane;

to keep the sabbath in its every detail, and the festivals and fasts in accordance with the practice laid down originally by the men who entered the new covenant in 'the land of Damascus';[23]

to pay their required dues in conformity with the detailed rules thereof;

to love each man his neighbor like himself;

to grasp the hand of the poor, the needy and the stranger;

to seek each man the welfare of his fellow;

to cheat not his own kin;

to abstain from whoredom, as is meet;

to bring no charge against his neighbor except by due process, and not to nurse grudges from day to day;

to keep away from all unclean things, in accordance with what has been prescribed in each case and with the distinctions which God Himself has drawn for them;

not to sully any man the holy spirit within him.[24]

Howbeit, for all that perform these rules in holiness unimpaired, according to all the instruction that has been given them—for them will God's Covenant be made good, that they shall be preserved for a thousand generations, even as it is written: 'He keepeth Covenant and loyalty with them that love Him and keep His commandments, even unto a thousand generations' [Deut. 7.9].

Of family life (vii, 6a–9)

If members of the community happen to be living in encampments,[25] in accordance with a usage which obtains in this country, and if they marry and beget children,[26] they are [in such matters] to follow the precepts of the Law [*Torah*] and the disciplinary regulations therein prescribed for the relationship of husband to wife and of father to child.**

Of the future requital (vii, 9–viii, 21)
of the disobedient

All that reject these things shall be doomed to extinction when God visits the world to requite the wicked—that is, when that ensues which is described by the prophet Isaiah the son of Amoz in the words: 'He will bring upon thee and upon thy kindred and upon thy father's house days the like of which have not come since the time that Ephraim departed from Judah' [Isa. 7.17]. In other words, the same situation will then obtain as obtained at the time of the great schism between the two houses of Israel, when Ephraim departed from Judah. At that time all who turned back were delivered to the sword, whereas all who stood fast were vouchsafed escape to 'the land of the north'.[27]

It is to this that allusion is also made in the statement: 'I will exile Sikkuth your king and Kiyyun your image, the star of your God . . . beyond Damascus' [cf. Amos 5.26].

The expression 'Sikkuth your king' refers to the Books of the Law, [for the word 'Sikkuth' is to be explained from the like-sounding *sukkah*, 'tabernacle']†† as in the passage of Scripture which says: 'I will raise up the fallen *sukkah* [tabernacle] of David' [Amos 9.11].

** Heb. even as God has said: 'Between a man and his wife and between a father and his son'—a loose quotation from Num. 30.17.

†† These words have here been inserted in order to bring out the word-play in the Hebrew original.

The expression 'king' denotes the congregation;[28] and the expression 'Kiyyun your image' refers to the books of the prophets[29] whose words the House of Israel has despised.[30]

As for the 'star', that refers to every such interpreter of the Law as indeed repairs to 'Damascus',[31] even as it is written: 'There shall step forth a star out of Jacob, and a sceptre shall rise out of Israel' [Num. 24.17].[32] The 'sceptre', it may be added, is the leader of the community, for in the exercise of his office he shall 'batter all the sons of pride',[33] as the Scripture says.

In the former visitation, these faithful men escaped, while those that turned back were delivered to the sword. Such will be the fate also of those who in the latter days will have entered God's Covenant but not held fast to these things. Them will God punish unto extinction by the hand of Belial.

The day on which God will carry out the punishment will be that to which the prophet alluded when he said: 'The princes of Judah have become like them that remove landmarks; I will pour out My wrath upon them like water' [Hos. 5.10]. They shall hope for healing, but the blem<ish> shall cl<i>ng to them. They are all of them apostates in that they have not turned from the way of the treacherous but have sullied themselves with wantonness and with wicked lucre and with the nursing of grudges against their fellows and with hatred of their neighbors. They have cheated their own kin and have had contact with lewdness and have been overbearing by virtue of wealth and possession and have done every man of them what was right in his own eyes, and have preferred the stubbornness of their own hearts, and have not kept aloof from the rabble, but have behaved lawlessly and highhandedly, walking in the way of the wicked.

Concerning them has God said: 'Their wine shall prove the poison of serpents and the cruel venom of asps' [Deut. 32.33]. The 'wine' in question is their conduct; the 'serpents' are the kings of the nations; and the 'venom [Heb. rô'sh] of asps' is the chief [Heb. rô'sh] of the Grecian kings who will come to wreak vengeance upon them.

Those that have been 'builders of the rickety wall' and 'daubers of veneer upon it'[34] have never considered all this, because the man who walks in wind, who raises whirlwinds, who spouts lies—the kind of man against all of whose ilk God's wrath has always been kindled—has kept spouting at them.

Howbeit, what Moses said of old, 'Not for thy righteousness nor for the uprightness of thy heart art thou going in to possess these nations but because of His love wherewith He loved thy forefathers and because He would keep the oath' [cf. Deut. 9.5],[35] applies equally to those in Israel who in those latter days show repentance and eschew the way of the rabble. The same love which God showed to the men of old who pledged themselves to follow Him will He show also to their successors. The ancestral Covenant shall stand good for them.

But inasmuch as He hates and abominates all that 'build a rickety wall', His anger has been kindled against them; and all who reject His commandments and forsake them and go on walking in the stubbornness of their own hearts will be visited with such judgment as has been described. It is to this that Jeremiah was referring when he spoke to Baruch the son of Neriah,[36] and Elisha when he spoke to his servant Gehazi.[37]

All those that entered into the new covenant in 'the land of Damascus' but subsequently relapsed and played false and turned away from the well of living waters shall not be reckoned as of the communion of the people nor inscribed in the roster of it throughout the period from the time the teacher of the community is gathered to his rest until that in which the lay and the priestly messiah [anointed] assume their office.[38]

The same applies also to all that entered the company of the 'specially holy and blameless'[39] but were loath to carry out the rules imposed upon the upright. Every such man is, as it were, like 'one molten in the furnace' [Ezek. 22.22]. When his deeds come clearly to light, he shall be cast out of that company as being one who has no share among the disciples of God. Men of knowledge shall reprove him according to his perfidy until he repent and thereby resume his place among the specially holy and blameless—that is, until it become clear that his actions are again in accordance with the interpretation of the Law adopted by the specially holy and blameless. Meanwhile, no man shall have commerce with him in matters either of property or of employment, for he has been cursed by all the holy ones of God on high.

The same applies again—in the future as it did in the past—to all who commit their hearts to idolatry and walk in the stubbornness of their hearts. All such have no portion in the household of the Law [*Torah*].

The same applies, once again, to all of their fellows that relapse in the company of scoffers. These too shall be judged; for they will have spoken error against the righteous ordinances and have rejected the Covenant of God and the pledge which they swore in 'the land of Damascus' —that is, the new covenant.[40] Neither they nor their families shall have a portion in the household of the Law [*Torah*].

About forty years will elapse from the death of the teacher of the community until all the men who take up arms and relapse in the company of the Man of Falsehood are brought to an end.[41] At that time, the wrath of God will be kindled against Israel, and that will ensue which is described by the prophet when he says: 'No king shall there be nor priest nor judge nor any that reproves aright' [cf. Hos. 3.4].

But they of Jacob that have repented, that have kept the Covenant of God, shall then speak each to his neighbor to bring him to righteousness, to direct his steps upon the way. And God will pay heed to their words and hearken, and He will draw up a record of those that fear Him and esteem His name,[42] to the end that salvation shall be revealed for all God-fearing men. Then ye shall again distinguish the righteous from the wicked, him that serves God from him that serves Him not. And God will 'show mercy unto thousands, unto them that love Him and keep

His commandments'—yea, even unto a thousand generations.

As for those schismatics[43] who, during the era when Israel was behaving perfidiously and defiling the sanctuary, indeed departed from the Holy City, relying (solely) on God, but who subsequently, without much [ad]o,‡‡ reverted to the popular [tre]nd—all of those shall be subjected to judgment by the sacred council,[44] each according to his character.

Those too who indeed entered the Covenant but subsequently broke through the bounds of the Law—all of those shall be 'cut off from the midst of the camp' at the time when God's glory is made manifest to Israel. And along with them shall go those that sought to turn Judah to wickedness in the days when it was being put to the test.

Of the future reward   (B. xx, 27-34)
of the faithful

Howbeit, all that hold fast to these enactments, going and coming in accordance with the Law; that hearken to the voice of the Teacher; that make confession before God, saying: Just and truthful are Thy judgments against us, for we have done wickedly, both we and our fathers, in that we have gone contrary to the statutes of the Covenant; all who raise not their hands against His holy statutes or His righteous judgments or His truthful ordinances; all who learn the lessons of the former judgments wherewith the men of the community were adjudged in time past; all who give ear to him who imparts the true interpretation of the Law and who do not controvert the right ordinances when they hear them—all of these shall rejoice and their hearts shall be strong, and they shall prevail over all that dwell in the world. And God will accept their atonement, and because they took refuge in His holy name they shall indeed see salvation at His hand.

‡‡ *Literally*, with fe[w] words.

[III]

*   *   *

II [IV—*cont.*]

A. CODE FOR URBAN COMMUNITIES

Of laying capital charges   (ix, 1)

The law which says that no person under doom from men shall be bought off, but must be put to death [cf. Lev. 27.29], is to be understood in the sense that any man who, as the result of a private vow, gets a fellow human being doomed to death under the laws of the Gentiles is himself to be put to death.[45]

Of grudges   (ix, 2–8)

And as to the law which says, 'Thou shalt not take vengeance nor bear any grudge against the children of thy people' [Lev. 19.18]—if any of those that have entered the Covenant bring charges against his neighbor without proving them by witnesses, or if he bring such charges merely through temper, or if he tell tales to his superiors simply to bring his neighbor into contempt, he ranks as one who takes vengeance and bears a grudge. Scripture says of God Himself that it is only upon His adversaries that He takes vengeance, and only against His enemies that He bears a grudge [Nah. 1.2]. Accordingly, if a man keep silent from day to day and then bring a charge against his neighbor in the heat of anger, it is as if he were laying capital charges against him, for he has not carried out the commandment of God Who said to him, 'Thou shalt surely reprove thy neighbor lest thou incur sin on his account' [Lev. 19.17].

Of involuntary oaths   (ix, 8–10)

Now regarding oaths. The principle that 'thou art not to take the law into thine own hands'[46] implies that a man who compels another to take an oath in the open field and not in the presence of judges or at their order has taken the law into his own hands.

Of lost property (ix, 10–15)

In the case of a loss, if it is not known who stole the particular article from the property of the camp in which the theft occurs, the owner is to be required to make a solemn deposition on oath. Anyone who hears it, knows the culprit and does not tell, is then to be considered culpable.

If a man makes restitution for expropriated property and brings the required guilt-offering, but there are no claimants to that property, he is to make his confession to the priest, and everything except the actual ram of the sin-offering is to go to the latter.

Lost property that is found but unclaimed is to be entrusted to the priests, because the man who retrieved it may not know the law about it. If the owners cannot be discovered [at the time], the priests are to take it into custody.

Of testimony (ix, 16–x, 3)

In the case of offenses against the Torah, if a man sees such an offense committed but is alone at the time, and if the matter be one of a capital nature, he is to disclose it to the overseer by bringing a charge in the presence of the alleged culprit. The overseer is then to make a record of it. If the man repeat the offense, this time also in the presence of one man only, and if the latter come in turn and inform the overseer—in that case, i.e., if the offender do it again and be again caught by only one person—the case against him is to be regarded as complete.

However, if there be two witnesses, and they concur in their statements, the culprit is to be excluded from his customary degree of purity only if those witnesses are trustworthy and if they lay information before the overseer on the very day when they saw the man [committing the offense].

In cases involving property, *two* trustworthy witnesses are required.[47] In those, however, that involve [no question of restitution but simply of] exclusion from the degree of purity, one alone is sufficient.

No man who has not yet completed his probationary period with the community and has not yet passed the statutory examination as a truly God-fearing person[48] is to be permitted as a witness before its judges in a capital case.

No man who has flagrantly transgressed the commandment is to be deemed a trustworthy witness against his neighbor until he has succeeded in winning re-acceptance into the community.

Of judges   (x, 4–10)

This is the rule concerning the judges of the community.

Periodically, a complement of ten men shall be selected from the community. Four of them shall belong to the tribe of Levi and Aaron, and six shall be laymen.[49] They shall be men versed in the Book of Study[50] and in the fundamentals of the Covenant. Their minimum age shall be twenty-five, and their maximum sixty. No man over sixty shall occupy judicial office in the community; for through the perfidy of man the potential span of human life has been reduced, and in the heat of His anger against the inhabitants of the earth, God decreed of old that their mental powers should recede before they complete their days.

Of ritual ablutions   (x, 10–13)

Now concerning purification by water. No one is to bathe in dirty water or in water which is too scant to fill a pail (?).[51]

No man is to purify himself with water drawn in a vessel or in a rock-pool where there is insufficient to fill a pail (?). If an unclean person come in contact with such water, he merely renders it unclean; and the same is true of water drawn in a vessel.

Of the Sabbath   (x, 14–xi, 18)

Now concerning the proper observance of the Sabbath.

No one is to do any work on Friday from the moment that the sun's disk stands distant from the gate by the length of its own diameter; for this is what Scripture implies when it says explicitly, Observe the Sabbath day to keep it holy.[52]

On the Sabbath day, no one is to indulge in ribald or empty talk. No one is to claim repayment of debts. No one is to engage in lawsuits concerning property and gain. No one is to talk about labor or work to be done the next day. No one is to go out into the field while it is still Sabbath with the intention of resuming his work immediately the Sabbath ends. No one is to walk more than a thousand cubits outside his city.[53] No one is to eat on the Sabbath day anything that has not been prepared in advance. He is not to eat anything that happens to be lying about in the field, neither is he to drink of anything that was not [previously] in the camp. If, however, he is travelling, he may go down to bathe and may drink wherever he happens to be.

No one is to commission a Gentile to transact business for him on the Sabbath day. No one is to wear soiled clothes or clothes that have been put in storage unless they first be laundered and rubbed with frankincense. No one is to observe a voluntary fast on the Sabbath. No one is to follow his beast to pasture for a distance of more than two thousand cubits from his city. No one is to raise his hand to strike it with his fist. If the beast be stubborn, he is not to take it outdoors. No one is to take anything out of his house, or bring anything in from outside. If he is [lodging] in a booth, he is likewise to take nothing out nor bring anything in. No one is to break open a pitch-sealed vessel on the Sabbath. No one is to carry ointments upon his person or walk around with them§§ on the Sabbath. No one is to pick up rock or dust in a dwelling place. Nurses are not to carry babies around on the Sabbath. No one is to put pressure on his male or female servant or on his hired help on the Sabbath. No one is to foal a beast on the Sabbath day. Even if it drop its young into a cistern or a pit, he is not to lift it out on the Sabbath.

No one is to stop for the Sabbath in a place near the heathen. No one is to desecrate the Sabbath for the sake of wealth or gain.

If a human being falls into a place where there is water or fire,[54] one may bring him up by means of a ladder or a rope or some other instrument.

No one is to present any offering upon the altar on the Sabbath except the statutory Sabbath burnt-offering—as the Scripture puts it, 'your Sabbath-offerings exclusively' [Lev. 23.38].[55]

Of the defilement　　　(xi, 18–xii, 2)
of holy places

No one is to send to the altar either burnt-offering or meal-offering or frankincense or wood by the hand of one suffering from any of the proscribed impurities, thus permitting him to render the altar impure; for Scripture says, 'The sacrifice of the wicked is an abomination, but the mere prayer of the righteous is like an acceptable offering' [Prov. 15.8].

As for those who come to the house of worship, no one is to come in a state of uncleanness requiring ablution. Such a man is either to anticipate the sounding of the trumpets of assembly or else to stay behind, so that [the rest] will not have to stop the entire service.

[　　　]; it is holy.

§§ Literally, 'go or come'.

No one is to lie with a woman in the city of the sanctuary, thereby defiling the city of the sanctuary with their impurity.

Of demoniacal possession   (xii, 2–6)

Any man who is dominated by demonic spirits to the extent that he gives voice to apostasy is to be subject to the judgment upon sorcerers and wizards. If, however, a man desecrate the Sabbath or the festivals through (mental) aberration, he is not to be put to death. In that case, it is the duty of men to keep him under observation. If he recovers, they are to watch him for seven years, and only thereafter may he be readmitted to public assemblies.

Of relations with the heathen   (xii, 6–11)

No one is to put forth his hand to shed the blood of a heathen for the sake of wealth or gain. Moreover, to prevent the levelling of defamatory charges, no one is to expropriate any of their goods except by the decision of an Israelite court.

No one is to sell clean beasts or fowl to the heathen, lest they use them for sacrifices. No one is to sell them any of the produce of his threshing-floor or winepress or any of his possessions. Nor is he to sell to them any of his male or female servants that may have joined him in the Covenant of Abraham.[56]

Of food   (xii, 11–15)

No one is to defile his person by eating any unclean animal or reptile. This rule includes the larvae of bees and any living entity that creeps in water.

Fish are not to be eaten unless they are ripped open while still alive and their blood poured out.[57]

As for the various kinds of locust, these are to be put in fire or water while they are still alive; for that is what their nature demands.

Of contagious impurity   (xii, 15–18)

When wood, stone or dust is contaminated by human uncleanness, the degree of the contamination is to be determined by the rules governing that particular form of uncleanness; and it is by this standard that all contact with them is to be gauged.

When a dead body lies in a house, every utensil—even a nail or a peg in the wall—is to be regarded as defiled, just as much as implements of work.

Epilogue   (xii, 19–22)

The foregoing is the rule concerning the various regulations for distinguishing clean from unclean and for recognizing holy from profane, such as it is to obtain in the urban communities of Israel. It is by these ordinances that the enlightened man may correctly determine his human relations on this or that particular occasion; and it is in this manner that the progeny of Israel is to conduct itself in order to avoid damnation.[58]

B. CODE FOR CAMP-COMMUNITIES

Prologue   (xii, 22–xiii, 7)

Here, however, is the rule for such camp-communities as may come into existence throughout the Era of Wickedness—that is, until the priestly and the lay 'messiah' again assume office.[59] The people who follow these rules must consist in any given instance of a minimum of ten,[60] and beyond that must be grouped by thousands, hundreds, fifties and tens.

In any place where there are ten, a priest versed in the Book of Study is not to be absent; 'by his word shall they all be ruled' [Gen. 41.40]. If, however, he is not experienced in all these matters, the members of the camp may elect by vote one of the levites, 'by whose orders they may come and go'.[61] Nevertheless, whenever a decision has to be rendered involving the law of bodily blemishes, the priest is to come and officiate in the camp, the overseer instructing him in the detailed interpretation of the Law. Moreover, if the priest be feeble-minded, that official must simply keep him under lock and key at all other times; or it is nonetheless by the priests that the decision in such matters must be rendered.[62]

Of the overseer[63]   (xiii, 7–19)

This is the rule for the overseer of the camp.

It is his duty to enlighten the masses about the works of God, and to make them understand His wondrous powers. He is to tell them in detail the story of things that happened in the past. He is to show them the same compassion as a father shows for his children. He is to bring back all of them that stray, as does a shepherd his flock.[64] He is to loose all the bonds that constrain them, so that there be no one in his community who is oppressed or crushed.

He is also to examine every new adherent to his community regarding his conduct, intelligence, strength, valor and wealth, and to register him in his due status, according to his stake in the portion of Truth. No member of the camp is to have authority to introduce anyone into the community in defiance of the camp's overseer.

No one who has entered the Covenant is to have any traffic with the 'men of corruption' [i.e., outsiders] except in spot cash transactions. No one is to enter into any sort of commercial partnership without informing the camp's overseer. Moreover, if he has made an agreement, but does not. . . . [*Four fragmentary lines.*]

Epilogue   (xiii, 20–xiv, 2)

Such, then, is to be the disposition of the camps throughout the Era of Wickedness. Those who do not adhere to these things shall not succeed in reoccupying their native soil [   ]. These, in fact, are the regulations for the social conduct of the 'enlightened' until God eventually visits the earth, even as He has said: 'There shall come upon thee and upon thy people and upon thy kinsfolk days the like of which have not been since Ephraim departed from Judah' [Isa. 7.17]. With those that follow them God's covenant will be confirmed; they will be delivered from all the snares of corruption. The foolish, however, will [   ] and be punished.

Of rank and precedence   (xiv, 3–12)

This is the rule for the disposition of all camp-settlements.

Everyone is to be registered by name in a census; first, the priests; second, the levites; third, the laymen; and fourth, the proselytes. Each individual is to be registered by name, one after another; first, the priests; second, the levites; third, the laymen; and fourth, the proselytes. It is in this order that they are to be seated at public sessions, and in this order that their opinions are to be invited on all matters.

The priest who holds office over the masses is to be from thirty to sixty years old, versed in the Book of Study and in all the regulations of the Torah, so as to be able to declare them on each appropriate occasion.

As for the overseer of all the camps, he is to be from thirty to fifty years old, adept in human relations and in all the varied languages of men.[65] It is as he determines that those who enter the community are to be admitted, each in his assigned order. Anything that any one has to say in a matter of dispute or litigation, he is to say to the overseer.

Of the communal economy   (xiv, 12–18)

This is the rule for regulating public needs.

Their wages for at least two days per month are to be handed over to the overseer. The judges are then to take thereof and give it away for the benefit of orphans. They are also to support therefrom the poor and needy, the aged who are dying, the [   ] persons captured by foreign peoples, unprotected girls, unmarriageable virgins, general communal officials [   ].

This, in specific form, is the way [   ] is to be disposed [   ] [com]munally.

Of personal morality   (xiv, 18–22)

And these, in specific form, are the regulations which they are to follow throughout the Era of Wickedness, until the priestly and lay 'messiahs' enter upon their office and expiate their iniquities.

No one is to practice conscious falsehood in matters of money [   ]; he is to be mulcted [of his rations] for six days.

If a man utter [   ], [or harbor an] unjustified [grudge against his neighbor, he is to be mulcted for one] year [   ].

III [IV, *init.*]

Of oaths   (xv, 1–xvi, 20)

No one is to take the oath by EL–* or by AD–,† but only by a formula of assent which invokes the curses prescribed in the Covenant [cf. Lev. 26.14–45].[66] Nor is he to make mention in this connection of the Law of Moses, for (the name of God is spelled out in that Law); so that if he swears by it and then transgresses, he commits profanation of the Holy Name; whereas if he swears before the judges by the curses of the Covenant—then, if he transgresses, he becomes liable only for a guilt-offering, confession and restitution, but does not have to pay the penalty of death.[66a]

It is to be a perpetual ordinance for the whole of Israel that whoever enters into the Covenant is to impose the

---

* The initial letters of *ELohim*, the Hebrew word for 'God'.
† The initial letters of *ADonai*, the Hebrew word for 'Lord'.

oath of the Covenant also upon his sons when they reach
the age for the preliminary examination.

Similarly, it is to be the rule throughout the Epoch of
Wickedness that anyone who repents his corrupt conduct
is to be enrolled, on the day when he speaks of it to the
general overseer, with an oath binding him to the Covenant
which Moses made with Israel—that is, with a covenanted
obligation that [in all] the varied activities of his life he
will return to the Law of Moses with all his heart and soul.
No one, however, is to acquaint him with the regulations
of the community prior to his actually standing in the presence of the overseer, lest, when the latter examines him,
he turn out to be a dolt. But once the overseer has sworn
him by oath to return to the Law of Moses with all his heart
and soul, he is to be liable to punishment for any breach
of faith. If he fail to understand anything in the Law which
is patently revealed to the normal mind, the overseer is
to [   ] and then issue an order concerning him that
he be kept in confinement for a full year on the grounds
of its having been ascertained that he is feeble-minded and
deranged.

In the case of one who is a chronic imbecile or is in-
sane, the judge is to come and [   ]. Such a man is
not to appear in public. . . . [*The next two lines are fragmentary, and four more have been lost.*]

There is an ancient text which says: 'It was by the Law
of Moses that God made the covenant with you and with
all Israel'.[67] It is for this reason that the man [who enters
the Covenant] must pledge himself 'to return to the Law
of Moses'. Therein is everything explicitly spelled out,
while an exact specification of the time when Israel will
be blind to all these things is spelled out with equal exact-
ness in the Book of the Divisions of the Times into their
Jubilees and Weeks.[68]

On the day that a man pledges himself to return to the
Law of Moses, the Angel of Obstruction[69] will start reced-
ing from him—that is, if he keep his word. It is in line with
this that Abraham underwent circumcision on the day that
he attained true knowledge.

In all cases where a man pledges himself by a binding

oath to perform any precept of the Law, he is not to free himself therefrom even at the price of death. For this is what Scripture means when it says, 'That which is gone out of thy lips thou shalt observe', i.e., 'to make good' [Deut. 23.23]. On the other hand, in all cases where a man pledges himself by a binding oath to depart from the Law, he is not to confirm it even at the price of death.

Now, concerning a woman's oath. Scripture says that it is her husband's duty in certain cases to void her oath [cf. Num. 30.14]. He is not to do so, however, if he does not know whether it is one that ought to be made good or voided. If it involves transgression of the Covenant, he is to void it and not make it good. The same rule applies also to her father.

Now, concerning the rules for free-will offerings. No one is to vow for the altar anything acquired by violence; nor, indeed, are the priests to accept from a layman anything so acquired. No one is to offer polluted food for sacred purposes. That is what Scripture means when it says, 'They trap each man his neighbor in respect to the consecrated thing' [Mic. 7.2]. . . . [*Five fragmentary lines.*]

[V]

*   *   *

THE LETTER OF THE LAW: ORDINANCES

* * *

Cp. Deut. 23.25–26

If any man thereof[1] construct a threshing floor or a wine press, anyone belonging to the community of Israel[2] who comes upon it and himself has nothing[3] may feed himself from it and gather for himself and [his] hou[sehold]. Within the field he may eat to his satisfaction,[4] but he may not bring anything home to deposit it (there).[5]

Cp. Exod. 30.11–16

Regarding the assessment of half a shekel which everyone is to furnish as coverage for his own person,[6] (for this) there is to be a single [scale of value] throughout his life:[7] the shekel is to be estimated as twenty gerahs, in accordance with the standard used for sacred purposes.[8] (Thus,) the 600,000 men (with Moses in the Wilderness)[9] would have had to pay (a total of) one hundred talents;[10] each of the three (customary divisions of the armed forces),[11] half a talent;[12] and a contingent of fifty men,[13] half a mina, i.e. 25 shekels . . .

(*There follows a specification of equivalencies, but the text is too fragmentary for translation.*)
Ephah and bath are equivalent.[14]

* * *

. . . .[15]

Cp. Lev. 25.42

They may not serve as slaves to Gentiles, (living) among foreigners, [for when the LORD brought them out of the land of] He enjoined upon them the commandment that they should not be sold as a slave is sold.
[For the settlement of legal disputes there shall be a coun-

cil of te]n laymen and two priests,[16] and it is to these
twelve that recourse must be had . . .
If, within (the community of) Israel, a capital charge be
preferred, these men's opinion must be sought.

Cp. Jos. 1.18

Anyone who offers defiance and takes the law into his own
hands,[17] is to be put to death.

Cp. Deut. 22.5

A woman is not to put on the accoutrements of a man;
and a man is not to clothe himself in the cloak of a woman,
nor wear a woman's shift; for that is an abomination.[18]

Cp. Deut. 22.14–21

If a man impugn the virtue[19] of an Israelite virgin, alleg-
ing that he married her [under false pretenses], she shall
be reliably examined, and if he has not lied about her, she
shall be put to death. But if (it be shown that) he has borne
[false] witness against her, he shall be fined two minas,
and he may not[20] divorce her for the rest of his life . . .
(The rest is fragmentary)

Our God and God of our fathers,

bless us with the threefold blessing in the Law,
written by the hand of Thy servant Moses,
spoken by the mouth of Aaron and his sons,
the priests, Thy holy people:

'The Lord bless thee, and keep thee;
The Lord make His face to shine upon thee
and be gracious unto thee;
The Lord lift up His countenance upon thee,
and give thee peace'.

Ancient Jewish Prayer; based on NUMBERS 6.24–26

A FORMULARY OF BLESSINGS

A. For blessing laymen

Form of blessing (greeting) to be used by the 'enlightened' in blessing (greeting) those who fear [God, do] His will, keep His commandments, hold fast to His holy Covenant and walk blamelessly [in all the ways of] His truth —that is, such men as He has chosen to be partners in an eternal Covenant [which shall] stand for ever.

THE LORD BLESS THEE [from His holy habitation] and open for thee from heaven the perpetual spring un[failing].[1]

[   ] in/at thy hand, and FAVOR THEE with all manner of blessing, and make thee [privy] to that knowledge which is possessed by the Holy Beings.[2]

[Verily, with Him is] a perpetual spring, and He [withholds] not [living waters from] such as thirst (for them). So mayest thou too [drink therefrom].[3]

[THE LORD KEEP THEE from all evil and] deliver thee from all [domination by Belial],[4] and may the frenzy thereof be (destroyed) without re[mnant].

[THE LORD KEEP THEE and deliver thee] from every satanic spirit* [and from every corrupting spirit].[5]

[There follow three broken lines, in two of which there is specific mention of 'holiness' (or of something holy) and the third of which refers to 'holy teaching.'

This is followed in turn by three more broken lines, the first and last of which contain specific reference to 'eternity'

---

* Heb. 'satan', i.e., adversary.

(or to something eternal), and the second of which alludes to 'all appointed times'.]

THE LORD KEEP [unto thee the covenant sworn to] thy fathers.[6]

[*There follow five broken lines containing various elaborations of the formula,* THE LORD LIFT UP HIS COUNTENANCE UNTO THEE.]

THE LORD FAVOR THEE with [His salvation] [   ] and cause thee to delight in peace [abounding].[7]

THE LORD FAVOR THEE also with [   ].

THE LORD FAVOR THEE with the holy spirit, with loving-kindness [   ].

THE LORD FAVOR THEE also with [His] eternal covenant and [   ] thee [   ].

THE LORD FAVOR THEE by visiting upon thee just judgment, [that] thy [foot may not] stumble [upon thy way].[8]

THE LORD FAVOR THEE also in all thy works [and in all that] thy [hand undertaketh] and in all the [   ].[9]

[THE LORD FAVOR THEE also with insight into] eternal truth.

[THE LORD GIVE PEACE unto thee and] unto all thine offspring [   ].

B. For blessing the high priest

[*Introductory words missing.*]

THE LORD LIFT UP HIS COUNTENANCE UNTO THEE and [accept] the sweet savor of [thy sacrifices][10] and choose as His own all them that abide in [thy] priestly care, and take note of all thy sacred acts[11] and be pleased with all thy seas[onal offices,[12] and increase] thy seed.

THE LORD LIFT UP HIS COUNTENANCE unto all thy congregation.

THE LORD LIFT UP upon thy head [a crown of honor],[13] and may thy [   ] [abide] in glory [eternal], and may He hallow thy seed with glory everlasting.

THE LORD LIFT UP [HIS COUNTENANCE UNTO THEE] and

grant thee grace [and peace everlast]ing, and [an inheritance in] the kingdom of [heaven].[14]

[THE LORD LIFT UP thy soul and raise thy spirit] out of
the flesh[15] and [set it] amid the holy angels.[16]

[THE LORD LIFT UP His banner[17] and] do battle for thee
[at the head of] thy thousands [against this] iniquitous
generation.

[*Three fragmentary lines.*]

[THE LORD LIFT UP His sword for thee][18] to humble
many peoples before thee [   ], and mayest thou not
[rely] upon worldly wealth, to become estranged from the
perpetual spring, [but find it when] thou seekest it.

Verily, God stayeth the foundations of the earth. [So
may He stay thy steps.]

[Verily, He stablisheth the world upon its basis. So] may
He stablish thy wellbeing[19] for ever.

C. *For blessing the priests*

> Formula of blessing to be used by the 'enlight-
> ened' in blessing the sons of Zadok—that is, the
> priests whom God has chosen to keep His
> covenant firm for ever, to act as the testers of
> all matters involving the performance of His
> rules among His people and to teach them ac-
> cording to that which He hath commanded, to
> the end that they may confirm His covenant in
> truth and supervise correctly [the perform-
> ance] of all His ordinances and walk in the
> way which He hath chosen:

THE LORD BLESS THEE from His holy habitation and set
thee crowned in majesty[20] in the midst of the Holy Beings,
and renew unto thee the covenant of priesthood everlasting, and give thee place in the holy habitation.[21]

By thine offices may all princes be judged, and all the
[lords] of the peoples by thine unstained lips.

May He give thee as thine inheritance the first-fruits
of all delights,[22] and at thy hand may He bless all mortal
designs.

May He be pleased with [all] the steps of thy feet, and make thee acceptable in the eyes of men and of the Holy Beings.

May He apportion unto thee[23] [   ] and mayest thou immerse thyself therein. And all mortal [   ] and delights [   ].

May He set eternal blessings as a crown upon thy head, and fill thine hands with holiness and [   ].

[*Line missing.*]

May He cause thee to do rightly in all thy ministrations. For thee hath He chosen [to perform the office] and to carry out the charge at the head of them that be sacred, and to give His blessing unto thy people, and thee [hath He appointed] that the men of the company of God may be [rendered pure?] at thy hand and not at the hand of any monarch or [potentate; and with thee He speaketh] as a man unto his neighbor; and thou art as a ministering angel in the holy habitation. [Mayest thou serve ever] unto the glory of the God of Hosts, and mayest thou be about Him as one that ministereth in a royal palace. And mayest thou share the lot of the ministering angels† and be one in the company of [the Holy Beings] for all time and for all the epochs of eternity. [For He hath entrusted thee with] His judgments, and hath made thee an holy thing among His people, to be as a light [   ] to [illumine] the world with knowledge and to enlighten the faces of men far and wide.

May He set upon thine head a diadem to proclaim thee holy of holies,[24] for [it is thou that evincest His] holiness and showest forth the glory of His name.

And may His Holy Beings [wait upon thee].

D. *For blessing the king*

[*Introductory words missing.*]

Thou hast been set apart from [all other men] [   ] them that see thee [   ].

† Heb. 'angel(s) of the Presence'.

May He renew unto thee [   ].

[*Line missing.*]

[   ] who hath commissioned thee [   ] for all time and for all the seasons of eternity. And may He not gi[ve] thy glory [unto another].

May God [set] the fear of thee upon all that hear tell of thee, and be thy majesty [upon all that] [   ].

E. For blessing the prefect of the community[24a]

Formula of blessing to be used by the 'enlightened' in blessing (greeting) the prefect of the community—that is, the man whom God hath chosen to represent His power and through whom He renews the covenant contracted with the community, to the end that He may maintain the sovereignty of His people for ever, and [whom He has appointed to judge the needy in righteousness] and to reprove in equi[ty the me]ek of the earth,[25] and to walk blamelessly in all the ways of [His truth], and to confirm His holy covenant when distress befalls them that seek Him:

THE LORD LIFT thee up unto the summit of the world, like a strong tower on a lofty wall.[26]

Mayest thou [smite nations] with the vehemence of thy mouth. With thy rod mayest thou dry up the [fountainheads] of the earth, and with the breath of thy lips mayest thou slay the wicked.[27]

[THE LORD FAVOR THEE with a spirit of sound counsel] and with perpetual strength and with a spirit of knowledge and with the fear of God.[28]

May righteousness be the girding [of thy loins and faithfulness] that of thy thighs.[29]

May God make thy horns of iron and thy hoofs of brass;[30] and mayest thou gore the [iniquitous] like a steer [and trample nations] like mire in the streets.[31]

For God hath appointed thee to be the scourge of rulers.[32] They shall [come] before thee [and make obeisance unto thee, and all peoples] shall serve thee. By His holy Name may He give thee power that thou be as a lion [which raveneth and as a wolf which smi]teth the prey, with none to retrieve it. And may thy chargers ride abroad[33] over [all the broad places of the earth].

NOTES*

The Manual of Discipline

1. Jer. 3.17.
2. Cp. Num. 15.39; Ezek. 6.9.
3. Luke 16.8; John 12.36; Eph. 5.8. Cp. also Luke 1.79; Rom. 2.19.
4. So too among the Essenes: Josephus, *War*, II, viii, 3; Philo, quoted by Eusebius, *Praep. Ev.*, viii, 11; Porphyry, *On Abstention from Animal Food*, p. 381 (ed. Leyden, 1620). Likewise among the early Christians: Lucian, *De morte Peregrini*, c.13.
5. Variant calculations of the calendar were a regular bone of contention among normative Jews and dissident sects, as also between Jews and Samaritans.
6. The word 'truth' is often used in the Scrolls in the specific sense of the Mosaic Law (*Torah*). So, too, the Samaritans commonly refer to it as 'the Verity' (*Qushtâ*).
7. Cp. Mishnah, *Berachoth*, V, 4.
8. Cp. *Jubilees*, 1.20; *Testament of Reuben*, ii; *of Levi*, iii; *of Zebulun*, ix; *of Naphtali*, ii; *of Benjamin*, vi. Cp. also *Didachē*, xxi.3.
9. 'Amen' (or 'Amen, amen') was the standard response to an oath: Num. 5.22; Deut. 27, *passim*; Mishnah, *Shebu'oth*, V, 2.
10. Ps. 106.6. This is the regular formula of confession on the Day of Atonement.

* The Dead Sea Scriptures are cited according to the columns and lines of the original texts. Old Testament references follow the numeration of the *Hebrew* text, which sometimes differs by a verse or two from the English version. Where the discrepancy is likely to be troublesome, the English numbering is indicated in parentheses.

11. Cp. the development of this idea in Eph. 1.11; Rom. 8.17; Gal. 3.29, etc., and cp. G. Dalman, *The Words of Jesus* (1902), pp. 125ff.

12. An expansion of the Priestly Benediction, Num. 6.22–27.

13. Cp. Mat. 18.9; Mark 9.43; Dalman, *Words*, p. 161.

14. The Hebrew is obscure, and various interpretations have been proposed.

15. By a scribal error, the word for 'every one that hath come' has been transferred in the original text to follow 'enter' rather than 'cursed be'.

16. Ezek. 7.19; 14.3, 7.

17. Deut. 29.19. The same passage is quoted in the same sense in the Syriac *Teachings of the Apostles*, ii, 23.

18. The Heb. term *gillulîm*, commonly rendered 'idols', was understood by early Jewish commentators on the Bible to mean 'filthiness'. Our author evidently had the same tradition.

19. This was the regular order of precedence among Jews; cp. Mishnah, *Horayoth*, III, 8.

20. The Brotherhood regarded itself as part of the ideal, sempiternal congregation of God—the Church Invisible.

21. Cp. II Cor. 5.1.

22. This is one of the most puzzling phrases in the entire document, and the translation is therefore uncertain. The Hebrew says: 'in the *se'ôn* of wickedness is his plowing'. The word *se'ôn* occurs only in Isa. 9.4(5), where it means 'sandal, boot'—a meaning which does not fit here. The medieval Jewish commentators, however, tended to equate it with the like-sounding Aramaic *seyan*, 'mud', and it is in this sense, I suggest, that our author likewise understood it. Furthermore, the notion of 'plowing wickedness' was clearly influenced by the occurrence of a similar expression in Hos. 10.13.

23. Cp. Mat. 3.11; Mark 1.8; Luke 3.16; John 1.33; Acts 1.5, etc.

24. The Hebrew word is that rendered 'teachers' in Dan. 11.33, 35; 12.3, 10. The *Formulary of Blessings* bears the same heading. Both texts were probably designed as 'assists' for the teachers of the Brotherhood,

this one being a kind of sermon—possibly delivered as an exposition of the Scriptural Lesson, Deut. 30.15ff.: 'See, I have set before thee this day life and good, and death and evil', etc.

25. Cp. I Sam. 2.3.

26. Cp. *Didachē; Testament of Levi*, 5.30; Mat. 7.13f.; Barnabas, xiv.3ff. The same doctrine occurs in the pseudepigraphic *Testament of Asher*, 1.3–9, and in the *Testament of Judah*, 20.1. It developed into the Jewish concept of the *yeṣer tob* (good inclination) and *yeṣer ra'* (evil inclination) in every man. On the background of the concept, see A. Dupont-Sommer, *The Jewish Sect of Qumran and the Essenes* (1954), pp. 118–30. Cp. also Slavonic Enoch, 30.13f.

27. Mentioned again in the *'Zadokite' Document*, v.18. Possibly, this is the real meaning of II Cor. 11.14, 'Satan himself is transformed into an angel of light', i.e., Satan disguises himself as *the* Angel of Light and then misleads.

28. In *Testament of Levi*, xix and in *Testament of Joseph*, vii, xx, Belial is called 'the spirit of darkness'.

29. The term used in the Hebrew (viz. *mastemah*) is related to the word 'Satan'. It is personified in *Jubilees* 11.5; 17.16; 18.9.

30. The angel in question is probably Gabriel, for not only is Gabriel the revealer of God's truth—he revealed the basic Koran to Mohammed—but he is also the champion of the faithful in the final battle against the powers of darkness; cp. *War of the Sons of Light*, etc.

31. Josephus (*War*, II, viii, 7) says that the Essenes were sworn not to divulge their doctrines to outsiders.

32. The text reads: 'These are the foundations of the spirit for the children of the truth of the world'. It is obvious that the scribe has erroneously altered the true order of the words; see above, n. 15.

33. Cp. I Peter 5.4. The Mandaeans attach great importance to the 'lustrous crown' (*Kelilâ de-zivâ*).

34. Cp. Rev. 6.11; 7.9. 'All God's chillun got robes'.

35. Cp. the lists of vices in Gal. 5.19ff.; Rom. 1.29ff.; I Cor. 6.9ff.; Col. 3.5, 8. Rendel Harris (*Teaching of*

the Apostles [1887], pp. 82ff.) derives these lists from the catalogue of sins recited in the confessions on the Day of Atonement. Others claim that they were borrowed from the Stoics, and cite similar texts in A. Dieterich, *Nekyia,* pp. 163ff.

36. Cp. Jer. Talmud, Sheb., vi. 37a. Cp. also Slavonic Enoch, 53.3; 56.1.

37. Cp. Isa. 44.3; Joel 2.28–29; Acts 2.17; 10.45; Titus 3.5–6.

38. This idea was common in the Graeco-Roman world; see F. Cumont, *After Life in Roman Paganism* (1923), p. 121.

39. Cp. John 12.43.

40. Cp. Isa. 65.17, and especially Mat. 19.28. Cp. also Dalman, *Words,* pp. 177ff.; Cumont, *op. cit.,* p. 13.

41. See General Introduction, p. 5.

42. Evidently, non-Jewish proselytes are meant.

43. Josephus tells us (*War,* II, viii, 6) that the Essenes avoided taking oaths. The only exception was the oath of allegiance on being admitted to the Brotherhood. Jesus counselled his disciples in the same sense (Mat. 5.33–37). It is interesting to observe that this rule obtained also among the Waldenses.

44. I.e., the curses prescribed in Deut. 28–29, known in Jewish tradition as 'the Commination' (Heb. *tôchechah*). When the passage is read in the Synagogue, it is customary among the Ashkenazim (German-Polish Jews) to 'call to the Law' the humblest member of the congregation—usually, the beadle or sexton. The Sephardim (Spanish-Portuguese Jews), however, insist that the rabbi (*haham*) must be 'called', to show that the Law is no respecter of persons!

45. This is not a protest against baptism, as has been supposed, but rather against the idea that the act of immersion can *by itself* absolve sins.

46. The Scriptural text refers specifically to *falsehood*.

47. The Scriptural text was evidently taken to mean 'whose spirit lies only in his breath', i.e., not in his 'soul'.

48. Philo (*Quod Omnis Probus Liber*, §13) commends the Essenes for their 'cheerfulness of temper'. So, too, Josephus (*War*, II, viii, 6) says that 'they are just dispensers of their anger, curbers of their passions . . . ministers of peace'.

49. The text says, 'the small is to obey the great'; but this evidently refers to rank, not age. However, Philo says of the Essenes that in synagogue the younger sat below the elder (*Quod Omnis Probus Liber*, §12).

50. So too among the Essenes: Philo, *loc. cit.*; Josephus, *War*, II, viii, 5.

51. Ten persons is the minimum required in Jewish law to form a congregation. So too, apparently, among the Essenes: Josephus, *War*, II, viii, 9.

52. So too among the Essenes: Josephus, *War*, II, viii, 5. In early Christian usage, the first act at an *agape* (lovefeast) was to bless the cup. The duty devolved on the bishop, if present; see Dom Conolly, *Didascalia Apostolorum* (1929), pp. lii,ff.

53. I.e., in order to expound it to them; cp. I Cor. 14.28. The *Didascalia Apostolorum* prescribes that the bishop is to be the 'interpreter'.

54. For the conjunction of 'studying' and 'worshiping' (lit. blessing'), cp. Mishnah, *Yômâ*, VII, 7.

55. Josephus (*War*, II, viii, 5) says of the Essenes that 'no noise or uproar ever desecrates their house. Rather do they let everyone take part in the conversation in turn'.

56. Josephus (*War*, II, viii, 9) says of the Essenes that 'when ten of them [i.e., the minimal quorum] sit together, no one will speak if the other nine do not agree to it'.

57. The Hebrew word is the exact equivalent of the Greek *episkopos*, 'bishop'. We thus see the original form of this office, which later assumed sacerdotal functions. Comparable also is the 'steward' or 'overseer' of the Essenes, mentioned by Philo (in Eusebius, *Praep. Ev.*, viii, 11) and Josephus (*War*, II, viii, 3).

58. Josephus (*War*, II, viii, 10) mentions four categories among the Essenes, and tells us also (*ib.*, 7), that a postulant was not admitted to 'the holier water of

purification' until after a year's probation. The 'common or general purity' (literally, 'the purity of the many') was evidently the lowest degree. The system was a special development of the four degrees of purity recognized in Jewish law and specified in the Babylonian Talmud, Ḥagigah 18b.

59. So too among the Essenes, according to Josephus (loc. cit.).

60. The Didascalia (54.26) likewise excludes initiants from the common meal. So too among the Essenes (Josephus, loc. cit.).

61. Josephus (loc. cit.) says that those who wished to join the Essenes had to spend a trial year 'outside' and two full years (in varied degrees of probation) 'inside' before they were eligible for admission. There is no real discrepancy between his statement and our author's, for the latter starts, as it were, from the moment the postulant has entered 'within'.

62. Deut. 28.58. Cp. James 2.7.

63. For the terms employed in the Hebrew, cp. Mishnah, Yômâ, VII, 7. For the office involved, cp. Mishnah, Berachôth, V, 5; Rôsh Ha-Shanah, IV, 9.

64. The point is that the left hand is used in the Near East for all unclean purposes.

65. According to Josephus (War, II, viii, 8), expulsion was the penalty among the Essenes for heinous offenses.

66. In imitation of the priestly triumvirate of Aaron, Eleazar and Ithamar during Israel's sojourn in the wilderness; cp. Num. 3.4.

67. Cp. Isa. 65.9; Ps. 105.43; II John 1; I Peter 2.9; Rev. 17.14, etc. The Mandaeans likewise call themselves 'the elect' (Lidzbarski, Mandäische Liturgien, pp. 75, 106f.; id., Johannesbuch, ii, pp. 69, 102, 221). So too the Manichaeans styled themselves (vičidagan).

68. Quoted in the same sense in I Peter 2.6.

69. Philo tells us (Quod Omnis Probus Liber, §12) that when the Scriptures were read publicly among the Essenes, on the sabbath, the 'expert' who expounded them 'passed over that which is not generally known,' i.e., within the grasp of the rank and file.

70. The same quotation is used in the same sense by John the Baptist; Mat. 3.3; John 1.23.
71. Literally, 'the Messiahs (i.e., anointed) of Aaron and Israel'. See above, p. 6.
72. The expression derives from Deut. 32.35, according to the text found in the Samaritan Recension, the Greek (Septuagint) Version, and a fragment discovered at Qumran itself. It recurs at Isa. 34.8, 61.2, and 63.4, and is the standard term for Doomsday among the Samaritans.

The 'Zadokite' Document

1. Based on Ezek. 4.5, 'For I have appointed the years of their iniquity to be unto thee a number of days, even three hundred and ninety days'. It is perhaps worthy of note that in the 'Chain of High Priests' supplied by the Samaritans to Rev. John Mills and published by him in his *The Modern Samaritans* (1864), pp. 333f., 'the kingdom of Nebuchadnezzar' is said to have lasted 390 years, viz. from 3488 until 3877 A.M. This must represent an independent tradition, for the Samaritans do not accept any Scripture other than the Five Books of Moses.
2. As Isaac Rabinowitz has pointed out (*Journal of Biblical Literature*, 73 [1954], 11), the reference is to the events narrated in Neh. 1.1ff., 'Now it came to pass in the twentieth year [of the reign of King Artaxerxes Longimanus]'. I should prefer, however, to see in the 'right-teacher' Ezra rather than Nehemiah. First, as explained in the Introduction, it seems to me that the 'right-teacher' was in all epochs necessarily a priest—and that Ezra was. Second, it was indeed Ezra who expounded the Law (Neh. 8.2ff.).
3. Here we have the term usually rendered 'Teacher of Righteousness'.
4. The reference is obscure. Possibly it is to Sanballat (Neh. 4.1ff.), though it is not recorded that he and his followers were annihilated. However, our text may be a general polemic against the Samaritans.

5. An ancient Jewish morning-prayer, ascribed by some to the Essenes, speaks of 'Knowledge and Discernment' as encompassing God like attendants.

6. Common figures of rabbinic lore; cf. also Enoch 56.1.

7. I.e., the anointed priests, custodians and teachers of the Law, which is here called 'the Truth', as regularly among the Samaritans and Mandaeans.

8. The reference is to the widespread post-Biblical legend of the rebel angels (headed by 'Lucifer') who were cast out of heaven. The legend is fully discussed in B. Bamberger's excellent work, *Fallen Angels* (New York, 1954). The name 'Watchers' is taken from Dan. 4.13, 17, 23.

9. The allusion is to Gen. 6.1–4. The Hebrew word usually rendered 'mighty men' was interpreted in antiquity as 'giants'.

10. The reference is to the generation of the Flood. Compare especially Gen. 6.17.

11. Gen. 9.20–28.

12. Note that the same example is cited, with the same point, in James 2.23.

13. Ps. 106. 18.

14. Cp. Jer. 2.13; 17.13; *Odes of Solomon*, 6.7; 30.1–2.

15. The point depends on a play on words: the Hebrew for 'associate oneself' is *l-v-h*, which at once suggests Levi.

16. I.e., the prototypes of the 'men of special holiness' mentioned in the *Manual*.

17. The Hebrew word for 'boundary' also means 'statute', and is used especially of the statutes, or provisions, of the Covenant.

18. The source of this quotation is unknown. It does *not* occur in the pseudepigraphical *Testament of Levi*, as one might expect.

19. RV. 'Neither shall he multiply wives unto himself'.

20. Lev. 15.19.

21. Cp. II Tim. 3.8. For the legend in Jewish sources, cp. L. Ginzberg, *The Legends of the Jews*, vi, 144.

22. The Hebrew word for prince is *sar*. The point obviously depends upon some fanciful interpretation of this

term, that now eludes us. Possibly it was connected on the one hand with the word *shur*, 'to look around for something', and on the other with a root appearing in the Assyro-Babylonian *shâru*, 'to belie, traduce'.

23. This passage has been taken to indicate that the Covenanters later betook themselves to Damascus, and it has been assumed that our present document emanates from that settlement. I agree entirely, however, with the view of I. Rabinowitz (*Journal of Biblical Literature*, 73 [1954], 11–35) that the language is purely figurative, being based on Amos 5.27. See above, p. 5.

24. See *Manual*, vols. iii–iv.

25. Josephus tells us clearly that not all of the Essenes lived in the desert (*War*, II, viii, 4), and the present document subsequently lays down rules for urban communities and for 'camps' respectively. Obviously, then, this literature did not emanate from, nor was it exclusive to, the particular group at Qumran.

26. Josephus tells us that while some Essenic groups discountenanced marriage, others did not (*War*, II, viii, 13). The Qumran group apparently fell in the latter category, for skeletons of women have been disinterred from its cemetery.

27. Comp. Zech. 6.8.

28. The text is defective, and it is therefore not quite clear how the author actually interpreted the Scriptural passage. C. Rabin makes the attractive suggestion that we should read: 'The King is the [prince of all the congregation; the image(s) are the instructors of the] congregation'. The point, he says, depends on a play on words, whereby the Hebrew *ṣelem*, 'image' is fancifully interpreted (by metathesis) as *meliṣ*, 'interpreter'. An alternative suggestion is, however, that the author was playing on the words of Deut. 33.4–5, 'Moses commanded us a law as an inheritance, O congregation of Jacob. And there was a King in Jeshurun, when the heads of the people were gathered, all the tribes of Israel together'.

29. Possibly, the writer was fancifully interpreting the word *Kiyyun* (really the name of the planet Saturn)

as containing the initial letters of the Hebrew expression, *Kitbê Nebi'îm*, 'writings of the prophets'. An exactly parallel mode of interpretation appears in the Commentary on Habakkuk, xiii, 2 (on 2.20).

30. The writer is playing on the words of Ps. 73.20, 'Their image wilt Thou despise'.

31. See above, n. 23.

32. The pseudepigraphic *Testaments of Levi* (18.3) and *Judah* (24.1) likewise refer this to the Messiah. Rev. 22.16 refers it to Jesus.

33. The writer interprets the Hebrew word *sheth* of the Biblical quotation—really, the name of a nomadic people called the Shûtu—as equivalent to *se'eth*, 'pride'. The same interpretation obtains among the Samaritans. Jeremiah (48.45) took the words somewhat similarly.

34. Ezek. 13.10.

35. The writer manipulates the Biblical text to suit his purpose and does not quote it accurately.

36. Cp. Jer. 45.1, 4–5: The word that Jeremiah the prophet spoke unto Baruch, the son of Neriah . . . 'that which I have built will I break down, and that which I have planted will I pluck up; the same is the whole land . . . for, behold, I will bring evil on all flesh'.

37. Cp. II Kings 5.26–27, where Elisha curses Gehazi for disobedience.

38. The reference is to the future (prophetic) teacher who will precede the eventual restoration of the priesthood and sovereignty; see above, p. 6.

39. See *Manual*, viii, 1–19.

40. This is *not* a 'New Testament' in the Christian sense. It refers simply to the future reaffirmation of the old covenant. See above, pp. 4ff.

41. Rabbinic tradition likewise assigns a period of forty years for the 'ministry' of the Messiah before the final restoration of Israel. The identity of the Man of Falsehood is unknown, and this is one of the major points of controversy among students of the Scrolls. I believe, however, that the reference is purely general, and refers to 'Belial' or 'Antichrist'—a regular figure of Jewish

(and later of Christian) eschatology from about the
second century B.C. onwards.

42. This idea recurs in the *Book of Hymns*, xvi, 10. Cp.
    also *Odes of Solomon*, 9.12.

43. Heb. 'the house of Peleg' (cf. Gen. 10.25)—a fanciful
    designation based on the fact that the Hebrew word
    p-l-g means 'divide'. The reference is to men who orig-
    inally withdrew from the faithless rabble, but later
    weak-heartedly rejoined it.

44. See *Manual*, vi, 8–13.

45. The interpretation of these lines is much disputed, and
    the translation here given must be considered only as
    tentative. For another view, see C. Rabin, *The
    Zadokite Documents* (1954), p. 54, n. 8.

46. Not in the Bible.

47. Cf. Mishnah, *Makkôth*, I.7.

48. This may also mean: no man who has not yet reached
    the age when he is eligible for enrollment in the Broth-
    erhood, i.e., no one under twenty; cp. xv, 6.

49. Cf. Mishnah, *Sanhedrin*, I.3, which implies a court of
    ten.

50. Heb. 'Book of Hagu', which has been the subject of
    considerable speculation. The fact is, however, that the
    word *hagu* actually occurs in the *Hymns* (xi, 2, 21)
    in the sense of 'meditation', and the cognate word de-
    notes 'study' in late Hebrew. There is thus no diffi-
    culty about the term.

51. The meaning is uncertain. The Hebrew word is *mar'il*,
    which is probably the Talmudic *mir'al*, 'pannier'.

52. I.e., the emphasis is on the word 'day', which was reck-
    oned from sunset to sunset. The moment indicated
    would thus imply the imminence of the sabbath day,
    Friday's sun being now about to set.

53. For the regular Jewish rule (2000 cubits), see Mish-
    nah, *Sotah*, V.3.

54. The text seems to say: 'If a human being falls into a
    place of water or into a place of . . . let no man bring
    him up by a ladder or a rope or by any other imple-
    ment'. But this would be against the universal Jewish
    rule that sabbath laws may be broken in cases of life

and death. Hence some scholars have assumed that a word has dropped out by haplography and read: 'If a human being fall . . . whence he cannot come up, one is to bring him up by means of a ladder', etc. But this involves bad grammar. I therefore adopt Vermes' ingenious emendation of *esh* ('fire') for the obscure *al* of the manuscript.

55. The Scripture says, 'apart from your Sabbath offering'; but our author took the word rendered 'apart from' as an adverb meaning 'exclusively'.

56. I.e., accepted Judaism. Cp. Bab. Talmud, *Yebamot*, 48b. The expression is a trifle odd, because it refers properly to circumcision.

57. Ritual slaughtering of fish is discussed in Bab. Talmud, *Ḥullin*, 27b.

58. I.e., in order to avoid the curses specified in Deut. 28–29.

59. See Introduction, pp. 6, 29.

60. See *Manual of Discipline*, note 51.

61. Num. 27.21. The *Didachē* likewise provides for a junior substitute, if the bishop is incapacitated or incompetent.

62. Lev. 13.2ff. Cp. Mishnah, *Nega'im*, III, 1.

63. Cp. *Manual of Discipline*, note 57.

64. So too in the *Apostolic Constitutions*, ii, 6, 7, in defining the duties of a bishop ('pastor').

65. Literally, 'In all communion with men and in every language according to their several families'. This scarcely means that he is to be a polyglot, but simply —as we should say—that he is to be adept at 'talking the other fellow's language'.

66. Swearing by AD . . . and by YH (the initial letters of YHVH, the Ineffable Name of God) is mentioned in Mishnah, *Shebu'oth*, IV, 13.

66a. Blasphemy was punishable by death: Lev. 24.10–23. Cp. Mishnah, *Sanhedrin*, VII, 5.

67. The quotation is not from the Bible.

68. I.e., the Book of Jubilees.

69. Heb. *Mastemah*, mentioned again in Jubilees 11.5; 17.16; 18.9. Cp. *Manual of Discipline*, note 29.

The Letter of the Law: Ordinances

1. I.e., of the community of Israel.
2. Literally, 'who is in Israel'.
3. Cp. Exod. 22.2.
4. Literally, 'He may eat of the field with his mouth'.
5. The law in Deut. 24.25–26 permits access only to the standing, but not to the threshed, corn.
6. Literally, 'as ransom (*kopher*) for his person'. On the varied meanings of the Hebrew term, see S. R. Driver's careful note in ICC, *Deuteronomy* (1895), pp. 425f.
7. Allegro restores the defective text to read, 'only once shall he give it during his lifetime', i.e., in contrast to the annual assessment in postexilic times. But it is difficult to see how the Temple could be maintained as a going concern on such a basis. Obviously, what is meant is that the value of the due is to remain constant, and not fluctuate (e.g., in accordance with the man's income; cp. Exod. 30.15), or even that, once he has paid it, no one is to be 'dunned' for more by way of supplementary or indirect taxation. (State and Federal legislators please note!)
8. Literally, 'according to the sacred shekel', see R. de Vaux, *Ancient Israel* (repr. 1965), p. 203.
9. Cp. Exod. 12.37; Num. 11.21.
10. A talent consisted of 60 minas; a mina, of 50 shekels.
11. Literally, simply 'the Third'. Allegro points out that David divided the people into three companies for military purposes; cp. II Sam. 18.2; 23.18–19. This seems, indeed, to have been a regular military tactic; cp. Judges 7.16; 9.43; I Sam. 11.11; 13.17.
12. The computation implies a force of 3000 men. It is therefore pertinent to observe that in various offensives Saul recruited just this number; cp. I Sam. 13.2; 24.3 (2); 26.2. Three thousand, however, was also simply a round number; cp. Judges 15.11; I Kings 5.12; I Chron. 29.4; II Chron. 25.13; 29.33; 35.7. So was 300,000; cp. I Sam. 11.8; II Sam. 17.14; II Chron. 25.5; 26.13. And so too was 300; cp. Judges 11.26;

15.4; II Sam. 21.16; II Kings 18.14; Esther 9.15, etc. (Similarly in classical literature; e.g., Catullus, ix, 2; xii, 10; Horace, *Sat.*, I, v, 10; Tibullus, I, iv, 69; Martial, xii, lxx; and in ritual contexts, Vergil, *Aeneid*, iv, 510; vii, 273, etc.)

13. Likewise a military contingent; cp. Exod. 18.21, 25; Deut. 1.15; I Sam. 8.12; *War*, iv, 3, 4; *'Zadokite' Document*, xiii, 1.

14. Cp. Ezek. 45.11.

15. The reading of this line is doubtful, and the text is defective.

16. In *Manual*, viii, 1ff. the judicial council consists of 12 laymen and 3 priests; in *'Zadokite' Document*, x, 4ff., of 6 laymen and 4 priests.

17. Literally, 'who has acted high-handedly'; cp. Num. 15.30; *Manual*, v, 12; viii, 17, 22; ix, 1; *'Zadokite' Document*, viii, 8; x, 3; xix, 21.

18. The Biblical commandment was probably directed in the first instance against cultic transvestism, for the word rendered 'abomination' usually refers to the ritual practises of the heathen; see T. H. Gaster, *Myth, Legend, and Custom in the Old Testament* (1969), §102.

19. Literally, 'brings a bad name upon . . .'

20. I have assumed a scribal error in the text, for otherwise it is in flat contradiction to the law of Deut. 22.19. It is possible, however, that the Brotherhood modified the ancient legislation on the compassionate assumption that an innocent woman thus slandered would find life intolerable with the man who had defamed her.

A Formulary of Blessings

1. Based on Deut. 28.12. The same passage is quoted in connection with the Priestly Benediction in *Sifrê*, §43.

2. Cp. *Sifrê*, §41.

3. Based on Ps. 36.9, 'For with Thee is the wellspring of life; in Thy light do we see light'. The passage naturally came to mind in connection with the Priestly Benediction's 'May He cause His face to *shine upon* (literally, *give light to*) thee'. Cp. also Jer. 2.13; 17.13.

4. Cp. *Manual of Discipline,* col. iii.

5. Cp. the Palestinian Targum's paraphrase of Num. 6.24: 'The Lord . . . keep thee from liliths and things that cause terror and from demons of noonday (cp. Ps. 91.5–6) and of morning, and from malign spirits and phantoms' (tr. Etheridge). Similarly, *Sifrê,* §40.

6. Based on Deut. 7.12, the passage being suggested by the expression 'and *keep* thee' in the Priestly Benediction. Similarly, *Sifrê,* §40.

7. Suggested by the expression, 'and give thee *peace*'. Cp. *Sifrê,* §42: 'Rabbi Eleazar ha-Kappar (2nd cent.) saith, Great is peace, for every blessing is sealed with it, as it is said, The Lord bless thee . . . and grant thee peace'.

8. Based on I Sam. 2.9, 'He *keepeth* the feet of His devoted servants'. Similarly, *Sifrê,* §40.

9. Cp. Deut. 28.8.

10. Cp. Lev. 26.31. This shows clearly that the passage is addressed to a *priest*.

11. I.e., the sacred offerings of the priests.

12. Cp. Neh. 10.34.

13. A reference to the crown of the high priest; cp. Ex. 29.6; Lev. 8.9.

14. Perhaps suggested by reference to the *crown*.

15. Cp. *Hymns,* iii, 20; xi, 12; xviii, 28–29. This suggests at once a play on the words 'lift up'.

16. A play on the fact that the high priest officiates on earth in the midst of 'holy ones', i.e., the other priests.

17. The allusion to leading troops into battle suggests yet another play on the expression 'lift up', viz. *lift up a banner;* cp. Isa. 5.26; 11.12; 18.3; Jer. 4.6; 50.2, etc.

18. The restoration is based on the assumption that there is once again a play on the expression 'lift up'—this time in the sense of *lift up a sword;* cp. Isa. 2.4; Mic. 4.3. Cp. also Deut. 9.3; Ps. 81.15; I Chron. 17.10.

19. Or, 'thy peace'.

20. Cp. Ezek. 16.14.

21. Service in the earthly sanctuary is to be but a prelude to similar office in the heavenly sanctuary. The latter,

in which the angel Michael officiates as high priest, is mentioned in Talmud, *Ḥagigah*, 12b.

22. A reference to the fact that the priest received the first-fruits or the prime part of certain offerings; cp. Num. 18.12; Deut. 18.4; Ezek. 44.30.

23. A reference to the priestly 'portion' of offerings; cp. Lev. 7.33; II Chron. 31.4.

24. A reference to the priestly diadem; cp. Ezek. 29.6; 39.30; Lev. 8.9.

24a. Hebrew, *nasî*. The title probably denotes the *ethnarch*, the civic chief of the Jewish community. Concerning this office, see: I Macc. 14.47; 15.1–2; Josephus, *Ant.*, xii, 6, §7; xiv, 8, §5; 10, §2; Y. Yadin, *Megillath Milḥamath Benê Ôr bi-Benê Ḥôshech* (1956), p. 285. In the *'Zadokite' Document*, v, 1, the law of Deut. 17.15, which refers to the *king*, is said to refer to the *nasî*, and *ib.*, vii. 20, the 'rod' which, according to Balaam's prophecy (Num. 24.17), will someday 'rise out of Israel', is interpreted as the future *'nasî' of the entire community'*. In normative Judaism of the intertestamental period, the *nasî* was paired with the 'father of the court' (*ab bêth dîn*) as joint president of the Sanhedrin. The title itself derives from the Bible (Ex. 16.22; Lev. 4.22; Jos. 9.15, 18; 17.4, etc.), where, however, it denotes simply any one of the tribal chieftains of Israel.

25. Cp. Isa. 11.4.

26. Cp. Isa. 30.13.

27. Cp. Isa. 11.4.

28. Cp. Isa. 11.2.

29. Cp. Isa. 11.5.

30. Cp. Mic. 4.13.

31. Cp. Mic. 7.10; Zech. 9.3; 10.5; Ps. 18.43, etc.

32. Cp. Isa. 14.5.

33. The word rendered 'chargers' is used in *The War of the Sons of Light and the Sons of Darkness* to denote 'light-armed troops' (the Roman *velites*). The suggestion is, therefore: 'May thy troops spread far and wide'.

THE PRAISE OF GOD

Hymns and Psalms

My soul thirsteth for Thee; my flesh longeth for Thee, in a dry and weary land, where no water is.

PSALM 63.1

INTRODUCTION

The chanting of psalms was one of the basic elements of worship in the Second Temple, and continued as a main feature of public devotions in the synagogue and church. In course of time, however, the Biblical repertoire was supplemented by more 'modern' compositions in the same style.

I

The Brotherhood possessed its own *Book of Hymns* written in this vein. It is contained in one of the scrolls discovered by the Bedouin boys in 1947 and extends to eighteen columns plus a large number of fragments too disjointed to translate. The end of each hymn was marked carefully by a blank space, but since the lower portion of each column has been eaten away, this indication must often have occurred in places where it is no longer evident. Hence, we cannot tell how many compositions even the main portion of the scroll originally contained, nor is it always possible to distinguish any one of them from the next. This is especially the case in the latter part of the manuscript, where the best that can be done in a translation is simply to indicate where a new column begins.

In cases where their beginnings can still be recognized, the hymns often open with the words, 'I give thanks unto Thee, O Lord'. For this reason they have come to be known as the *Psalms* (or *Hymns*) *of Thanksgiving*—a title which is all the more appropriate when it is remembered that in the early synagogue and church, 'thanksgiving' was a technical term for a clearly defined type of liturgical composition. Some of the pieces, however, begin with the alternative formula, 'Blessed art Thou', and this is equally significant in view of the fact that 'blessing' seems likewise to have denoted in antiquity not only a formula of benediction but also a specific type of hymn. Accordingly, the joint title, *Blessings and Thanksgivings* (Hebrew, B^erachôth we-Hodayôth) would appear to be the most adequate.

The hymns represent the most original literary creation in the Dead Sea Scriptures. It is true that they are, in the main, mosaics of Biblical quotations and that they often exhibit all the learned and tortured exploitation of Scripture that we find later in the medieval poetasters (*payyetanim*) of the synagogue. This, however, is merely the trammel of literary convention, and it should no more dull our ears to the underlying passion and authenticity of feeling than do the mannered conceits of a Donne or a Herbert or a Vaughan.

Especially noteworthy is the prevalence in these hymns of the vocabulary which Evelyn Underhill and others have recognized as the standard and characteristic idiom of mystical experience. There is the same harping on the wilderness of isolation; the same reference to the 'ascent' to God and to 'the height of eternal things'; the same metaphor (particularly in Hymn No. 5) of the New Birth and the 'travail of the world'; the same intensive apprehension of Divine providence, communion and 'enlightenment'; and the same sense of nursing a precious secret against the day of revelation. Apprehension of these notes is of the essence in understanding the spirit of the hymns in particular and of the Brotherhood in general.

It has been suggested that some of the hymns, which speak of deliverance from froward assailants ('the company of Belial' or 'the men of corruption'), were designed for the use of soldiers who had escaped their adversaries or defeated them. To the present writer, such a view seems singularly and unperceptively overliteral; it confuses the 'slings and arrows of outrageous fortune' with concrete bazookas and guided missiles. Similarly, there seems no good reason for assuming, as has been done, that Hymn No. 8 must necessarily have been written by 'the teacher of Righteousness' simply because it speaks of one who sought to impart God's law to his brethren but was constantly thwarted and abused by 'preachers of lies' and 'prophets of deceit'. What the text is describing is the normal and typical frustration of the mystic—the experience of *every* man who believes that he has seen God and that he is burning a small candle in the darkness of a world unredeemed.

To the main body of hymns we have here prefixed another, which the ancient librarians of Qumran attached to a copy of the *Manual of Discipline*. If one reads it carefully, one will find that it repeats almost verbatim the list of obligations and the basic oath of allegiance laid down in that document for new members of the Brotherhood. It may therefore be regarded as a hymn chanted by initiants when they were formally received into the community; and this would in turn explain why the ancient librarians considered it an appropriate liturgical 'appendix' to the *Manual*. On this hypothesis we have called it *The Hymn of the Initiants*. The Scrolls themselves, it may be added, bear no titles; those assigned by modern scholars are therefore in any case quite arbitrary.

II

Several further hymns are included in a compendium (preserved in several incomplete copies) the major part of which contains portions of the Biblical Book of Psalms. This compendium, which has been somewhat tendentiously called 'The Dead Sea Psalm Scroll', and presumed to be a variant form of the canonical collection, was probably compiled for liturgical purposes.[1]

Three of the extracanonical hymns have been known hitherto from late Syriac manuscripts—none earlier than the fourteenth century. Evidently once current in the services of the Eastern Orthodox Church, they are part of a group

of five fancifully attributed to David,[2] who is indeed credited, in a kind of colophon to our scroll, with no less
than 4050 effusions![3]

a. *David (Psalm 151)*. The first of these three 'Davidic'
compositions to be here presented (though in fact the last
in the manuscript) is an old acquaintance: it is the poem
appended to the Greek (Septuagint) Version of the canonical Psalter and there entitled, *A genuine, though supernu-
merary, Psalm of David, composed when he engaged Goliath in single combat.*[4] There are, however, some varia-
tions and additions, and that the latter were part of the
original text, and no mere interpolations by some Qumranite redactor, is evident from the fact that they complete
the chain of ideas and give coherence to what in the Greek
Version appears as a string of somewhat inconsequential
sentences. To put it mildly, the translator was something
of a clod.

The psalm relates, in the first person and in an artless
style characteristic more of folk poetry than of sophisti-
cated literary invention, the story of how David, the youngest son of Jesse, was relegated by his father to the humble
task of tending sheep and goats (v. 1); how he made a
Panpipe and lyre in order to pay honor thereon to God
(v. 2); how he was inwardly aware all the while that the
mute mountains and hills were incapable of conveying to
God what they had witnessed of his piety, and the rustling
leaves of relaying his praises, and the sheep of reporting
how well he was tending them (v. 3); how, though he was
himself left wondering who or what could possibly bring
word of his activities, God, Lord of the Universe, nevertheless saw and heard all, without need of intermediaries (v.
4); and how, in consequence, he was selected by God's
envoy, the prophet Samuel, to be the future leader of Israel
and was anointed with sacred oil, in preference to his older
and seemingly more attractive brothers (vv. 5–7).

This, to be sure, is but one interpretation of the text,
but it is supported by the fact that echoes of it are indeed
to be heard in later Jewish legend (midrash), where we

are told that God chose David to shepherd His people precisely because He saw how well he shepherded his father's flocks,[5] and also—a notion repeated in the Koran—that when He heard his songs of praise, He commanded birds and sheep thenceforth to join in.[6]

There is, however, an interesting alternative. By reading a single word somewhat differently,[7] some scholars have extracted the sense that, though mountains and hills were indeed inarticulate and seemingly unresponsive, trees and flocks 'recognized the excellence' of David's words and music.[8] On this basis it has then been suggested that the poet was influenced by a popular fancy of his day which assimilated the 'sweet singer of Israel' to the classical Orpheus who, as Shakespeare puts it, 'With his lute made trees/ And the mountain-tops that freeze/ Bow themselves when he did sing'. In support of this suggestion it is pointed out that in a prominent position in the synagogue at Dura-Europus there is a fresco depicting an Orpheus-like figure by some identified as David;[9] that a representation of the same scene occurs in a Jewish catacomb at Rome;[10] and that in various manuscripts of the Psalter David is indeed portrayed as Orpheus.[11] Though all of them considerably later than our Qumran scroll, these representations are taken to attest the persistence of an ancient tradition.

In my opinion, this interpretation overshoots the mark. In the first place, there is no solid evidence that David was ever identified with Orpheus at an earlier date.[12] Secondly, the notion that inanimate things or nature in general can be charmed by music in fact occurs in folktales from several parts of the world,[13] so that, even if this is what our text means, it by no means implies a *specific* identification of David with Orpheus. Thirdly, this interpretation overlooks the essential distinction between the inability of the rustling leaves to repeat David's *words*—that is, his songs of praise—and that of the sheep to apprise God of his *acts* —that is, his proficiency and solicitude as a shepherd. It is just this combination, as later midrash insists, that fitted him for the leadership of Israel. Fourthly, the proposed rendering, *The hills do not tell forth* (*God's glory*), involves the grammatical anomaly of making a *feminine* noun govern a verb with *masculine* form.

There is also a difference of opinion about the meaning of the succeeding verse (v. 4). In the *editio princeps* this is rendered:

> *For who can proclaim and who can bespeak*
> *and who can recount the deeds of the Lord?*
> *Everything has God seen,*
> *everything has He heard and He has heeded.*[14]

This, I think, misses the sense. The words are a continuation of David's inner thought, and what they say is, quite simply, that although he was initially left wondering who or what could ever report his activities, God as Lord of All nevertheless saw and heard everything without any such mediation. In support of this interpretation a number of points can be made. First: as several scholars have pointed out,[15] the Hebrew word *'ādôn*, which has been rendered 'the Lord', is nowhere else used in this absolute form in reference to God, the usual style being *Adonai*. Second: our author elsewhere employs the Tetragrammaton (*YHWH*), which, to boot, he writes reverently *in archaic script* (vv. 2, 6). Third: by construing the word *all* as part of the title, viz., *Lord of All*, rather than as the object of the verb *saw*, we recover an expression which indeed occurs elsewhere in intertestamental literature[16] and which is also found in precisely the same Hebrew form in the famous *'Alēnū*-prayer, commonly regarded as of pre-Christian origin.[17] Fourthly, the rendering, *He has heeded*, misses the specific point of the Hebrew word, which means properly, *gave ear* and thus states that God was able all by Himself (Heb. *He*—emphatic) to hear what David was singing, even though it was not reported to Him.

It is perhaps worth suggesting that our author wrote under the influence of secular Hellenistic poetry. Thus the reference to David's making a Panpipe and lyre (v. 2), though obviously based on the Scriptural allusions to his musical skill (I Sam. 16.18, 23), may be intended at the same time to depict him as the typical shepherd of Greek pastoral idyl.[18] Pious David, however, plies his instruments to the glory of God—not, as do the Greek swains, merely for diversion or in order to sing 'amorous ditties all a summer's day'. Again, when nature is here portrayed as unresponsive to his warblings, this is perhaps a sly jibe at the conventional cliché, common in Theocritus (and later imitated by Vergil), that the whole woodland responds to the sounds of the flute.[19] So too, when it is said of David's brothers (v. 6) that they were not only tall and handsome, but also 'graced with comely locks' (a detail absent from the Septuagint Version!), may we not detect a Hellenic note, for this is quite frequently mentioned in Greek poetry,[20] whereas—as my friend and former student, Mr. Murray Lichtenstein, has pointed out to me—in Ancient Near Eastern verse the big thing in descriptions of bodily beauty is usually the *eyes*. It should be observed, however, in connection with this last point, that later midrash does indeed make much of the seductive properties of Joseph's locks,[21] and it is possible that our author had some earlier form of this legend specifically in mind, seeing that he describes the brothers in terms which the Bible applies to Joseph (Gen. 39.6).

Finally, it should be noted that the encounter with Goliath, which is incorporated into the Greek Version and which gives it its title, is, in the Qumran scroll, made the subject of a separate psalm, with its own superscription. Only a few fragments of the initial verses, however, have survived.

b. Invitation. The second of the extracanonical hymns is a summons to join in acclaiming the glory of God in public assembly and in imparting to the ignorant a knowledge of His majesty and power. This, it is said, is the true role of wisdom, and whoever is responsive to this duty is as acceptable to God as one who offers sacrifice or as the savor of incense. The voice and song of Wisdom ring out from the homes of the godly, but ignorant and intemperate men keep away from it. When the righteous and godly sit at meals, their talk is of wisdom and the Lore (Torah) of God—things of which the wicked and arrogant neither speak nor know. The righteous, however, have their reward: God looks compassionately upon them, and will surely deliver them from 'the evil time'—that is, more specifically, from the period of turmoil and distress which will precede the Messianic Age and which the men of Qumran already saw all around them. The psalm concludes with a call to bless God as the redeemer of the humble and oppressed, the sure restorer of Israel's glory, and as the One who will govern the world from the midst of Israel, 'spread His tent' in Zion, and be ever at hand in Jerusalem.

The psalm has been read as a call to 'service' addressed specifically to the Qumran Brotherhood, the words *join company*, which occur in the third verse, being rendered, *form a community*.[22] I would suggest, however, quite a different interpretation—namely, that this is really what is termed in rabbinic literature a *Birkath Zimmūn*, a call to an assembled company to join in the Grace after Meals, coupled with an invitation to participate in the 'talk about Torah' which was a customary concomitant of such gatherings. Such an invitation to 'say Grace' is issued by a delegated member of the group whenever three or more persons dine together, the custom being as old, according to the Palestinian Talmud (*Berachôth*, vii.2) as Simon ben Sheṭaḥ, who lived during the reigns of Alexander Jannaeus and Salome (104–69 B.C.E.). The meal must be accompanied by 'words of Torah'; otherwise, as later sages put it,[23] it is no better than a 'session of scoffers' (cp. Ps. 1.1) or than 'sacrifices offered to the dead' (cp. Ps. 106.28).[24]

This suggestion derives especially from the explicit reference (v. 3) to the fact that when the godly 'eat their fill and drink', the voice of Wisdom—a common rabbinic synonym for Torah—rings out, and their talk is of the Lore (Torah) of the Most High and is designed to further knowledge of His power. It finds further support in the fact that all the original elements of the Grace, as they are prescribed in the Talmud (*Berachôth*, 48a), viz., the reference to 'eating to satiety and blessing God' (a quotation from Deut. 8.10); to the eventual 'raising of the horn', i.e., enhancement of the status, of God's people; and to the establishment of His abode in Zion, find place in this composition;[25] while the statement (v. 12) that the song of

Wisdom rings out may readily be seen as an allusion to the chanting of psalms at meals—a custom familiar especially from the Last Supper (Matt. 26.30; Mark 14.26) and still current in Jewish practise. Moreover, the assertion (vv. 10–11) that he who acclaims the majesty of God (in response to the direct summons in v. 1) is as one who offers oblation accords significantly with a passage in the Hymn of the Initiants (below, p. 138) which says explicitly,

> At the common board,
> or ever I raise my hand
> to enjoy the rich yield of the earth,
> with the fruit of my own lips
> I will bless Him as with an oblation.

The concluding invocation, *Bless ye,* likewise accords with the suggestion that our poem was really a prelude to the Grace after Meals, for it is indeed the formula prescribed in the mishnah when many dine together.[26]

Finally, it is perhaps worthy of note that in the Qumran compendium the poem follows Psalm 145, for this may have been due to the occurrence in that psalm of the verses (15–16)

> The eyes of all wait upon Thee,
>   and Thou givest them their food in due season.
> Thou openest Thy hand
> and givest in full measure to all living
> that which they desire;

—the latter of which is actually incorporated into the opening benediction of the traditional Grace.

c. Plea for Grace. The third of the 'psalms' already known from the Syriac manuscripts is composed in the form of an alphabetical acrostic and is a plea for the remission of punishment for sins. Not impossibly, it was designed for recitation in illness, this being regarded as a requital for misdeeds. The hymn is largely a pastiche of Biblical verses, and the original acrostic has occasionally been disturbed (as in the first chapter of Nahum) by later editing or by such distortion as is apt to arise when a poem gains popular currency.

Of the three hymns hitherto unknown, the first (here entitled *Supplication*) is likewise a prayer for forgiveness of sin and remission of punishment. It belongs, though in a more personal vein, to the liturgical genre known later as *Selîhôth* (or *Baqashôth*), i.e., Pleas for Pardon. There is, however, a notable difference between this composition and those which find place in the traditional Jewish prayer book, inasmuch as the latter seek forgiveness for sins actually committed, whereas here the major emphasis is on immunity from the proclivity to sin and from demonic possession. Such immunity is the natural outcome of that enlightenment and insight which accompanies a sense of the divine and which the Qumran Brotherhood claimed as their special endowment.

The second of the entirely new hymns has been called by its first editor *An Apostrophe to Zion*.[27] It is, however, more than a mere patriotic anthem, such as we find, for instance, in Psalm 87, for while it certainly celebrates the glories of Zion and of her ancient inhabitants, its main thrust is to provide consolation and assurance of deliverance from its foes. Indeed, one is tempted to suggest that the poem may have been composed during the time of the First Jewish Revolt, when the Roman troops were closing in.

The last of the 'new' hymns is, without doubt, the gem of the collection.

It is an ancient Jewish belief that every daybreak is a renewal of creation. For this reason, the appropriate moment for the initial devotions of the day is when the glimmer of dawn first appears in the sky, and the world is reborn.[28] The recital of the *Shema'*—a cardinal element in the morning and evening services—is preceded in the former by a series of benedictions the first of which celebrates the creation of daylight and is known as *Yôṣer*, because God is specifically described in it as *yôṣer 'ôr*, 'creator of light'. The traditional form of this prayer has been attributed by some authorities to the Essenes, and in subsequent generations hymnodic elaborations of the central theme formed a distinct genre of Hebrew liturgical poetry. What we have here entitled *Morning Hymn* is a composition of this type.

The hymn is perhaps the most imaginative in the entire Qumran repertoire. It plays successively on the several features of daybreak—the rising of the sun, the dissipation of darkness, the increased movement of the sea, the growing intensity of the light, the lifting of mists from the mountains, the gradual emergence to view of the green and dew-drenched meadows. Each of these features is regarded as a manifestation at once of God's power and grace.

The all-seeing sun was envisaged in remoter Semitic antiquity as the god of justice and was said to be attended by twin sons, Right and Equity, who stood respectively on his right and left. This ancient concept was later developed into a description of essential qualities associated with God (cp. Ps. 85.11). In our text, Loving-kindness and Truth are said to encompass Him, and Justice and Right to be the mainstays of His throne. Similarly, in the traditional form of the *Yôṣer*-hymn, Purity and Rectitude stand before His throne, Loving-kindness and Compassion before His glory, while Knowledge and Understanding surround Him.[29] The notion is then in turn developed in kabbalistic lore, where such qualities (arranged in pairs) are regarded as constituent elements of a pluralistic Deity.

The idea need not be discarded in our own times as a mere outworn fantasy. It is susceptible of still further development. The assertion that Knowledge and Understanding circle around God may be understood today not in the sense that He is enveloped by them, but rather that all empirical perception and science can at best but skirt His essence. Similarly, the affirmation that Loving-kindness and Compassion stand before His glory may mean for us today that the benevolence and compassion revealed (one might say, inbuilt) in the order of Nature—such factors as the inevitable return of spring, the instinctive love of mother for child, the ability both to remember and to forget—take precedence over its outward majesty as manifestations of God, and that He attaches more importance to them than to the physical display of His splendor.

The association of daybreak with creation is brought out in our poem by a direct reference to a passage in the Book of Job (38.7) where it is said that at the dawn of the world all the celestial hosts (styled 'sons of God') and all the morning stars burst into song. The verse is exquisitely chosen, for the earthly counterparts of those 'sons of God' are the faithful and sensitive among men, while those of the morning stars are the illumined 'children of light' whom the men of Qumran claimed (or, at least, aspired) to be. The implication is, therefore, that in their daily matins the latter are in fact emulating what their heavenly archetypes did at the first dayspring.

III

The *Lament for Zion* is not part of the 'psalmodic' compendium, but has been pieced together out of two separate fragments retrieved from another cave.[30] In style and content it is the forerunner of the dirges which came later to be chanted in the synagogue on the Fast of Ab, the anniversary of the destruction of the Temple. Like those compositions, it draws heavily on the Biblical Book of Lamentations (likewise part of the service), and punctuates the several stanzas with the refrain, *Woe unto us!*[31] The archaeological evidence makes it clear that the poem was composed before 68 C.E., the year in which the Qumran 'monastery' was abandoned. The Temple which the poem mourns is therefore the *First* Temple, destroyed by the Babylonians in 586 B.C.E., and if it be asked why such mourning should have continued when a second temple was in fact standing, the answer is that, by reason of the venality of the Jerusalemitan priests, the men of Qumran regarded the latter as polluted and no longer recognized its sanctity.

At first, no doubt, dirges of this kind were inspired more

immediately by nostalgia on the part of those who had actually witnessed the disaster and by despair at the loss of relatives and friends—an intense personal trauma like that experienced in our own day by survivors of the Nazi holocaust. In course of time, however, Zion came to take on a wider meaning. Just as the Temple was, while it stood, the outward symbol of God's presence among His people and of their own reciprocal devotion to Him, so its destruction became that of His seeming withdrawal (or 'exile') and of their own defection from Him. The dirges then tended to become stereotyped in the form of literary clichés and imitations of the Biblical Book of Lamentations, and this is what we find in our poem. It can scarcely be described as either a spontaneous *cri du coeur* or as a literary masterpiece; it lacks both the artistry and inventiveness of (say) the great lament in *The Apocalypse of Baruch*[32] and the simple pathos of (say) Jane Elliot's famous *Lament for Flodden*.[33] Indeed, the sound of tears seems to have degenerated into little more than a liturgical bleat.

Just the opposite note is sounded in two short poems contained in a fragmentary hymnal retrieved from Cave 4. These are songs of consolation, holding out the hope of an imminent era of prosperity, the rout of the wicked (Belial), and the restoration of past glories. They are little more than pastiches of Biblical verses and lack any real creative originality.

NOTES

1. I see no reason for assuming that the Qumran compendium represents an alternative canonical Psalter. A crucial objection to this view (which no one seems yet to have pointed out) is that, while there are no less than 154 quotations from our standard Psalter in *The Book of Hymns* and other Qumran writings (see below, pp. 144ff.), there is nary a one from the 'extra' hymns included in the present collection. This surely proves that the latter were not 'familiar in men's mouths' as words of Scripture.

2. For details, see J. A. Sanders, ed., *DSD IV: The Psalms Scroll from Cave 11* (1965), pp. 53f. The standard edition is that of Martin Noth, in *Zeitschrift für die alttestamentliche Wissenschaft*, 48 (1930), pp. 1–23, which includes a retroversion into Hebrew.

3. Such attribution has nothing whatsoever to do with the question of canonization. Nor is it of any real importance that there are differences between the Qumran text, the Masoretic recension, and the Greek (Septuagint) Version concerning the Davidic authorship of certain psalms. Such variant ascriptions were not uncommon in antiquity, even as they are today among classical scholars. Some rabbis, for instance, even attributed the Book of Job to Moses! Moreover, the Talmud (*Babâ Bathrâ*, 14[b]) records a tradition that David put together a vast corpus of psalms, some of which went back to Abraham!

4. Pseudo-Philo, *Biblical Antiquities*, 59.4, quotes another psalm which David is said to have indited when he fought Goliath. The title, *A Hallelujah*, found in

the Qumran scroll, recalls the later statement by R. Arika ('Rab'; c. 220 c.e.), cited in *Midrash T^ehillim*, 1, that this is the most appropriate designation of the Psalter as a whole.

5. *Midrash T^ehillim*, 78.20; *Exodus Rabba*, ii.2.
6. Koran, Suras xxi.79; xxxiv.10.
7. For *'^alê ha-'êṣîm*, 'the leaves of the trees', they read *'illū ha-'eṣîm*, giving to the former word the meaning which it bears in post-Biblical Hebrew.
8. Cp. Sanders, *op. cit.*, p. 62.
9. Cp. E. R. Goodenough, *Jewish Symbols in the Graeco-Roman Period*, iii (1953), fig. 604; v (1956), figs. 117–19. For the identification with David cp. C. H. Kraeling, *The Excavations at Dura-Europus, Sixth Season* (1936), p. 370; Rachel Wischnitzer, *The Messianic Theme in the Paintings of the Dura Synagogue* (1948), p. 95.
10. In the Vigna Randanini, on the Via Appia; cp. Robert Eisler, *Orphisch-Dionysische Mysteriengedanken* (1925), pp. 4–5.
11. Cp. Eisler, *op. cit.*, p. 11.
12. In later midrash he is sometimes identified with Hermes, as inventor of the lyre, and it is even said that he sits in heaven twanging his harp under the name of Hermesiel!
13. Cp. Stith Thompson, *Motif-Index of Folk Literature*, D.1275.1; T. H. Gaster, *The Oldest Stories in the World* (1952), pp. 131f. One thinks, for instance, of Wänäimöinen's music in the Finnish Kalevala.
14. The Greek Version substitutes, *And who will report (this) to my Lord?* The Syriac, with no less lack of sequence, has, *Who will show me my Lord? He, the Lord, has become my God.* Neither translator could read poetry.
15. E.g., S. Rabbinowitz, in *Zeitschrift für die alttestamentliche Wissenschaft*, 76 (1964), pp. 193ff.
16. E.g., II Maccabees, 9.5; 12.22; 15.2; III Macc. 2.21; *Sibylline Oracles*, frag. i.4, ed. Geffcken.
17. S. Singer, ed., *The Authorized Daily Prayerbook* (1890), p. 76.

18. Cp. Theocritus, *Id.*, iv, 28; vii, 71.

19. Cp. Theocritus, *Id.*, vi, 43–44; vii, 74; Vergil, *Ecl.*, v, 62f.; vii, 2.22f.; x, 9.

20. E.g., Theocritus, *Id.*, v, 91; cp. also Horace, *Odes*, iii, 20, 14.

21. Cf. L. Ginzberg, *Legends of the Jews*, ii, 5, 44, 48. This detail finds place also in the retelling of the story in the Persian poet Jami's *Yusuf and Zuleikha;* see J. D. Yohannan, ed., *Joseph and Potiphar's Wife in World Literature* (1968), pp. 176, 180.

22. This rendering depends on taking the Hebrew word *yaḥad*, 'together', as the noun which elsewhere designates the Qumran Brotherhood. But this is forced, since the expression is modelled directly on Psalm 122.3.

23. Mishnah, *Abôth* iii, 3, 4. The sayings are attributed respectively to Ḥananiah b. Teradion (martyred, 135 c.e.) and Simeon b. Yoḥai (c. 100–70 c.e.).

24. In the Mishnaic context, the reference is probably to the Roman *feriae novendiales*, a sacrifice and funeral repast on the ninth day after burial (cp. Juvenal, *Sat.*, v, 85; Servius, on Vergil, *Aen.*, v, 64) or to the *silicernium*, a meal near the grave (cp. Terence, *Adelphi*, iv, 2, 48; Servius, on Vergil, *Aen.*, v, 92).

25. The elements of 'building Jerusalem' (cp. Ps. 147.2) and of 'causing the horn of David to flourish' (cp. Ps. 132.17) occur in succession in the Eighteen Benedictions (xiv, xv) in the Jewish liturgy, while references to 'deliverance in the day of trouble', the redemption of Israel, the building of the City, the 'flourishing of the horn' both of David and of Israel, and God's choice of Zion appear also in the hymn which is inserted in the Genizah text of Sirach, after 51.12.

26. The Mishnah (*Bᵉrachôth*, vii.3) says that if three, or a hundred, or a thousand, or a myriad others be present, the formula must begin, *Bless ye*, rather than *Let us bless*, as when there are but three persons in all. R. Akiba and R. Ishmael assert, however, that *Bless ye* is the formula in all cases. This corresponds to the Christian *Benedicite*. To 'say Grace' is still called col-

loquially 'to *bensh*', i.e., a Judaeo-German (Yiddish) corruption of that word.

27. A second copy has now been identified in a fragmentary scroll from another cave at Qumran.
28. Mishnah, *B**rachôth*, i.1; cp. *Wisdom of Solomon*, 16.28.
29. S. Singer, ed., *Authorized Daily Prayerbook* (1962), p. 39.
30. There are also sundry minor scraps too fragmentary to translate.
31. Most of these compositions are, to be sure, medieval, and many of them commemorate later catastrophes. For those of the Ashkenazic rite, see S. Baer, ed., *Seder ha-Qinôth* (Rödelheim, 1913). Those of the Sephardic rite derive mainly from the Spanish school of Jewish poets and are of far superior literary quality. For representative translations see T. H. Gaster, *Festivals of the Jewish Year* (1953), pp. 207ff.; Nina Davis, *Songs of Exile* (1901). An interesting specimen of the same genre is the Judaeo-Greek lament published by Benjamin Schwartz in *The Joshua Bloch Memorial Volume* (New York, 1960), pp. 107–44.
32. x.6–9.
33. Richard Aldington, ed., *The Viking Book of Poetry of the English-speaking World* (1941), pp. 582f.

THE HYMN OF THE INITIANTS
[*Manual of Discipline*, cols. x–xi]

1 [Day and night will I offer my praise]
and at all the appointed times which God has prescribed.

When daylight begins its rule,
when it reaches its turning-point,[1]
and when it again withdraws to its appointed
abode;

When the watches of darkness begin,
when God opens the storehouse thereof,[2]
when He sets that darkness against the light,[3]
when it reaches its turning-point,[4]
and when it again withdraws in face of the light;

When sun and moon shine forth from the holy Height,
and when they again withdraw to the glorious
Abode;[5]

When the formal seasons come on the days of new
moon,[6]
when they reach their turning-points,[7]
and when they yield place to one another,
as each comes round anew;*

5 When the natural seasons come, at whatever time
may be;

* The text here incorporates a series of esoteric glosses which
have been omitted from the translation.

when, too, the months begin;
   on their feasts and on holy days,
   as they come in order due,
   each as a memorial in its season[8]—
I shall hold it as one of the laws
engraven of old on the tablets[9]
to render to God as my tribute
   —the blessings of my lips.[10]

When the (natural) years begin;
   at the turning-points of their seasons,
   and when each completes its term
   on its natural day,
   yielding each to each—
   reaping-time to summer,
   sowing-time to verdure;

In the (formal) years of weeks,
   in the several seasons thereof,
   and when, at the jubilee,
   the series of weeks begins[11]—
yea, throughout my life,
I shall hold it as one of the laws
engraven of old on the tablets
to offer to God as my fruits—
   the praises of my tongue,
and to cull for him as my tithe
   —the skilled melody of my lips.[12]

All my music shall be for the glory of God;
   my lyre and my harp shall be devoted
   to tell of His holy dispensation;
I shall put the flute to my lips
   to rehearse the due poise of His judgments.

10   With the coming of day and night
      I shall come ever anew
      into God's covenant;
   and when evening and morning depart,
      shall ob<ser>ve how He sets their bounds.[13]

Only where God sets bounds
—the unchangeable bounds of His Law—
will I too set my domain.[14]
I shall hold it as one of the laws
engraven of old on the tablets
to face my sin and transgression
and avouch the justice of God.
    I shall say unto God:
    'Thou, for me, art the Right!'
    and unto the Most High:
    'For me Thou art cause of all good!'

Fountain of all knowledge,
Spring of holiness,
Zenith of all glory,
Might omnipotent,
Beauty that never fades,
    I will choose the path He shows me,
    and be content with His judgments.

Whenever I first put forth my hand or foot,
I will bless His name;[15]
when first I go or come,
when I sit and when I rise,[16]
when I lie down on my couch,
I will sing unto Him.
    At the common board,
or ever I raise my hand
to enjoy the rich yield of the earth,
with the fruit of my own lips
    I will bless Him as with an oblation.[17]

At the onset of fear and alarm,
or when trouble and stress are at hand,
I will bless him with special thanksgiving
and muse upon His power,
and rely on His mercies alway,
and come thereby to know
that in His hand lies the judgment of all living,
and that all His works are truth.[18]

Whenever distress breaks out,
   I still will praise Him;
and when His salvation comes,
   join the chorus of praise.[19]

I will heap no evil on any,
but pursue all men with good,[20]
knowing that only with God
lies the judgment of all living,
and He it is will award
each man his deserts.

I will not be envious
of the profit of wickedness;
   for wealth unrighteously gotten my soul shall not
      lust.[21]

I will not engage in strife
with reprobate men,[22]
   forestalling the Day of Requital.[23]

I will not turn back my wrath
from froward men,
   nor rest content until justice be affirmed.

I will harbor no angry grudge
against those that indeed repent,[24]
but neither will I show compassion
   to any that turn from the way.

I will not console the smitten
until they amend their course.

I will cherish no baseness in my heart,
nor shall there be heard in my mouth
coarseness[25] or wanton deceit;
neither shall there be found upon my lips
   deception and lies.[26]
The fruit of holiness shall be on my tongue,
and no heathen filth be found thereon.

> I will open my mouth with thanksgiving,
> and my tongue shall ever relate
> the righteousness of God
> and the perfidy of men
> until men's transgressions be ended.

> Empty words will I banish from my lips;
> filth and perverseness from my mind.

> I will hedge in knowledge with sound counsel,
25 > and protect [it] with shrewdness of mind.

> I will [set] a sober limit
> to all defending of faith
> and exacting of justice by force.
>   I will bound God's righteousness
> by the measuring-line of occasion.
>   [I will temper] justice [with mercy],
> will show kindness to men downtrodden,
xi,1 > bring firmness to fearful hearts,
> discernment to spirits that stray,
> enlighten the bowed with sound doctrine,
> reply to the proud with meekness,
> with humility answer the base
> —men rich in worldly goods,
> who point the finger of scorn
> and utter iniquitous thoughts.

> To God I commit my cause.
> It is His to perfect my way,
> His to make straight my heart.
> He, in His charity,
>   will wipe away my transgression.

> For He from the Wellspring of Knowledge
> has made His light to burst forth,
> and mine eye has gazed on His wonders;
> and the light that is in my heart
> has pierced the deep things of existence.

He is ever the stay of my right hand.[27]
The path beneath my feet
is set on a mighty rock[28]
unshaken before all things.
  For that rock beneath my feet
5 is the truth of God,
and His power is the stay of my right hand;
from the fount of His charity
my vindication goes forth.

  Through His mysterious wonder
light is come into my heart;
mine eye has set its gaze
on everlasting things.
A virtue hidden from man,
a knowledge and subtle lore
concealed from human kind;
a fount of righteousness,
a reservoir of strength,
a wellspring of all glory
wherewith no flesh has converse—
these has God bestowed
on them that He has chosen,
to possess them for ever.
He has given them an inheritance
in the lot of the Holy Beings,
and joined them in communion with the Sons of
    Heaven,[29]
to form one congregation,
one single communion,
a fabric of holiness,
a plant evergreen,[30]
  for all time to come.

But I—— I belong to wicked mankind,
to the communion of sinful flesh.
  My transgressions, my iniquities and sins,
and the waywardness of my heart
10 condemn me to communion with the worm
and with all that walk in darkness.

For a mortal's way is [not] of himself,
neither can a man direct his own steps.
The judgment lies with God,
and 'tis His to perfect man's way.

Only through His knowledge
have all things come to be,
and all that is, is ordained by His thought;
and apart from Him is nothing wrought.[31]

Behold, if I should totter,
God's mercies will be my salvation.
If I stumble in the waywardness of flesh,
I shall be set aright
through God's righteousness ever-enduring.
If distress break out,
He will snatch my soul from perdition,
and set my foot on the path.
   For He, in His compassion,
has drawn me near unto Him,[32]
and His judgment upon me shall be rendered in His
      mercy.
   In his righteous truth He has judged me,
and in His abundant goodness
will shrive my iniquities,
and in His righteousness cleanse me
from all the pollution of man
15   and the sin of human kind,
that I may acknowledge unto God His righteousness,
and unto the Most High His majestic splendor.

Blessed art Thou, O my God,
Who hast opened the heart of Thy servant unto
      knowledge.
Direct all his works in righteousness,
and vouchsafe unto the son of Thine handmaid
the favor which Thou hast assured to all the mortal
      elect,
to stand in Thy presence for ever.

For apart from Thee no man's way can be perfect,
and without Thy will is nothing wrought.
Thou it is that hast taught all knowledge,
and all things exist by Thy will;
and there is none beside Thee
to controvert Thy plan;
none to understand all Thy holy thought,
none to gaze into the depths of Thy secrets,
none to perceive all Thy wonders and the might of
 Thy power.

20 Who can compass the sum of Thy glory?
And what is mere mortal man
amid Thy wondrous works?
And what the child of woman
to sit in Thy presence?
For, behold, he is kneaded of dust,
and his [ ] is the food of worms.
He is but a molded shape,[33]
a thing nipped out of clay,[34]
whose attachment is but to the dust.
 What can such clay reply,
 or that which is molded by hand?
 What thought can it comprehend?

THE BOOK OF HYMNS
OR
PSALMS OF THANKSGIVING

. . . .

5   [Thou art the source of all might]
and the wellspring of all power;
[yet art Thou also rich in wisdom]
[and] great in counsel.²
    Thy fury [is vented] in the presence of [   ];
[yet are Thy mercies] beyond number.
    [Thou art a God that visits wrongdoing;]
[yet also a God] longsuffering in judgment.³
    In whatsoever Thou doest,
Thou hast ever done justly.

In Thy wisdom didst [Thou call into being]
[spirits] immortal,
and ere Thou didst create them,
didst foreknow their works for all time.
    [Apart from Thee] can naught be done,
    and naught apprehended save by Thy will.⁴
Thou it is formed every spirit,
[and set due rule] and role for all their works.

10   When Thou didst stretch out the heavens for Thy
        glory,
and [command] all [their host] to do Thy will,⁵
Thou didst also make potent spirits
to keep them in bounds.

Or ever spirits immortal
took on the form of ho[ly] angels,[6]
Thou didst assign them to bear rule
over divers domains:
over the sun and moon,
to govern their hidden powers;
over the stars,
to hold them to their courses;
over [rain and snow,]
to make them fulfill their functions;
over meteors and lightnings,
to make them discharge their tasks;[7]
[and Thou didst set them in] promptuaries[8]
[whence Thou didst cause them to issue]
for their several purposes,
to govern the mysteries of these things.[9]
 When, too, in Thy power Thou didst create
earth and seas and deeps,
in Thy wisdom[10] didst Thou set [with]in them
[spirits immortal],
15 thereby to dispose to Thy will
all that therein is.
 [So hast Thou made (his) flesh
a promptuary] in (this) world
for that spirit of man which Thou didst create[11]
to last throughout all time
and for ages infinite,
that it might gov[ern his deeds].
 Thou hast assigned the tasks of men's spirits
duly, moment by moment,[12]
throughout their generations;
and Thou hast determined the mode
in which they shall wield their sway,
season by season;
yea, [Thou hast prescribed] their [works,]
age after age—
alike when they shall be visited with peace
and when they shall suffer affliction.[13]

Thou hast [man's spirit]
and duly assigned its role
for all his offspring
throughout the generations of time;
and [Thou hast   ] it
for all years of eternity.
And in Thy knowing wisdom
Thou hast ordained its fate,
or ever it came into being.

20   By [Thy will all things exi]st,
and without Thee is nothing wrought.[14]

Shapen of clay and kneaded with water,
a bedrock of shame and a source of pollution,
a cauldron of iniquity and a fabric of sin,
a spirit errant and wayward,[15]
distraught by every just judgment—
what can I say that hath not been foreknown,
or what disclose that hath not been foretold?
All things are inscribed before Thee
in a recording script,[16]
for every moment of time,
for the infinite cycles of years,
in their several appointed times.

25   No single thing is hidden,
naught missing from Thy presence.

How can man say aught
to account for his sins?
How argue in excuse of his misdeeds?
How can he enter reply
to any just sentence upon him?
    Thine, O God of all knowledge,[17]
are all works of righteousness
and the secret of truth;
while man's is but thralldom to wrongdoing,
and works of deceit.
    The spirit that lies in man's speech,
Thou didst create.
Thou hast known all the words of man's tongue

and determined the fruit of his lips,[18]
ere those lips themselves had being.
It is Thou that disposeth all words in due sequence[19]
and giveth to the spirit of the lips
ordered mode of expression;[20]
that bringeth forth their secrets
in measured utterances,[21]
and granteth unto spirits
means to express their thoughts,
that Thy glory may be made known,
30 and Thy wonders told forth
in all Thine unerring works,
and that Thy righteousness [may be proclaimed,]
and Thy name be praised in the mouth of all things,
and that all creatures may know Thee,
each to the meed of his insight,
and bless Thee alway.

Moreover, in Thy mercy and great lovingkindness
Thou hast given man's spirit the strength
to endure afflictions,
and the power to come forth clean,
though never so great its transgressions;
showing thereby unto all Thy works
what wonders Thou canst perform.
[So, for my own part,
what I tell is, to sim]ple minds,
but a tale of my sufferings
and how just they are;
but to the world at large
'tis a tale of miracles
which Thou hast evinced through me
in the sight of all mankind.

Hear, then, ye that are wise,
and sanely reflect;
Ye that are simple-minded,[22]
learn to think with more depth![23]
Ye that are righteous
put an end to perversity!
Ye that are blameless of conduct

keep a firm stance!
Be patient and spurn not correction!
Though men that are foolish at heart
cannot understand these things,
God's ways are ever just;
while men who behave unbridled
will (be left to) gnash their teeth.[24]

. . . .

2

II, 2-19

[I give thanks unto Thee, O Lord,]
for Thou art my strength and [my stronghold,[1]]
and Thou hast delivered my soul
from all works of unrighteousness.
    [For Thou hast] put [truth in my heart]
and righteousness [in my spirit,]
along with all gifts of Thy wisd[om;]
5   and hast crushed the loins [of them]
[that have risen up against me.[2]]

    Thou bringest me cheer, O Lord,[3]
amid the sorrow of mourning,
words of peace amid havoc,
stoutness of heart when I faint,
fortitude in the face of affliction.

    Thou hast given free flow of speech
to my stammering lips;
stayed my drooping spirit
with vigor and strength;
made my feet to stand firm
when they stood where wickedness reigns.[4]

    To transgressors I am a snare,
but healing to them that repent,
prudence to the unwary,
temperance to the rash.

10   Thou hast made me a reproach and a derision
        to them that live by deceit,
        but a symbol of truth and understanding
        to all whose way is straight.

        I am become an eyesore
        unto the wicked,
        a slander on the lips of the unbridled;[5]
        scoffers gnash their teeth.
        A song am I unto transgressors,[6]
        and the hordes of the wicked rage against me;[7]
        like ocean gales they storm
        which, when their billows rage,
        cast up mire and dirt.[8]

        Yet, Thou hast set me as a banner
        in the vanguard[9] of Righteousness,
        as one who interprets with knowledge
        deep, mysterious things;
        as a touchstone for them that seek the truth,
        a standard for them that love correction.[10]

        To them that preach misguidance
        I am but a man of strife;[11]
15   but to them that see straight,[12]
        [a very symbol of pe]ace.

        To them that pursue del[usion]
        I am but a gust of zeal;[13]
        men that live by deceit
        roar against me like the roar of many waters.

        Naught is there in their thoughts
        save mischievous designs.
        When, opening the fount of knowledge
        to all that have understanding,
        Thou hast set a man's life to rights
        by the words of my mouth,
        and hast taught unto him Thy lesson
        and put understanding in his heart

—they thrust him back into the pit.
   In place of these Thy gifts
they offer a witless folk—[14]
stammering lips and barbarous tongue,[15]
that, wandering astray,
they rush headlong to their doom.[16]

3

II, 20-30

20   I give thanks unto Thee, O Lord,
for Thou hast put my soul in the bundle of life[1]
and hedged me[2] against all the snares of corruption.

   Because I clung to Thy covenant,
fierce men sought after my life.[3]
But they—a league of Falsehood, a congregation of
    Belial—
they knew not that through Thee I would stand.
For Thou in Thy mercy dost save my life;
for by Thee are my footsteps guided.

   Of Thy doing it was that they assailed me,
to the end that by Thy judgment on the wicked
Thy glory might stand revealed,
and that Thou mightest show forth through me
25   Thy power over mankind;
for by Thy mercy I have stood.

   Mighty men, I said, have pitched their camp
    against me;
their weapons have compassed me,
their shafts have been loosed unceasing;
the flash of their spears is like fire devouring timber,
and the roar of their voices like the roar of many
    waters.
Like a floodburst bringing ruin far and wide,[4]
all weak things and frail
they crush in a pounding cascade.[5]

Yet, while my heart was dissolving like water,
my soul held firm to Thy covenant,
and they—their own foot was caught
in the net they had spread for me;
in the traps they had hidden for my soul
themselves they fell.[6]

'Now that my foot on level ground doth rest,
30   *Far from the madding crowd, I call Thee blest'.*[7]

4

II, 31-36

I give thanks unto Thee, O Lord,
for Thine eye is ever awake,
watching over my soul.
    Thou hast delivered me
from envy of them that preach falsehood,
and hast freed this hapless soul[1]
from the congregation of them
that seek smooth things
—men who sought to destroy me
and spill my blood in Thy service.

    Little did they know
that my steps were ordered of Thee,
when they made me a mock and a reproach
in the mouths of all men of deceit.
    But ever, O my God,
hast Thou holpen the soul
of the needy and weak
and snatched him from the grasp
35 of him that was stronger than he.[2]
    So hast Thou freed my soul
from the grasp of mighty men,
nor suffered me so to be crushed by their taunts
that for fear of the mischief which the wicked might
        wreak
I should forsake Thy service,

or change for wild delusion
the sound spirit which Thou hast vouchsafed me.

. . . .

5

III, 3-18

[I give thanks unto Thee, O Lord,]
for Thou hast illumined [my face]
[with the vision of Thy truth;]
[wherefore I yet shall wa]lk in glory everlasting
along with all [the holy that hear the words of] Thy
     mouth;
5   and Thou wilt deliver me from [the pit and the
     slough.]

Howbeit, at this hour
my soul is [sore dism]ayed.
Men deem me a [worthless shard]
and render my life like a ship stormtossed on the deep,
or like a bastion city[1] beleaguered by the [foe.]

Yea, I am in distress
as a woman in travail
bringing forth her firstborn,[2]
when, as her time draws near,
the pangs come swiftly upon her[3]
and all the racking pains[4]
in the crucible of conception.

For now, amid throes of death,
new life is coming to birth,[5]
and the pangs of travail set in,
as at last there enters the world
the man-child long conceived.
   Now, amid throes of death,
that man-child long foretold
is about to be brought forth.[6]
10   Now, 'mid the pangs of hell,[7]

there will burst forth from the womb
that marvel of mind and might,[8]
and that man-child will spring from the throes![9]

From the moment that he was conceived
pangs have been sweeping apace
over the whole wide world;[10]
new things have been coming to birth
amid racking pains,
and tremors have beset
the wombs in which they lie.

And when he comes to birth,
all those pangs of travail
that rack the world's great womb[11]
—that crucible of conception—
will take a sudden turn;[12]
what has been conceived
with all the bale of a viper[13]
will end, at the moment of birth,
in mere racking pain,
and all the tremors be but labor lost.[14]
For lo, the wall shall rock
unto its prime foundation,
even as rocks a ship
stormtossed on the waters.
The heavens shall thunder loud,
and they that now do dwell
on the crumbling dust of the earth
be as sailors on the seas,
aghast at the roaring of the waters;
and all the wise men thereof
be as mariners on the deep
15 when all their skill is confounded[15]
by the surging of the seas,
the seething of the depths,[16]
as high o'er the swirling tides[17]
the billows [surge], the breakers roar,
while the gates of Hell[18] burst open,
and at every step they take,

they face Perdition's shafts,[19]
and only the raging deep
hears their cries.[20]
  Yet anon shall the gates of [salvation][21] be
    opened;
  all baleful deeds [will cease],[22]
  while the doors of Perdition shall close
  on all that Perverseness has conceived,
  and everlasting bars[23]
  shut in all baleful spirits.

6

III, 19-36

  I give thanks unto Thee, O Lord,
  for Thou hast freed my soul from the pit[1]
  and drawn me up from the slough of hell[2]
20 to the crest of the world.
    So walk I on uplands unbounded
  and know that there is hope[3]
  for that which Thou didst mold out of dust
  to have consort with things eternal.
    For lo, Thou hast taken a spirit
  distorted by sin,[4]
  and purged it of the taint of much transgression,[5]
  and given it a place
  in the host of the holy beings,
  and brought it into communion
  with the sons of heaven.
  Thou hast made a mere man to share
  the lot of the Spirits of Knowledge,[6]
  to praise Thy name in their chorus[7]
  and rehearse Thy wondrous deeds
  before all Thy works.[8]

    I, that am molded of clay,
  what am I?
    I, that am kneaded with water,
  what is my worth?

I, that have taken my stand
where wickedness reigns,[9]
25 that have cast my lot with the froward;
whose soul has lodged like a beggar
in a place of wild unrest;[10]
I, whose every step
has been amid ruin and rout[11]—
on what strength of mine own may I count
   when Corruption's snares are laid,
and the nets of Wickedness spread,
when far and wide on the waters
Frowardness sets her drags,[12]
when the shafts of Corruption fly[13]
with none to turn them back,
when they are hurled apace
with no hope of escape;
   when the hour of judgment strikes,*
when the lot of God's anger is cast
upon the abandoned,
when His fury is poured forth[14] upon dissemblers,[15]
when the final doom of His rage
falls on all worthless things;
   when the torrents of Death do swirl,[16]
and there is none escape;
when the rivers of Belial[17]
burst their high banks
—rivers that are like fire
devouring all . . . ,
rivers whose runnels destroy
30 green tree and dry tree alike,[18]
rivers that are like fire
which sweeps with flaming sparks
devouring all that drink their waters
—a fire which consumes
all foundations of clay,
every solid bedrock;
   when the foundations of the mountains
become a raging blaze,[19]

* Heb. 'When the line falls upon judgment'; cf. Isa. 28.27.

when granite roots are turned
to streams of pitch,[20]
when the flame devours
down to the great abyss,[21]
when the floods of Belial burst forth
unto hell itself;
    when the depths of the abyss are in turmoil,
cast up mire in abundance,[22]
when the earth cries out in anguish
for the havoc wrought in the world,
when all its depths are aquake,
and all that is on it quails
and quivers in [mighty] havoc;
    when with His mighty roar
God thunders forth,[23]
and His holy welkin[24] trembles
as His glorious truth is revealed,
35   and the hosts of heaven give forth their voice,
and the world's foundations rock and reel;
    when warfare waged by the soldiers of heaven
sweeps through the world[25]
and turns not back until final doom[26]
—warfare the like of which
has never been?

7

III, 37-IV, 4

[Fragment]

I give thanks unto Thee, O Lord,
for Thou hast been unto me a strong wall[1]
against all that would destroy me
and all that would [traduce me.]
    Thou dost shelter me from the disasters
of a turbulent time,
[   ] that it come not [   ]

. . . .

iv,3   [Thou hast set] my foot upon a rock[2]

. . . .

[I will walk] the age-old way
and the paths which Thou hast chosen.

. . . .

8

IV, 5-V, 5

5   I give thanks unto Thee, O Lord,
for Thou hast illumined my face
with the light of Thy covenant.
    [Day by day] I seek Thee,
and ever Thou shinest upon me
bright as the perfect dawn.[1]

    But as for *them*—
they have [dealt treacherously] with Thee,
have made smooth their words.[2]
Garblers of truth are [they all,]
witlessly stumbling along.[3]
They [have turned] all their deeds to folly;
they have become abhorrent unto themselves.
    Though Thou show Thy power through me,
they regard me not,
but thrust me forth from my land
like a sparrow from its nest;
all my friends and familiars
are thrust away from me,
and deem me a broken pot.[4]

    Preachers of lies are they,
10   prophets of deceit.
They have plotted mischief against me,
to make Thy people exchange for smooth words
Thy teaching which Thou hast engraven on my heart.
They have kept the draught of knowledge
from them that are athirst,
and given them in their thirst
vinegar to drink,[5]

to feast their eyes upon them
as they wander astray,[6]
make sport of them as they falter
and are caught in their snares.

But Thou, O God, wilt spurn
all the schemes of Belial.
Thy plan it is will prevail,[7]
and the thought of Thy heart endure for ever.

Crafty men are they;[8]
they think base thoughts,
seek Thee with heart divided,
stand not firm in Thy truth.
In their every thought is a root
which blossoms to wormwood and gall.[9]
15 In the stubbornness of their hearts
they wander astray
and go seeking Thee through idols.
They make their iniquity
a stumbling-block before them,[10]
and come to inquire of Thee
from the mouths of lying prophets,
men by error seduced.
Then, with stammering tongue
and with alien lips[11]
they speak unto Thy people,
seeking guilefully
to turn their deeds to delusion.
They have [paid no heed to] Thy teaching,
nor given ear to Thy word,
but have said of the vision of knowledge,
'It is not sure',
and of the way Thou desirest,
'There is no such thing'.

But Thou, O God, wilt give them their answer,
judging them in Thy power
for all their idolatrous acts
and their manifold transgressions,

to the end that they shall be caught
in their own designs[12]
who have turned away from Thy covenant.
20   Thou wilt sentence all men of deceit
to be cut off,[13]
and all the prophets of error
will be found no more.

    For in all Thou doest there is no delusion,
and in all Thou thinkest no deceit.
And they that are pleasing to Thee
shall stand in Thy presence for ever,
and they that walk in the way Thou desirest
rest firm for all time.

    So, for mine own part,
because I have clung unto Thee,
I shall yet arise and stand upright[14]
against them that revile me;
and my hand shall yet be upon all
that hold me in contempt.
    Though Thou show Thy power through me,
they regard me not.
Howbeit, Thou in Thy might
hast shed upon me the Perfect Light,
and bedaubed not their faces with shame[15]
that have let themselves be found
when that I sought them out;
who, in a common accord,
have pledged themselves to Thee.
    They that walked in the way Thou desirest
have hearkened unto me
and rallied to Thy cause
25   in the legion of the saints.[16]
And Thou wilt vindicate them
and plainly show forth the truth;[17]
and suffer them not to stray
at the hand of froward men,
what time these plot against them.
    Thou wilt yet cause Thy people
to stand in awe of them.

But for them that transgress Thy word
Thou shalt ordain dispersal
among all the peoples on earth,
passing sentence on them
that they be cut off.

Through me hast Thou illumined
the faces of full many,
and countless be the times
Thou hast shown Thy power through me.
For Thou hast made known unto me
Thy deep, mysterious things,
hast shared Thy secret with me
and so shown forth Thy power;
and before the eyes of full many
this token stands revealed,
that Thy glory may be shown forth,
and all living know of Thy power.

Yet, never could flesh alone
attain unto this,
nor that which is molded of clay
do wonders so great
30 —steeped in sin from the womb
and in guilt of perfidy unto old age.
Verily I know
that righteousness lies not with man,
nor perfection of conduct with mortals.
Only with God On High
are all works of righteousness;
and ne'er can the way of man
be stablished save by the spirit
which God has fashioned for him,
to bring unto perfection
the life of mortal man;
that all His works may know
how mighty is His power,
how plenteous His love
to all who do His will.

When I called to mind
all my guilty deeds
and the perfidy of my sires
—when wicked men
opposed Thy covenant,
35   and froward men Thy word—
trembling seized hold on me and quaking,
all my bones were a-quiver;
my heart became like wax
melting before a fire,
my knees were like to water[18]
pouring over a steep;[19]
   and I said: 'Because of my transgressions
I have been abandoned,
that Thy covenant holds not with me'.

But then, when I remembered
the strength of Thy hand
and Thy multitudinous mercies,
I rose again and stood upright,
and my spirit was fortified
to stand against affliction;
for I was stayed by Thy grace.
Thou in Thy plenteous compassion
   dost wipe out sin,[20]
and with Thy righteousness
purge away man's guilt.
Man alone cannot do
as Thou hast done;
for Thou it is didst create
both the righteous and the wicked.
   And I said: 'Through Thy covenant
I shall go strengthened for ever,

. . . .

[and on Thy gra]ce [be stayed.]
40   For Thou Thyself art truth,
and all Thy works are righteousness'.

. . . .

9

5   I give thanks unto Thee, O Lord,
for Thou hast not forsaken me
though I dwell as a sojourner
among an alien people,[1]
[nor cast me forth from Thy sight,]
[nor] judged me according to my guilt,
nor abandoned me to my lusts;
      but hast rescued my life from the pit.

    Though Thou hast set [my soul] amid lions[2]
prompt to spring on the guilty
—fearful lions that break men's bones,
mighty lions that drink their blood—
and though Thou hast placed me full oft
in ready reach of their haul
who spread their nets for the froward
like fishers upon the waters,
or seek, like hunters, to trap them,[3]
      yet, when Thou hast placed me there,
      Thou hast dealt justly with me.[4]

    For Thou hast set firm in my heart
Thy deep, deep truth;
and to them that seek after that truth
Thou bindest Thyself in pledge.
    So hast Thou put a lock
upon the mouths of those lions,
10   whose teeth are like a sword,[5]
whose fangs like a sharp spear,[6]
<whose breath> is the venom of serpents.[7]
    Though ever they seek to raven,
and though ever they lie in wait,
      they have oped not their jaws against me.

Thou hast sheltered me, O my God,
in the face of all mankind,
and hidden Thy teaching [within me],
until it be shown unto me
that the hour of Thy triumph is come.[8]

In all the distress of my soul
Thou hast not abandoned me.
In the bitterness of my spirit
Thou hast heard my cry,
and in my sighing discerned
the song of my pain.

When I have found myself
in a very den of lions,[9]
whetting their tongues like a sword,[10]
Thou hast rescued me in my plight.
Yea, O my God, Thou hast locked their teeth
lest they rend a hapless man apart;
and Thou hast drawn back their tongue
15 like a sword into its sheath,[11]
lest it [do hurt] to Thy servant.

Moreover, to show forth Thy power
in the sight of all men,
Thou hast singled me out, a hapless wretch,
and worked a wonder in me,
passing me [like gold] through a furn[ace,]
even through the action of fire,
and like silver that is refined
in the crucible of the smith,
to come forth sevenfold pure.[12]

The wicked rush wildly upon me
to [grasp] me in their vice,
and they crush my spirit all day,
but Thou, O my God, dost turn the storm to a
calm.[13]

From the jaws of very lions
Thou hast snatched a poor lost soul,
[when it was nigh] to be rent.

10
V, 20-VI, 35

20   Blessed art Thou, O Lord,
for Thou hast never abandoned the orphan
neither despised the poor.
    [Unbounded is] Thy power,
and Thy glory hath no measure.

    Angels of wondrous strength
minister unto Thee,
and [they walk] at the side of the meek
and of them that are eager for right-doing,[1]
and of all the lost and lorn
that stand in need of mercy,
lifting them out of the slough[2]
when that their feet are mired.[3]

    So, for mine own part,
to them that were once my [familiars]
I am become [a reproach],
an object of strife and discord[4]
unto my friends;
an occasion of fury and anger
unto my fellows;
of murmuring and complaint
to all mine acquaintances.
[All] that ate of my bread[5]
have lifted their heels against me;[6]
all that shared my board
have mouthed distortions about me;[7]
and they with whom I [consorted]
have turned their backs upon me
and defamed me up and down.

25   By reason of the secret
which Thou hast hidden within me
they have spread slander against me
to men that were bent on mischief.

Because they have he[mmed in my w]ay[8]
and because they are laden with guilt,
Thou hast (perforce) kept hidden (from them)
the fount of understanding
and the secret of truth,
while they—they go on contriving
the mischief of their hearts,
opening their shameless [mouths,]
unleashing their lying tongues
which are like the venom of adders[9]
fitfully spurting forth;[10]
like reptiles they shoot forth their his[sing]
—vipers that cannot be charmed.[11]
    It becomes like a constant pain,[12]
a fretting wound[13]
in the body of Thy servant,
causing his spirit to droop,
wearing down his strength,[14]
until he cannot withstand.
    They have o'ertaken me between the straits,[15]
and I have no escape.

• • • • • • • • • • • • • • • • •

30   They have thundered abuse of me
to the tune of the harp,
and in jingles chorused their jeers.
    Confusion and panic beset me,[16]
horrendous anguish[17] and pain,
like to the throes of travail.
My heart is distraught within me;
I clothe me in mourning garb;[18]
my tongue cleaves to the roof of my mouth.[19]
[In] their hearts they rev[ile me,]
and openly vented their spleen.

The light of my face is turned to darkness,
my radiance to gl[oom].

   Thou, O my God,
hast enlarged my heart,
but ever they seek to constrict it.
They have hedged me about with thick darkness.
I eat my bread amid sighs,
and my drink is mingled with tears[20]
which have none end.
Mine eyes are dimmed with anguish,[21]
and with all that beclouds the daylight[22]
my soul is over[cast.]
Sorrow and sighing are all about me,
35   and the pall of shame o'er my face.
The very bre[ad] that I eat
seems to be quarreling with me,
the very drink that I drink
to be at odds with me.
   They purpose to trammel my spirit,
to wear down all my strength
with blasphemous mystic lore,
converting the works of God
into that which they guiltily imagine.
   I am bound with unbreakable cords,
with fetters that cannot be sundered.
A strong wall [is upreared against me;]
bars of iron [restrain me]
and doors of brass.[23]

. . . .

Over my soul swirl the torrents of hell.[24]

. . . .

vi,2 My heart [is sore distraught]
because of their obloquy
which they have heaped upon me.

. . . .

   [Ruin encompasses me,]

disaster which knows no bound,
destruction which hath no [end.]

· · · · · · · · · · · · · · · ·

[Howbeit, O my God,]
Thou hast opened mine ear withal
to the lessons which they impart
who reprove with justice,[25]
[and hast thereby delivered me]
5   from company with the vain
from fellowship with crime
and hast brought me into communion
[with Thy holy truth],
[purging my soul of] guilt.
So am I come to know
that in [Thy] loving[kindness]
lies hope for them that repent
and for them that abandon sin,
[and confidence for him]
who walks in the way of Thy heart
without perversity.
Therefore, though peoples roar,
though kingdoms rage,[26]
when that they gather together,
I shall go comforted.
I shall [not] be dismayed,
knowing that in a space
Thou wilt raise a reviving for Thy people
and grant to Thine inheritance a remnant,[27]
and refine them, to purge them of guilt.
Whenas in all their deeds
they have done as Thy truth† enjoined,
Thou wilt judge them with lovingkindness,
with plenteous compassion
and abundance of forgiveness,
guiding them according to Thy word,
10   stablishing them by Thy counsel,‡
by Thine unswerving truth.

† I.e., the Scriptures.
‡ Or, 'in Thy council'.

¶Thou hast acted for Thyself and for Thy glory,
that the Law may come to [fruition,]
and hast [sent] among mankind
men that be schooled in Thy counsel
to tell forth Thy wonders through the ages,
world without end,
to [rehea]rse Thy deeds of power
without surcease,
that all nations may know Thy truth,
and all peoples Thy glory.

All them that follow Thy counsel
hast Thou brought into [com]munion with Thee,
and hast given them common estate
with the Angels of Thy Presence.[28]
There stands no intermediary among them
to appr[oach Thee in their behalf
and] bring them back Thy word[29]
filtered through his mind (?);[30]
for they themselves are answered
from out of Thy glorious mouth.
They are Thy courtiers,§
sharing the high estate
of [all the heavenly beings.]

15 ¶[For these hast Thou planted a tree]
which blooms with flowers unfading,
whose boughs put forth thick leaves,
which stands firm-planted for ever,
and gives shade to all [   ];
[whose branches tower] to hea[ven],
whose roots sink down to the abyss.[31]
All the rivers of Eden
[water] its boughs;[32]
it thrives beyond [all bounds],
[burgeons beyond all] measure.
[Its branches stretch] endless across the world,
[and its roots go down] to the nethermost depths.

§ Heb. 'princes'. The word is commonly used in post-Biblical Hebrew to denote angels.

Moreover, there shall well forth for them a fountain of light
a perpetual spring unfailing.
Howbeit, in its [fiery] sparks
all [infamous] men shall be burned;
it shall be as a flame devouring the guilty,
until they are destroyed.

These men who were once my comrades,
pledged to the selfsame task
of bearing witness to Thee,
have let themselves be seduced
by garbl[ers of truth],
[that they are concerned no more]
with working for righteousness.
20   Thou hadst given them commandments, O God,
that they might have profit of their lives
by walking Thy ho[ly way,]
whereon the uncircumcised and unclean
and profane may not pass.[33]
But they veered from the way of Thy heart
and ensnared themselves in their lusts.
Belial has been counseling their hearts[34]
and, through their wicked devisings,
they have been wallowing in guilt.
   Wherefore on their account
I was as a sailor in a ship
when the seas do froth and foam.
All the breakers thereof
kept pounding against me,
and the whirlwind[35] blew about me,
[and there was no] moment of calm
wherein to catch my breath,
neither could I steer
a course upon the waters.
The deeps echoed my groaning,
and I [came near] to the gates of death.[36]

¶But now I am as one
25   that hath reached a fortified city,

found refuge behind a high wall
until deliverance come.
For I have stayed myself on Thy truth, O my God,
knowing full well
that Thou foundest Thy structure on a rock,
that Righteousness is the line
by which Thou layest its bricks,
that Justice is the gauge
Thou usest to set its footing,
that of solid stone[37] is its wall,
unshakeable;
that all who repair unto it
shall never be moved,
for there shall no stranger invade it.
Its doors are a sheet of protection
which none may force,
and its bars are strong bars
which cannot be broken.
No armed band can storm it,
neither all the war hosts of wickedness together.

But anon, in the Moment of Judgment,
the sword of God will be swift
and all who acknowledge His truth
will rouse themselves to [do battle]
30 [against the forces of] wickedness,
and all the sons of guilt
will be no more.
The Warrior[38] will bend his bow,
and lift the siege for ever,
and open the gates everlasting
to bring forth His weapons of war;
and His legions shall go marching
from end to [end of the earth,]
[and there shall be no es]cape
for the guilty impulse of men.
They shall trample it to destruction,
that naught re[main thereof.]
[There shall be no] hope for it
in [weapons] never so many,

neither any escape
for all that fight in its cause.
   For the [victory] shall belong
unto God on High,

. . . .

and though they that lie in the dust
will have raised their flag,[39]
and though this worm which is man[40]
will have lifted up his banner
to do [battle against the truth,]
[yet shall they be] cut off
35 when battle is joined with the presumptuous;
and he that sought to bring
the scourge of a flood overflowing[41]
will never reach that stronghold.

. . . .

10a

VII, 1-5

   Lo, I am stricken dumb,
[for naught comes out of men's mouths
but] swearing [and lying].
My arm is wrenched from its socket;[1]
my foot is sunken in mire;
mine eyes are dimmed[2] from looking on evil;
mine ears are deafened from hearing of bloodshed;
my heart is numbed with thinking on evil;
for wheresoever men show
the temper of their being,
there is the spirit of baseness.
   The structure of my being
is rocked to its very foundation;
my bones are out of joint;[3]
mine inwards heave like a ship
5 when the searing eastwind soughs;[4]
my heart is sore distraught.
   In the havoc of their transgression
a whirlwind swallows me up.

11

VII, 6-25

I give thanks unto Thee, O Lord,
for by Thine own strength hast Thou stayed me,
and hast wafted o'er me Thy holy spirit
that I cannot be moved.

Thou hast braced me for all the battles
that Wickedness wages against me,
and hast let not the havoc dismay me
to break faith with Thee.

Thou hast made me like a strong tower
upon a lofty wall,[1]
founded upon a rock,[2]
reared on eternal foundations,
whose walls are a proven bulwark
that cannot be shaken
10   —a tower which Thou hast provided, O my God,
for (this) holy community
—these men that rise as on wings.[3]

[Thou hast brought me into] Thy covenant.
Words flow free on my tongue,
as it were trained by Thee,[4]
while the Spirit of Havoc stays speechless,
and the reprobate ope not their mouth.
Through me Thou hast kept Thy pledge:
'False lips shall be stricken dumb'.**

All them that challenge me
Thou makest to stand condemned,
distinguishing through me
the right from the wrong.

¶Thou knowest the impulse of every act,
and discernest the purport of every speech,

** Ps. 31.18.

yet, by Thy guidance†† and truth
Thou hast directed my heart,
to set my steps straight forward
on paths of righteousness,
and walk where Thy Presence is,
15 within bounds of [holiness],
on roads of infinite glory and peace,
ending all [waywardness] for ever.

Thou knowest also the nature
of this Thy servant,
how that I have not relied
[upon the things of the world,]
lifting [my heart] in pride,
vaunting my strength.
No refuge have I in flesh,
nor righteousness [in my soul,]
that I may be saved from the snare
except by Thy pardon.
On [Thy mercy alone] I rely,
and for Thy grace I hope,
to bring [what I have plan]ted to flower,
to make the shoot to grow,
to find cause for vaunting strength,
for [lifting heart.]

¶And Thou, O God of mercy,
hast in Thy bounty given me place
20 among those to whom Thou art pledged;[5]
and unto Thy truth will I cling.
Thou hast [shown me Thy grace] and set me
as a father to them Thou holdest dear,[6]
and as a nurse unto them
whom Thou hast made exemplars of men.[7]
They open their mouths for my words,
like sucklings [at the breast,]
and like as a babe that plays
on the bosom of its nurse.

†† Heb. *Torah.*

Thou hast raised high my horn[8]
over all that revile me,
and all who wage battle against me
are rou[ted without remnant,]
and all that contend with me
are as chaff before the wind;[9]
and all impiety bows to my sway.

For Thou, O my God, hast holpen my soul
and raised high my horn.

I am lit with a light sevenfold,
with that same [lustre] of glory
which Thou didst create for Thyself.[10]
25   For Thou art unto me as a light eternal[11]
guiding my feet upon [the way.]

12

VII, 26-33

I give [thanks unto Thee, O Lord,]
for Thou hast given me insight into Thy truth
and knowledge of Thy wondrous secrets.

In lovingkindness to [lowly] man,
in abundance of mercy to wayward hearts,
who is like Thee among the gods, O Lord,[1]
and what truth is like Thine?

Who can prove righteous in Thy sight
when Thou bringest him unto judgment?
Not even a spirit can answer Thy charge,
and none can withstand Thy wrath.
Yet, all that are children of Thy truth
30   Thou bringest before Thee with forgiveness,
[clean]sing them of their transgressions
through Thine abundant goodness,
and, through Thy plenteous mercies,
causing them to stand in Thy presence for ever.

For Thou art a God everlasting,
and all Thy ways hold firm for all time;[2]
and there is none else beside Thee.
But what is man—vain, empty man,
that he should understand Thy great wondrous works?

13
VII, 34-VIII, 3

[I give thanks] unto Thee, O Lord,
for Thou hast cast not my lot in the congregation of
the false,
nor set my portion in the company of dissemblers.

35   Behold, in Thy mercy [I trust],
in Thy pardon [confide],
and on Thine abundant mercies [I lean],
when all [just] judgments are passed upon me.
[For Thou dost tend me as a mother tendeth]
her babe,
and [like a child] on the bosom of [its nurse dost Thou
sustain me].

. . . .

Thy justice holdeth firm for ever,
for [Thou dost] not [abandon them that seek Thee].[1]

14
VIII, 4-36

I give thanks unto Thee, O Lord,
because, in a dry place, thou hast set me beside
a fountain;
in an arid land, beside a spring;[1]
5   in a de[sert], beside an oasis;
like one of those evergreen trees—
fir or pine or cypress—
planted together to Thy glory,[2]

which, hidden 'mid other trees—
trees that stand beside water—
are fed from a secret spring,
and which put forth blossom unfading
upon an eternal trunk,
striking firm root ere they burgeon,
spreading their roots to the stream;[3]
a tree whose stem is exposed to living waters,
and whose stock lies beside a perpetual fount;
a tree on whose flowering leaves
all the beasts of the woodland can feed;
whose roots are so widespread
that all wayfarers cannot but tread them;[4]
upon whose dangling boughs
there is room for every bird.[5]

　All those other trees—
those trees that stand beside water—
keep railing against it,[6]
because *they* grow entangled in their plantations,[7]
10　and can send not their roots to the stream,
while this one,
which puts forth the shoot of Holiness upon the stock
　　of Truth,
keeps its secret hidden, unknown,
sealed and unsuspected.
Moreover, O God, Thou has hedged in its fruit
by the mystic power of stalwart angels,[8]
by holy spirits,
and by a flaming sword turning this way and that;[9]
that [the wicked] may not [drink]
from the Fountain of Life
nor, like those evergreens,
imbibe the waters of Holiness;[10]
that he never may bring his fruit to blossom
through the [sho]wers of heaven,[11]
because, though indeed he has seen it,
he has never sensed what it was,[12]
nor, though he has had notion thereof,[13]
has he ever believed in the Fountain of Life,
but, instead, keeps la[ying violent hands]

on what is really a flower unfading.
Behold, I was (aforetime)
like lands which torrents have ravaged,[14]
15 casting their silt upon me,[15]
but Thou, O my God, hast, as it were, put in my
mouth
early and latter rain
(falling) all [the year round],
an outpouring of living waters,
which never fail,
opening the heavens without surcease,[16]
so that (those waters) are become
like a river in flood,[17]
spilling over its banks,[18]
and like seas un[fathomable]
which, long hidden in secret,
suddenly burst forth [   ],[19]
and quicken [every tree],
green and dry alike,[20]
and serve as a pool for wild beasts.

The tr[ees of the wicked shall fall]
like lead in mighty waters,[21]
20 and a fire [shall break out], and they shall wither,
and the planting of that fruit [prove in vain].
[But the trees of the righteous]
shall [bloom fa]ir for ever,
a glorious richness, a flower of beauty.
At my hands hast Thou opened a wellspring for them,
yielding runnels of water,
that their roots may be firmly set
and their trees planted in line of the sun,[22]
in light [unfailing;]
that their [boughs] may yield glorious foliage.

When I apply my hand
to dig the furrows thereof,[23]
its roots strike even on granite,
its stocks are firm-grounded in the earth,[24]
and in the time of heat it secures protection.

But if I relax my hand,
it becomes like a [heath in the desert,][25]
and its stocks like nettles in a salt-marsh,
25   and out of its furrows grow thorns and thistles;[26]
[it turns] to briars and brambles,[27]
and its [   ] change to stinking weeds,[28]
its leaves fade before the heat;
it is not exposed to water.
It suffers mishap and disease
and becomes a [target] for all manner of blight.

Then I become like a man
abandoned in [a desert];
no refuge have I,
for then whatever I planted
blossoms but into wormwood.
Constant is my pain,[29]
and cannot be stayed.
[My soul is disqui]eted,[30]
like them that go down to Sheol;
my spirit sinks low[31] among the dead.
My life has as good as reached the Pit,[32]
and my soul waxes faint[33] day and night without rest.
30   There bursts forth, as it were a blazing fire
held in my [bones,][34]
the flame whereof devours unto the nethermost seas,
exhausting my strength every moment,
consuming my flesh every minute.
Disasters hover about me,
and my soul is utterly bowed down.[35]
For all my strength has ceased from my body,
and my heart is poured out like water,
and my flesh melts like wax,
and the strength of my loins is turned to confusion,
and my arm is wrenched from the shoulder.[36]
I [cannot] move my hand,
and my [foot] is caught in a shackle,
and my knees dissolve like water.
I can take neither pace nor step;
[heaviness] replaces my fleetness of foot;

35 [my steps] are trammeled.
    Once Thou didst put into my mouth
a powerful tongue,
but now it is taken away.
I cannot lift my voice
in any articulate [speech]
to revive the spirit of the stumbling
or encourage the faint with a word.[37]
Lips which were once so fluent[38]
are now stricken dumb.

· · · · · · · · · · · · · · · · · ·

15

IX, 2-X, 12

· · · · · · · · · · · · · · · · · ·

Though [mine eye] sleep [not] at night,
[though Belial assail me] without mercy,
though in anger He stir up His fury[1]
[and pursue me] unto destruction;
though the breakers of death swirl around me,[2]
though Sheol‡‡ be upon my couch;
though my bed take up a lament,[3]
and [my couch] a cry of anguish;
5 though mine eye smart as through the smoke of an
    oven,[4]
though my tears flow like rivers;[5]
though mine eyes fail,[6] and I have no rest;
though [my strength] stand afar off,
and my life be put aside;
though I go from rout to ruin,[7]
from pain to plague,
from pangs to throes.

Yet will I muse on Thy wonders;
for Thou, in Thy lovingkindness,
hast at no time cast me off.

‡‡ I.e., the netherworld.

My soul will delight every moment
in the abundance of Thy mercies,
and I shall have wherewith to reply
to him that would confound me,
and to gainsay him that would abase me.
I shall refute his case,
and vindicate Thy judgment.
10 For I have come to know Thy truth;
I accept Thy judgments upon me,
and am content with my afflictions.

I have learned to put hope in Thy mercy;
for Thou hast placed in the mouth of Thy servant
the power to win Thy grace,[8]
and hast not mortally rebuked him,
neither renounced his wellbeing,
neither frustrated his hope.
Rather hast Thou braced his spirit
to withstand affliction.

Thou it is emplanted§§ my spirit,
and Thou knowest its every intent;
and so in my straitness
Thou hast given me reassurance.
I delight in the promise of pardon,
and repent my former transgression;
for I know that in Thy mercy lies hope,
and confidence in Thine abundant power.

15 For none can prove himself righteous
when Thou bringest him unto judgment,
neither can [any prevail]
when Thou enterest suit against him.
Though man may prove more righteous than man,
though a human may prove wiser than [a beast,]
though flesh may rank higher than dumb [clay,]*

§§ Heb. 'founded'.
* Literally, 'than that which is molded out of clay'.

though one spirit may prove mightier than another,
yet naught can match [Thy power] in strength.
Thy glory hath no equal,
Thy wisdom no measure,
Thy tr[uth no bound;]
and all that have forfeited them
[are doomed to perdition.]

¶Behold, for my own part,
through Thee have I pr[ospered my way,]
[through Thee maintained] my stand;
for Thou hast not [abandoned me]
[unto them that se]ek my hurt.
20 Whenever they plot against me,
Thou [savest me from their grasp,]
and if they are bent to disgrace me,
Thou in Thy mer[cy dost confound] them.
If mine enemy vaunt himself against me,
it proves to his own undoing;†
and they that battle against me
[are overwhelmed] with disgrace,
and shame overtakes them that revile me.

For at [every] time, O my God,
Thou dost fight my fight.[9]
Though now, in Thine inscrutable wisdom, Thou re-
    buke me,
yet art Thou but hiding the truth until [its time]
and [Thy glory] until its season.
Then will Thy rebuking of me
be turned into gladness and joy;
25 my plague shall be turned to perpetual health,
the scorn of my foes to a diadem of glory,[10]
my halting steps to enduring strength.
    Lo, through Thy Name and through Thy glory
light has shone forth upon me.
Thou hast brought me light out of darkness,
hast given me [health] in place of plague,[11]

† Literally, 'stumbling'.

wondrous strength in place of stumbling,
and abiding enlargement for the straitness of my soul.

[Thou art] my refuge and my tower,
my rock of retreat and my stronghold;
in Thee do I take refuge from all that [pursue me,]
[and Thou art] mine escape evermore.

¶Or ever my father begat me,
30   Thou didst know me;
from the womb of my mother Thou didst shower me
      with Thy grace‡
and from the breasts of her that conceived me
Thy mercies have been shed upon me.
On the bosom of my nurse [Thou didst sustain me,]
and from my youth up
Thou hast enlightened me with understanding of Thy
      judgments,
held me firm by Thy truth,
and caused me to delight in Thy holy spirit:
and even unto this day
Thou dost stay my goings.

Though Thy just rebuke be with my body,
yet will my soul be saved
by Thy watch over my wellbeing.
    With every step I take
Thine abundant forgiveness enfolds me,
and when Thou arraignest me,
Thy mercies overwhelm me.
    Even unto old age
Thou wilt yet sustain me.
35   For my father hath renounced me,
and my mother hath abandoned me to Thee;[12]
yet Thou art a father to all that [know] Thy truth,
and Thou wilt rejoice over them
like a mother who pitieth her babe,

‡ The Hebrew word can also mean 'Thou didst wean me'.
There is thus a *double-entendre*.

and Thou wilt feed all Thy works
as a nurse feeds her charge at the bosom.[13]

. . . .

¶[Who can fathom the des]igns of Thy heart?
Apart from Thee hath nothing existed,
and without Thy will will nothing be;
yet can none understand Thy wis[dom]
nor gaze upon Thy [sec]rets.

What is man, mere earth,
kneaded out of [clay,]
destined to return unto the dust,[14]
that Thou shouldst give him insight into such wonders
and make him privy to things divine?

x,5   As for me,
I am but dust and ashes.
What can I devise except Thou hast desired it?
And what can I think apart from Thy will?
And how be strong except Thou hast stayed me,
or use my mind,[15] except Thou hast created it?
How speak except Thou hast opened my mouth?
How reply except Thou hast given me sense?
Lo, Thou art the Prince of the angels,
and the King of all that are in glory,
and the Lord of every spirit,
and the Ruler of every deed.
Without thee nothing is wrought,
and without Thy will can nothing be known.[16]
None there is beside Thee,

10   and none to share Thy might,
and none to match Thy glory,
and Thy power is beyond price.
Which among all Thy great wondrous works
has power to stand before Thy glory?
How much less, then, can he who returns to his dust
    attain to [such power.]

Only for Thine own glory hast Thou done all these
    things.

16

 Blessed art Thou, O Lord,
Thou God of compassion and mercy,
for giving me knowledge [of Thy truth]
15 and [insight] to [tell forth] Thy wonders,
unhushed day and night.

. . . .

 Because I have come to rely
on that truth of Thine,
[I will put my trust] in Thy mercy,
[my hope] in Thy great goodness
[and in Thine abundant] compassion.

. . . .

 Except Thou [keep hold,] there is no standing;
and except [Thou let go, no falling];
except Thou rebuke, no stumbling;
no affliction, but Thou hast foreknown it;
[no healing but] by Thy [will].

20 Now that I know [Thy tru]th,
that I clearly behold Thy glory,
now that I understand
[the mysteries of Thy ways],
[I now will put my trust]
in the moving§ of Thy compassion,
[my hope] in Thine acts of forgiveness.

 The high and mighty draw their strength
from abundance of (worldly) delights;
in profusion of corn and wine and oil
[they find their joy],
25 and pride themselves in goods and possessions.[1]

 Cho[osing] mortal delights
and thinking to glut themselves

§ Or, abundance.

on earthly things,
[they picture themselves] as trees
green beside running streams,[2]
which cannot but put forth leaves
and branches full many.[3]

But the joy and the bliss which Thou hast given
to these lowly servants of Thine[4]
is a joy and a bliss unending,
and only by the measure of his knowledge
does one outrank another.[5]

So, in (this) knowledge of Thy truth
hast Thou bestowed on me,
a lowly servant of Thine,
a rich inheritance;
and by virtue of that knowledge
he now is come to ho[nor].[6]

30   The soul of (this) Thy servant
abhors all wealth and gain;
in abundance of (worldly) delights
his heart has no pleasure.[7]
    Nay, in Thy covenant
does my heart rejoice,
and Thy truth it is that regales my soul.

Wherefore, with heart exposed
to a spring unfailing,
drawing my strength from on high,[8]
I shall blossom like a lily,[9]
[while all the fruit of the wicked
shall be but travail] and woe;
they shall wither like a flower before [the heat].

35   Howbeit, when I hear tell
how Thou wilt yet come to judgment
along with Thy stalwart angels,[10]
how Thou wilt yet enter suit
in company with Thy host of Holy Beings,[11]

my heart is sorely racked,
my loins are all a-quake,
my groans reach down to the nethermost depths
and penetrate withal
into the chambers of Hell;[12]
and I am full stricken with terror.

For [judgment Thou surely wilt wr]eak
[over the whole wide earth],
justice on all that Thou hast made;
and [Thy] right[eousness] wilt Thou evince
over the hordes of Belial.[13]

. . . .

[My soul is com]moved with ter[ror];
[tr]ouble [is not hidden] from mine eyes;[14]
Gri[ef and sorrow o'erwhelm]
the musing of my heart.

17

XI, 3-14

I give thanks unto Thee, O my God,
for Thou hast wrought a wonder with dust
and hast shown forth Thy power
in that which is molded of clay.
    For Thou hast made me to know Thy deep, deep
        truth,
and to divine Thy wondrous works,
and hast put in my mouth the power to praise,
and psalmody on my tongue,
5   and hast given me lips unmarred[1]
and readiness of song,
that I may sing of Thy lovingkindness
and rehearse Thy might all the day
and continually bless Thy name.

I will show forth Thy glory
in the midst of the sons of men,

and in Thine abundant goodness
my soul will delight.
　For I know that Thy mouth is truth,
and in Thy hand is bounty,
and in Thy thought all knowledge,
and in Thy power all might,
and that all glory is with Thee.

　In Thine anger come all judgments of affliction,
but in Thy goodness pardon abounding;
and Thy mercies are shed upon all
who do Thy will.
　For Thou hast made them to know Thy deep, deep
　　truth
10　and divine Thine inscrutable wonders;
and, for Thy glory's sake,
Thou hast granted it unto man
to be purged of transgression,
that he may hallow himself unto Thee
and be free from all taint of filth
and all guilt of perfidy,
to be one with them that possess Thy truth
and to share the lot of Thy Holy Beings,
to the end that this worm which is man[2]
may be lifted out of the dust
to the height of eternal things,
and rise from a spirit perverse
to an holy understanding,
and stand in one company before Thee
with the host everlasting and the spirits of knowledge
and the choir invisible,[3]
to be for ever renewed
with all things that are.[4]

18

XI, 15-27

15　　I give thanks unto Thee, O my God,
　　I extol Thee, O my Rock,[1]

and because Thou hast wrought wonders with me
[I bless Thy name.]
For Thou hast made me to know Thy deep, deep
    truth;
  Thy wonders hast Thou revealed unto me,
and I have beholden [Thy truth]
[and witnessed Thy] deeds of lovingkindness.

  So am I come to know
that though Thou art ever just,
yet in Thy lovingkindness
lies sal[vation for men],
and that without Thy mercy
[theirs is but doo]m and perdition.

20   Lo, for mine own part,
when I mark the nature of man,
how he ever reverts [to perversity and wrongdoing],
to sin and anguish of guilt,
a fountain of bitter mourning
wells up within me;
[my tears flow like rivers],[2]
and sorrow is not hidden from mine eyes.[3]
These things go to my heart
and touch me to the bone,
that I raise a bitter lament
and make doleful moan and groan,
and keep plying my harp in mournful dirge
and bitter lamentation,
till wrongdoing be brought to an end,
and men have no more to suffer
punishing plague and stroke.

  But when that time shall come,
then shall I ply my harp
with music of salvation,
and my lyre to tune of joy;
I shall ply the pipe and flute
in praise without cease.

Though none there be among all Thy works
can rehearse the full tale of Thy [wonders],
yet then, in the mouths of them all
shall Thy name be praised;
25   then with mouth of [   ]
they shall go blessing Thee for ever,
and along with the [Holy Being]s
chorus their song of joy.[4]
For sorrow and sighing shall be no more;[5]
wrongdoing shall be [at an end],
and Thy truth shall burst forth as the dayspring
in never-ending glory
and peace perpetual.

19
XI, 27-XII, 35

Blessed art Thou, [O Lord,]
Who hast given unto man the insight of knowledge,
to understand Thy wonders,
[discern Thy truth,]
tell forth Thine abundant mercies.

Blessed art Thou, O God of compassion and grace,
for the greatness of [Thy] power,
the abundance of Thy truth,
the profusion of Thy mercies
30   over all Thy works.

Rejoice the soul of Thy servant in Thy truth,
and in Thy righteousness make me clean,
even as when [aforetime] I waited on Thy bounty
and hoped on Thy mercies,
and Thou didst bring release to my travail,[1]
and even as when I leaned on Thy compassion,
and Thou didst comfort me in my sorrow.

Blessed art Thou, O Lord,
for Thou it is hast wrought these things,
and placed in the mouth of Thy servant

[power to pray] and to win Thy grace,
and all readiness of tongue;
and hast prepared for me the guerdon of [righteous-
ness]
[and the reward of devotion],
35 that I may attain to [stand in Thy presence].

. . . .

[   ] my soul will exult[2]
[because it hath come to abide in Thy presence]
[and to dwell] secure in [Thy] ho[ly] abode,
in calm and quietude.
[In] my tent [I will chant]
[songs of joy] and salvation,[3]
and in the midst of them that fear Thee
tell forth the praise of Thy name
to all ages to come,
pouring forth prayer and supplication[4]
always, at all times and seasons;[5]
when daylight comes forth from [its abode];
xii,5 when, in its ordered course,
day reaches its turning-point,
in accordance with the rules of the sun;
and again at the turn of the evening,
when daylight departs,
as the rule of darkness begins;
and again in the season of night,
when it reaches its turning-point,
and when the morning breaks;
and when, in the presence of the daylight,
night withdraws to its abode;
when night departs and day comes in,
alway, at all the birthdays of time,
at the moments when seasons begin;[6]
when they reach their turning-points;
when they come in order due
according to their several signs,[7]
as these have dominion in due order assured,
[decreed] by the mouth of God
and by the law of existence

—that law which shall ever be
10   and beside which is none else,
for the God of Knowledge it is
that hath determined it,
and along with Him there never hath been
nor ever shall be another.

Behold, for mine own part,
I have reached the inner vision,
and through the spirit Thou hast placed within me,
come to know Thee, my God.

I have heard Thy wondrous secret,
nor heard it amiss.[8]
Through Thy holy spirit,
through Thy mystic insight,
Thou hast caused a spring of knowledge to well up
    within me,
a fountain of strength,
pouring forth waters unstinted,
a floodtide of lovingkindness and of all-consuming
    zeal.
Thou hast put an end to [my darkness],
15   and the splendor of Thy glory has become unto me as
    a light ev[erlasting].

Wickedness hath been [consumed] altogether,
and deceit [existeth] no more.
[Perverseness is gone down] to perdition,
for [   ] existeth no more [   ]
Bluster[9] is at an end,
for it [cannot withstand] Thine anger.
[The sins which I committed aforetime]
[I committed in] overhaste;
for [now am I come to know that] no man is righteous
    with Thee.
20   For there is none can understand all Thy hidden
    things,
nor answer Thy charge against him;
but all must needs wait upon Thy goodness,
for Thou, in [Thy] lovingkindness [wilt reveal to them
    Thy truth,]

that they may come to know Thee;
and when Thy glory bursts upon them, they shall re-
    joice.

Only to the measure of each man's knowledge
and to the meed of his understanding
hast Thou given men access [to Thee],
to serve Thee in their several domains,
even as Thou hast assigned their roles,
[but] never to overstep Thy word.

And I—I was taken from dust,
nipped out of clay;
I was but a source of filth
25   and of shameful nakedness,
a heap of dust,
a thing kneaded with water,
a dwellingplace of darkness,
a shape moulded of clay,
which must needs revert to dust in due season
[and lie once more] in the dust
whence it was taken.
And how can (such) dust and [clay]
give answer to [Him who shapes] it;
or how understand what He doeth,
or how stand before its Accuser?
Even the holy [angels,]
the everlasting [spirits,]
the reservoirs of glory,
the wellsprings of knowledge and power,
30   —even they [cannot] tell forth all Thy glory,
nor stand against Thine anger,
nor answer Thy charge.
For Thou art ever righteous,
and none can gainsay Thee.
How much less, then, he who returns to his dust?

Lo, I am stricken dumb.
What can I say against this?

I have spoken but according to my knowledge
and only with such sense of right
as a creature of clay may possess.
But how can I speak except Thou open my mouth,
and how understand, if Thou give me not insight;
or how contend, save Thou open my heart;
or how walk straight save Thou gu[ide my feet?]
35 How can [my] fo[ot] stand,
how can I be strong in power,
how can I endure [save by Thy grace?]

• • • • • • • • • • • • • • • • • • • •

(*From this point it becomes impossible to distinguish the
separate hymns.*)

XIII, 1-21

When first the world began
[Thou didst shed an] holy [sp]irit
[on all Thou didst bring into being,]
and make them all to attest
Thy wondrous mysteries.[1]

• • • • • • • • • • • • • • • • • • • •

[Thou didst show Thy] handiwork
in all that [Thou] didst make.
[Thou didst reveal Thy glory
in all their varied shapes,]
[Thy] truth [in all] their works.

• • • • • • • • • • • • • • • • • • • •

¶On all that [keep Thy charge]
[Thou bestowest grace abounding]
5 and mercies never failing;
but upon all things that defy Thee
Thou bringest perdition eternal.
[So, if mortal men
keep faith with Thee,
behold, Thou crownest their he]ads
with glory everlasting[2]

and [compassest their] works
with perennial joy;
but [the face of] the wicked
[Thou coverest with shame.]

On those whom Thou hast set [in] glory[3]
[to show forth] the full measure of Thy works,
yea, on the hosts of Thy spirits,
the congregation of [Thy Holy Beings,]
[the heavens] with all their array,
the earth with all its produce,
all things in lakes and seas
—on those, ere Thou didst create them,
Thou didst impose a task
10   and a perpetual charge.
For when first the world began
Thou didst so order them
and appoint the work of each
that they would spell out Thy glory
throughout Thy dominion,
making known thereby
what none would else have seen,
how ancient things pass over,
and new things are ever created,[4]
how Thou doest away with outworn forms,
yet [main]tainest eternal nature,[5]
for Thou art a God everlasting,
and Thou wilt endure for all time.

In Thine inscrutable wisdom
Thou hast assigned to all these
natures diverse and varied
wherein to show forth Thy glory.
But how can a spirit of flesh
understand of these things?
How can it conceive
Thy so great mystery?
Yea, how can one born of woman
attest Thy tremendous plan?

15 Creature of dust that he is,
    moulded of sodden clay,
    [a heap of filth],
    whose foundation is naked shame,
    and who is ruled by a spirit perverse,
    through his constant misdeeds*
    does he not (rather) serve
    as a thing of unending [revulsion],
    a portent for all generations,[6]
    an object of abhorrence to all flesh?[7]

        Nay, it is only through Thy goodness
    and through Thy mercies abundant
    that Man can ever do right.
    For it is with Thine own beauty
    that Thou dost beautify him,
    and only of Thy free bounty
    dost Thou shower him with delights
    and grant him peace unending
    and length of days.

        And [Lord,] when once Thou hast spoken
    ne'er is Thy word revoked.[8]

        So, for mine own part,
    through the spirit Thou hast planted within me,
    I, Thy servant, am come to know
    that [all Thy judgments are truth,]
    and righteousness all Thy works,
    and ne'er is Thy word revoked.

20 None of the terms and times
    which Thou hast foreordained
    [hath failed to come to pass]
    —all of them duly chosen
    for their appointed ends.[9]

        Therefore I know full surely
    [that yet the time will come]
    [when Thou wilt reward the righteous,]
    and the wicked be utterly [doomed.]

* Heb. 'If he do wrong'.

XIV, 1-27

[I give thanks unto Thee, O Lord,
for Thou hast granted a remnant]
unto Thy people
and a re[vival]
[unto Thine inheritance.]¹
   [Thou hast raised up among them]
men of truth
and sons [of light,]²

. . . .

men of abundant compassion,
men of stalwart spirit,
men of tempered [soul,]
men steeled to [sustain] Thy judgments.
   [Through them hast Thou kept Thy covenant]
5   and fulfilled Thy pledge,
to render us unto Thee
[a kingdom of priests and] an holy [nation]³
for all generations of time
and for all the [ages to come.]
   [Verily, O Lord, Thou dost sustain]
them that have vision of Thee.

Blessed art Thou, O Lord,
Who puttest the sense of discernment
into the heart of Thy servants,⁴
[that they may walk blamelessly before Thee,]
and be steeled against all the dev[ices] of wickedness,
and that they may bless [Thy name,]
10   [loving] all that Thou lovest
and abhorring all that [Thou hatest,]⁵
[and stray not in the waywar]dness of men,
but, through the spirit of [discern]ment which is
     theirs,
[distinguish] the good from the wicked
[and keep] their deeds undefiled.

Behold, for mine own part,
through that discernment which Thou hast bestowed,
I have indeed attained to such knowledge;
for by virtue of Thy good pleasure
I have been granted a share in Thy holy spirit,
and Thou hast brought me close
to an understanding of Thee.
The nearer I draw to Thee,[6]
the more am I filled with zeal
against all that do wickedness
and against all men of deceit.
For none that draws near to Thee
can see Thy commandments defied,
15   and none that hath knowledge of Thee
can brook change of Thy words,
seeing that Thou art the essence of right,
and in all Thine elect Thy truth is engrained.

Thou wilt bring eternal doom
on all frowardness and transgression,
and Thy righteousness will stand revealed
in the sight of all Thou hast made.

Lo, through Thy great goodness
I have come to know these things,
and committed myself by oath
never to sin against Thee
nor do aught that is evil in Thy sight;
and I have been granted admittance
to [this] community.
So, for mine own part,
I will admit no comrade
into fellowship with me
save by the measure of his understanding,
and only to the degree
of his share in this common lot
will I show friendship to him.
I will not countenance evil,
neither recognize fraud.

20 I will not barter Thy truth for wealth,
    nor all Thy judgments for a bribe.
    Only as Thou drawest a man unto Thee
    will I draw him unto myself,
    and as Thou keepest him afar,
    so too will I abhor him;
    and I will enter not into communion
    with them that turn their back upon Thy covenant.[7]

        Blessed art Thou, O Lord,
    Who, in the greatness of Thy power,
    in Thy manifold, infinite wonders
    and in the greatness of Thy forbearance
    forgivest them that repent their transgression,
    but visitest the iniquity of the wicked.
        Verily, [on the righteous]
    Thou bestowest freely [Thy love,]
25 but perversity Thou hatest for ever.[8]
    So hast Thou graced me, Thy servant,
    with the spirit of knowledge and truth,[9]
    that I should cherish the paths of righteousness
    and abhor all froward ways.
        So, for mine own part,
    I in turn will love Thee freely[10]
    and with all my heart will I [choose]
    [to walk in] Thy paths.
    For by Thy hand has this thing been wrought,
    and without [Thy will can naught be done].

· · · · · · · · · · · · · · · · · · · ·

                                    XV, 9-26

· · · · · · · · · · · · · · · · · · · ·

    [   ] they love Thee alway.

        So, for mine own part,
    [I will] [   ]
10 and love Thee right freely
    with all my heart and soul.[1]

Yea, I have cleansed [my heart]
[to adhere to Thy] ho[ly Law]
[and never to] turn aside
from aught that Thou hast commanded;
and I have made Thy commandments
to take firm hold upon many
that they abandon not
any of Thy statutes.

Moreover, through the discernment
which Thou hast bestowed upon me
I am come to know
that not by means of the flesh
can a mortal order his way
neither can any man
direct his own steps.[2]
I know that in Thy hand
is the shaping of each man's spirit,
and ere Thou didst create him
Thou didst ordain his works.[3]
And how can any man
change what Thou hast decreed?

15   Thou alone it is
that hast created the righteous,
conditioning him from the womb
to rank among the favored
at the end of days,[4]
to be safeguarded ever by covenant with Thee,
to walk alway [undaunted]
through the moving of Thy compassion,
to open all the straitness of his soul
to everlasting salvation[5]
and perpetual peace unfailing.
Thou hast raised his inner glory
out of the flesh.

But the wicked hast Thou created
for the time of Thy [wr]ath,[6]
reserving them from the womb

for the day of slaughter,
because they walk in the way of the bad
   and spurn Thy covenant,
and their soul abhors Thy [statutes],
and they take no pleasure in all Thou hast commanded,
but choose that which Thou hatest.

All [them that hate Thee] hast Thou destined
to the wreaking of great judgments upon them
20 in the sight of all Thou hast made,
to serve as a sign [and a token] for ever,
that all may have knowledge how great
is Thy glory and strength.

How can flesh have reason,
or the earth-bound direct his steps,
except that Thou hast created spirit*
and ordained the working thereof?
By Thee is the way of all the living ordained.

So am I come to know
that no wealth can equal Thy truth,
and Thy holiness hath no match;
and I know that Thou preferest these things to all
   else,
and that They attend on Thee alway.

Thou wilt accept no bribe [for wrongdoing],
and Thou wilt accept no ransom
for deeds of wickedness.
25 For Thou art a God of truth
and [hatest]† all perverseness;
[and no iniquity]
shall endure in Thy presence.
   And I am come also to know

---

* Heb. 'Thou it is that createdest spirit', etc.
† Or, 'wilt destroy'.

that [righteousness] is Thine,
[and a]ll [Thy works are truth.]

· · · · · · · · · · · · · · · · · ·

XVI, 1-19

[Thou hast shed] Thy holy spirit
on righteous and [wicked alike,]
[and Thou wilt judge all men]
[according to their deeds.]

Thy holy spirit can [pass] not [away.]
The fulness of heaven and earth [attests it,]
and the sum of all things
[stands witness to] Thy glory.[1]
I know that through [Thy] good wi[ll] towards man
Thou hast bestowed upon him
a rich heri[tage in Thy Law]
[that he may walk] in all [his ways]
as Thy truth [inst]ructs;
and (Thou hast vouchsafed unto him)
5 to maintain a proper stance
through Thy [truth] which Thou hast entrusted to
     him,
lest he go as[tr]ay [   ],
and Thou [hast lain hold on him]
that he stumble not in any of [his steps].[2]
Because that all these things
are present in my mind,
I would put into words
my prayer and confession of sin,
my constant search for Thy spirit,
the inner strength which is mine
through the holy spirit,
my devotion to the truth of Thy covenant,
the truth and sincerity
in which I walk,
my love of Thy name:

Blessed art Thou, O Lord,
creator of all things,
mighty in deed,[3]
by Whom all things are wrought.
Behold, Thou hast granted mercy to Thy servant
and shed upon him in Thy grace
Thine ever-compassionate spirit
and the splendor of Thy glory.
Thine, Thine alone, is righteousness,
for Thou it is hast done all these things.

10 ¶Moreover, because I know
that Thou dost keep a record
of every righteous spirit,[4]
therefore have I chosen
to keep my hands unstained,
according to Thy will;
and the soul of Thy servant has abhorred
all unrighteous deeds.
    Nevertheless I know
that no man can be righteous
without Thy help.
Wherefore I entreat Thee,
through the spirit which Thou hast put [within me,]
to bring unto completion
the mercies Thou hast shown unto Thy servant,
cleansing him with Thy holy spirit,
drawing him to Thee in Thy good pleasure,
[   ] him in Thine abundant lovingkindness,
granting to him that place of favor
which Thou hast chosen for them that love Thee
and observe Thy commandments,
that they may stand in Thy presence for ever.
    [Suffer not Beli]al [to ari]se
and immerse himself in Thy servant's spirit,
15 neither let [a spirit] perverse
[rule over] any of his deeds.[5]
Let not affliction confront him
to make him to falter from the statutes of Thy cove-
    nant,

but [crown him] with glory and truth.
   [For Thou art a God gracious] and merciful,
longsuffering and abounding in lovingkindness and
      truth,
forgiving transgression [   ]
and relenting of [evil]
[unto them that love Him] and keep His command-
      [ments][6]
—even unto them that return unto Thee
in faithfulness and wholeness of heart
to serve Thee [and do what is] good in Thy sight.
   So turn not away the face of Thy servant
neither [reject] the son of [Thine] handmaid;
[for to Thee, O Lord, belongeth forgiven]ess,
and by Thine own words have I call[ed upon Thee.][7]

· ·

XVII, 1-XVIII, 30

(*Eleven lines too fragmentary to translate seem to de-*
scribe the doom which awaits the wicked.)

[*For divine forgiveness*]

   In Thine [abundant] mercy
Thou hast said by the hand of Moses
that Thou wouldst [forgive all] iniquity and sin
and shrive all [guilt] and treason.[1]
And verily, though the roots of the mountains [have
      blazed]
and though the fire [has devoured]
to nethermost hell,[2]
yet, whensoever Thou hast wrought Thy judgments
them hast Thou ever [redeemed]
that were fa[ithful to Thee],
that they might serve Thee in constancy
and that their seed might be ever in Thy presence;[3]
and Thou hast ever confirmed unto them Thine
      o[ath]

15 [to pass over all transg]ression[4]
and to cast away all their iniquities,[5]
and to give them for their inheritance
every mortal glory
and abundance of days.

So, for mine own part,
by virtue of the spirits[6]
which Thou hast set within me,
I will give free rein to my tongue
to tell forth Thy bounteous acts
and Thy forbearance towards me
and the deeds of Thy strong right hand,
and to [confess] my former transgressions
and to make prayer and supplication[7] before Thee
concerning mine [evil] deeds
and the waywardness of [my heart.]
For I have been wallowing in filth,
and [turned] from communion with Thee,
and I have not att[ach]ed myself
[unto Thy congregation.]

20 Thou—with Thee lies bounty,
and of Thy nature it is
ever to dower blessing.[8]
[Proffer,] then, Thy bounty
and redeem [my soul,]
and let the wicked be brought to an end!

[*For spiritual strength*]

Moreover, I have come to understand
that Thou hast ever directed the course
of such as Thou hast chosen,
bestowing insight upon him
to spare him from sinning against Thee,
repaying unto him
all his affliction of heart
in Thy chastisements and Thy [trials].

Thou hast delivered Thy servant
from sinning against Thee
and from stumbling in doing Thy will.
    Strengthen, then, the stand of this Thy servant
against all spirits of perverseness,
that he walk in all the ways which Thou lovest,
reject all that Thou hatest,
and do what is good in Thy sight.
    Yea, [   ] within me,
for of flesh is the spirit of Thy servant.

[For inner enlightenment]

    [I am come also to know]
25 Thou hast ever wafted Thy holy spirit
on him who is Thy servant,
i[llumi]ning for him
the [dark places] of his heart
[with light like the sun.]
But I—behold, I look
to all covenants made by man,
[and all are nothing worth;][9]
[while they that seek after Thy truth]
do surely find it,
[for on them Thy light] shineth;
and they that love it [are illumined]
[and walk in the glow of] Thy light for ever,[10]
and Thou raisest [their hearts] out of the dark[ness].

.   .   .   .

    Let, then, Thy light [shine ever on Thy servant]

.   .   .   .

for with Thee is light everlasting.

[For divine protection]

    [I am come also to know]
that once Thou didst [   ]
and open the ear of one
who was but dust

[that He might hear Thy teaching]
[and deliver Thy chosen people]
[from folly] and delusion

xviii,5 and from the uncleanness which [.]
And Thou didst [   ] Thy [   ],
and [the hands] of Thy servant were steadied by Thy
    tr[uth,]
and have remained so for ever,
that he might announce Thy wondrous tidings
and reveal them to all who would hear.
[Thou didst strengthen him] by Thy strong right hand
    to lead [   ]
and Thou didst [   ] [him] by Thy mighty
    strength,
[that he might achieve renown] for Thy name
and triumph in glory.[11]

Withdraw not now Thy hand [from Thy people,]
that now too there might be among* them
men† that hold firm to Thy covenant,
10   that stand [blameless] before Thee!

[For power of speech]

Moreover, in the mouth of Thy servant
Thou didst open, as it were, a fount
and duly set‡ on his tongue
[the words of Thy Law,]
that through the understanding which Thou givest to
    him
he might proclaim them to human mold,
and serve as the interpreter of these things
to dust like myself.

That fount didst Thou open also
that he might reprove what is molded of clay
concerning its way

* Heb. 'unto'.
† Heb. sg., viz. 'a man' that holds firm, etc.
‡ Or, 'engrave' (despite the mixed metaphor!).

and that which is born of woman
concerning its guiltiness,
every man according to his deeds.

[*Thanksgiving for divine grace*]

But lo, that fount serves also
as a wellspring of Thy truth
for every man whose spirit
Thou hast stayed by Thine own strength,
that he [may walk] in Thy truth,
a herald of Thy good tidings,[12]
bringing cheer to the humble
through Thine abundant compassion,
15   sat[ing] from that fount
them that are [wounded] in spirit,
bringing to them that mourn
everlasting joy.[13]

. . . .
. . . .

[Were it not for Thy grace,]
I could not have seen this thing.
[For how can] I look on [Thy glory]
except Thou open mine eyes?
How hear [the words of Thy truth]
[except Thou unstop mine ears?]
20   Behold, my heart was amazed
that thus the Word was revealed
to one with ears unattuned,
and that a [wayward] heart
[was suffered to grasp these things.]
But now have I come to know
that for Thyself, O my God,
hast Thou done these things.
For what is mortal flesh
[that Thou shouldst so exalt it]
and work such wonders with it?

Howbeit, Thou wast minded§
to consummate all things
and ordain them unto Thy glory,
[and hast therefore called into being]
a host endowed with knowledge
to tell forth Thy mighty acts
unto mortal flesh,
and Thy sure ordinances
to that which is born [of woman.]
And Thou hast brought [Thine elect]
into covenant with Thee
and opened their heart of dust
that, through Thy compassionate Presence,
they may be guarded from [   ]
25 [and escape] the traps of judgment.

So, for mine own part,
molded [of clay] that I am,
with an heart of stone,[14]
lo, of what worth am I,
that I should attain unto this?
Yet, behold, Thou hast set [Thy word]
in this ear of dust,
and graven upon this heart
eternal verities;**
and Thou hast brought to an end
[all of my frowardness,]
to bring me into covenant with Thee,
that I may stand [before Thee]
evermore unshaken††
in the glow of the Perfect Light,[15]
till the end of time,
where [no] darkness is for ever,
30 and where all is peace unbounded
until the end of time.

. . . .

§ Heb. 'it was in Thy thought'.
** Heb. 'realities'.
†† Heb. 'in an eternal station'.

FRAGMENTS

1

[The ho]ly [angels]¹ which are in heaven—
[even they do not know Thy gr]eat name,
for it is a mystery;²
neither can they ever [recount all] Thy [wonders]³
nor claim knowledge⁴ of all [Thy secrets].
    [How much less, then, can one
who is destined to re]vert
to the dust whence he came?⁵

5   Rebellious that I was,
wallowing [in filth],⁶
[tain]ted with the guilt
of wickedness,⁷
I had been [living, as it were],
through more than one Day of Wrath,⁸
[fearful how I could with]stand
the blows that were raining upon me,⁹
how I might be protected
[from the punishing stroke].
Yet, [through that inner discernment
which Thou hast vouchsafed to us,
we of this brotherhood]
have been [made awa]re of these things:
that there (always) is hope for a man¹⁰
[who turns back from sin
that Thou wilt cleanse him] of taint.
    Wherefore, O my God,
mere creature of clay though I be,¹¹
now have I placed my reliance
[on Thy mercy and faithfulness],
10   knowing full well
that [what comes from Thy mouth] is truth,¹²
[that Thy word is never re]voked.¹³

    So, throughout the time
that is yet allotted to me¹⁴

I shall hold firm [to Thy judgments],
and I shall maintain my stance
in the station wherein Thou dost set me;
for [Thou, a God of mercy,
dealest mercifully with all] men
and Thou dost provide for them
a way of return.

. . . .

*   *   *

2

*   *   *

[None is there in Thy heavens
neither upon] Thine earth,
none among angels or m[en
can] render Thee [fitting] praise
or tell forth all of Thy glory.
How much less, then, can I
who was taken from dust?
5   Howbeit, O my God,
'tis but to attest Thy glory
that Thou hast made all of these.

Wherefore, in accordance
with Thine abundant mercy,[1]
grant that the sense for rightdoing
which issues from Thee
may serve ever as a safeguard [to Thy servant]
to deliver him from doom,[2]
and that, at his every step,
there may be men about him
to interpret to him what he should know[3]
and, [in all of his ways,]
men to impress upon him
the lessons of truth.[4]
For, [do whatever he may,]
how else can man achieve aught,

who is but dust,
in whose ineffectual hands
lies nothing but ashes?

    Yet lo, [on such a creature of] clay
[hast Thou shed Thy grace,
giving him Thy] command[ments
in] Thy good will.
    Thou hast shaped that clay on the wheel[5]
and passed it through Thy test,
that it may find its way
into Thy lot;[6]
and when cracks appear in it,
Thou mendest them.[7]

10   Yea, over mere dust
hast Thou wafted Thy [holy] spirit,
[and hast so molded that] clay
that [it can have converse with] angels
and be in communion
with beings celestial.

    [Mere flesh hast Thou lit
with a light] perpetual,
that there be no reversion to darkness,
for [   ],
and a light hast Thou revealed
that it never can be turned back.

· · · · · · · · · · · · · · · ·

    Thou hast wafted Thy ho[ly spirit
o'er these humble servants of Thine],[8]
clearing away all guilt[9]
[and purifying them],
that, along with Thine (heavenly) host,
they too [may minis]ter to Thee,
and, stayed upon Thy truth,

15   walk [upon level ground
and str]ay [not] from Thy presence.
    These men hast Thou singled out, [O my God,]
(to bear witness) to Thy glory,

and through that sense for rightdoing
[which Thou hast vouchsafed to them
Thou hast delivered them from sin
and purged away from them
a]ll the frowardness
of their tainted mold.

      *   *   *

3

      *   *   *

[Unto the children of light]
a way has indeed been opened
[that they may walk upon] peaceful paths[1]
and show how miraculously[2]
[God rescues human] flesh
[from thralldom to sin].

My own feet had been [falling]
into all manner of hidden traps[3]
which Sin[4] had been laying,
and into all manner of nets
which it had been spreading.[5]

5   [How, thought I,] will I (ever) preserve
(this) fabric of dust from crumbling,
this waxen mold [from dissolving]?
Mere heap of ash that I am,
how will I (ever) withstand
the stormy blast?[6]

Howbeit, God has been keeping it
for His mysterious ends;
because He has been aware
[of how frail it is,
He has not suffered it (?)]
to be wholly destroyed.[7]

Though men keep laying (for it)
traps never so many,
and [tightening all about it]

the toils of frowardness,[8]
yet will all guileful bent
be brought to an end,
10   [and all wickedness] come to naught
and every deceitful intent[9]
and all the works of guile
cease to exist.

I am but a creature [of clay,
a fabric of dust;]
and what strength does such possess?
    Thine, O God of [all knowledge][10]
is [the power and the might];[11]
Thou it is didst make all things,
and but for Thee [can naught exist].

[Yet, creature] of dust though I be,
by virtue of the spirit
which Thou hast set within me,
I have now come to know
that [Thou wilt yet call to account
all guil]ty (men)[12]
that flock unto[13] frowardness and guile,
and the wellspring of sin will be dammed.[14]
[For] that which is wrought in uncleanness
can bring naught else but disease,[15]
condign plague[16] and decay.

• • • • • • • • • • • • • • • • • • •

Thine, [O my God,] is a blazing wrath
and a ven[geful] passion.[17]

• • • • • • • • • • • • • • • • • • •

4

* * *

[The sons of Thy covenant
are come to know
that alway, at every moment,

continually, ev]ening and morning,
[Thou dost vouchsafe unto them
the blessing of salvation]
and [heal]ing [from all the afflic]tions of men
and pa[ins of humankind].
5 Wherefore they stand as sentinels,
[posted] upon their watch,[1]
[knowing that] Thou wilt exorcize
every noisome devil[2]
and [every evil spirit].

Moreover, Thou hast unstopped mine ear
(and made me aware)
that through such spirits as these*
[men who have bound themselves
to] (human) [pledge] and pact
have (ofttimes) been seduced
and will (someday) come before Thee
to face Thy charge.
Wherefore, I for my part
have been living in terror of Thy judgment
10 [for who can prove innocent be]fore Thee,
and who can gain acquittal
when Thy sentence is passed?[3]
To what will man amount
when Thou arraignest him,
and to what he that turns back to his dust [   ]?

Howbeit, O my God,
Thou hast opened mine heart
to the insight which comes from Thee,
and unstopped mine ear [to Thy teaching],
that, although my mind be unquiet[4]
[on account of hidden wrongdoings],
and although my heart has been melting like wax[5]
because of transgression and sin
which I have kept [concealed],[6]
I am come to rely upon Thy goodness.

* Heb. 'through them'.

15   Blessed be Thou,
Thou God of (all) knowledge,[7]
Who hast (so) ordained,
and vouchsafed, for Thine own sake,
that this fortune should fall upon Thy servant.
For now that I am come to (this) knowledge,
so long as I have being
I will put my hopes in Thy [mercy].
    Confirm, then, [Thy word] unto Thy [ser]vant.
Forsake us not in (these) times [of trial,[8]
that so we may bear witness alway
to Thy grace] and Thy glory and [Thy] go[odness].

       *   *   *

5

With a wondrous shew of [Thy power
Thou wilt visit upon them
Thy] righteous [judg]ment,[1]
[sundering and] severing them for ever
from standing among [Thy] sa[ints][2]
[and from all] communion
with Thy Holy Beings.[8]
    The spirits of wickedness[4]
wilt Thou ba<ni>sh from the ear[th],[5]
5   [and they that incite to] evil
shall exist no more.
    Thou wilt appoint a place of un[rest[6]
for all] spirits of frowardness,[7]
the which shall be brought to their ruin,
(doomed) to [perpetual] mourning
and everlasting grief.[8]
    When wickedness reaches its height
in a climax of mighty uphea[val],[9]
there shall come upon them
anguish absolute.[10]
    Howbeit, that all may take knowledge of Thy glory
and s[ee] how soothfast is Thy judgment,[11]

[Thou wilt also shew forth]
in the sight of all Thou hast made
how wondrous Thy mercies can be.[12]
    Thou hast opened human ears[13]
[and imparted unto them
the designs of] Thy heart,[14]
and hast given to [mortal] minds
the means to understand
that a time is yet to come
when 'witness will be borne'.[15]
    (Here) on earth wilt Thou enter suit[16]
with them that dwell thereon,[17]
and [Thou wilt] also [wreak vengeance
on the children of] darkness,[18]
vindica[ting the ri]ghteous
and cond[emning the wicked],[19]
and suffering not [the children of light][20]
to be sundered [from bl]essing [evermore].

POEMS FROM A QUMRAN HYMNAL

Sing unto the Lord a new song

I

DAVID

(PSALM 151)

A Hallelujah; ascribed to David, the son of Jesse

v.1   Smaller[1] was I than my brothers
and the youngest[2] of my father's sons.
So he set me as herdsman of his sheep
and ruler over his kids.[3]

v.2   My hands fashioned a Panpipe,
and my fingers a lyre
that I might pay honor to the 𝕷𝖔𝖗𝖉.*

v.3   I kept saying within myself:
"The mountains cannot tell Him
what indeed they witness,[4]
neither can the hills.
The leaves of the trees have no speech for my words,[5]
nor the sheep for my acts.[6]
v.4 Nay, who is there that can tell,
who is there that hath speech and can relate
what it is that I am doing?"

Yet, He Who is the Lord of All Things
saw it indeed;
He Who is the God of All Things—
He heard and Himself gave ear.

v.5   So He sent His prophet to anoint me,
even Samuel to bring me to greatness.[7]

* Written in archaic script.

My brothers went out to meet him,[8]
handsome and comely withal,[9]
v.6 tall of stature,[10] with splendid locks;
but *them* the 𝕷𝖔𝖗𝖉 God did not choose.
v.7 *I* it was He sent for and fetched
from behind the sheep,[11]
and He had me anointed with holy oil,
and made me the leader[12] of His people
and the ruler of the Children of His covenant.

It may be of interest here to reprint a curious and forgotten version of Psalm 151 quoted in Holland's *Psalmists*
(1848) as the work of a certain 'R.B.', said to be Richard
Braithwait, whose versified rendering of I Samuel, ch. 17, in
no less than sixty four-line stanzas, appeared in London in
1628. Holland says that the Psalm is included in Arabic,
Anglo-Saxon, and Greek liturgies and was recognized as canonical by Athanasius. Actually, what is presented is, at best,
an abbreviation of 'R.B.'s' version, and it has been suggested
that it may in fact have been composed by William Tennant,
who held the Chair of Hebrew at St. Andrew's University,
Scotland, in the middle of the nineteenth century; see *Notes
and Queries*, VI, v (1882), p. 357.

1. Among my brethren I was least,
    And of my father's stock
  I was the youngest in his house—
    The shepherd of his flock.
2. Rare instruments of music oft
    My hands, well-practised, made;
  And on the sacred psaltery
    My skilful fingers play'd.
3. But who of me shall speak to God,
    and tell him of my care?
  The Lord himself, lo, even now,
    Doth hearken to my prayer.
4. He sent his messenger and took
    Me from the shepherd's toil;
  And on my head—sweet unction!—pour'd
    His own anointing oil.
5. My brethren, beautiful and tall,
    Held theirs a happy lot;
  But in them and their comeliness
    The Lord delighted not.
6. To meet the boasting alien chief
    I went forth on their part;
  He cursed me by his idols and

Despised me from his heart.
7. But having slain, I with his sword
   Cut off his head at once.
   And took away the foul reproach
   Of Israel's daunted sons.

II
INVITATION TO GRACE AFTER MEALS

1   [Loudly acclaim
the majesty of God;
where many are foregathered
Let His majesty resound!

2   Amid the throng[1] of the upright
proclaim how majestic He is,[2]
and along with the faithful
tell stories of His greatness![3]

3   [Join company][4] with the good and the blameless
in confessing the majesty transcendent;[5]

4   unite[6] in making known
His saving power,
nor be laggard in showing to the mindless
His might and majesty!

5   For it is that the glory of the 𝕷𝖔𝖗𝖉* may be made known
that wisdom has been given,

6   and that the richness[7] of His works may be told
has it been imparted to man,

7   to the end that the witless may have knowledge of
His power,
and the mindless a sense of His greatness—

8   men who keep far from her doors,
remote from all access to her.

9   Although the Most High, forsooth,
is Jacob's special Lord,[8]
yet does His majesty reach out

* Written in archaic script.

over all that He has made,
10 and a mortal who avows it[9]
is no less pleasing to Him
than one who brings offerings of grain,
11 or presents to Him he-goats and bullocks,
or fills the altar with ashes
of burnt-offerings never so many[10]—
yea, than fragrant incense
proffered by righteous men.

12   Wisdom's voice rings out
from behind the doors of the righteous;
wherever the godly foregather
(is heard) her song.
13 Whenso they eat and are filled,[11]
the word is of her;
when they drink in fellowship together,
14 their talk is of the lore† of the Most High;
the aim of their discourse is to further
the knowledge of His power.
15   (But oh, how far from the wicked
is any word of her;
how far from all the proud
any wish to have knowledge of her!)

16   Behold, the eye[12] of the 𝕷𝖔𝖗𝖉
looks with compassion on the good,
17 and great is His tenderness to them
that avow His majesty;
He will save them from the time of trouble.[18]

18   [Bless ye] the 𝕷𝖔𝖗𝖉,
Who redeems the humble
from the grasp of the proud,
[and deli]vers [the blameless]
[from the hand of the wicked;]
19 [Who will yet raise Ja]cob [to honor],[14]
and [from Israel] govern [the world];[15]

† Heb. 'Torah'.

20 [Who will spread His tent in Zion
and be present in Jerusalem for ever!][16]

III
PLEA FOR GRACE*

𝕷𝖔𝖗𝖉,† I have called on Thee;
pay heed unto me.[1]
I have (duly) spread forth my palms
toward Thy holy abode.[2]
Bend Thou, (then,) Thine ear[3]
and grant me what I ask,[4]
nor withhold from me what I seek.

5   Build up my soul,
and cast it not down,
neither be it left naked[5]
in face of the wicked.

Let the evil that I have earned[6]
be turned away[7] from me,
O Thou Who judgest right truly.[8]
   Sentence me not, O 𝕷𝖔𝖗𝖉,
according to my sin,
for there is no man living
can be justified in Thy presence.[9]

Cause me, O 𝕷𝖔𝖗𝖉,
to understand what Thou teachest;‡[10]
school me in Thy rules,[11]
that men far and wide may hear tell of how Thou actest,
and peoples acknowledge how illustrious is Thy glory.[12]

10   Remember me; do not forget me,
neither involve me
in things too hard for me.

* In the Hebrew, this poem is an alphabetical acrostic.
† Written in archaic script.
‡ Heb. 'Thy Torah'.

The sins of my youth put far from me,
and let not my transgressions
be remembered against me.[13]

Cleanse me, O Lord, of noisome plague,[14]
and let it never return[15] unto me.
Let its root wither from me,[16]
and its l[ea]ves blossom not upon me.

15   Mighty[17] art Thou, O Lord;
wherefore by Thine own power
fulfil[18] what I ask;
(for) unto whom (else) can I cry
that He might grant it to me,
and what pow[er] more (than Thine)
do mere mortals possess?[19]

From Thee comes my confidence, O Lord.
Whenso I have called upon the Lord,
He (alway) has answered me[20]
[and mended] my broken heart;
whenso I have slumbered or [sl]ept or dreamed,
[(alway) Have I awoken;§[21]
whenso my heart has been smitten,[22]
Lord, Thou hast (ever) upheld me,[23]
and I have had cause to cry out!]
" 'Tis Thou, Lord,
[hast rescued me!]"[24]

20   [So, at this present time,
I shall yet behold
the hopes of the wicked confounded;**[25]
but no such confounding will be mine
because it is in Thee
that I have taken refuge.][26]

§ Passages in smaller type are supplied from the Syriac version.

** Heb., simply, 'I shall yet behold their disappointment'.

[Ransom Israel, O 𝕷𝖔𝖗𝖉,[27]
to whom Thou art pledged,[28]
even the house of Jacob
whom Thou hast chosen.]

IV
SUPPLICATION

<Poor am I and weak,>*
for the worm cannot confess Thee,
nor the maggot rehearse Thy lovingkindness;
the living alone can do so,
the living alone.[1]
　　Whenever Thou showest men Thy kindness,
what time their foot has slipped,
they needs must confess Thee (and own)
that in Thy hand it is
that the souls of all living lie,
and that Thou it is hast given
breath to all flesh.[2]

5　¶Deal with us, then, O 𝕷𝖔𝖗𝖉,†
after the manner of Thy goodness,
Thine abundant compassion and Thy justice.[3]
　　The 𝕷𝖔𝖗𝖉 hath (alway) heard the voice
of them that love His name,[4]
and ne'er hath He abandoned
His lovingkindness[5] toward them.

¶"Blessed is the 𝕷𝖔𝖗𝖉,
Who dealeth bountifully.[6]
Who crowneth with loyal love and compassion
them that are loyal to Him."[7]
　　(So) hath mine own soul
come to acclaim Thy name
in a roar of praise,

* Supplied from another fragmentary copy.
† Written in archaic script.

confessing Thy loyal love
in joyous song,
telling forth the tale
of Thy constancy.[8]
  (Endless, indeed, is the praise
that is due unto Thee!)

10   ¶I too had been marked for death
on account of my sins,
my wrongdoings had sold me to Shëol;‡[9]
but Thou, in accord with Thine abundant compas-
    sion,
Thou, in accord with Thy bounteous ways,
didst rescue me, O 𝕷𝖔𝖗𝖉.

¶I too have loved Thy name,
sought shelter in Thy shade;[10]
in calling to mind Thy power
my heart finds strength,[11]
and upon Thy loyal love
have I come to lean.

  Wherefore forgive Thou my sin, O 𝕷𝖔𝖗𝖉,[12]
and purge me of my wrongdoing.[13]
Vouchsafe Thou unto me
a spirit of constancy
and knowledge (of Thy truth).[14]
  Let me not stumble in waywardness.[15]

15   Suffer no devil[16] nor spirit unclean[17]
to bear sway over me;
let not pain or evil bent
gain mastery over my body.
For Thou, O 𝕷𝖔𝖗𝖉, it is
from Whom comes (all) my worth,[18]
and on Thee have I alway pinned my hopes.[19]
  Let my brethren and father's house
who now are desolate

‡ That is, the netherworld.

rejoice along with me
in the dowering of Thy grace.

. . . .

Let me find in Thee
an [everl]asting joy.

V
THE CITY OF GOD

I will call down a blessing, O Zion,
on the memory of thee;[1]
with all my might have I loved thee:[2]
'Blessed for evermore
be the memory of thee!'[3]

Great has been thy hope, O Zion,
thy quiet, longing hope[4]
that salvation would come to thee;[5]
that men would be dwelling in thee
till the end of time;[6]
that successions[7] of godly men
would be there for thine ornament;
that men who now are yearning
for the day of thy salvation,
who find joy in thy manifold glory,
would yet drink in that glory of thine
like mother's milk,[8]
and stroll through thy beautiful squares
to the jingling of bells;[9]
that thou wouldst yet conjure up
the godly devotion of thy prophets
and find thy pride in the things
wrought by thy saints—
in the purging of all violence from within thee,
with (all) falsehood and frowardness cut off;
that thy children would make merry in thy midst,
and thy friends who have allied themselves with
thee.[10]

(How have they been hoping
for thy salvation,[11]
and mourning over thee!)[12]

This hope of thine, O Zion,
shall prove not a hope forlorn,[13]
nor shall this yearning of thine
become a forgotten thing.
Who ever perished, being righteous,[14]
or whom in his frowardness
has God ever allowed to go free?
Nay, there is never a man
that is not brought to trial
for the way he has trod,
and none but receives his deserts
for the deeds he has done.
Nevertheless, O Zion,
no foe ever compassed thee[15]
but was (in the end) cut down,
and none has nursed hate for thee
but was put to rout![16]

A scent[17] unto the nostrils
is the fame of thee, O Zion,
(diffused)[18] over all the world!

Over and over again
will I call down a blessing
upon the memory of thee:
with all my heart[19] invoke
(this) benediction upon thee:
   'Mayest thou yet attain
the triumph of righteousness
world without end,[20]
and receive the blessings shed
on men marked out for honor![21]
   Reap thou the harvest[22] *of that vision*[23]
that once was spoken of thee,
and may there ensue for thee
what the prophets dreamed!'[24]

Grow high and wide, O Zion!
Praise the Most High, thy Redeemer!
   When thou art brought to honor
my soul will rejoice.[25]

VI
MORNING HYMN

Great and holy is the 𝕷𝖔𝖗𝖉,*[1]
the holiest of the holy for all time.[2]

Before Him goes a splendor;[3]
behind Him a surge of many waters.[4]

Lovingkindness and Truth
are round about His presence;[5]
   Justice and Right
are the mainstay of His throne;[6]

Who has parted light from darkness[7]
and, through His discerning wisdom,[8]
   turned the glimmer of dawn
into bright day.[9]
   (When first all His angels saw it,
they sang for joy,[10]
   for what He was showing them
was a thing they had known not erst);[11]

Who crowns the hillsides with produce[12]—
choice food for all the living.

Blessed be He[13]
Who by His power made the earth,
by His wisdom founded the world,
by His understanding spread out the skies;
Who (first) brought forth [the wind]
out of His promptu[aries],[14]
made [lightnings for the ra]in,[15]
and lifted the mist[s from the] hori[zon].[16]

* Written in archaic script.

LAMENT FOR ZION

[God warned us that He would pu]nish
all our iniquities,
but because [we] did not listen to [the war]ning[1]
that all these things would befall us,
now is there naught we can do.[2]
By the evil of [our deeds[3]
we have cancelled] His covenant (with us).[4]

Woe unto us!
5   [Our temple] has gone up in flames;[5]
the [shrine] which was our pride[6]
has been turned into [rubble];
no more is there within it
the sweet savor of sacrifices.

[Men have come trampling] in [their sandals][7]
the courts of our sanctuary.
[All the sacred] ve[ssels] have been [carried
away] (?).[8]

Jerusalem, which was once
a [joyous] city,
is made over to wild beasts,[9]
with no one to [rescue her].[10]
[Deserted] are her squares,
10   her mansions all [abandoned],
[her highways] desolate,
with never a pilgrim upon them.[11]

All the cities of [Judah
have been laid waste;[12]
the land of] our heritage
has become like a wilderness,
an un[inhabited] tract.[13]
No sound of merriment
is heard anymore within it,
[No one] seeks [our welfare,[14]
nor is there] any man
[who has carried the lo]ad of our pain;[15]
and (all the while) our foes
[have been lolling at ease].[16]

15   Our transgressions [are past all counting],
and our sins [have denounced us].[17]

I, ii

Woe unto us!
    God's anger flared [against us],[18]
and we shared the defilement of the dead,[19]
Is[rael became]
like a wife grown loathsome,
[Our mothers showed no pity] for their babes;
Our womenfolk were turned into harpies,[20]
5   [shorn of all the charm of] their youth.[21]

    Our sons were undone;[22]
[numbed] by winter's cold,
our daughters, instead of dwelling
[secure] in [their fathers'] homes,
[hugged] the dunghills[23] with wizened hands;
when they begged for water,
no one pou[red it for them].

    They that were worth their weight in gold
10   [were deemed but] worthless [shards],[24]
reared though they were in purple,[25]
decked in fine gold,

garbed in [linen] and lawn,
man[tled] in blue and brocade.[26]
    The (once) tender maidens of Zion
[became   ].

*   *   *

II

[Ah, how she sits] alone,
[the city once full of people!][27]
5 Once the princess of all nati[ons],[28]
now is she desolate,
like a woman abandoned!
.... all her daughters too
like a woman abandoned,
like a woman cast down and cast off.[29]

    Her mansions all and [her] wal[ls],
(empty of all life,)
are become like a barren wife,[30]
and all [her] roads like one
left destitute.[31]
Her..........are like a woman
in bitter grief,[32]
and all her daughters like those
who mourn their mates;
...her [matrons] are like (mothers)
bereaved of an only child.[33]

    Bitterly Jeru[salem] weeps,
[and her tears run] down her cheeks;[34]
on account of her sons [   ]
. . . .
10   she [has been wa]il[ing] and moaning.[35]

HYMNS OF TRIUMPH

I

    Let the [righteous] hail the LORD
in wild acclaim,[1]
for He is (even now) on His way
to pass judgment on all deeds,
to wipe out the wicked from the earth,[2]
that the froward exist no more.

    The skies will [drop] their dew,[3]
and blight shall come no more
within their borders,[4]
The soil will yield its tilth in due season,[5]
and its produce shall not be lacking.
Fruit trees will [burgeon and blossom],
and springs will not fail.
5   The poor will have to eat,[6]
and they that fear the LORD will be sated.

II

    Let heaven and earth unite
in a chorus of praise![1]
Let all the stars of evening
break out in hymns![2]
    Be right joyful, O Judah,
right merry and gay!
Make thy pilgrimages;
pay (in a purified Temple)
the offerings thou hast vowed,
for Belial shall no more be in thy midst![3]

Victory and triumph shall be thine;
for lo, thine enemies shall perish,
and all evildoers be scattered;[4]

5 but Thou, O LORD, art eternal
and Thine is a glory which endureth
world without end.[5]

Hallelujah.

NOTES

The Hymn of the Initiants

1. I.e., at noon.
2. 'Storehouses of darkness' are mentioned (metaphorically) in Isa. 45.3.
3. Literally, 'and sets against it (?)'; the text is somewhat obscure.
4. I.e., at midnight. The reference in these lines is to the three statutory times of daily prayer; cf. Mishnah, *Berachôth*, iv.1.
5. On the basis of such Biblical passages as Hab. 3.11; Deut. 26.15; Jer. 25.30 and II Chron. 30.27, the terms 'Height' (Heb. *Zebul*) and 'Abode' (Heb. *Ma'on*) came to be used in rabbinic literature as names of two of the seven heavens.
6. In the calendrical system underlying the pseudepigraphic books of *Jubilees* and *Enoch*, seasons formally begin at new moon.
7. I.e., at solstice and equinox.
8. Cp. Ex. 12.14; Lev. 23.24; Num. 10.10.
9. An allusion to the belief, still maintained by the Samaritans, that *all* the commandments given to Moses were engraven by God on tablets. Cp. Ex. 32.16.
10. An allusion to the obligation of bringing tribute at seasonal festivals; cp. Num. 15.19–20. Jewish tradition declares that prayer now substitutes for offerings, and the statutory services are still named for those offerings. The Essenes, says Josephus (*War*, I, iii, 5) did not make offerings but 'offered sacrifices within themselves'. This was also the attitude of the early Church. The *Didascalia Apostolorum* declare expressly that 'instead of sacrifices which then were, offer now

prayers and petitions and thanksgivings' (p. 86, ed. Conolly).

11. Cp. Lev. 25.8ff.

12. The expression occurs also in the Psalms of Solomon, 15.3: 'The fruit of the lips with the well-tuned instrument of the tongue, the first-fruits of the lips from a pious and righteous heart—he that offereth these shall never be shaken by evil'. There is a subtle play on words in the original, for the Hebrew word *azammerah* means at once 'cull' (strictly, 'trim vines'; cp. Lev. 25.3) and 'sing'. The concept of 'fruit of the lips' is derived from Isa. 57.19, and more especially from a variant reading of Hos. 14.3(2) preserved in the Greek (Septuagint) and Syriac (Peshitta) translation (and adopted by the Revised Standard Version).

13. Cp. Jer. 31.35–36. The point is that the Hebrew word for 'bound' also means 'statute, ordinance'. In observing the fixed order of day and night, the psalmist will be inspired likewise to abide by God's rules.

14. Literally, 'and where they [i.e., God's bounds, statutes] are will I set my boundary'.

15. The pious Jew offers a blessing every morning as soon as he takes his first steps, viz. 'Blessed art Thou, O Lord, our God, King of the Universe, Who directest the steps of man'.

16. An adaptation of the words, 'when thou liest down and when thou risest up', in Deut. 6.7. The pious Jew recites the *Shema*' (Deut. 6.4–9, etc.) when he lies down to sleep and when he wakes up in the morning —in the former case, in a recumbent position, in the latter standing up; cp. Mishnah, B^erachôth, i.3.

17. An allusion to the benediction pronounced before meals, viz. 'Blessed art Thou, O Lord our God, King of the Universe, Who bringest forth food (bread) from the earth'.

18. An allusion to the blessing offered by Jews on hearing bad news, viz. 'Blessed is He, the truthful Judge' (Mishnah, B^erachôth, ix.2). Cp. Mishnah, Ber. ix.5: 'Man is obliged to offer blessing for evil as well as for good'.

19. An allusion to the blessing offered by Jews on deliverance from danger, viz. 'Blessed art Thou, O Lord our God . . . Who bestowest good things on the undeserving, and Who hast bestowed a good thing upon me'.

20. An adaptation of Ps. 23.6.

21. Cp. *Manual*, ix.22.

22. Cp. *Manual*, ix.16.

23. The expression is derived from Deut. 32.35, according to the reading found in the Samaritan recension and in the Greek (Septuagint) Version, viz. 'Is not this stored up with Me . . . against the Day of Requital?' This reading is actually found in a fragment of Deuteronomy discovered at Qumran. See also Isa. 34.8; 61.2. 'Day of Requital' is the technical term among the Samaritans for Doomsday.

24. Cp. *Manual*, vii.8.

25. Cp. *Manual*, vii.9.

26. Cp. *Manual*, vii.5ff.

27. Pss. 16.8; 121.5.

28. Ps. 40.3(2).

29. Cp. Eph. 1.3; II Thess. 1.5. A similar expression occurs at the beginning of the *Apostolic Constitutions*.

30. Based on Isa. 60.21; 61.3. The *Apostolic Constitutions* speaks of 'God's planting and the holy vineyard, the church catholic, the elect', and so too does Epiphanius, *Haer.*, xiv.4.

31. Cp. John 1.3.

32. The word, I suggest, has a technical nuance, for Josephus (*War*, II, viii, 7) speaks of one who was admitted to the communion after the first year of probation as 'one who comes nearer'. I would therefore make a distinction between 'coming near' as indicating the first stage, and 'coming nearer' as indicating the second. The former is here intended, since the psalmist virtually repeats the *preliminary* oath described in *Manual*, col. i.

33. The Hebrew text is doubtful. Others read, 'a draining

of spittle', but I find this meaningless, because spittle
is *ejected*, not *drained.*

34. Job 33.6.

The Book of Hymns

1

1. This is perhaps the most intricate hymn in the collection, and in order to bring out the nexus of thought
I have had to resort to a certain amount of expansion
and paraphrase. The central idea appears to be that
God has appointed sentient spirits to inform and govern the various elements of the universe. The functions and operations of such spirits were determined
even before they were created. Man too is endowed
with such a spirit. Hence, God knows and determines
all that man will ever do, think or say. But since God's
power is matched by His benevolence, He also forti-
fies that spirit against the trials and afflictions of human existence; and when it gets tainted by worldly
corruption, He constantly cleanses it. Man can save
himself from error and profanation by adopting a so-
ber and temperate mode of life.

The doctrine of controlling spirits may owe something to Iranian ideas about the *yazatas,* who likewise
'animate' phenomena and bestow help upon men.

2. Cp. Jer. 32.19.
3. Cp. Ex. 34.6. The psalmist resorts to the common
rabbinic device of contrasting, or juxtaposing, the various attributes of God.
4. Cp. John 1.3.
5. Restored from Isa. 45.12.
6. The rabbinic tradition was that angels were created
only on the second or fifth day; cp. Genesis Rabbah,
i.3.
7. The language is borrowed from Num. 4.27.
8. The concept is based on such Scriptural passages as
Jer. 10.13; 51.16; Ps. 135.7 (promptuaries of winds);
Ps. 33.7 (of waters); Job 38.22 (of hail); and Isa.

45.3 (of darkness). It is elaborated in Enoch 17.3; 18.1; 41.4ff.; 60.12–24; 69.23; 71.4.

9. Cp. Enoch 41.3; 59.1; 71.4.

10. Note the contrast between the *power* and the *wisdom* of God, exemplifying the general statement made in the opening lines. The restoration is imposed by the basic theme of the psalm.

11. Cp. Zech. 12.1.

12. Literally, 'at their fixed times'.

13. Cp. *Manual of Discipline*, iii. 14–15.

14. Cp. John 1.3.

15. Cp. Isa. 29.24; Ps. 95.10; I John 4.6 ('the spirit of error').

16. Cp. *Hymns*, xvi.10; Slavonic Enoch, 50.1. See also T. H. Gaster, *Thespis*² (1961), pp. 288f.

17. Cp. I Sam. 2.3.

18. The phrase is based on Hos. 14.3, read as in the Greek (Septuagint) and Syriac (Peshitta) Versions.

19. Literally, 'settest words upon a line'.

20. Literally, 'and the expression of the spirit of the lips in due measure'.

21. Literally, 'and Thou producest lines for their secrets'.

22. Literally, 'ye of low intellect'.

23. Literally, 'increase prudence (subtlety)'.

24. Cp. *Hymns*, ii.11; Pss. 35.16; 37.12; 112.10; Job 16.9; Lam. 2.16.

2

1. Restored from Jer. 16.19.

2. Deut. 33.11.

3. Ps. 51.10.

4. Mal. 1.4.

5. Ezek. 36.3.

6. Job 30.9; Lam. 3.14.

7. Cp. Isa. 17.12.

8. Isa. 57.20.

9. Literally, 'the elect of righteousness' or 'the rightfully chosen'. But there is a play on words, for 'elect' was

the technical term in Hebrew (and already in the cuneiform documents from Mari, of the 18th cent., B.C.) for 'picked troops'. This explains the reference to the 'banner', which is understood in the sense of a military ensign.

10. Prov. 12.1.
11. Judges 12.2; Jer. 15.10.
12. Isa. 30.10. (RSV: 'Prophesy not unto us what is right'. But the word rendered 'prophesy' really means 'see, envision', and that rendered 'what is right' really means 'straight things'.)
13. Num. 5.14, 30. The poet gives his own interpretation of the words usually rendered 'spirit of jealousy' (or, 'zeal').
14. Isa. 27.11.
15. Isa. 28.11.
16. Cp. Hos. 4.14.

3

1. I Sam. 25.29. These famous words are usually rendered, 'The soul of my lord shall be bound up in the bundle of life [or, the living]', and it is in this sense that they are commonly inscribed on Jewish tombstones. But the word rendered 'bundle' can also mean 'pouch, wallet', and the poet evidently understood the sentence—as did several medieval Jewish commentators—to imply that God will keep the faithful, like a treasure in a wallet, safe from Death.
2. Job 1.10.
3. Pss. 54.5; 86.14.
4. Cp. Isa. 30.30.
5. A fanciful interpretation of the Hebrew text of Isa. 59.5 (American Jewish Version: 'And that which is crushed breaketh out into a viper'). By construing the words differently, the poet obtained the sense, 'By repeated crushings they split all trivial things'.
6. Pss. 9.16; 35.7–8.
7. An adaptation of Ps. 26.12.

4

1. Ps. 82.3.
2. Jer. 31.11.

5

1. I Sam. 6.18; II Kings 10.2; Jer. 1.18; Ps. 108.11.
2. Jer. 4.31.
3. I Sam. 4.19; Dan. 10.16.
4. A play on Mic. 2.10, for the Hebrew words which in that context mean 'grievous destruction' can also be construed in the sense of 'grievous throes'.
5. Cf. II Kings 19.3; Isa. 37.3.
6. Isa. 66.7.
7. II Sam. 22.6 (Ps. 18.6).
8. Literally, 'One who is wonderful in counsel, a hero divine', alluding to Isa. 9.5.
9. Cp. Job 38.8.
10. Literally, 'all the birth-throes are hastening'.
11. This line has here been inserted in order to clarify the expression 'crucible of conception'.
12. The Hebrew word which normally describes the onset of labor means properly 'turn, change', and the poet here plays on that sense.
13. The poet has in mind the words of Isa. 42.14, 'Like a woman in travail will I gasp', but he takes the Hebrew word for 'gasp', viz. *ef'eh*, in the sense of the noun *ef'eh* meaning 'viper'.
14. The pun has been introduced into the rendering in order to bring out the meaning.
15. Ps. 107.27 (RSV: 'They are at their wits' end').
16. Job 41.23(31).
17. A play on Job 38.16, where (by changing the vowels) the Hebrew words for 'springs of the sea' can be interpreted to mean 'eddies of the sea'. This, it may be added, is the way in which the ancient Aramaic translation (Targum) understood them, and our poet had the same tradition.

18. Isa. 38.10.
19. Disaster was often portrayed in antiquity as the loosing of divine or demonic arrows; cp. Ps. 91.5; Job 6.4. In the *Iliad* (i, 51), the plague which besets the Greeks before Troy is attributed to the arrows of Apollo, and in the Middle Ages, a man who was diseased was said to be 'elf-shot'. In later Jewish folklore, punishment in the grave includes the shooting of 'arrows of iron and fire'; cf. Zohar, Wayaqhel (§199.2); Ḥibbūṭ ha-Qeber, in Masseketh Simḥah, ed. M. Higger (1931), p. 259; A. Jellinek, *Beth ha-Midrash*, v. 49; J. Eisenstein, *Oṣar ha-Midrashîm* (1915), p. 94.
20. 'To cry to the deep' seems to have been a proverbial expression for futile screams; cf. *Hymns*, vi.24; x.33. Here, in the context of a storm at sea, the picture is somewhat more literal, and I have therefore rendered it by a paraphrase designed to bring this out.
21. The restoration is due to L. Silberman.
22. Cp. Jonah 2.6.
23. See above, n. 13.

6

1. Isa. 38.17.
2. Prov. 15.11; 27.20. The term rendered 'Perdition' was sometimes used as a synonym for 'hell' (Ps. 88.12; Job 26.6, etc.). It is the Hebrew Abbadon, which occurs in Rev. 9.11 as the name of the demon of the abyss.
3. Ezra 10.2.
4. The expression is based on Isa. 19.14 (RSV: 'spirit of confusion', literally, 'of distortions').
5. Ps. 19.14.
6. Cp. *Manual of Discipline* ii, 25; iv, 22; Eph. 2.19.
7. Cp. Isa. 52.8; Ps. 98.9; Job 38.7—all of which passages show that the Hebrew words mean simply 'sing together, in chorus', not 'sing in the Community', as some scholars have mistakenly rendered.

We may perhaps compare Plotinus, *Enneads,* vi, 9: 'When we behold Him, we attain the end of our existence and our rest. Then we no longer sing out of tune, but form a truly divine chorus about Him'.

8. Pss. 9.2; 26.7; 75.2.
9. Mal. 1.4.
10. Amos 3.9.
11. This is simply an approximate rendering. The Hebrew word occurs only once in the Bible (Isa. 14.4)—and even there the reading is uncertain—and its meaning is not yet definitely determined (RSV: 'insolent fury'; Moffatt: 'mad rage').
12. Based on Isa. 19.8.
13. See note 15 to Hymn No. 5.
14. Jer. 42.18; Nah. 1.6, etc.
15. The Hebrew word occurs only at Ps. 26.4. It is apparently derived from a verbal root meaning 'hide, conceal', and is therefore usually rendered 'dissemblers' (Moffatt: 'hypocrites'). However, it is quite common in the dialect of the Samaritans in the general sense of 'wrongdoers'.
16. Pss. 18.5; 116.3.
17. Ps. 18.5.
18. Ezek. 21.3(20.47).
19. Cp. Deut. 32.22.
20. Cp. Isa. 34.9.
21. Suggested by Amos 7.4.
22. Isa. 57.20.
23. I Sam. 2.10; II Sam. 22.14; Ps. 18.14; Job 37.4.
24. Isa. 63.15. The archaic 'welkin' conveys the effect of the Hebrew word, which really means 'eminence, lofty structure', but came in post-Biblical Jewish literature to be the name of one of the seven heavens.
25. Cp. Zech., ch. 14. The idea is fully developed in the *War of the Sons of Light and the Sons of Darkness.* Armed soldiers of heaven are mentioned in Slavonic Enoch 17.1, and in rabbinic literature, the heavenly hosts are sometimes described as an 'army'.
26. Dan. 9.27.

7

1. Cp. Isa. 26.1.
2. Restored from Ps. 40.3.

8

1. Hos. 6.3 (which the poet construed in the light of a similar expression in Prov. 4.18).
2. Prov. 2.16; 7.5.
3. Hos. 4.14.
4. Ps. 31.13(12). Compare 'crackpot'.
5. Ps. 69.22.
6. The phrase is suggested by Hab. 2.15. The traditional ('Masoretic') text reads: 'Woe to him that plies his neighbor with drink . . . so as to gaze on his [Heb. 'their'] nakedness' (*m^e'ôrêhem*). However, in the Dead Sea *Commentary on Habakkuk* the last word is read slightly differently (viz. *m^e'ôdêhem*), to yield the meaning 'their staggerings', and it is this reading that the poet follows.
7. Prov. 19.21.
8. See note 15 to Hymn No. 6.
9. Deut. 29.17(18).
10. Ezek. 14.3, 4, 7.
11. Isa. 28.11.
12. Ps. 10.2.
13. Extirpation from the community was the statutory punishment in Jewish law for blasphemy or idolatry; cf. Num. 15.30; Mishnah, *Kerithoth* ('Extirpations'), i, 1.
14. Ps. 20.9(8).
15. Cp. Isa. 44.18.
16. Heb. 'in the council of the holy beings' (cp. Ps. 89.7). Since the Hebrew word here rendered 'rallied' refers specifically to the marshalling of troops, and since the expression, 'have hearkened unto me' may very well allude to the Roman practise of reciting the military oath to new recruits, it seems permissible to recognize

a military metaphor, and for that reason the term 'legion' has been used.

17. Hab. 1.4.
18. Ezek. 7.17; 21.12(7).
19. Mic. 1.4.
20. Ps. 65.4.

9

1. Ex. 21.8.
2. Ps. 57.5.
3. Literally, 'And Thou hast placed me in the drag [Heb. *magor;* cf. Hab. 1.15], with many fishermen spreading their nets on the face of the waters [cp. Isa. 19.8] and (with) huntsmen (hunting) after wrongdoers'.
4. An interpretation of Hab. 1.12.
5. Pss. 57.3; 59.8.
6. Ps. 57.5.
7. Deut. 32.33. A word has evidently fallen out of the Hebrew text.
8. Cp. Isa. 56.1.
9. Nah. 2.12.
10. Pss. 64.4; 120.4; 140.4.
11. Jer. 47.6.
12. Ps. 12.7.
13. Ps. 107.29.

10

1. An interpretation of a word which in Isa. 32.4 and 35.4 is usually rendered 'rash'. It comes from a root meaning 'be hasty'.
2. An interpretation of Ps. 40.3(2) which is usually rendered, somewhat incongruously, 'He brought me up from the pit of tumult'. The poet understood the Hebrew word 'tumult', viz. *shaôn,* in the sense of the like-sounding Aramaic *seyan,* 'mud'—an interpretation which, it may be added, was proposed independently by the present writer many years ago.

3. Literally, 'in the mirings of [their] feet'. The poet employs a very rare term which occurs only in Isa. 14.23 and there means 'broom, besom'. However, ancient commentators and lexicographers connected it (perhaps correctly) with the like-sounding Hebrew word for 'mud'—the very word used in Ps. 40.3, which the poet has just quoted. It is evident that he had the same tradition.

4. Prov. 6.19; 10.12.

5. Obadiah 7; Ps. 41.10. Cp. 'com-pani-on'.

6. Ps. 41.10(9).

7. Cp. Prov. 4.24, where similar Hebrew words are rendered 'devious speech'.

8. Restored after Lam. 3.9.

9. Deut. 32.33.

10. The Hebrew expression is a clever adaptation of Hab. 2.3 which the poet read according to the text preserved in the Greek Septuagint Version rather than in the traditional Jewish recension.

11. Ps. 58.6(5).

12. Isa. 17.11.

13. Lev. 13.51.

14. An adaptation of Lam. 1.14.

15. Lam. 1.3.

16. Zeph. 1.15; Job 30.3; 38.27. The words may also be rendered 'ruin and devastation'.

17. Ps. 11.6 (interpreted metaphorically).

18. Isa. 50.3.

19. Ps. 137.6; Job 29.10.

20. Ps. 102.10(9).

21. Pss. 6.8(7); 31.10(9).

22. Job 3.5. I read *bi-merîrê yôm* in place of *bi-merôdê yôm* of the *editio princeps*.

23. Isa. 45.2; Ps. 107.16.

24. Ps. 18.4.

25. I Sam. 9.15; 20.12–13; II Sam. 7.27, etc.

26. Cp. Isa. 13.4; Ps. 46.7.

27. Ezra 9.8–9.

28. A common expression in post-Biblical Hebrew for the ministering angels who stand before God.
29. The Hebrew text is here faint and fragmentary, so that the rendering is largely a guess. (For *banîm* of the transcription, which makes no sense, I have emended *bênam*, after Gen. 42.23.)
30. The Hebrew text is here virtually illegible.
31. Suggested by Ezek. 31.3ff. and Dan. 4.8(11).
32. Inspired by Ezek. 31.4, 7.
33. Cp. Isa. 52.1.
34. Adapted from Nah. 1.11.
35. Isa. 19.14 (where the term is used figuratively).
36. Ps. 107.18.
37. Isa. 28.16.
38. I.e., God; cp. Isa. 42.13; Zeph. 3.17.
39. Military ensigns were certainly used in Israelite warfare (cp. Isa. 5.26; Jer. 4.6), but perhaps the poet is thinking more specifically of the *Roman* technical expression, *signa tollere*, 'to lift the ensigns', in the sense of 'to set the army on the march'.
40. Cp. Job 25.6.
41. Isa. 28.15, 18.

10a

1. Job 31.22.
2. Isa. 6.10.
3. Ps. 22.15(14).
4. An interpretation of an obscure term in Jonah 4.8, usually rendered 'sultry wind'.

11

1. Isa. 26.6; 30.13; Ps. 139.6; Prov. 18.19.
2. For the sake of clarity, I have slightly altered the structure of this sentence. In the original it reads: 'Thou hast set me as a strong tower on a high wall, and hast planted my structure firmly on a rock, and eternal foundations serve as my basis, and all my walls are a tested bastion that cannot be shaken'.

3. Scholars differ about the meaning of these lines. The Hebrew says literally, 'And Thou, O my God, hast given (provided) it for the *'āfîm* to the holy council'. The most natural meaning of *'āfîm* is 'those that wing their way'. In that case the picture would be that of the spirit soaring to transcendental heights and alighting at last atop a high tower. One may compare the great sentence in *The Mirror of Simple Souls* (Div. iv, ch. 1): 'This [soul] is the eagle that flies high, so right high and yet more high than doth any bird, for she is feathered with fine Love'. Cp. also Edgar Lee Masters, *Spoon River Anthology* ("Lydia Humphrey"): 'I knew of the eagle souls that flew high in the sunlight/ Above the spire of the church'.

4. Cf. Isa. 50.4.

5. Literally, 'in Thy covenant'.

6. In the *Didascalia Apostolorum* (p. 45, ed. Achelis-Fleming), the bishop is called 'Father in God'.

7. Zech. 3.8.

8. Ps. 92.11, etc.

9. Isa. 17.13; Pss. 1.4; 35.5.

10. Cp. Isa. 60.19; Rev. 21.23, 25; 22.6. The Talmud says that the light of the Messianic sun will be sevenfold strong; TB Sanhedrin, 91b.

11. Isa. 60.20.

12

1. Ex. 15.11.

2. Prov. 4.26.

13

1. Restored on the basis of Ps. 9.11(10).

14

1. Isa. 35.7; 49.10.

2. Isa. 41.19.

3. Jer. 17.8.
4. Cp. Dan. 4.9(12); Ezek. 31.6. Literally, 'Its stock (stump) is trampled by wayfarers'.
5. These lines may also be understood in the sense that the holy tree is now being ravaged and despoiled by birds and beasts (i.e., by the impious), and its roots are being carelessly trampled.
6. Cp. Ezek. 31.9.
7. Cp. Isa. 17.11, where RSV renders the verb as 'make them grow'. Our poet, however, took it, as did later Jewish commentators, to be a variant of the common word for 'entangle'.
8. Ps. 103.20.
9. Gen. 3.24.
10. Cp. Enoch 24.4–25.5; 28.1–3; 30.1; 35.3ff.
11. I restore: *'im [shef]'a sheḥaqîm.*
12. Literally, 'without recognizing (it)'.
13. Literally, 'though he has thoughts (about it)?'
14. Cp. Isa. 18.2, 7, where the versions so render the rare word *b-z-'*, which is probably to be read here.
15. Isa. 57.20.
16. Cp. Deut. 28.12. Literally, 'that they (i.e., the rains) depart not'.
17. Jer. 47.2.
18. Cp. Isa. 8.7.
19. The reference is to the subterranean springs which suddenly burst forth at the foot of the hills to relieve the summer drought; see G. A. Smith, *Historical Geography of the Holy Land,* p. 77.
20. Ezek. 21.3 (20.47).
21. Ex. 15.10. Cp. also Enoch 4.89.
22. For the Hebrew idiom, cp. Isa. 28.17.
23. Isa. 5.2.
24. Isa. 40.24.
25. Jer. 17.6; 48.6.
26. Hos. 10.8.
27. Isa. 5.6.
28. Isa. 5.2, 4 (commonly rendered 'wild grapes').
29. Isa. 17.11.

30. Pss. 42.6, 12(11); 43.5.
31. In the Hebrew, this is a combination of Ps. 77.7(6) and Ps. 88.6(5). In both passages, a word *ḥ-p-s* is employed. In the first, it actually means 'search out' (*ḥappes*); in the second, 'free, quit' (*ḥophshi*). But our author evidently equated it in both instances with a root akin to Arabic *ḥafatha*, 'be low, sordid'. In the Ras Shamra texts, of the fourteenth century B.C., the cognate term *ḥ-p-sh-t* denotes the 'charnel house' of the netherworld.
32. Ps. 88.4(3).
33. Ps. 107.5; Jonah 2.8.
34. Jer. 20.9.
35. Pss. 42.7(6); 43.5.
36. Job 31.22.
37. Isa. 50.4.
38. Literally, 'my circumcised lips'; see note 1 to Hymn 17.

15

1. Cp. Isa. 42.13.
2. II Sam. 22.5.
3. Cp. Ps. 6.7(6).
4. There is a slight error in the text: for *k'sh* we must read *k'shn;* cp. Ex. 19.18.
5. Lam. 2.18.
6. Ps. 31.11; Lam. 2.11.
7. Cp. Zeph. 1.15; Job 30.3; 38.27.
8. Literally, 'supplication'; but the Hebrew word is connected with the idea of grace.
9. Jer. 50.34; 51.36.
10. Cp. *Manual of Discipline*, iv, 7; I Peter 5.4.
11. I restore the Hebrew to read: [*marpe' lᵉ-maḥ*]*aṣ makkati;* cp. Isa. 30.26.
12. Ps. 27.10.
13. Cp. Num. 11.12.
14. Job 34.15; Eccl. 3.20.

15. The text reads, 'How can I *stumble*' (Heb. *ekshôl*),
    which makes no sense. A slight emendation (viz.
    askîl) yields the meaning given in the translation; cp.
    Hymns, xi.28; xii.13.
16. John 1.3.

16

1. Ezek. 38.12, 13.
2. Jer. 17.8; Ps. 1.3.
3. Ezek. 17.8, 23; 36.8, 30.
4. The Hebrew words could also mean, 'those that
   espouse (lit. the sons of) Thy truth', but it seems to
   me that a pointed contrast is intended between the
   lowly estate of the Brotherhood and the worldly wealth
   of the impious. For the Hebrew expression, cp. Pss.
   86.16; 116.16.
5. Cf. *Manual*, v.20–24.
6. Restoring *yk[bd]*. This supplies the necessary contrast
   between the 'lowly servant' and the 'high and mighty'.
7. Philo (*Quod Omnis Probus Liber*, 11) says of the
   Essenes, a group akin to, or identical with, the Qumran
   Brotherhood: 'They do not lay up treasure of gold and
   silver, nor acquire real estate out of a desire for rev-
   enues, but provide themselves only with the bare neces-
   sities of life'. Similarly, Josephus observes (*War*, II,
   viii, 2) that 'they despise riches', and Pliny (*Natural
   History*, v. 17) that 'they live without money'.
8. I.e., in contrast to the 'running streams' and produce
   of the earth on which the impious rely.
9. Hos. 14.6.
10. Cp. Ps. 103.20; *Hymns*, viii.11.
11. Final judgment with the aid of the angels is foretold
    in the Book of Enoch (e.g., 53.3; 63.1; 93.15) and
    in the Qumran *Sermon on the Last Jubilee;* cf. also
    Hymns iii.3; vi.29f.; *War*, xv.14. Based on Zech. 14.3,
    5.
12. Cp. Prov. 7.27.
13. Restored simply *ad sensum*.
14. Job 3.10.

17

1. Literally, 'circumcision of lips'. The expression is modelled on the Biblical 'one of uncircumcised lips'= 'stammerer' (Ex. 6.12, 30).
2. Isa. 41.14.
3. Literally, 'those versed in concerted song'. The Jewish Daily Morning Service speaks of the angelic choir as 'all of them opening their mouths in holiness and purity, in song and chant, blessing, praising, glorifying, and proclaiming both the awe and the holiness and the sovereignty of God . . . all of them giving accord to one another to praise their Creator in tranquillity of spirit and with holy chant; all of them taking up word as one and saying, Holy, holy, holy is the Lord of Hosts; the fullness of the whole earth is His glory'.
4. On regeneration as a mystical experience, see E. Underhill, *Mysticism* (ed. 1955), pp. 53f.

18

1. II Sam. 22.3, 47; Pss. 19.15(14); 28.1; 62.3, 7(2, 6); 144.1, etc.
2. Lam. 2.18.
3. Job 3.10.
4. Cp. Avesta, *Yasht* 31.20, etc.
5. Cp. Isa. 35.10; 51.11.

19

1. The metaphor is taken from childbirth.
2. Cp. Ps. 138.3.
3. Restored from Ps. 118.15.
4. Cp. note 7 to *Column XVII*.
5-6. Cp. *Hymn of the Initiants*, 1–10.
7. I.e., their several governing constellations.
8. Literally, 'I have heard faithfully (reliably)'.
9. Cp. Note 11 to Hymn 6.

[*From this point it becomes impossible to distinguish the separate hymns. The notes are therefore geared to the columns of the original text.*]

Column XIII

1. The restoration is tentative, but it is obvious from the sequel that these lines must have recited the doctrine that all things have been endowed with spirit and intelligence wherewith to perceive the truth and reality of God. This is scarcely to be confused with the later more elaborate doctrine of the Gnostics.
2. Cp. *Manual of Discipline*, iv.7; I Peter 5.4.
3. I.e., the angels. For this term, cp. *Hymns*, x.28; Enoch 24.6.
4. The reference is to the doctrine of the eschatological renewal of the world; see Analytical Index, E. 3, Rewards (*a*).
5. Literally, 'Abolishing ancient existences and [establi]shing the things that (currently) obtain in the world'.
6. Cp. Zech. 3.8. In rabbinic usage, the term is applied to a great scholar, i.e., a 'prodigy' of learning or piety.
7. Isa. 66.24. (Cp. also Dan. 12.2.)
8. Restored on the basis of Jos. 23.14.
9. Cp. Ps. 111.2 (which the author must have understood to mean 'sought out for their several purposes', rather than 'sought out [or, studied] by all who have pleasure in them', as usually rendered).

Column XIV

1. Restored on the basis of Ezra 9.8.
2. Another possible restoration is: 'men of truth and dis[cernment]'.
3. Restored from Ex. 19.6.
4. The fourth the Eighteen Benedictions which form a staple element of all Jewish devotions ends: 'Blessed art Thou, O Lord, Who gracest man with knowledge'.
5. Cp. *Manual of Discipline*, i.3–4.

6. Probably in the technical sense of admission to the Brotherhood; cp. *Hymn of the Initiants*, note 32.
7. Cp. *Manual*, ix.20.
8. Cp. *Manual*, iv.1.
9. See above, note 4.
10. Hos. 14.5.

Column XV

1. Hos. 14.5.
2. Ps. 37.23; Prov. 20.24.
3. Josephus (*Ant.*, XIII, 5, 9) says of the Essenes that they believed all things were pre-ordained.
4. Literally, 'Thou hast prepared him for the Era of Favor'; see Analytical Index, E. 1 (*c*).
5. Isa. 45.17.
6. See Analytical Index, E. 1 (*a*).

Column XVI

1. Isa. 6.3.
2. In general, I here follow the restorations suggested by J. Licht (*The Thanksgiving Scroll* [1957], p. 202), except that in line 4 I read *bᵉ-Toratᵉchāh* for his *bᵉ-goralᵉchāh* ('in Thy lot') and in line 5 I read [*wa-tᵉ'ammᵉṣêhû*] for his [*wa-tᵉyassᵉrēhû*] and, at the end, *bᵉ-kôl mi[ṣ'adāw]* for his *bᵉ-kôl mi[shpaṭêchah]* ('in all Thy judgments').
3. Jer. 32.19.
4. On this concept, cf. T. H. Gaster, *Thespis*² (1961), pp. 288f.
5. Cp. *Manual*, iii.20ff.
6. Exod. 34.5, 7–9.
7. The reference is to Ex. 34.5ff., just quoted. According to the Talmud (*Rôsh Ha-Shanah*, 17b), this formula was prescribed by God as that which Israel was to repeat when entreating forgiveness of sins. For that reason, it runs like a refrain through the Confessions on the Day of Atonement.

Columns XVII–XVIII

1. Ex. 34.5ff.
2. Deut. 32.22.
3. Cp. Ps. 102.29(28).
4. Ex. 34.6.
5. Cp. Mic. 7.19, and see T. H. Gaster, *Festivals of the Jewish Year* (1953), pp. 121–23.
6. The reference is to the *two* spirits described in the *Manual of Discipline*, cols. iii–iv.
7. The terms employed in the Hebrew (viz. *tefillah* and *taḥanun*) denote in Jewish usage statutory and spontaneous prayer.
8. An adaptation of Dan. 9.7, the Hebrew word *zedaqah*, which there means 'righteousness', being taken in in its later sense of 'charity, bounty'. Similarly, the common phrase, 'To Thy name pertains blessing', is taken to mean 'And of Thy nature it is to bestow blessing'.
9. The restoration is based on the obviously implied contrast between covenants made by men and those made by God.
10. Isa. 60.19–20.
11. The clue to this very difficult passage is to be found, I think, in the sequence of the phrases, 'The hands of Thy servant were steadied' and 'that he might triumph in glory'; for these expressions hark back to the incident related in Ex. 17.8–13. During the battle against Amalek at Rephidim, 'when Moses held up his hand, Israel *triumphed;* and when he let down his hand, Amalek *triumphed.* But Moses' hands grew heavy . . . so Aaron and Hur stayed up his hands on either side; *and his hands were steady* until the going down of the sun'. The allusion, therefore, is to Moses, though the poet obviously uses the Biblical expressions in an extended sense.
12. Isa. 61.1. (The prototype of the term 'gospel'!)

13. Isa. 61.2–3.
14. Ezek. 11.19; 36.26.
15. Heb. *Ôr-Tôm;* cp. Introduction, p. 21.

Fragments

1

1. For this designation, cp. *Manual,* vii.6; xii; *MFC* ii.8; *Blessings,* iii.6; *Oration,* ii.8; *War,* vii.6; x.ii; *AL(a).*
2. Cp. Judges 13.18.
3. Cp. *Hymns* i.30, 33; iii.23; vi.ii; x.20.
4. Cp. *Hymns* xii.12; frag. x.3.
5. Cp. *Hymns* x.12; xii.31; frag. iv.ii.
6. Cp. *Hymns* iv.19; vi.22.
7. Literally, 'in guilt of wickedness', cp. *Hymns* vi.22.
8. Literally, 'through Eras of Wrath'. For this eschatological term, cp. Analytical Index, E. 1 (a).
9. Cp. *Hymns* i.18, 32; ii.7; iv.36; ix.10, 12; xi.8, 12.
10. Cp. *Hymns* iii.30; vi.6; ix.14.
11. Cp. *Hymns* i.21; iii.24; iv.29; xii.26, 32; frag. xi.7 (?).
12. Cp. *Hymns* xi.7.
13. Cp. *Hymns* xiii.18–19.
14. Literally, 'in my time(s)'; cf. Analytical Index, E. 1.

2

1. Literally, 'in conformity with the abundance of Thy mercies'.
2. In the Hebrew, the image appears to be that of a city under siege.
3. Literally, 'mediators of knowledge (gnosis)'; cp. *Hymns* ii.13.
4. Literally, 'men who reprimand them in accordance with truth'.
5. For this use of the Hebrew word *('abnāyîm)*, cp. Jer. 18.3.

6. The picture is that of a craftsman inspecting his products and giving them the stamp of his approval; cp. T. H. Gaster, *Myth, Legend, and Custom in the Old Testament* (1969), §6.

7. The restoration is due to J. Licht, though he understands the Hebrew words in the sense of 'bandage his wound(s)', which misses the metaphor.

8. Cp. Lev. 12.8; 16.30; Num. 8.21.

9. See Analytical Index, F. 2 (c).

3

1. Prov. 3.17.

2. Cp. Joel 2.26.

3. Cp. Jer. 18.22; Pss. 140.6; 142.4.

4. The subject is supplied from the subsequent reference to '*its* traps . . . *its* net'.

5. Cp. Ps. 35.7; Prov. 29.5; Lam. 1.3.

6. Cp. Pss. 55.9; 107.25; 148.8.

7. The restoration is a mere guess.

8. Cp. Job 18.9.

9. Literally, 'every inclination to deceit'.

10. I Sam. 2.3; cp. *Manual*, iii.15; *Hymns* i.26; xii.10.

11. Cp. II Chron. 20.6.

12. Tentative restoration: [*lifqod kôl bᵉnê 'asha*]*mah;* cp. *Hymns* v.7; vi.30; vii.11.

13. Cp. Ps. 59.4.

14. Reading (with Yadin) *wᵉ-ḥadal zādôn.* The rendering attempts to reproduce the imagery of the latter word; commonly rendered 'arrogance, presumption', it actually derives from the root *z-y-d,* 'seethe, bubble up', and refers to the seething of wickedness within the soul.

15. For the sentiment, cp. *HabC,* xi.1. The metaphor is taken from the fact that filth and insanitary conditions (*niddah*) lead to symptoms of disease (*taḥᵃlū'îm*).

16. Literally, 'judgments of plague/stroke'; cp. *Hymns* i.33; xi.8.

17. Cp. *'Zadokite' Document,* ii.4.

4

1. Restored from Hab. 2.1.
2. Zech. 3.2. The word here rendered 'rebuke' carries the meaning 'exorcize', as in the incident in *The Memoirs of the Patriarchs* where Abram expels Pharaoh's sickness. The word rendered 'devil' is *satan*, here used generically, as in *Hymns* frag. xiv.3; *Blessings*, i.8.
3. Cp. *Hymns* ix.14–15.
4. Cp. Jer. 4.19; 48.26.
5. Ps. 22.15.
6. Restoring tentatively, [*kissî*]*timoh*.
7. I Sam. 2.3; cp. *Manual*, iii.15; *Hymns* i.26; xii.10.
8. A probable supplement is *qişşê* [*ḥārôn*], lit. 'the times of (Divine) Wrath'. For this eschatological term, cp. Analytical Index, E. 1 (*a*).

5

1. Cp. *Hymns* i.23, 26, 30.
2. Cp. *Hymns* iii.21; frag. vii.11 (?).
3. Cp. *War*, xii.7; *Hymns* frag. xxiv.2; *HFCi* 9.12; *Blessings*, i.5.
4. *War*, x.14.
5. The manuscript's unintelligible *tbw/yt* is, I think, a scribal error for t<*sh*>*byt*; cp. Ezek. 23.48.
6. Restoring *ro*[*gez*], after Job 3.19. An alternative, suggested by J. Licht, is *ri*[*sh'ah*], when the meaning will be, 'Thou wilt lay waste (every) place of wickedness'.
7. Cp. *Manual*, iv.13; *Hymns* ii.15; xi.22.
8. Literally, 'for the generations of eternity'; cp. *Hymns* i.16.
9. Tentatively restored: *li-me*[*hūmah*] *rabbah*; cp. *Hymns* xii.8.
10. The obscure word *'nînam* is here interpreted from the Heb. *'-n-n* (and Arabic cognate) meaning 'to feel inner grief', *le-chalah* being regarded as adverbial, as in, e.g., Exod. 11.1.

11. Restoring, with J. Licht, w^e-lif[$hôd$]; cp. Manual, iv.2; Hymns x.34; frag. iv.9.

12. Ps. 31.22; cp. War, xiv.9.

13. Literally, 'an ear of flesh . . . a mind of flesh'. Perhaps the poet is referring to a personal, not a general, revelation.

14. Cp. Hymns iv.13, 21.

15. Literally, 'Thou hast given to the heart of . . . an understanding of the Time (Era) of Witness'. For this eschatological term, cp. Hymns, frag. lix.3. For the concept, cp. Enoch, xcvii.4; xcix.8; c.10–11. The missing word may be b^e-[$hîrêchah$], 'Thine elect, chosen ones'.

16. Cp. Hymns x.35.

17. The expression is adapted from Isa. 24.21.

18. Cp. War, iii.6. See also Analytical Index, D. 3.

19. Restored after 'Zadokite' Document, iv.7.

20. See Analytical Index, A. 7.

POEMS FROM A QUMRAN HYMNAL

I. David

1. Cp. I Sam. 16.11. But here the word has special point, because kings were commonly required to be taller than any of their subjects. This is said explicitly of Saul (I Sam. 10.23), of Xerxes (Herodotus, vii, 187) and of the kings of Ethiopia (Athenaeus, xiii, 20). In the Akkadian 'Epic of Creation' (Enuma elish, i.99), Marduk, who assumes sovereignty over the gods, is said to be of exceptional stature. Conversely, in the Canaanite Poem of Baal (II AB, ii.59–60), the young Ashtar is rejected as successor to Baal because he is too small. See T. H. Gaster, Myth, Legend, and Custom in the Old Testament (1969), §127.

2. The Hebrew word combines the notions of youngest and least significant. Indeed, a late midrash asserts that David was the latter only, the youngest son of Jesse having been Elihu, mentioned in I Chron. 27.18. See L. Ginzberg, Legends of the Jews, vi.249, n. 23.

3. David is here described as the shepherd and 'ruler' of Jesse's lambs and kids (not even full-grown goats!) in contemptuous contradistinction to his eventual role as shepherd and ruler of God's flock. For 'shepherd'= 'king', cp., in the Old Testament, II Sam. 5.2; 7.7; Jer. 3.15. Mesopotamian and Homeric kings likewise affected this title.

4. Literally, 'cannot testify', but the word has the connotation of *oral* deposition; and that is here the point.

5. That is, my songs of praise.

6. That is, my proficiency in tending the sheep. (The word does not mean simply 'my works' in the sense of 'my compositions'.)

7. Cp. I Sam. 16.12.

8. Cp. I Sam. 16.7ff.

9. Cp. Gen. 39.6.

10. Cp. I Sam. 16.7.

11. Cp. I Sam. 16.8; Ps. 78.70–71.

12. For this title cp. I Sam. 9.16; 13.14; 25.30; Isa. 55.4.

II. Invitation to Grace After Meals

1. Literally, 'multitude'.

2. Literally, 'confess the majesty of His name'. The 'name' in Hebrew signifies also the outward manifestation.

3. Verses 1–2, missing in the Qumran manuscript, are here supplied from the Syriac version.

4. Literally, 'unite your (individual) selves'.

5. Literally, 'of the Most High'. The meaning is that there is a supernal power which works salvation.

6. The Hebrew means simply, 'join in fellowship together', the expression being modelled (as again in v.13) on Ps. 122.3. To render, 'form a community', and to draw therefrom a reference to the Qumran Brotherhood, strains the syntax.

7. Literally, 'multitude'.

8. The word, 'Lord' (Heb. '*Adôn*), has special point: the meaning is that although the Most High is the particular Lord of Israel, His sovereignty is universal.

9. Literally, 'avow the majesty of the Most High'.
10. For the Hebrew expression (though in a slightly different sense), cp. Num. 4.3; Ps. 20.4.
11. Cp. Deut. 8.10.
12. The manuscript has 'eyes', but the verb is in the singular. Hence the text must be corrected in accordance with the Syriac version.
13. For this expression cp. Isa. 32.2; Jer. 14.8; 15.11; 30.7; Ps. 37.39. In the Qumran texts it has a quasi-eschatological meaning, as in Dan. 12.1.
14. Literally, 'establish/upraise the horn'—a common Biblical expression for 'triumph'. It is not clear whether this refers to the triumph of Israel in general (as in Ezek. 29.21; Ps. 148.14) or, more specifically, to the raising up of a future Messianic King (as in Ps. 132.17). I think the former is more probable; see next note.
15. Literally 'and from Israel a judge of peoples'. It is not clear whether this means that God will raise up from Israel one who will be judge of all peoples, or that He Himself is such a judge. In light of Ps. 67.4, whence the expression is taken and where it refers to God, I think the latter more probable, the strict translation then being, '(Bless the Lord) . . . Who judges (all) peoples from Israel'. Nor do I think that 'judges' here refers to the Final Judgment; the Hebrew word means simply 'governs'. The sentiment is that of Isa. 2.3.
16. This expression echoes Exod. 33.7. The verse, missing from the manuscript, is here supplied from the Syriac version.

III. Plea for Grace

1. Jer. 18.19.
2. From v. 13 it is apparent that the poet is praying for relief from sickness, albeit only metaphorical. The verse therefore harks back to the words of I Kings 8.38f. (=II Chron. 6.29): 'If plague or sickness befall them, then hear the prayer or supplication of every man . . . as each one spreads out his hands (lit. palms)

towards this house; hear it in heaven Thy dwelling and forgive, and act' (NEB). For the expression, 'Thy holy abode', cp. also Deut. 26.15; Jer. 25.30; Zech. 2.17; Ps. 68.6; II Chron. 30.27.

3. Cp. Isa. 37.17; Pss. 17.6; 31.3; 86.1.

4. Cp. I Sam. 1.27; Ps. 106.15.

5. Reading *tipparē'a* (3rd sg. fem.), and taking the subject to be *nafshî* ('my soul') in the preceding line. Cp. Wolsey's 'If I had served my God with half the zeal/I served my king, He would not in mine age/ have left me naked to mine enemies': Shakespeare, *Henry VIII*, iii,2.

6. Vocalizing *gᵉmūlî*, rather than *gᵉmulê*, as in the *editio princeps*.

7. Reading *ȳashūb*, rather than *yāshîb*, as in the *editio princeps*.

8. This is the epithet applied to God in the traditional blessing on hearing bad news; cf. Mishnah, *Bᵉrāchôth*, ix.2.

9. Cp. Ps. 143.2.

10. Cp. Ps. 119.34.

11. Cp. Ps. 119.7, 108.

12. The expression is suggested by Ps. 145.5.

13. Cp. Ps. 25.7.

14. The expression is borrowed from the law concerning persons afflicted with skin diseases: Lev. 13.6, 17; 14.48. The words rendered 'noisome plague' there mean specifically 'foul blot, blotch'. Here they may be understood either literally or metaphorically.

15. Cp. Lev. 14.43.

16. Cp. Hos. 9.16; Job 18.16.

17. Emending after the Syriac version, *kabbîr* for the *kābôd* of the Qumran text. The point is that the might of God is contrasted with the ineffective power of men.

18. Vocalizing *shallemah* (imperat., with 3rd sg. fem. objective suffix), rather than *shᵉlēmah* (adj. 'complete'), as in the *editio princeps*.

19. Cp. Job 17.9.

20. Cp. Pss. 3.5; 120.1; Job 9.16.

21. Cp. Ps. 3.6.

22. Cp. Ps. 102.5.
23. Cp. Ps. 3.6.
24. Cp. Pss. 40.18; 70.16; 144.2, etc.
25. The Hebrew word *bôsheth*, usually rendered 'shame', also means 'disappointment', and this is the meaning here, in contrast to the preceding affirmation (v. 17), 'From Thee comes my confidence, O Lord'.
26. Cp. Ps. 25.20.
27. Cp. Ps. 25.22.
28. Heb. *ḥasîdêchā*, usually rendered 'Thy devout ones'; but *ḥesed* also denotes the mutual loyalty involved in a covenantal relationship.

IV. Supplication

1. For the sentiment, cp. Isa. 38.18–19, 'The netherworld cannot confess Thee; Death cannot shout Thy praise . . . The living, the living it is who (alone) can confess Thee'.
2. Job 12.10.
3. Literally, 'acts of *ṣedaqah*'. This word, which normally means 'righteousness', is here used in the post-Biblical sense of 'charity, benevolence'.
4. Cp. Pss. 5.12; 69.37; 119.132.
5. Ruth 2.20.
6. Ps. 103.6.
7. Ps. 103.4.
8. Ps. 92.3.
9. Cp. Isa. 50.1.
10. Cp. Isa. 30.2; Pss. 36.8; 57.2(1).
11. Cp. Targums to Deut. 15.7; Pss. 27.14; 31.25. For an analogous expression, cp. *'Zadokite' Document*, iii.3.
12. Num. 14.9; Jer. 33.8; Ps. 51.4.
13. Jer. 33.8; Ezek. 36.3.
14. Cp. in the 'Eighteen Benedictions' of the Jewish liturgy: 'Thou hast vouchsafed knowledge to man'. Here, the 'knowledge' is virtually gnosis.
15. For the quasi-Aramaic phrasing in the original, cp. Targum to Hos. 5.5; 14.2.

16. Heb. *satan*, but here probably in the sense of *a*, rather than *the*, satan, i.e., an adversary spirit. For this usage, common in later magical texts, cp. *Hymns* frags. iv.6; xiv.3; *Blessings*, ii.8. For the sentiment, cp. Ps. 119.113.

17. This expression, familiar especially from the New Testament (Mat. 10.1; 12.43; Mark 1.23ff.; 3.11, 30; 5.2, 8, 13; 6.7; 9.25; Luke 4.33, 36; 6.18; 8.29; 9.42; 11.24; Acts 5.16) and from later rabbinic writings, is not found elsewhere in the Dead Sea Scrolls thus far published.

18. Literally, 'Thou, O Lord, art (the object of) my praise'. What this means is not simply that the writer extols God, but that the indwelling spirit of God is the source of his human worth and esteem. This contrasts with the notion of demonic possession.

19. Ps. 25.5.

V. The City of God

1. Cp. Prov. 10.1.
2. Deut. 6.5.
3. Ps. 112.6.
4. Heb., by hendiadys, 'peace and longing hope'. Possibly, however, the meaning is that Zion hopes for peace; cp. Jer. 8.15; 14.19.
5. Isa. 56.1; Lam. 3.22.
6. Literally, 'for generation upon generation'.
7. Literally, 'generations'.
8. Literally, 'would suck the teat of thy glory'; cp. Isa. 66.11.
9. Suggested by the meaning traditionally assigned to a rare word ('-*k-s*) in Isa. 3.16.
10. The reference is to gentiles; cf. *Manual*, v.6; '*Zadokite*' *Document*, iv.3; Isa. 14.1; 50.5; 56.3; Zeph. 2.15.
11. Gen. 49.18.
12. Isa. 66.10. For *tmyk*, at the end of the line (which cannot mean 'thy perfect ones', since this would require *tmymyk*), I emend to the very similar *tmyd*, 'always'. The scribe evidently miscopied.

13. For the wording, cp. Ezek. 19.5; 37.11; Ps. 9.9; Prov. 10.28; 11.7; Job 8.13; 14.19.

14. Imitated from Job 4.7. (Possibly, 'righteousness' [*ṣdq*] is a scribal error for 'a righteous man' [*ṣdyk*].)

15. Literally, 'roundabout, on all sides'.

16. Cp. Targum Onqelos to Num. 10.35.

17. Literally, 'pleasant in . . .'

18. The causative form of the verb (if indeed it is a verb rather than simply the adverb meaning 'above') indicates that the image is that of an incense-offering whose aroma rises.

19. Deut. 6.5—the complement to 'with all my might' in v.1.

20. Cp. Dan. 9.24.

21. Literally 'blessings of men held in honor'. I take the genitive to be objective, rather than subjective. Zion is envisaged as a conquering hero receiving plaudits.

22. Literally, 'receive the vision'. This, I think, means 're-ceive what has been envisaged', rather than 'compre-hend the prophecy'.

23. The reference is more specifically to Dan. 9.24.

24. This line is obscure, involving a word—*ttb'k*—of un-certain meaning and seemingly anomalous form. My translation (which is provisional) is reached by taking it as a parallel to *qh* 'receive', rather than to *dūbar*, 'spoken', in the preceding line, by parsing it as a noun (on the pattern of *talmūd, takrîk*, etc.), and by deriv-ing it from a root akin to Arabic *t-b-'*, 'follow', in the sense of 'consequence'.

25. Literally, 'in thy glory/honor my soul will rejoice'. I take the 'glory/honor' to be that which will eventually be restored.

VI. Morning Hymn

1. Cp. Ezek. 28.23 and the opening words of the Jewish Kaddish-prayer.

2. Literally, 'from one generation to another'.

3. Cp. Ps. 96.6; I Chron. 16.27. Here the reference is, more specifically, to the splendor of sunrise.

4. The reference is to the swelling of tides at daybreak—an interpretation which I owe to my daughter, Corinna. The glow of dawn forms the foreground, the rush of the tides the background, of the daily theophany, when the sun seems to rise out of the ocean.

5. The image is that of courtiers in attendance on a king. For the wording, cp. Ps. 89.15. The unfolding scene at daybreak attests both the beneficence of God and His constancy (truth; Heb. *'emeth*) in maintaining His creation.

6. The manifestation of God's presence in the sunrise bespeaks His sovereignty over the world, but—in contrast to that of earthly monarchs—His is a sovereignty founded on Justice and Right. For the wording, cp. Ps. 97.2. (The manuscript reads, 'Truth and Justice and Right', but the word *Truth* overloads the meter; it is simply vertical dittography from the preceding line.)

7. Gen. 1.4, 18; Enoch 41.8.

8. Literally, 'by the knowledge of His heart/mind'.

9. At first blush, this line might be rendered, 'established the dawn'; but the Hebrew word for 'established' (viz. *hekîn*) here bears a technical sense, attested in Prov. 4.18 and Hos. 6.3 (which many modern scholars needlessly emend), and refers to the sun's eventually standing at the meridian. (The cognate Akkadian *kânu* is similarly employed of a celestial body's reaching its zenith.)

10. Cp. Job 38.7. The reason why the poet here introduces parenthetically a 'flashback' to the original creation is that, in Jewish belief, the birth of each new day is in fact a repetition of that primordial event. Says the *Yoṣer*-hymn for sabbaths and festivals: 'He reneweth every day continually the work of the Creation'.

11. For the wording, cp. *Hymns* xiii.11.

12. Cp. Ps. 65.12 (where, incidentally, for the anomalous *shᵉnath*, 'year', we should perhaps read, *maʻᵃnôth*,

'furrows'). Again a picture suggested by the landscape revealed at sunrise.

13. The following verses are taken from Jer. 10.12–13; 51.15–16; Ps. 135.7. Note that *knowledge* and *understanding* are mentioned in Exod. 31.3 as the special qualities of the *human* artisan, Bezalel.

14. Cp. also Enoch 41.3. The reference is here more specifically to the cool breezes at dawn—especially welcome in the torrid heat of the Dead Sea area!

15. The reference is more specifically to the electric storms which, in the Holy Land and in Syria, presage the onset of the 'early rains' in late September. Native Arabs have a saying, 'The lightning is a token of rain'; cp. T. H. Gaster, *Myth, Legend, and Custom in the Old Testament* (1969, 1975), §201.

16. A picture suggested more specifically by the rising of mountain mists in the early morning.

Lament for Zion

1. Reading [*dibrê ha-tᵉ'ū*]*dah*, with reference especially to Deut. 30.19; 31.28.

2. Cp. Deut. 28.32.

3. Again a reference to the wording of the 'Great Commination'; cp. Deut. 28.20.

4. Restoring, [*hefarnū*] *et bᵉrîtô*; cp. Deut. 31.14, 26.

5. Isa. 64.10.

6. Ibidem.

7. A tentative restoration, after Psalms of Solomon 2.2. This detail is mentioned likewise in the medieval dirge, *Zᵉchôr 'ᵃsher 'āśah ṣār*, chanted in the synagogue on the Fast of Ab (verse 6).

8. Or, ['meal-offering and libation have been cut off']; cp. Joel 1.8.

9. Cp. Zeph. 2.15.

10. Restoring *wᵉ'ên ma*[*ṣṣîl*]; cp. Isa. 5.29; Pss. 7.3; 50.22.

11. Cp. Lam. 1.4.

12. Cp. Jer. 9.10; 10.22; 34.22.

13. Restored after Jer. 6.8.

14. Cp. Jer. 38.4; similar is Ps. 142.5.
15. Tentatively restored after Isa. 53.4.
16. Literally, 'and all our foes [   ]'. Restored after Lam. 1.15.
17. Cp. Isa. 59.12.
18. Ps. 78.21.
19. I.e., the corpses of the slain defile the holiness of the city. Cp. *Baruch* 3.10. Cp. also Isa. 59.10.
20. Literally, 'cruel women'; cp. Lam. 4.3.
21. Restored *ad sensum;* cp. I Maccabees 1.26.
22. Cp. Lam. 1.16.
23. Restoring, [ḥibbᵉqū] 'ashpôtôt (= 'ashpātôt); cp. Lam. 4.5.
24. Cp. Lam. 4.2.
25. Cp. Lam. 4.5.
26. Cp. Ezek. 16.10–13. (The reading in the *editio princeps* is egregiously wrong!)
27. Cp. Lam. 1.1.
28. Ibidem.
29. Cp. Isa. 54.6. My rendering seeks to reproduce a play on words ('ᵃzūbah-'ᵃṣūbah) in the Hebrew.
30. There is a *double entente* in the original, the Hebrew word '-q-r denoting both the razing of a structure and the barrenness of a woman. The words inserted in parentheses are designed to bring out the point. The same metaphor is employed in the Babylonian recension of a traditional dirge for the Fast of Ab: S. Baer, ed., *'Abôdat Israel*, 96, line 8.
31. Allegro's reading, *u-kmskkt*, could mean only 'like a woman *who plaits, interweaves*', but this makes no sense, and his interpretation of the word as a passive participle meaning *who is shut away* is impossible. It seems to me that the correct reading is *u-kmsknt*, 'like a woman *left beggared*', i.e. dispossessed.
32. Cp. Gen. 26.35; I Sam. 1.10; Isa. 22.4; Ezek. 21.11.
33. Cp. Jer. 6.26; Amos 8.10; Zech. 12.10.
34. Lam. 1.2.
35. Restoring [ḥêlî]la[h] wᵉ-hagᵉtah; cp. Isa. 16.7; Jer. 48.31.

Hymns of Triumph

I

1. Cp. Ps. 148.13. Literally, 'sing hallelujahs to the name of the Lord'. The name is the visible presence.
2. Cp. Pss. 104.39; 144.20.
3. Cp. Deut. 33.28; Prov. 3.20.
4. Cp. Isa. 60.18. 'Their' refers to the righteous.
5. Cp. Lev. 26.4; Deut. 11.17; Ezek. 34.27; Ps. 67.7.
6. Cp. Ps. 22.7.

II

1. Cp. Ps. 69.35.
2. There may be a subtle point in this phrase: in Job 38.7 it is said that the stars of morning chanted in chorus at the dawn of creation. Now it will be the stars that have been glimmering through Israel's dark night that will do the same.
3. Cp. Nahum 2.1.
4. Cp. Ps. 92.10.
5. Cp. Ps. 104.31.

THE MERCY OF GOD

A Prayer for Intercession

O Thou Who art all-good, whose mercies never fail; Thou Who art all-merciful, whose graces never end: ever have we hoped in Thee.

JEWISH DAILY SERVICE

INTRODUCTION

The *Prayer for Intercession* is preserved in an incomplete scroll which also contains liturgical pieces for the various days of the week. It is followed immediately by a rubric reading *Hymns for the Sabbath Day*. On the back of the scroll are inscribed two words—evidently a librarian's notation—which mean literally 'words of the luminaries (heavenly lights)'. The purport of this legend has yet to be discovered. It has been proposed by the first editor of the document that this prayer was believed to be one uttered by the heavenly lights as part of the celestial liturgy of the angels. The concept of such a liturgy is certainly well attested in Jewish mystical literature,* and fragments of two extracts from an angelic order of service have indeed turned up at Qumran.† It seems difficult, however, to reconcile this explanation with the marked emphasis throughout our text on the particular fortunes and misfortunes *of Israel,* or with the fact that in speaking of the latter, the writer constantly says 'we, us, our'. The suggestion may therefore be offered that the enigmatic legend is simply the equivalent of 'matins', the prayer being designed for recital in the early morning service. In support of this suggestion, it may be pointed out that an essential and ancient element of the traditional Jewish morning service is indeed the blessing of God as creator of the luminaries (*yôṣer ha-ME'OROTH*, the same Hebrew word), and that the Mishnah says explicitly (Megillah iv.6) that no man should recite the morning Shema' who

---

* See S. Baer, *Seder 'Abodath Israel* (1868), p. 120; L. Ginzberg, *Legends of the Jews,* v (1947), p. 25.

† See below, pp. 285ff.

is blind and cannot actually behold the luminaries (*me'ôrôth*). Just as that traditional Jewish prayer came to be known conventionally as *Yôṣer*—from the words *yôṣer ha-me'ôrôth*, 'Creator of the luminaries'—so the men of Qumran may have called its equivalent *Me'ôrôth*—simply 'Luminaries'—for short.

The place of the piece in the collection, viz. *after* the prayers for the several days of the week and *before* those for the sabbath, may simply indicate that it was recited on *all* days of the week and not, as were the others, on any one or other particular day.

The theme of the prayer is the eternal forbearance of God in the face of constant provocation by His people. A continuance of the same forbearance is besought in their current hour of distress. I have been especially careful in my translation to bring out this *leitmotif*, for it is the essence of the piece.

In view of the foregoing considerations, it has seemed to me best to give this composition the neutral title *Prayer for Intercession*.

PRAYER FOR INTERCESSION

LORD, we beseech Thee, do as Thou art,[1]
in accordance with the greatness of Thy power,[2]
Thou Who (of old) didst forgive our fathers,
what time they rebelled against Thy word.[3]
Though Thou wast angry with them, to destroy them,[4]
yet, through Thy love of them and for Thy Covenant's
    sake,
Thou didst spare them,
in that Moses won clearance of their sin.[5]

So now, we beseech Thee,
to the end that Thy great power may be known,
and the abundance of Thy mercies also,
unto all generations for ever,
let Thine anger and Thy wrath be turned away from Thy
    people Israel,
and, besides their sins,
remind Thyself also of Thy peculiar favors[6]
which Thou hast (alway) wrought for us in the sight of
    the nations,
because Thou hast claimed us as Thine own.[7]

[Vouchsafe, we beseech Thee,
to tu]rn us again unto Thee with all our heart and soul,[8]
and so to plant Thy teaching‡ in our hearts[9]
that we depart not from it to right or left,
Thou having cured us of madness and blindness and be-
    wilderment of heart.[10]

‡ Heb. *Torah.*

¶Behold, when (of old) we were sold by our wrongdoings,[11]
even amid our transgressions didst Thou call us[12]
. . . and didst rescue us from (further) sinning against
Thee.
[Moreover, Thou didst vouchsafe unto us
to know the mysteries of Thy Tru]th[13]
and to understand the evidences (of Thee),
in that Thou didst [gre]at . . . .

. . . .

III

¶Behold, all the nations were deemed as naught before
Thee,
as emptiness and nothingness in Thy presence,[14]
but us—since we owned ourselves Thine alone,[15]
and since Thou hadst created us unto Thy glory[16]—
us didst Thou treat as Thy children[17] in the sight of the
nations,
calling Israel, 'My son, My firstborn'.[18]
And though Thou didst chastise us,
as a man might chastise his son,[19]
yet didst Thou grant us increase
throughout the years of our generations.
Thou didst not [abandon us
neither suffer] hunger or thirst, plague or sword [to consume us]
but didst ever fulfill Thy Covenant (with us).

¶(So too,) because Thou hadst chosen us for Thine
own[20]
[out of all the peoples of] the earth,
therefore although, when Thine anger was kindled,
Thou didst pour on us Thy wrath and Thy fiery rage,
and cause to cleave unto us[21] [all] Thy [plagues and
str]okes
which Moses had prescribed[22]
and (likewise) Thy servants the prophets

whom Thou didst send to [procla]im unto us the evil
which was to befall us in latter times[23]
—when [our priests (?)] and kings [brake faith with Thee]
by taking to wife the daughters of [the heathen],[24]
thereby [   ] and acting corruptly[25]—
[yet didst Thou not abjure] Thy Covenant, neither [reject
    us,
to wipe out] the seed of Israel

. . . .

  (Nay,) Thou dost ever deal justly with them that cl[ing
    unto Thee],[26]
and dost [   ]

. . . .

                                     IV
  ¶(So too,) because Thou didst love Israel above all
    peoples,
and didst choose the tribe of Judah,
[Thou didst set] Thy dwelling [in Zion],
[and] a resting-place [for Thy glory] in Jerusa[lem],[27]
[the city which Thou hadst chos]en out of all the earth,
that Thy [name] might abide§ there for ever;
and Thou didst also fulfill Thy covenant with David
that he should be shepherd, leader o'er Thy people,[28]
and that (his offspring) should sit alway in Thy presence
on the throne of Israel.[29]
And all the nations beheld Thy glory,
ensconced as Thou wast in holiness amid Thy people Israel,
<and they made obeisance to Thee> and to Thy great
    name,
and brought their tribute of silver and gold and precious
    stones
together with all the choice things of their lands,
to do honor unto Thy people,
and unto Zion, Thy holy city,
and unto Thy glorious House.[30]
Nor was adversary there nor misfortune,[31]

  § Heb. 'be'.

but only peace and blessing;
men ate and filled themselves and waxed fat[32] [   ]

. . . .

V

¶(So too,) though they had forsaken that fount of liv-
    ing waters[33]
[which Thou hadst opened for them for] their [hall]owing,
and though they practised idolatry[34] in their land, and their
    soil was destroyed by their foemen,
when, in Thy fiery passion, Thy fury and hot anger [were
    poured] out,
so that it was turned to a wasteland,
where no man came nor went,[35]
yet, despite all of this, Thou didst not reject the seed of
    Jacob,
neither contemn Israel, to make an end of them,[36]
and abjure Thy Covenant with them.
Nay, Thou alone art a living God;
and there is none beside Thee.
Therefore, remembering the Covenant
by which Thou hadst brought us forth in the sight of the
    nations,[37]
Thou didst not then abandon us among those nations,
but in all [the] lands whither Thou didst thrust them[38]
Thou didst still show kindness to Thy people Israel,
that they might be minded to return unto Thee and to
    hearken to Thy voice,[39]
even to all which Thou hadst commanded through Thy
    servant Moses,
For Thou didst shed Thy holy spirit[40] upon us,
(so) bringing to us Thy blessings,
that we might take thought on Thee when trouble befell us,
and murmur our prayers (to Thee) whenso Thy chastise-
    ment pressed sore.[41]
(And troubles indeed have we encountered,
[pla]gued and tortured by the fury of oppressors!)[42]

Moreover, although *we*, for our part,
'drove God hard with our wrongdoings,

and, with our sins, laid hard service on our Rock',[43]
yet, when *Thou* didst lay service upon *us*,
Thou didst so for our advantage,
guiding <us> in the way we should walk.[44]
[And] though we paid no heed to [Thy word],

.   .   .   .

[yet didst Thou   ]

.   .   .   .

                                                        VI

.   .   .   .

and, ever true to Thyself,**
[Thou didst ca]st away from us all our transgressions,[45]
and purge us of our sin.
    It is Thou, O LORD, (not us), that hast dealt rightly,[46]
for all these things hast Thou done.[47]

    ¶Howbeit, now, this day,
when our hearts are bowed down,[48]
have we not paid the price of our own and our fathers'
        wrongdoing
—the price of our perfidy and of our contrariness?[49]
For we have not spurned Thy trials,
neither have our souls demurred††[50] against Thy strokes,
abjuring our Covenant with Thee
through all the distress of our souls.
(Thou Who hast sent our enemies against us
hast Thyself also given us courage!)
    Therefore, we beseech Thee, O LORD,
to the end that we may bear the tale of Thy power to all
        generations for ever,
even as throughout all time Thou hast wrought peculiar
        favors,
so now let Thine anger and Thy wrath be turned away
        from us,

    ** Heb. 'for Thy sake'.
    †† Heb. 'felt revulsion'.

and look Thou on our woe and our trouble and our stress,[51]
and grant unto Thy people Isra[el
in all] the lands, near and far,[52] whither [Thou hast thrust
them],
yea, unto everyone that is inscribed in the Book of Life,[53]
that they may succeed in serving Thee and giving thanks‡‡
to [Thy holy name].
[Deliver them also] from all their needs[54] [   ].
[But bring Thou Thy retribution on dissemblers(?)]
who are causing [Thy people(?)] to stumble[55] [   ]

*　　*　　*

¶[Blessed be He who   ],
Who hath delivered us from all distress.
AMEN, [AMEN]

‡‡ Or, 'praise'.

NOTES

1. I.e., act in accordance with Thy divine nature and attributes.
2. Cp. Num. 14.17–20.
3. Deut. 1.43; 9.23.
4. Deut. 9.8.
5. Cp. Ex. 32.30.
6. The Hebrew word, usually rendered 'wonder, marvel', means properly a singular and special act, and the corresponding verb is often employed in the Old Testament in connection with the bestowal of favor or the fulfillment of obligations of loyalty (*hesed*).
7. Literally, 'Because Thy name hath been called over us'.
8. Deut. 4.29; 10.12; 11.13; 30.2, 10.
9. Cp. Isa. 51.7.
10. Deut. 28.28.
11. Cp. Isa. 50.1.
12. Cp. Isa. 50.2.
13. I restore tentatively, [*l^ehôdî'enu razê ha-eme*]t.
14. Isa. 40.17.
15. Literally, 'Since we made mention of Thy name alone', or perhaps, 'Since we alone were designated by Thy name'.
16. Cp. Isa. 43.7.
17. Cp. Deut. 14.1.
18. Ex. 4.22.
19. Deut. 8.5.
20. Cp. Deut. 14.2.
21. Deut. 18.11.
22. Deut. 31.21.
23. Deut. 31.29.

24. Cp. Ezra 9.1–2; Neh. 12.25–26.
25. Cp. Deut. 31.29.
26. I restore tentatively, *tiṣdaq la-mᵉḥa[kkîm lak]* (or, *la-maḥᵃ[ziqim bak]*).
27. Pss. 95.11; 132.14. Cp. also Isa. 66.1.
28. II Sam. 5.2; 25.30.
29. Cp. II Sam. 7.13; I Kings 2.4; 4.5; 8.25; I Chron. 17.12, 14.
30. Isa. 60.7; 64.10.
31. I Kings 5.18(4). The phrase became something of a cliché; cp. Jubilees 23.29; 40.9; 46.1, 2, 5. Also in the Jewish prayer book: Singer, p. 7 (cp. TB Berachoth 60b).
32. Deut. 31.10.
33. Jer. 17.13.
34. Literally, 'worshipped a strange (alien) god.'
35. Zech. 7.14; 9.8.
36. Lev. 26.44; Jer. 14.19.
37. Lev. 26.45.
38. Cp. Deut. 30.1.
39. Deut. 30.2, 8.
40. Isa. 44.3; cp. Enoch 91.1.
41. Isa. 26.16.
42. Isa. 51.13.
43. Isa. 43.23–24.
44. Cp. Isa. 48.17. The point of the sentence lies in the contrast between Israel's *belaboring* God with its sins, and God's *laying service* on Israel for its benefit. (The original editor's restoration, 'Thou didst *not* lay service on us', therefore gives just the wrong sense.)
45. Ezek. 18.31.
46. Dan. 9.7; cp. *Hymns* xvi.9.
47. Jer. 14.22; a cliché in the *Hymns*, e.g. x.12; xviii.21; frag. ii.5.
48. Lev. 26.41.
49. Lev. 26.24, 27, 40, 41.
50. Lev. 26.15.
51. Deut. 26.7.
52. Ezek. 21.4–5.

53. Dan. 12.1.
54. The manuscript is not clear. Tentatively, I read and restore: *we-haṣṣilem mi-kol ṣorᵉkᵉhemah.*
55. Cp. *Florilegium,* i.8.

GLORY TO GOD IN THE HIGHEST

The Litany of the Angels

Praised be Thy name for ever, O our King, creator of ministering spirits, all of whom stand in the height of the universe . . . and open their mouths in holiness and purity, with song and psalm, while they bless, praise, glorify, reverence, and ascribe sovereignty to the name of the Divine King. . . . With tranquil spirit, with pure speech, and with holy melody they all intone in unison and exclaim with awe:

Holy, holy, holy is the Lord of Hosts, the fullness of the whole earth is His glory.

And the Ophanim and the Holy Creatures with a noise of great rushing upraise themselves towards the Seraphim, and over against them offer praise and say:

Blessed be the Glory of the Lord from the place thereof.

JEWISH MORNING SERVICE

INTRODUCTION

Jewish folklore, deriving its inspiration from the famous visions of Isaiah (6.2–3) and Ezekiel (ch. 10), has insisted throughout the ages that when Israel offers public worship to God, its devotions are accompanied by a corresponding act of divine service performed by the angels. This poetic fancy, which finds expression also in the *Sanctus* of the Christian Communion service, forms the background of what is here designated *The Litany of the Angels.* This document, only two short extracts from which have thus far been published, describes elements of the celestial liturgy.

The first extract is based squarely on the vision of Ezekiel (1 and 10) and depicts the angels rising in their several classes and contingents to give praise to God seated aloft on His Chariot-throne. The main interest of the extract is historical: it pushes back to a remoter antiquity that lore of the Heavenly Chariot (*Merkabah*) which formed a staple of later Jewish mysticism and which some scholars have attributed to the Essenes. Moreover, the passage bears a remarkable resemblance to some of the ancient prayers (*Yoṣer*) embodied in the traditional Jewish morning service—prayers which some nineteenth-century savants likewise ascribed to that ascetic brotherhood.

The second extract is in many ways the more interesting. It sets forth a series of blessings said to have been pronounced, as part of the celestial liturgy, by each of seven archangels. The point is, however, that these blessings are evidently conceived as the angelic counterpart of the

Priestly Benediction (Num. 6.24–27) anciently recited in the Temple and now a staple element of all Jewish public worship. The similarity is close and arresting:

(a) Each blessing is divided into three parts, matching the structure of the Aaronic formula, and according especially with the statement in the Mishnah (*Tamîd*, vii.2) that outside of Jerusalem this formula was indeed reckoned and recited as *three* blessings.

(b) Each blessing is pronounced *in the name* of a divine quality or attribute, e.g., God's sovereign majesty, sublime truth, mystical power, or holiness, and each is designed to convey a particular benefit upon its recipients. This is in direct accord with the words of the Aaronic formula: *So shall they put My name upon the children of Israel, and I will bless them* (Num. 6.27).

(c) The entire benediction ends with the word *peace*, again in accordance with the Aaronic formula (Num. 6.26).

(d) We may perhaps go even a step further. Besides those 'who have walked uprightly', 'who have been eager to do God's will', 'whose way has been blameless', and the like, one passage (Blessing #5) makes curious mention—according to one possible rendering—of 'those who have given thanks to Him'. True, one reason for this specification is that it lends itself to a play on words between the majesty (*hôd*) which they are to receive as their guerdon and the act of thanksgiving (*môdîm*) by which they have earned it. It is also possible, however, that what suggested this somewhat curious particularization was the fact that in the service of the synagogue the Priestly Benediction (or a substitute for it) is actually recited in the Standing Prayer (*'Amidah*) immediately after the Blessing of Thanksgiving, which begins, *We give thanks* (môdîm) and ends, *Blessed art Thou, O Lord . . . to whom it is fitting to give thanks*. This usage is believed to be ancient.

It is not clear whether the blessings were thought to be pronounced upon angels or human beings. In Blessing #4 there is indeed a specification of 'the godly beings who have upreared the structure of true knowledge', and this is a not uncommon description of angels. On the other hand, phrases like 'those whose way has been blameless' are certainly more suggestive of human beings, and in Blessing #6 the benefit conferred is that the recipients 'may take their stand beside the beings eternal'—a phrase which can scarcely refer to angels who themselves are those eternal beings. It may therefore be suggested that the blessings were thought to be pronounced upon *the sainted dead*, who thus received their heavenly reward. That these should be designated 'godly beings' is not at all extraordinary; the very point of the designation may lie in the hyperbole.

This interpretation is strongly supported, if not actually confirmed, by the fact that in later rabbinic tradition mention is made of seven classes of saintly persons who are privileged to enjoy the Beatific Vision in seven compartments of paradise, each of them being there translated into a category of angels, and in several cases they are designated by the same names as in our text. Thus, as enumerated in *Seder Gan Eden** (which is thought to have been compiled from ancient sources), they are: (i) the 'righteous' [*zaddiqîm*], to whom correspond the angelic Arelîm; (ii) the 'upright' [*yesharîm*], to whom correspond the angelic Ḥashmalîm; (iii) the 'blameless' [*temîmîm*], to whom correspond the angelic Tarshîshîm; (iv) the 'saintly' [*qedôshîm*], to whom correspond the angelic Holy Beings; (v) the 'penitent', to whom correspond the angelic Ōphānîm; (vi) school children, to whom correspond the angelic Cherubîm; and (vii) the 'pious' [*hasîdîm*], to whom correspond the angelic Holy Creatures (*hayôth*). Each of these is headed by a Scriptural paragon, viz. (i) Joseph; (ii) Phinehas; (iii) Eleazar, son of Aaron; (iv) Aaron; (v) King Manasseh of Judah; (vi) Joshua; the leader of the seventh class being left unnamed.

Thus, what is envisaged in our text would be a blessing by the corresponding leader of the heavenly contingent

* A. Jellinek, *Beth Ha-Midrash*, iii, 131–40; J. D. Eisenstein, *Oṣar Midrashîm*, i,86.

either upon its counterpart still on earth or else upon those members of it who have already attained celestial status.

Finally, it is worth observing that the divine qualities in whose names the blessings are pronounced accord in several instances with those associated with God in the elaborate kabbalistic system of the Sephiroth, e.g., majesty, power, etc. Nor should it be overlooked that there is a subtle correspondence between the qualities of those on whom the blessings are conferred and of the angels who confer them. Thus, those who have upheld true knowledge (gnosis) become one with the angels who possess such knowledge and who are elsewhere described in the Scrolls (*Hymns* iii.22) as 'spirits of knowledge' or as possessed of the 'wisdom of the sons of heaven', (*Manual*, iv.22). Similarly, those who have laid firm foundations for nobility and knowledge qualify (by implication) as the equals of those personified celestial 'foundations' (elements, στοιχεια) of the world who are in fact angelic beings; while those who have 'shown prowess of mind' become the companions of the angels who are elsewhere described as 'stalwarts' (*Hymns* viii.11; x.34–35; cp. Ps. 103.20).

THE LITANY OF THE ANGELS

A

. . . the angels that minister to the Presence of God's Glory[1] in that compartment of heaven[2] where abide [the beings who possess (true)] knowledge.[3] They fall[4] before the [cheru]bim and intone their blessings.[5]

While they are soaring aloft,[6] there sounds a murmur of angel voices [   ],[7] and the lifting of their wings is accompanied by a clamor of joyous song. It is the murmur of angels blessing the Chariot-like Throne[8] above the firmament of the cherubim,[9] while they themselves, from below the place where the Glory dwells, go acclaiming in joyous song the [splen]dor of that radiant expanse.

(Whenever the wheels (of that Chariot) are in motion,[10] angels of sanctification[11] dart to and fro[12] all around it, between its glorious wheels. Like fiery apparitions are they,[13] spirits most holy, looking like streams of fire, in the likeness of burnished metal[14] or of lustrous ware; clothed in garments opalescent, a riot of wondrous hues, a diffusion(?)[15] of brightness; live angelic spirits,[16] constantly coming and going beside the glorious wonderful Chariot.[17] Amid all the noise of their progress sounds also that murmured intonation of blessings, and whenever they come round, they shout their holy hallelujahs.)

When (the angels) soar aloft, they soar in wondrous wise; and when they alight,[18] they stay standing.[19]

Then the sound of the paean is hushed, and the murmur of angelic benedictions pervades all the camps[20] of those godly beings. Anon, from the midst of their every contingent,[21] they [give forth] a sound of praise, as, in [holy] wor[ship], each of their several ranks[22] breaks forth into joyous song, one after another, in their several stations.[23]

B

*   *   *   *   *   *   *

4

¶Next, with seven words[1] of nobility[2]
the fourth of the arch-princes[3]
blesses[4] in the name of His[5] kingly nobility
all who have walked uprightly;
   and with seven words of [   ]
he blesses all who have laid foundations for [nobility];
   and with seven words of vindication[6]
he blesses all those godly beings who have upreared the
     structure of true knowledge;[7]
     that they may be blessed with His glorious mercy.

5

¶Next, with seven words of sublime truth
the fifth of the arch-princes
blesses in the name of His mystical powers[8]
all who have [led lives of] purity;
   and with seven words of [   ]
he blesses all who have been eager to do His will;
   and with seven words of majesty
he blesses all who have acknowledged His majesty;[9]
     that they may be blessed with [   ] majesty.

6

¶Next, with seven words of His mystical prowess
the sixth of the arch-princes
blesses in the name of angelic prowess[10]
all who have shown prowess of mind;[11]
   and with seven mystical words
he blesses all whose way has been blameless;[12]
     that they may take their stand beside the beings
     eternal;[13]
  and (again) with seven mystical words
he blesses all who have waited on Him;[14]

that they may obtain in return[15] the mercy of
His tender love.

7

¶(Finally,) with seven words of His mystical holiness
the seventh of the arch-princes
blesses in the name of His holiness
all the saintly beings among those who have laid foundations for (true) knowledge;
   and with seven mystical words
he blesses all who have avouched the sublimity of His
judgments;[16]
      that they may be blessed with stout shields;
   and with seven words of [   ][17]
he blesses all who have enlisted in the cause of righteousness,[18]
who have sung continually the praises of His glorious
kingdom;[19]
      that they may be blessed with peace.[20]

¶THEREUPON all the arch-princes (in concert)
[acclaim the praise of] the God of the angels,
and all the [

NOTES

A

1. See Analytical Index, F. 2 (*b*)–(*c*).
2. Literally, 'dwelling', but the term bears this specific meaning in the Hechaloth-literature, e.g., in *Massecheth Hêchalôth*, ch. 7, (=Eisenstein, *Oṣar Midrashîm*, i.110b).
3. See Analytical Index, F. 5.
4. Possibly this is all one sentence, with the ministering angels as the subject. But it seems to me more natural to suppose that these, with the cherubim, are the beings who reside in the highest heaven, just below the Throne, and whom the soaring angels encounter.
5. See Analytical Index, F. 6. The Kedushah ('Sanctus') in the Jewish liturgy for sabbaths and festivals describes them as responding to the Trisagion uttered by the seraphim with the words, 'Blessed be the glory of the Lord from the place thereof' (cp. Isa. 6.3; Ezek. 10.3). *Massecheth Hêchalôth*, ch. 5, elaborates: 'By day they sing the Sanctus; at night, the Benedictus'. It is the latter, rather than a general benediction, that may here be meant.
6. Cp. Ezek. 10.16, 17, 19.
7. The low murmur (whisper) of the angels is a common theme in rabbinic literature; e.g., *Sifrê* i.58. It is mentioned explicitly in the Kedushah; cp. L. Zunz, *Gottesdientl. Vorträge der Juden,*[2] 173, 363. *Hechaloth Rabbathi*, ch. 26 (Eisenstein, *op. cit.*, i.121a) says that 'the Holy Creatures stand posted before Thee in a soft murmur'. Similarly, Slavonic Enoch 20.3 says that the angels sing 'with small tender voices'; cp. also ib., 21.1 (A); 22.3.

8. I.e., the Merkabah of later Jewish mysticism, which concept some scholars have indeed attributed to the Essenes. The expression occurs also among the Mandaeans: *John Book* ii.76f. The phrasing in our text is adapted from I Chron. 28.18.
9. Cp. Ezek. 10.1. These several 'firmaments', i.e., storeys of heaven, are mentioned specifically in the Hechaloth-literature, e.g., Jellinek, *Bêth ha-Midrash*, iii.168.
10. Cp. Ezek. 10.9, 11.
11. See Analytical Index, F. 2 (*d*). As in Enoch, these are here identified with the 'holy creatures' of Ezekiel's vision.
12. The phrase is taken from Ezek. 1.14 (read as in the Vulgate, with a slight deviation from the traditional Jewish Masoretic text).
13. Cp. Ezek. 1.13, 27. See also Slavonic Enoch 29.13.
14. Cp. Ezek. 1.27. But the exact meaning of the Hebrew word *ḥashmal* is uncertain. In rabbinic lore, it came to denote a class of angels!
15. The reading, and hence also the translation, is uncertain. I have guessed.
16. *Not* 'spirits of a living God', as the words might formally mean. This is a paraphrase of the expression 'holy creatures' (lit. 'holy *living beings*') in Ezekiel's vision.
17. The text reads 'chariots', in the plural. These are indeed mentioned in the Hechaloth-literature, but it seems more probable that the scribe has made a slip, and that the reference is to the Throne-chariot (Merkabah) of God.
18. The curious use of the Hebrew word *sh-k-n* in this sense may be illustrated from Syriac, where one of its meanings is indeed 'sink down in flying'.
19. Cp. Ezek. 1.24–25. Isa. 6.2 says expressly that 'the seraphim *stood* above him'. Standing was the ancient posture in prayer, though the expression 'stand beside' was a good Semitic way of saying simply 'serve'.
20. The phrase derives from Gen. 32.3 (RSV: 'God's army'). The 'camps' of the angels are frequently mentioned in the Hechaloth-literature (e.g., Eisenstein, op.

cit., 110a, 123a), and the angels—as the 'host of heaven'—are often depicted as a militia.

21. A *military* term; cp. Num. 2, passim; *War* vi.1, 4, 5; viii.14; ix.4, 10; xvii.10.
22. Again a military term; cp. Isa. 13.4, etc.
23. Once more a military term; cp. *War* vi.1, 4, 5; viii.3, 6, 17; ix.10; xvi.5; xvii.11.

B

1. I.e., phrases redolent of (nobility, etc.).
2. Or, majesty, splendor.
3. I.e., archangels. The expression is adapted from Ezek. 38.2; 39.1. See Analytical Index, F. 2 (*a*).
4. Or, will bless, is to bless.
5. Note that the name of God is never mentioned directly in the blessings.
6. Or, righteousness.
7. Literally, 'raise high' in contrast to 'lay the foundations'. Slight paraphrase has been necessary to bring out the point.
8. The Hebrew word means properly 'something singular, extraordinary', and is used constantly in the Scrolls of things heavenly and transcendental. 'Mystical' seems the nearest equivalent.
9. The word may also be rendered, 'who have given thanks to Him'. Perhaps it plays on the fact that in the service of the synagogue, the Priestly Blessing, of which this is the angelic counterpart, is recited after that section of the Standing Prayer ('*Amidah*) which begins, 'We give Thee thanks' and ends, 'Blessed art Thou, O Lord . . . to whom it is beseeming to give thanks'. There is also a word-play between 'majesty' (*hôd*) and 'give thanks' (*môdîm*).
10. Cp. *Manual*, xvii.6.
11. In allusion to the fact that the angels themselves are called 'those who show prowess of strength'; see Analytical Index, F. 1 (*h*).
12. Ps. 119.1.
13. For this notion, see Analytical Index, A. 12.

14. Isa. 30.18.
15. Scarcely, 'that they may obtain a return (restoration) of His tender love', as the words might formally mean, because the doctrine of the Scrolls is that, despite all Israel's defections, God's tender love remains constant.
16. Literally, 'who have exalted His judgments (i.e., dispensation)'—again in contrast to 'lay the foundations'; see above, n. 7.
17. Cp. TB *Berachôth* 27ᵇ, where men of advanced insight are described as 'shield-bearers'; v. Kohut, *Aruch Completum*, viii.282.
18. A military metaphor; cp. note 16 to Hymn 8, and see Analytical Index, A. 10.
19. The point is that they have done what the angels themselves are continually doing, viz. singing the 'eternal song' of God. The Kedushah ('Sanctus') in the Jewish liturgy says explicitly that the earthly congregation recites God's sanctity and grandeur continually *as do the angels*.
20. In imitation of the Priestly Blessing, which ends with 'peace' (Num. 6.26). In the Jewish liturgy, it is followed immediately by a prayer beginning, 'Grant peace', and ending, 'Blessed art Thou, O Lord, Who blessest Thy people Israel with peace' (cp. Ps. 29.11).

THE WORD OF GOD

The Study of Scripture

The grass withereth, the flower fadeth; but the word of our God shall stand for ever.

ISAIAH 40.8.

Remember the days of old.

DEUTERONOMY 32.7.

I. EXPOSITIONS OF SCRIPTURE

Introduction. Believing firmly that they stood on the threshold of the New Age, the members of the Brotherhood were especially interested in searching the Scriptures for intimations of current events. A form of interpretation thereby developed in which the words of the ancient prophets were deftly applied to the contemporary scene. Such interpretations were doubtless propounded not only in the course of general study but more especially when portions of the Law and the Prophets were read during the public devotions on the sabbath. Philo tells us distinctly concerning the Essenes that 'on the seventh day . . . they go to the sacred places called synagogues . . . and listen with becoming attention. Then one of them takes the Scriptures and reads, while another, selected from those most versed in the subject, comes forward and expounds it, passing over more recondite points. For they philosophize on most things by construing them symbolically [literally, by symbols], in accordance with ancient usage'. Similarly, in the Gospel of Luke we are told (4.16ff.) how Jesus once attended synagogue at Nazareth on the sabbath, read publicly the Lesson from the Prophets and then proceeded to expound it in terms of current events: 'Today hath this scripture been fulfilled in your hearing'.

This type of exposition is represented by a series of texts which, for purposes of convenience, scholars have called *commentaries*. However, they are not commentaries in the modern sense of the term. Their keyword is, in Hebrew, *pesher*, and *pesher* means properly the interpretation of a dream or the unravelling of a puzzle. It is the correlative of the term *raz*, 'secret, mystery', which is often applied in the Scrolls to the supposedly arcane and latent meaning which underlies the Word of God revealed in the Scriptures.

Significantly enough, while the other sectarian texts from Qumran, such as the *Manual of Discipline,* the *'Zadokite' Document,* and the *Hymns,* are each represented by several copies, the 'commentaries' all exist in only one copy.* This would seem to indicate that they were not in the category of standard traditional literature, but were simply *ad hoc* products—texts of, or rough notes for, 'sermons' delivered by the various official 'interpreters'.

The fragmentary commentaries on Isaiah, Hosea and Micah scarcely deserve special comment, since they contain nothing of importance save the rather general polemic against the priests in Jerusalem.

The special interest of the *Commentary on Nahum* lies in the fact that it contains the only explicit historical allusion thus far found in the Scrolls—namely, a reference to an incident which occurred in 88 B.C. and which is related in detail by Josephus. This establishes beyond doubt the date before which it could not have been written; and if it really came from the library of the Qumran 'Monastery' and was cached at the approach of the Roman legions in 68 A.D., the time of its composition can thus be fixed within about one hundred and fifty years. It would be hazardous, however, to conclude that this necessarily settles the date of *all* the 'commentaries', though it clearly strengthens the hypothesis that they belong to the Roman rather than to an earlier period. Nor, further, should it be supposed that because the commentator illustrates a particular passage of Scripture by this reference to Demetrius Eucerus and Alexander Jannaeus, all other references to 'men of lies' and 'wicked priests' necessarily refer to the same persons. In other words, there is no warrant for the assumption that the *Commentary on Nahum* establishes a definitive frame

---

* To be sure, there are sometimes variant commentaries on the same Scriptural text, but that is something else.

of reference for the commentaries as a whole and hence
a date for the Scrolls in general.

The *Commentary on Habakkuk* has aroused special interest for two reasons. The first is that an observation contained in it—namely, its comment on Habakkuk 2.15—has
been taken by several scholars to imply that the Brotherhood believed in a Christ-like Teacher of Righteousness
who suffered a martyr's death but subsequently 'reappeared
in glory' to his disciples. The second is that the various
allusions in this document to the 'teacher of righteousness',
the 'wicked priest', and the 'man of falsehood' have been
thought to constitute a connected biographical narrative
which, once the characters are identified, might provide a
definitive clue to the antiquity of the text and thence possibly to that of the Scrolls as a whole. With the untenability
of the former theory and with the precariousness of the
latter we have already dealt in the General Introduction
to this volume. Nothing further, therefore, needs here be
said on these matters.

On the other hand, there is a little detail in the *Commentary on Habakkuk* which appears to have been overlooked, but which may prove of considerable importance
for the identification of the Brotherhood. Interpreting the
prophet's words (2.17), 'The violence of Lebanon shall
overwhelm thee', our author observes, 'Lebanon stands for
the Communal Council'. The basis of this interpretation
is, I suggest, that the name Lebanon really means 'white'
(Heb. *laban*); and what the author had in mind was that
the Communal Council was white-robed. His statement
would then chime perfectly with Josephus' assertion (*War*,
II, viii, 3) that 'the Essenes dressed in white'—a custom
still observed by the Samaritans and Mandaeans. In other
words, this comment might provide evidence that the
Brotherhood were indeed Essenes.

The only noteworthy point in the *Commentary on Psalm
Thirty-seven* (again fragmentary) is the reference to the
forty-year period of 'Messianic tribulation', harmonizing
with what is said in the *War of the Sons of Light and*

the Sons of Darkness, and with a well-known rabbinic tradition.

Concerning the *Commentary on Psalm Forty-five* (of which only the opening lines remain) there is nothing to be said except that it anticipates by several centuries the fanciful interpretation of the title (v. 1) which is found later in rabbinic sources.

ISAIAH[1]

CHAPTER FIVE

(5) [*And now I would have you know   what I shall
do to My vineyard*]   *take away its hedge,   that it
go to rack and ruin,   make a gap in its fence,   that
men come trample it down.* The meaning of this passage
is that God has abandoned them . . .

(6) And as to the statement, *Thorns and thistles shall
grow up,* [this refers to] . . .
And as to the term . . . , [this refers to] . . . of the
way . . . their eyes.[2]

(10?) *Ten acres of vineyard shall yield but eight gal-
lons,   and the harvest be only one tenth of what is
sown.*[3] This statement has reference to the Latter Days,
to the price of guilt which, through warfare and famine,
the earth will then have to pay. This will occur at the time
of the Visitation of the Earth.[4]

(11–14) *Woe to them that rise early,   to go chasing
after strong drink,   that stay late in the cool of the evening,   while wine lights fires within them!   Those
carousals of theirs   are but rounds of strumming and
drumming,   of hooting and tooting—and wine.*[5] *Quite
oblivious they are   to what the LORD is about,   too
blinded ever to see   what He is actually doing.*
      *That is the reason why   My people, likewise uncon-
scious,   have likewise been 'carried away'   —away to
an alien land,   their gentry starving for hunger,
their masses parched for thirst. That too is the reason why
      it is Hell that now stretches its gorge,   and Hell*[6]
that now holds its mouth   limitlessly agape,   while

down goes all their proud show,   all their racket and riot,   and all that made merry therein!

The persons here in question are those men of impiety[7] who are in Jerusalem. These are the men of whom it is said:

(24–25) *They have spurned the Law[8] of the LORD, and held in contempt the word   of Israel's Holy One.*

Therefore has the LORD's anger   been kindled against His people.   He has stretched forth His hand against them,   and struck them till mountains quaked, and their carcases lay like refuse   in the midst of the streets.

Yet, despite all of this,   His anger is still unabated, and His hand is still outstretched.

This refers to the men of impiety who are in Jerusalem.

(29–30) [*Their roaring is like a lion's,   like young lions they roar;   they growl and seize their prey, snatch it,*] *and none can rescue.*

[(*So God Himself*) *will roar   against them in that day*]   *like the roar[ing of the sea.*]   *And if one look to the land,   lo, darkness closing in,   and all the day-light darkened   by lowering banks of clouds.*

· · · · · · · · · · · · · · · · · · · ·

CHAPTER SIX

(9) [And as for] the statement, [*Hear and hear, but do not understand*]; *see and s[ee, but do not perceive].* . . . [the term] *understand* [means]. . . .

CHAPTER TEN

(12) *When* [*the Lord*][9] *has brought to completion that which He means to do   on Mount Zion and in Jeru-salem,   I then will call to account   the king of A[s-syria]   for the fruit of his arrogant heart   and the pride[10]   of his haughty looks.   For* (*see*) *what he has been saying: 'By my own brain and brawn*

*(for oh, how clever I am!) I have accomplished it (all)—
shifted the bounds of peoples and rifled their stores.*
The reference is to the annihilation of Babylon.[11] . . .
[The *bounds of peoples*] are the statutory Laws of [God's]
people[12]   [which the Man of Lies (?)[13] summarily sets
aside; while the *rifling of the stores* refers to the] deception
which he practises on the masses. . . .

. . . .

(20) *When that day comes, those of Israel that are left
and those of the house of Jacob that survive will no longer
stay themselves on one who (merely) smites*[14] *them, but
rather on the Lord, Israel's Holy One.*

(21) *A remnant there will be [   ] that then will
find its way back   to the one true Paladin,   Who is
God Himself.*[15]

(22) *Israel, though now your people [   ] be
countless as sands of the sea, only a remnant among them
[   ] will find its way back.*   In an eschatological
sense, this means that [the bulk of the people] will go into
capti[vity] . . . ; [while the statement that they are
now countless as the   sands of the sea][16] implies that
there will (eventually) be a diminution [of their numbers];
as the text puts it:

(22ᵈ) *A decisive end will there be,   a floodtide of
their just deserts;*[17]

(23) *for a final decisive end   is the Lord, the Lord
of Hosts   making throughout the earth.*

(24) *Wherefore thus says the Lord, The Lord [of
Hosts]* . . .

(ANOTHER COMMENTARY)

(21) *A remnant there will be   that then will find its
way back to the one true Paladin, Who is God Himself.*
[This remnant of Is]rael denotes [the congregation of the
elect(?),]   the godly champions of righteousness, while
the [   ] are the ranks of the priests, for . . .

(22) And as to the statement, *Israel, though now your
people, etc.,* [this means that   ] many will perish
[when judgment is rendered] on the earth. In truth . . .

(28–32) *Now has he reached 'Aiath,   now left*
[Migron] behind,   [now stored his gear at Michmas.
*   Now are they over] the pass,   at Geba' halt for the*
night.   Now is [Ramah] a-trem[ble,   Saul's Gibe'ah
in flight.   Now shr]iek, O maid of Gallim!   [O
Laishah], catch the sound!   [Re-echo it, 'Anathoth!]
*   Madmenah [takes to its heels];   they that dwell in*
Gebim seek cover.   Ere [this day be done   he shall
be standing at Nob,   shaking] his fist* *at the mount of*
maid Zion,   the hill of Jerusalem. This statement [has
reference] to the end of days, to the coming of [the Redeemer   ], at the point when he marches up from
the valley of 'Acho<r>[18] to wage [a migh]ty unparalleled
[battle] against [   ]. Through all the ci[ties of
[19] will he pass and will eventually reach] the boundary of Jerusalem.

(33ᵃ) [*Behold, the Lord, the Lord of hosts,   shall*
lop the boughs with terror.]   [The meaning is that He will
wreak judgment] upon all the [and upon] the
[Kit]taeans who [   ] and [upon] all the heathen, and
[His] pow[er shall be made manifest upon them].

(33ᵇ–34) [*And those of high] stature shall be hewn*
down,   [and the lofty shall be brought low].
[   ] *And the thickets of [the forest]   shall be cut*
down with [an ax].†   [This state]ment [has reference] to
the war against the Kittaeans.[20]   ['Those of high stature'
are the] Kittaeans who will be consign[ed to   ]* * *
[And as for the statement, *The thickets of the forest shall*
be cut down] *with an ax,   and Lebanon with [its] sym-*
bols of grandeur‡ [be felled,   this refers to those who have
been oppressing(?)] Ju[dah and] Israel and the humble
of [the land]. Grandiose [though they appear], they shall
[   ] and quail, and [their] he[arts] shall melt. These

---

* Heb. 'hand'.
† Heb. 'iron'.
‡ Heb. 'its majestic ones', i.e., cedars.

['symbols of grandeur'] are the soldiers of the Kit[taeans,
while the thickets of the for]est [that shall be cut down]
with an ax are their [allies], and (the words,) *Lebanon
with [its] sym[bols of grandeur shall be felled* mean that
their ringleader will meet his doom] at the hands of the
notables in his own entourage,§[21] [and will not succeed
in escaping to] safety[22] when he flees before [   ].

CHAPTER ELEVEN

   (1–4) [*But out of the stock of*] Jesse [*shall come forth
a shoot*],   *and a scion [shall sprout] from his roots.
   And upon him [shall re]st [the spirit of the Lord,
the spirit of wis]dom and discernment,   the spirit of
counsel [and of might],   the spirit of knowledge [and
of the fear of the Lord.   And He will inspire him with
fear of] the 𝔏𝔬𝔯𝔡**   and [he shall not judge after] the
sight of [his eyes,   neither dec]ide [after the hearing of
his ears],   but judge [the poor with righteousness
and decide with equity for the humble of the land].*
[The reference is to the scion of] David[23] who will exercise his office at the end [of days]. His [ene]mies [will be
felled],[24] but him will God uphold [by bestowing upon
him   po]wer, a throne of glory, a h[oly] crown and
broidered robes.[25] A [[26] shall be placed] in his
hand, and he shall bear sway over all the hea[th]en, and
Magog [shall be vanquished by him],[27] and his sword shall
wreak judgment upon all the peoples. And as for the statement, *He shall not [judge after the sight of his eyes] neither
decide after the hearing of his ears,*   the reference here
is to the fact that [he will follow the instructions of the
priests; only] as they direct him will he judge, and by their
advice [will he decide].[28] [   ] one of the (more) distinguished priests will come forth, bearing in his hands the
vestments of [royalty][29]* * * *

§ Heb. 'his great ones'.
** Written in archaic script.

CHAPTER FOURTEEN

(4–7) . . . This refers to the annihilation of Babylon.

(8) *The cypresses make merry over you,* (*and*) *the cedars of Lebanon,* (*saying*): *'Now that you are laid low, no one comes up to fell us!'* The cypresses and the cedars of Lebanon mean allegorically . . .

* * *

(26) And as to the statement, *This is the plan that has been planned against the entire earth,* and this is the hand stretched forth over the nations (*all*).[30] *Yet when the Lord of Hosts it is that has laid the plan, who can bring it to naught?*

When His is the hand stretched forth, who can turn *it back?* This refers to [; for does not] Scripture assert in the Book of Zechariah:[31] . . .

CHAPTER THIRTY

(15–18) *Thus saith the LORD, the Holy One of Israel: 'In going back to your homes, in dwelling tranquilly, you shall achieve your real triumphs; in quiet, un- ruffled living shall lie the proof of your strength'.*

But you would have none of it. 'No! To horse!' you said. 'We must be off and away!' Then off and away shall you be —away in a headlong flight!

Or, again, you said, 'But we like to gallop around'. Then galloping you shall have —of men chasing after you! At the threat of one single man —or, at best, of a handful of men, a thousand of you shall flee, till your lone survivors are left like a mast on a moun- tain top, an ensign on a hill.

This is the reason why the LORD is biding His time before He shows favor to you, why He is keeping aloof from showing compassion for you: the LORD is a God of justice. (Yet happy, withal, are they who stand in wait for Him!)

This passage refers to the Latter Days and to the congregation of those, in Jerusalem, who 'seek after smooth things.' These are the men who . . . the Law and do not st[udy it whole]heartedly, for/but . . . they have spurned the Law . . .

(19–21) *Howbeit, O people in Zion,   who dwell in Jerusalem,   nothing is here for tears!   At the mere sound of your cry,   He will straightway show favor to you.   No sooner has He heard (it)   than He (always) has answered you.   So, what though the LORD now give you   meagre bread and scant water,   as in time of siege, men there yet will be,   no longer muffled up,*[82]   *to point the way for you.*[83] *Your eyes will see those men   pointing the way for you,   and your ears hear a word behind you,   saying, Though now you be turning   either to right or left,*[84]   *this is the way; walk upon it!* The reference is to the wrongdoing[35] of the con[gregation of] . . .

CHAPTER FIFTY-FOUR[36]

(11) *Behold, I will set your stones in antimony,*
This refers to the fact that . . . all Israel like antimony around the eye(?).
and lay your foundations with sapphires.
This refers to the fact that they have founded the deliberative council of the community out of priests and laity—a veritable congregation of God's elect—like a sapphire among gems.

(12) *And I will make your pinnacles of agate,*
This refers to the twelve . . . who shine after the manner of the Urim and Thummim. Even the more inferior of them were like the sun in all its radiance and like . . .
and your gates of carbuncle.
This refers to the heads of the tribes of Israel . . . each man [filling] his assigned role, (together constituting) the rotas of . . .

HOSEA

CHAPTER TWO

(7) [*For their mother hath played the harlot, she that conceived them hath done shamefully; for she said, 'I will go after my lovers, that gave me my bread and my water, my wool and my linen, my oil and my drink.'* This means that . . .] and they took delight in . . . and walked crookedly . . .

(8) [*Behold, I will hedge up her way*] *with thorns, and her paths* [*shall she not find.* This means that God smote them with madness] and blindness and bewilderment [of heart,[1] for throughout the era of wickedness] and the era of their perfidy[2] they did not [follow His guidance]. The persons in question are (also) the generation of the Visitation[3] . . . [and] the [ge]neration of the La[tt]er [Days] . . . in throughout the eras of Wrath,[4] for . . .

(9) [*So she said, 'I will go back to my fi*]*rst* [*husband*], *for* [*then I fared better than now.* This refers to the fact that] when the Exile was restored . . .

(10) [*But she knew not that*] *it was I that gave her corn* [*and must and oil*], *and that multiplied* [*the silver*] *and gold which they used* [*for Baal.* This means] that [they ate and drank and] filled themselves, and then forgot God who . . . They cast behind their backs His commandments which He sent to them [through] His servants the prophets, and hearkened and paid honor (instead) to men who led them astray, and, in their blindness, they stood in dread of them as though they were gods.

(11) *Therefore will I take back My corn in the time thereof, and My must [in the season thereof], and shall snatch away My wool and My linen that it cover not [her nakedness]. And now will I discover her shame before the eyes of [her] lovers, and no [man] shall deliver her out of my hand.* This means that God has smitten them with famine and nakedness, that they are become a thing of sha[me] and reproach in the eyes of the nations on whom they relied. Those shall not save them from their woes.

(13) *I will make all her merriment to cease, her festivals, new moons and sabbaths, and all her seasonal feasts.* This means that . . . which they accommodated to the festivals of the heathen, and that all their joy has been turned into mourning.

(14) *I will lay waste [her vine and her fig tree] whereof she said, 'These are my hire [which] my [lovers gave unto me.]' I will turn them into a woodland, and the be[asts of the field] shall devour them.*

MICAH

(5) *All this is because of the transgression of Jacob, and the sins of the house of Israel. What is the transgression of Jacob? Surely, Samaria! . . . So I will turn Samaria into a heap in a field, a place for the planting of a vineyard.* This refers to the preacher of falsehood, who leads the simple-minded astray.[1]

But what are the (true) 'high places' of Jewry? Surely, Jerusalem! This on the other hand refers to those who expound the Law correctly to God's people and to all who are willing to join His elect—that is, the doers of the Law —when the latter meet together in the communal council. These will be delivered from the Day of Judgment.[2]

(6) As to the words: *I will turn Samaria into a heap in a field, a place for the planting of a vineyard; and I will roll down her stones into the valley, and uncover her foundations* [   ], this refers to the Jerusalemitan priests who are leading God's people astray. [God will thrust them forth, to become sojourners in a foreign land; and He will drive all] His enemies [into exile.][3]

* * *

(8) *I will go stripped and naked . . . for it is come unto Judah; it reacheth unto the gate of my people, unto Jerusalem.* [   ] [God] will wreak judgment on His enemies [   ] [them who sought] to betray Him.[4]

(9) As to the words: *It reacheth into the gate of my people,* this means that God's glory will move (once more) from Se'ir to Jerusalem. [   ] For God will come forth from [   ].[5]

NAHUM

CHAPTER ONE

(3) *In gust and gale[1] is His way, [and] clouds are
the du[st at his feet].* [The gust and gale connote] the
ex[pan]ses of His heaven and His earth,[2] which [will be
convulsed] when [He comes do]wn.[3]

(4) *He rebukes the sea and dries it up.*[4] The 'sea' connotes the Kittians,[5] (and what is meant is that) He will
wreak such judgment upon them as to wipe them out from
off [the face of the earth] together with [   ] and its
rulers, whose dominion will be brought to an end. *A-wilt
are Bashan and Carmel; a-wilt too is Lebanon's bloom.*
This means that through Him the towering pride of wickedness[6] [will be abased, and the dominion of Belial brought
low (?)]. 'Lebanon' connotes the latter's rulers.[7] *A-wilt
too is Lebanon's bloom.* This connotes his (i.e., Belial's)
abettors.[8] They will perish in the face of [and of]
the elect of [   ].[9] [Judgment will fall on (?)] all
that dwell in the world.

(5) *Mountains quake before Him.* This means that
[   ] will tremble at His presence(?).[10]

(6) *In the face of His fury who will stand? Who abide
the blaze of His wrath?* This means [   ].[11]

CHAPTER TWO

(11) *Where is the abode of the lions, which was the
feeding place of the young lions—* [This refers to Jeru-

salem which has become] an abode for the wicked men of the heathen.[12]

where the lion and lioness walked, and the lion's whelp, [and none made them afraid]? [This refers to Deme]-trius, the king of Greece, who, at the instance of them 'that sought smooth things', sought to enter Jerusalem.[13] [Never] from the days of Antiochus[14] until the time when the rulers of the Kittians[15] arose, [has that city daun]ted the kings of Greece; and eventually it will be trodden under.

(12) *The lion rent the limbs[16] of his own whelps, and strangled his own lionesses for prey.* [This refers to] the Young Lion of Anger[17] who proceeded to smite his own great men and his own confederates.

and filled his caves with prey, and his abodes (dens) with torn flesh. [This refers to] the Young Lion who [wrought venge]ance on them 'that sought smooth things', in that he proceeded to hang them up alive.[18] [Such a thing had never] before [been done] in Israel, for the Scripture designates a man hung up alive as ['a reproach unto God'].[19]

(13) *Behold, I am against thee, saith the Lord of Hosts, and I will burn thy multitude[20] in smoke, and the sword shall devour thy young lions, and I will cut off thy prey from the earth.* [This refers to   ]. 'Thy multitude' means the great men of his army [and] his [confederates]. His 'young lions' are [   ], and his 'prey' is the property which [the priests of] Jerusalem amas[sed][21] (and) which [   ]. [E]phraim [shall become]   ; Israel shall be rendered [   ].[22] [*And the voice of thy messengers shall no more be heard.*] . . . his 'messengers' are his ambassadors, whose voice shall no more be heard among the nations.

CHAPTER THREE

(1) *Woe to the bloody city! It is all full of fraud and rapine.* This alludes to the city of Ephraim[23]—to those

(future) 'seekers after smooth things[24] who, in the Latter Days, will walk in fraud and lies.

The prey departeth not, nor do (2) *the crack of the whip, the whir of wheels, the prancing horses, the bounding chariots* (3) *the charging horsemen, the flashing* [*sword*], *the glittering spear, the multitude of slain, the great heap of carcasses. No end is there to the bodies; men stumble over those bodies.* This alludes to the period when the 'seekers after smooth things' hold sway. Never will the sword of the gentiles depart from the midst of their community, nor yet captivity, spoliation and internecine strife, nor exile through fear of an enemy. Many a guilty corpse shall fall in their days, and there shall indeed be no end to the slain. Moreover, through the guilty counsel (policy) of these men, men will indeed stumble in the body of their own flesh.

(4) *Because of the manifold whoredoms of the well-favored whore, that mistress of witchery, who sells whole nations through her whoredom, and whole families through her wit*[*cher*]*y.* This alludes to those who will go leading Ephraim astray, those by whose false teaching,[25] lying tongue, and guileful lips many shall indeed be led astray —kings, princes, priests, laymen, and affiliated strangers— and through whose counsel (policy) their cities and families shall go to ruin, and through whose tongues nobles and rulers will fall.

(5) *Behold, I am against thee, quoth the LORD of* H[*ost*]*s, and thou shalt* (*yet*) *uncover* [*thy*] *skirts over thy face, and show the nations* [*thy*] *nakedness, and the kingdoms thy shame.* This alludes to . . . the cities of the east, for the 'skirts' are . . . the gentiles their . . . their filthy abominations.

(6) *And I will cast abominable filth upon thee, and make thee vile and render thee loathsome.*[26] (7) *And it shall come to pass that all who see thee shall flee from thee.* This alludes to the 'seekers after smooth things'

whose evil works will, at the end of the present epoch, become manifest to all Israel. Many will then discern these people's iniquity and come to hate them and to hold them loathsome on account of their guilty arrogance. Moreover, when (eventually) the glory of Judah suffers dishonor, those in Ephraim who have hitherto been duped will flee from the midst of those men's congregation and, renouncing them that led them astray, attach themselves (once more) to (the true) Israel.[27]

And they will say, Nineveh is ravaged, (but) who bemoans her? Whence can I seek any who will condole with thee? This alludes to the 'seekers after smooth things' whose counsel (policy) will come to naught and whose synagogue[28] will be dispersed. No longer will they lead the congregation astray, and those who were previously duped will no longer hold to their counsel.

(8) *Art thou better than <Nô> Amon, that was situate by the rivers?*[29]   The allusion in the term 'Amon' is to Manasseh. The 'rivers' are the grandees of Manasseh, the nobles of . . . who . . . the . . .
Water was all around her; her rampart (ḥayil) was the sea; water also formed her walls. The allusion is to the men of her army (ḥayil), her warriors. . . .[30]

(9) *Ethiopia is her strength; Egypt too, and it is endless.* This alludes to the . . . who . . .
Put and Lubim[31] *are among her supporters.* This alludes to the wicked men of . . . ,[32] that divisive group[33] who ally themselves with Manasseh.

(10) *She too is gone into exile, into captivity; her babes are dashed in pieces at the top of every street; over her nobles men cast lots, and her grandees are bound in chains.*
This alludes to Manasseh in the final era, when its kingdom will be brought low at [the hand of] . . . Its womenfolk, babes, and infants will go into captivity; while its warriors and its honored men [will fall] by the sword.

(11) *Thou too shalt become drunken, become all be-clouded.* This alludes to the wicked men of Ephraim whose cup (of doom)[84] will follow that of Manasseh, and who will become . . .

Thou too shalt go seeking in the city a refuge from the foe. This alludes to the . . . [who will go seeking escape] from their enemies within (their own) cities.

All thy strongholds shall be like fig trees. . . .

*   *   *

HABAKKUK

CHAPTER ONE

(4) *Therefore the law is numbed.* This refers to the fact that they have rejected the *Torah*—that is, the Law—of God.

For the wicked besets the righteous . . . The reference (in the word 'righteous') is to the teacher who expounds the Law aright [   ].

Therefore justice goes forth perverted.

. . . .

(5) *Look, ye traitors,[1] and see: marvel and be astonished. For it is in your own days that the deed is being done. Ye do not believe when it is told.* This refers to the traitors who have aligned themselves with the man of lies. For they did not believe what he who expounded the Law aright told them on the authority* of God. It refers also to those who betrayed the new covenant,[2] for (the word rendered 'believe' also means 'keep faith' and therefore alludes to the fact that)[3] they have not kept faith with the Covenant of God, but have profaned His holy name. Again, it refers to future traitors—that is, to the lawless men who will betray the Covenant and not believe when they hear all the things that are to come upon the final age duly related by the priest whom God appoints to interpret in those days all the words of His servants the prophets by whom He has told of that impending disaster.

(6) *For lo, I raise up the Chaldeans, that wild and impetuous nation.* This refers to the Kittaeans,[4] who are indeed swift and mighty in war, bent on destroying peoples

* Literally, 'from the mouth of'.

far and wide and subduing them to their own domination.
They dispossess [   ] but do not believe in the ordinances of God [   ]. Over lowland and plain they
come to smite and pillage the cities of the land. This is
what the Scripture means when it speaks of them as coming *to possess dwellings that are not their own.*

(7) *Dreadful and awful it is: out of itself proceed both
its standard of justice and its (lust for) deception.*[5] This
refers to the Kittaeans, the terror and dread of whom are
upon all the nations. Moreover, when they meet in their
council,[6] all their plans are directed to doing evil; and they
behave towards all peoples with knavery and deceit.

(8, 9) *Swifter than leopards are its steeds, and keener
than evening wolves. Their horsemen spread out and ride
abroad: they come flying from afar like a vulture that
hastes to devour. They all of them come for violence: the
serried mass of their faces is a veritable eastwind*[7]. This
refers to the Kittaeans who thresh the earth with their
horses and their beasts. Like a vulture they come from
afar, from the isles of the sea, to devour all the nations;
and they are insatiable. In the heat of fury, in searing rage,
in scorching anger and with tempestuous mien[8] they speak
with all the peoples; and this is what the Scripture means
when it says, *the serried mass of their faces is a veritable
eastwind, and they amass spoil like sand.*

(10) *At kings it scoffs, and lordlings are a derision unto
it.* This refers to the fact that they scorn the great and
mock the noble, make sport of kings and princes, and scoff
at any numerous people.
*It derides every stronghold: piles up an earthmound and
takes it.* This refers to the rulers of the Kittaeans who
scorn the strongholds of the peoples and tauntingly deride
them, surrounding them with a great host in order to capture them.[9] Through alarm and terror the latter are surren-
dered into their hands; and they overthrow them through
the iniquity of those who dwell in them.

(11) *Then the wind sweeps by and passes: and an-other,*[10] *whose might is his God, proceeds to wreak devas-tation.*[11] This refers to the rulers of the Kittaeans. In their guilt-ridden Council House[12] they keep replacing those rulers one after another, and each comes in turn to destroy the earth.[18]

Another whose might is his God. This refers to [   ] all the peoples.

(12b–13) *Him hast thou appointed, O Lord, to wreak the judgment: and him hast thou established, O Rock, to proffer the charge—him who has kept his vision pure, that it could not look upon perverseness.*[14] This refers to the fact that God will not exterminate His people by the hand of the heathen, but will place the execution of judgment on all the heathen in the hands of His elect. Moreover, it is through charges proffered by the latter that the wicked among His own people will stand condemned—that is, the people who kept His commandments only when they were in trouble. This is what the Scripture means by the words, *him who has kept his vision pure that it could not look upon evil.* The reference is to the fact that [God's elect] did not go a-whoring after (the lust of) their eyes during the Era of Wickedness.

(13) *Why dost thou look (idly) upon traitors, and keep silent when the wicked confounds*[15] *him that is more right-eous than he?* This refers to the 'house of Absalom'[16] and their cronies who kept silent when charges were lev-elled against the teacher who was expounding the Law aright, and who did not come to his aid against the man of lies when the latter rejected the *Torah* in the midst of their entire congregation.[17]

(14–16) *Thou hast made men like fishes of the sea, like crawling things, that he may have dominion over them.*[18] *He takes up all of them with the angle and hauls them in his net, and gathers them in his drag. Therefore he sacri-fices to his net: therefore he rejoices and makes merry; therefore, too, he burns incense to his net: because thereby his portion is rich* . . . This again refers to the Kittaeans. What with all their plunder, they keep increasing their wealth like a shoal of fish. And as for the statement, *therefore he sacrifices to his net and burns incense to his drag,* this refers to the fact that they offer sacrifice to their ensigns and that their weapons are objects of veneration to them.[19]

For thereby is their portion fat and their food rich. This refers to the fact that they apportion among all the peoples annual assignments of forced labor† and tribute designed to provide them with food, thereby devastating many lands.[20]

(17) *Therefore does he bare his sword,*[21] *and never spares to slay nations.* This refers to the Kittaeans who destroy many by the sword—youths, adults (?)[22] and old men, women and children alike—and have not pity even on the fruit of the womb.

CHAPTER TWO

(1, 2) *I will take my stand on my watch and post myself on my tower, and scan the scene to see whereof He will denounce me and what answer I might give when He arraigns me. And the Lord took up word with me and said: Write the vision, and make it plain upon tablets that he who runs may read.* God told Habakkuk to write down the things that were to come upon the latter age, but He did not inform him when that moment would come to fulfilment. As to the phrase, *that he who runs may read,* this refers to the teacher who expounds the Law aright, for God has made him *au courant*[23] with all the deeper implications of the words of His servants the prophets.

(3) *For the vision is yet for the appointed time. Though it lags*[24] *toward the moment, it will not be belied.* This refers to the fact that the final moment may be protracted beyond anything which the prophets have foretold, for

† Literally, 'their yoke'.

'God moves in a mysterious way His wonders to perform'.[25]

*Though it tarry, yet await it; for it will surely come, it
will not delay.* This is addressed‡ to the men of truth, the
men who carry out the Law [*Torah*], who do not relax
from serving the Truth even though the final moment be
long drawn out. Assuredly, all the times appointed by God
will come in due course, even as He has determined in His
inscrutable wisdom.

(4) *Behold, his soul shall be swollen, not reduced
therein*§[26] This refers to the fact that they will pile up
for themselves a double requital[27] for their sins, and shall
not be quit of judgment for them.

But the righteous through his faithfulness shall live.
This refers to all in Jewry[28] who carry out the Law
[*Torah*]. On account of their labor and of their faith in
him who expounded the Law aright, God will deliver them
from the house of judgment.

(5, 6) *Moreover, because wealth*[29] *betrays, a man
grows prurient*[30] *and behaves unseemly,*[31] *in that he
grows greedy like Sheol*[32] *and insatiable as death. All the
nations are gathered unto him, and all the peoples are
amassed unto him. Shall not they all take up a parable
against him and heap on him jesting satire and say: 'Woe
unto him who amasses what is not his! How long shall it
last! He is merely heaping pledges (which must someday
be returned)!'*[33] This refers to the wicked priest who,
when first he came to office, enjoyed a reputation for
truth,[34] but who, when he came to rule in Israel, grew arrogant and abandoned God, betraying His statutes for the
sake of wealth, plundering and amassing for himself the
kind of wealth usually acquired by criminals who have rebelled against God. He also took public property, thereby

‡ Literally, 'this refers'.
§ Literally, 'Behold, his soul is swollen, not levelled therein'.
In the Hebrew, the contrast is between a protuberance and level
ground. But it is virtually impossible to reproduce this effect
in English.

merely heaping upon himself the penalty of guilt. Furthermore, he practised abomination, involving every kind of impurity and filth.[35]

(7, 8[a]) *Will not they suddenly rise who will 'put their bite'*[36] *on thee, and will they not (suddenly) 'sting'*[37] *who shall rudely disturb thee? . . . Because thou hast plundered nations aplenty, all the rest of the peoples (will) plunder thee?* This refers to the priest who rebelled [and violated] the statutes of God, thereby causing himself to be smitten with the judgments of wickedness. The horrors of evil diseases acted upon him and he paid the price of his misdeeds in the body of his flesh.[38] And as for the phrase, *because thou hast plundered nations aplenty, all the rest of the peoples will plunder thee,* this refers to the final priests of Jerusalem who will amass for themselves wealth and gain by plundering the people, but whose wealth and plunder will ultimately be delivered into the hands of the army of the Kittaeans, i.e. 'the rest of the peoples'.

(8[b]) *Because of human bloodshed and the violence done to land and city and to all that dwell therein.* This refers to the wicked priest. Because of the mischief which he had done to him who taught the Law aright and to the men associated with him, God delivered him into the hands of his enemies, that they might torture him with scourging and wear him out with bitterness of spirit for acting unrighteously against His elect.

(9–11) *Woe unto him who gets evil gain for his house, setting his nest on high, to be safe from the reach of harm! Thou hast planned but shame for thy house—the cutting off many peoples, and thou hast sinned against thine own self! For the stone shall cry out from the wall, and the beam from the woodwork respond!* This refers to the [   ] who planned to build himself a mansion in such a way that its very stones would be furnished through oppression and the beams of its woodwork through robbery.[39] And as for the phrase *the cutting off of many peoples and thou hast sinned against thine own self,* this refers to the House of

Judgment where God will render His judgment in the midst of many peoples. Thence will He in turn transport him for the execution of sentence, and in their midst He will condemn him and sentence him to the fire of brimstone.

(12, 13) *Woe unto him who builds a city by bloodshed and founds a town by wrongdoing! Behold, will it not come from the Lord of hosts that peoples shall labor only for fire, and nations weary themselves for naught?* This statement refers to the preacher of lies who misled many people into building a worthless city by bloodshed and into establishing a community by falsehood,[40] directing their efforts[41] to the service of vanity and instructing them in deeds of falsehood. The result will be that all their labors will prove in vain, since they will encounter the judgments of fire for having abused and defamed God's elect.

(14) *For the earth shall be filled with the knowledge of the glory of the Lord as waters cover the sea.* This statement refers to the fact that when God eventually restores them to their former glory, [   ] falsehood [will] [   ], and thereafter knowledge will be revealed to them, abundant as the waters of the sea.

(15) *Woe unto him that plies his neighbor with drink, that pours out his flask* [ḥemathô], *yea, makes him drunk, in order to gaze on their festivals!*[42] This refers to the wicked priest, who chased after the true exponent of the Law, right to the house where he was dwelling in exile,[43] in order to confuse him by a display of violent temper [ḥᵃmathô], and who then, on the occasion of the rest-day of Atonement, appeared to them in full splendor in order to confuse them and trip them up on the day of the fast, the day of their sabbatical rest.[44]

(16) *Thou art sated with disgrace instead of with honor. The cup in the Lord's right hand will come around unto thee, and basest disgrace will fall upon thine honor.* This refers to the priest whose disgrace exceeded his

honor, because he did not circumcise the foreskin of his heart, but kept walking in the ways of drunken debauch in order to slake his (insatiable) thirst. The cup of God's wrath will confound him, so that all he will really increase will be [shame, disgrace] and anguish.

(17) *The crime (committed) against Lebanon shall overwhelm thee and the violence done to dumb beasts shall crush you,*[45] *because of human bloodshed and of violence done to land and city and to all that dwell therein.* The statement refers to the wicked priests and means that God will mete out to him the treatment that he meted out to the needy. 'Lebanon' stands here for the Communal Council,[46] and 'dumb beasts' for the simple-minded Jews who have been carrying out the Law [*Torah*]. God will condemn him to annihilation, even as *he* plotted to annihilate the needy. And as to the statement, *because of blood shed in the city and violence done against the land,* the 'city' refers to Jerusalem wherein the wicked priest wrought his abominable works and wherein he defiled the sanctuary of God; while the 'violence done against the land' refers to the cities of Jewry[47] wherein he plundered the property of the needy.

(18) *What value has a graven idol, when its maker has graven it, or a molten image, or teachers of lies? For the maker is but trusting in his own creation, is simply making dumb idols!* This statement refers to the idols which the heathen make to serve and worship. On the day of judgment these will not deliver them.

(19) *Woe unto him that says to a stock, awake: to a dumb stone, arise!* This refers to [   ].

(20) *Hush before the Lord, all the earth!* This refers to all the heathen who have been worshipping stock and stone. On the Day of Judgment God will annihilate all who worship idols and all the wicked from the earth.

PSALM 37

*　　*　　*

(7) *Wait quietly for the 𐤉𐤄𐤅𐤄,** *be patient till He comes;
fret not over him whose way runs smooth, the man who
achieves his ends.* The reference is to the Man of Lies,
who has been seducing the masses by falsehoods, in that
they have come to choose ungodliness and have given no
ear to him who has been mediating (true) knowledge; for
these men will (eventually) perish by sword, famine, and
plague.

(8, 9) *Refrain from anger and abandon wrath; fret
not thyself, it tendeth only to evil-doing. For evil-doers
shall be cut off.* This applies to those who return to the
Law [Torah] and do not refuse to repent their evil-doing.
Those, however, who are defiant about repenting their iniquity will be cut off.
*But they that wait upon the 𐤉𐤄𐤅𐤄—those shall inherit
the earth.* The reference in the word 'those' is to the congregation of God's elect, the men who do His will.

(10) *Yet a little, and the wicked shall not be. Though I*[1]
look closely at his place, he shall not be. This refers to
all <who practise>[2] wickedness. At the end of forty years
which are (first) to be completed,[8] no wicked man shall
be found on earth.

(11) *But the meek shall inherit the earth and delight in
peace abounding.* This refers to the congregation of the
men who are poor[4] (currently) having to accept a period
of affliction, but who will eventually be delivered from all

* Written in archaic script.

snares of Belial and thereafter enjoy all the [riches] of the
earth and regale themselves on all the delights of the flesh.

(12, 13) *The wicked schemes against the righteous and
gnashes his teeth over him; but the 𝕷𝖔𝖗𝖉 will laugh at him,
for He has seen that his day is coming.* This refers to
those in the house of Judah who violate the Covenant in
that they scheme to make an end of all in the council of
the community who carry out the Law. God, however, will
not abandon the latter into their hands.

(14, 15) *The wicked have drawn out the sword and
bent their bows to cast down the poor and needy and to
slay such as walk the straight road. Their sword shall enter
their own heart, and their bows shall be broken in pieces.*
This refers to the wicked men of Ephraim and Manasseh[5] who seek to assail the priest and the men of like counsel when this time of testing is come upon them. Howbeit,
God will rescue the latter out of their hand, and thereafter
they themselves will be delivered into the hands of heathen
desperadoes, that judgment may be executed upon them.

(16) *The little that is owned by one righteous man is
worth more than the wealth of many who are wicked.*
This refers to those who carry out the Law and do not
[abandon themselves] to evil things.

(17, 18) *For the arms of [the wicked will be broken],
but the 𝕷𝖔𝖗𝖉 will uphold the righteous. The 𝕷𝖔𝖗𝖉 [knows
that the blameless will have their day, and their heritage
will endure for ever.* This refers to those who do] His
will [   ].

(19) *They shall suffer no hurt[6] through [evil times.
. . .* This refers to] those who will (eventually) come
back from the wilderness[7] and live in safe[ty][8] for a thousand generations.[9] The whole heritage of Adam shall be
theirs and their seed's for ever.[10]

(20) *But the wicked shall perish.* This means that God will sustain such men when they go hungry in this period of affliction, whereas the masses who did not participate in that exodus and who [refused] to go along with the congregation of God's elect will perish through famine and plague.

Howbeit, they that love the 𝔏𝔬𝔯𝔡[11] *shall be like prized lambs.*[12] This means that they will become leaders and princes [among His people, like] <bellwethers>[13] among their flocks.

(But those others) shall vanish like smoke; they shall be brought to an end.[14] This refers to those princes of (the realm of) wickedness who have been oppressing God's holy people. They shall vanish like the smoke of a firebrand [in the] wind.

(21, 22) *The wicked borrows and does not repay, but the righteous is generous and gives. Verily, they that are blessed of God shall inherit the earth, but they that are cursed of Him shall be cut off.* This refers to that congregation of poor men who have been willing to [make over] their entire estate to the [common fund].[15] These shall obtain as their possession that 'most eminent of Israel's mountains'[16] and revel in Him who sits in holiness upon it. But as to the 'cursed' who are to be 'cut off'—these are the wicked men in Israel who violate the Covenant. They shall be cut off and [destroyed] for ever.

(23, 24) *The goings of a man are ordered by the 𝔏𝔬𝔯𝔡, and He is concerned*[17] *with his every step. Though he fall, he shall not be flung headlong, for the 𝔏𝔬𝔯𝔡 [grasps his hand] in support.* This refers to the Priest who expounds the Law correctly,[18] whose office God has bespoken, whom He has appointed to build for Him a congregation[19] of [holiness(?)] and to whom He has given a straight way to His truth.

(25, 26) *I have been young, and now am old; yet have I not seen the righteous forsaken, nor His seed begging bread. All the day long He is gracious and lends, and His seed becomes a blessing.* This refers to him who expounds the Law [correctly   ].

*   *   *

(28) [*Wrongdoers*] *are destroyed for ever, and the offspring of the wi*[*cked are cut off*]. These are the men who violate [the Covenant and spurn] the Law.

(29) *The righteous* [*shall inherit the earth and dwell for*] *ever upon it.* [This refers to the fact that they will endure] through a thousand [generations].

(30, 31) [*The mouth of the wicked utters*] *wisdom, and his tongue speaks* [*justice. He gives mind to the guidance given by his God (wherefore) his steps do not slip.* This refers to] the Truth which [God] has spoken [   ], He has told them [   ].

(32, 33) *The wicked watches out for the righteous, and seeks* [*to put him to death. The* 𝔏o]r𝔡 [*will not abandon him into his hand, nor*] *suffer him to be condemned when he is arraigned.* This refers to the Wicked [Pri]est[20] who watc[hes out] for the right[eous and seeks] to put him to death [so as to subvert the Covenant] and the Law which God has transmitted to him. Howbeit, God will not aban[don him] nor [suffer him to be condemned when] he is arraigned, but will deal to (that villain) his deserts by delivering him into the hands of heathen desperadoes, to execute [judgment] upon him.

(34) [*Wait for the*] 𝔏or𝔡, *and keep to His way, and He will exalt thee to possess the earth. Thou wilt see the wicked cut off.* This refers to the fact that they will see wickedness adjudged, and rejoice along with God's elect in an inheritance of truth.

(35, 36) *I have seen the wicked flourishing wild in all his naked pride,*[21] *like a flowering tree in its native soil; but anon I passed by*[22] *[and lo, he] was gone. I s[ought him] but he could not [be found.* This refers] to the Man of Lies[23] [who has been vaunting himself] against God's elect [and see]king to stop [the sons of righteousness from ob]ser[ving the precepts of the Law] whereby they might do [deeds] of justice.[24] Highhandedly has he been venting his presumption [   ].

(37) [*Mark the blameless man and behold] the upright, [for there is pos]te[rity for the ma]n of peace.* This refers to [. They will enjoy] a peaceful [futu]re.

(38) *But transgressors shall be destroyed one and all, and the posteri[ty of the wicked shall be cut off].* This means that [   ] will perish and be cut off from the midst of the congregation of the community.

PSALM 45

(In order to render these comments intelligible, it is necessary to present the Scriptural text and our author's literal understanding of it side by side.)

Scriptural Text

(1) From the collection of the Choirmaster.

From the collection of the Choirmaster.

To the tune of "lilies . . ." From the repertoire of (the guild of temple musicians known as) 'the sons of Korah'.

Concerning (those who may be described as) 'lilies', i.e., the sons of Korah.[1]

A poem of the genre called *maskîl*.

A didactic poem (*maskîl*).

An erotic song.

A song expressing (God's) affection.

————[The 'sons of Ḳoraḥ' here typify] the seven classes of penitents in Is[rael . . .

(2) My heart is astir with a goodly matter (lit. word).

My heart has been bubbling over with (God's) Good Word.

I indite my verses (lit. works for a king).

My works (deeds) are done for a King.[2]

————This refers to [the influence of] the Holy Spir[it],[3] for [

and my tongue is the pen of a ready writer.

and my tongue is the pen of an expert scribe.

————The reference is to the authoritative expositor of
the Law (Torah).[4] God has endowed him with power of
expression. . . .[5]

*   *   *   *

NOTES

Isaiah

1. The comments are culled from four different manuscripts; for details, see the list of sources, below,
pp. 541ff. Comments on other passages are too fragmentary for translation, and in some cases only the
Scriptural text, without the interpretation, is preserved.
2. The author is evidently interpreting the *thorns and
thistles* to refer symbolically to those that seek to ob-
struct Israel from following the true path. The words,
their eyes, may be the conclusion of a sentence saying
that, in consequence of these men's machinations, the
bulk of the people are following the sinful inclination
of their hearts and eyes (cf. *M.* v.5) or doing what is
right in their own eyes (cf. *Z.* viii.7; xix.20).
3. For the convenience of the reader, I have borrowed
Moffatt's rendering, which turns the Hebrew measures
into English equivalents.
4. This is a precise eschatological epoch; cp. *Manual,*
iii.18; iv.19, 26, '*Zadokite*' *Document,* xix.10.
5. Literally (RSV), *They have lyre and harp, timbrel
and flute and wine at their feasts.*
6. Heb. *Sheol,* i.e., the netherworld.
7. Literally, 'men of scoffing'—the same expression as in
the '*Zadokite*' *Document,* xx.11; cp. also ib., i.14.
8. Heb. *Torah.*
9. Although the point is irrelevant to our author's interpretation, it may be suggested that in the Scriptural
verse, *the Lord* is an interpolation due to wrong exegesis, the subject of the sentence being really the king of
Assyria, who was in fact turned back at the very gates
of Jerusalem; cp. Isa. 37.36–37. In that case, the sense

of the verb would be inchoative, i.e., 'when he is about to consummate what he is doing', etc.

10. As a parallel to 'fruit', the Hebrew word *tiph'ereth*, which usually means 'pride, splendor', may perhaps here be derived from the root *p-'-r* II (whence *p'ūrah*, 'branch') and rendered 'burgeoning'.

11. Actually, the prophecy was directed against Assyria, but in applying it to current events the author may be using the name Babylon, as frequently in rabbinic literature, as a cautious pseudonym for Rome.

12. The point is that the Hebrew word *ḥôq* means both 'bound' and 'statute'.

13. Since the whole purpose of the commentary is to give the prophecy a contemporary relevance, this seems the obvious restoration.

14. In the Scriptural context, the reference is, of course, to the king of Assyria. It should be observed that the verb here rendered 'stay themselves' is also used specifically of leaning on a staff, so that the words 'one who merely smites them' continue this image.

15. The Hebrew words mean literally, 'God, the Warrior' or 'a divine champion'; the implication being that instead of relying on an earthly emperor, they will recognize God as the true conquering hero.

16. Restored *ad sensum*.

17. NEB: 'justice in full flood'. The picture is suggested, of course, by the preceding reference to '*sands of the sea*'.

18. The manuscript appears to read '*Acco*, i.e., the seaport of Acre. From the other places named, however, it is plain that the Redeemer is imagined as advancing upon Jerusalem from the east and northeast, through the territory of Benjamin—consonant with the words of Isa. 41.2 (originally referring to Cyrus): 'Whom hath He roused from the east', etc. (Cp. also *Sibylline Oracles*, iii.652f.) Acre therefore lies in the wrong direction, besides being too far away, and we must assume a scribal error for '*Achor* (Jos. 7.24; 15.7; Isa. 65.10; Hos. 2.17), i.e., the valley of the Wadi Dabr

and the Wadi Mukelik, east of 'Aiath (Ai), Michmas Geba', etc.

19. The context suggests the restoration, '[Benjamin]'.

20. Cp. *War*, passim; Introduction, pp. 27–28.

21. The Scriptural text is usually taken to mean, 'Lebanon with its majestic ones (i.e., cedars) shall fall'; but the Hebrew is ambiguous, and our author evidently understood it (as a strict parallel to 'with an ax') in the sense of 'Lebanon by the agency of its own majestic ones shall fall'.

22. I restore: [*sha*]*lôm*.

23. Cp. Jer. 23.5; 33.15; Zech. 12.6.

24. I restore ['*oyᵉ*]*baw*, preceded by a verb antithetical in sense to 'uphold'.

25. These are standard appurtenances of the messianic king. For the 'throne of glory', cf. Isa. 22.23; for the 'holy crown', cf. Ps. 132.18 (where the Ancient Versions read significantly, 'upon him shall *My* crown flourish' instead of '*his* crown', as in the Masoretic text). A similar description is given in the late Jewish *midrash* entitled 'Chapters about the Messiah' (J. D. Eisenstein, ed., *Oṣar Midrashim* [1928], ii, 393b): 'In that hour the Holy One, blessed be He, will adorn the Messiah with a crown and set upon his head a helmet of salvation [Isa. 59.17], and endue him with a majestic sheen and lustre, and attire him in glorious garments and make him stand upon a high mountain to herald glad tidings to Israel; and he will proclaim, "Salvation is nigh!" '

26. A gap in the text prevents our knowing what was supposed to be placed in the hand of the messianic king. A clue might perhaps be found in the words of Isa. 22.21, 23–to which verses, indeed, our passage is indebted: the priest, there envisaged as exercising the royal office, is said to be clothed in the regal robe and girdle and to have *the government* (or *the insignia of government?*) committed into his hand. Alternatively, we may think of the later Jewish belief (attested, for instance, in the Persian version of *The Apocalypse of*

Daniel) that the Messiah would carry in his hand the wonder-working rod of Moses—a belief which appears also in Samaritan sources (e.g., *Asāṭir* xii.24; Cowley, *Samaritan Liturgy*, 511ff.; *Ma'lf*, § 49; *Scroll of Itamar*, quoted in M. Gaster, *Samaritan Eschatology* [1932], 263).

27. See above, pp. 27–28; cf. also Analytical Index, E. 2 (*i*).

28. In the future dispensation, the anointed king is to be subject to the authority of the anointed priest; see below, pp. 392, 441. The point is made explicitly in the pseudepigraphic *Testament of Judah*, iv.2–4.

29. What is envisaged is, of course, the investiture of the messianic king.

30. It may be suggested that in the Scriptural text these words, usually taken to refer to God's plan, really refer sarcastically to the grandiose schemes of the king of Assyria, the following verse then providing a crushing counterblast.

31. The defective state of the manuscript prevents our determining the verse in Zechariah which our author has in mind. Perhaps it is Zech. 1.6: 'Like as the Lord of Hosts purposed to do unto us, according to our doings, so has He dealt with us'.

32. In view of the statement, 'your eyes shall see', I interpret the Hebrew word *yikkaneph* (a denominative verb from *kanaph*, 'edge of a garment') in the sense in which the cognate term is used in Arabic.

33. In Hebrew the word means also 'teachers', inevitably suggesting the future true expounders of the Law (*vulgo* 'teachers of righteousness').

34. This is usually rendered (RSV), *When you turn to the right and when you turn to the left,* but it is difficult to see how any path can be described as the right one, if one can turn off it arbitrarily to either side! I therefore take the words to constitute a concessive clause. (It may be suggested that the true reading of the Scriptural text is *kōh . . . weḵōh*, rather than *kî . . . weḵî*, i.e., 'here you must turn to the right, and there to the left'.)

35. The Hebrew word for 'wrongdoing' means properly 'deviation, aberration', and this is the basis of the interpretation.

36. A fragmentary comment on these verses (*DJD* V, No. 176, frags. 8–11) refers them to a period during which Israel will be in a state of exhaustion waiting for the words of consolation and the abounding glory which God will vouchsafe and to the discomfiture of Belial who will no longer be able to afflict his servants. The fragments are too mutilated to allow of translation.

Hosea

1. Cp. Deut. 28.28.
2. Cp. *'Zadokite' Document*, i.3; xx.23.
3. An eschatological era; cp. *Manual*, iii.18; iv.19, 26; *'Zadokite' Document*, vii.9; viii.3; xix.6, 10, 15.
4. Cp. *'Zadokite' Document*, i.7; *Hymns* iii.28. See also Analytical Index, E. 1 (*a*).

Micah

1. This interpretation is based on the fact that the Hebrew words rendered *a place for the planting of a vineyard* could also be translated (purely formally), *them that lead the vineyard astray*. Since Israel is described in Scripture as God's vineyard (Isa. 5.1; 27.2), our author fancifully took the verse to mean that God would eventually 'dump' the false teachers who misled His people.

2. What the prophet meant, of course, was that Jerusalem had been turned into the equivalent of a pagan 'high place' or sanctuary. But our author took the words to imply the converse of what had previously been said. Israel, he declares, has turned to idolatry; but the true 'high place' of the Jews is the temple in Jerusalem. His further interpretation is based on the fact that the name Jerusalem can be fancifully ex-

plained as containing the two elements, *y-r-h*, 'teach', and *shalom*, 'peace'. The true sanctuary, he suggests, is that built by the righteous teachers who ensure peace and security on the Day of Judgment!

3. This is a tentative restoration, seeking to recover what may have been our author's way of interpreting the Scriptural text. It is based on the fact that the Hebrew word rendered *roll down* resembles that which means *sojourn*, while the word rendered *uncover* is identical in form with that meaning *drive into exile*. The 'stones' and 'foundations' of idolatry would readily have been identified with the venal priests of Jerusalem.

4. The basis of this interpretation is that the gate of the city was the place of judgment.

5. This interpretation is suggested by the fact that the Hebrew word for 'gate', viz. *sha'ar*, resembles the name Se'ir, and thus calls to mind Deut. 33.2: 'The Lord came from Sinai, and rose from Se'ir unto them'. Cp. also Judges 5.4.

Nahum

1. This rendering attempts to reproduce the alliteration in the Hebrew. The expression is something of a cliché; cp. Isa. 29.6; Amos 1.14; Ps. 83.16.

2. The basis of this interpretation would seem to be that the Hebrew word for 'expanse' (viz. *raqî'ᵃ*) suggests the verb *r-q-'* meaning 'stamp to dust' (II Sam. 22.43; Ezek. 6.11; 23.6).

3. The restoration (viz. *br[dtô yzd'zū*, vel. sim.]) is simply a guess.

4. In the Scriptural context, this is a transference to Yahweh of an older Canaanite myth relating how Baal discomfited the Lord of the Sea. The myth is related on tablets discovered at Ras Shamra-Ugarit, and has Mesopotamian and Hittite parallels; cp. T. H. Gaster, *Thespis*[2] (1961), pp. 137–53. In the Bible, the phrase is virtually demythologized.

5. See above, General Introduction, pp. 27–28.

6. For this expression cp. *Hymns* frag. 5.7.

7. Cp. the exposition of Isa. 10.34; above, pp. 306–7.

8. Literally, 'the men of his counsel'; for this expression, cp. *HabC.* v.10; ix.10; *Hymns* vi.10; 11.13; *MFC* i.3. Note that the scheming of Belial is specifically mentioned in Nahum 1.11.

9. See Analytical Index, A. 5.

10. Cp. Isa. 5.25; 63.19; 64.2; Jer. 4.24; Micah 1.4; Ps. 18.18.

11. Not impossibly, the mention of the Lord's 'blazing wrath' was taken to refer to the eschatological 'Era of Wrath', concerning which see Analytical Index, E. 1 (*a*).

12. The interpretation is based on Pss. 26.8; 68.6; 76.3; II Chron. 36.15, where Jerusalem (Zion) is designated as God's 'abode'; and on Jer. 2.15, where the adversaries of Israel are described as 'young lions'.

13. The comment alludes to an incident described by Josephus (*Ant.*, XIII, 14.1–2) in connection with an uprising of the Jews against the cruelty of Alexander Jannaeus, around 88 B.C.: 'They sent also to Demetrius Eucerus [king of Syria] and besought him to make common cause with them in their defense. So Demetrius came with an army and took those that had invited him, and pitched camp near Shechem. Thereupon, Alexander, with his 6,200 mercenaries and about 20,000 Jews who were of his party, went forth against Demetrius, who had 3,000 horsemen and 40,000 foot soldiers . . . (Eventually) they joined battle. Demetrius won, and all of Alexander's mercenaries were slain . . . Alexander took to the hills'. (The story is told also in *War*, I, 4.4–5.) Evidently, after his victory, Demetrius sought to enter Jerusalem and claim the throne.

14. Evidently, Antiochus IV Epiphanes (175–164 B.C.).

15. The 'Kittians' are here evidently identified with the Romans, as later in the Aramaic Version (Targum) of Num. 24.24 and in the Vulgate.

16. The comment shows that the author read the Hebrew word *BeDê*, 'sufficient for', as *BaDDê*, 'limbs' (cp. Job 18.13).

17. Warriors or heroes are called 'mighty lions' in II Sam. 23.20; Isa. 33.7—according to a traditional interpretation—and 'whelps' (Ezek. 32.2). A similar expression is frequent in Arabic (e.g. Yaqut, III. 437, 17; 615, 13). Comparable also is Aeschylus, *Choephori*, 939, where Orestes and Pylades are so described. Cp. also Euripides, *Orestes*, 1401.

18. Cp. Josephus, *loc. cit.*: 'Some 6,000 Jews, moved to pity by the change in Alexander's fortune, gathered together and joined him. At this, Demetrius grew alarmed, and withdrew from the country. The Jews then turned on Alexander, but were defeated and slain in great numbers. When he had shut up the most powerful of them in the city Bethone, he besieged them therein; and when he had captured the city and brought those men into his power, he had them transported to Jerusalem and perpetrated upon them one of the most barbarous acts in the world. For while he was carousing with his concubines, in full view of the citizenry, he ordered some eight hundred of those men to be crucified; and, while they were still alive, he ordered the throats of their children and their wives to be slit before their eyes. This was by way of revenge for the injury they had done him' (Whiston's translation, slightly revised).

19. The Mishnah (*Sanhedrin*, 6.4) records the opinion of the sages that 'none is hanged save the blasphemer and the idolator'. This is an interpretation of the Scriptural text (Deut. 21.23) that 'he that is hanged is a curse (reproach) to God', in the sense that hanging presupposes blasphemy.

20. The comment shows that our author read *RBKH*, 'thy multitude', not *RKBH*, 'its chariotry', as in the traditional (Masoretic) text. His reading agrees with that of the Greek (Septuagint) and Syriac (Peshitta) Versions.

21. Cp. *Commentary on Habakkuk* 2.5–6 (below, pp. 322ff.).

22. 'Ephraim' and 'Israel' denote the Samaritans, who claimed to be the remnant of the Northern Kingdom and to be descended from Ephraim and Manasseh.

23. I.e., the Samaritans, who claimed descent from Ephraim and Manasseh, and betrayed the Jews on numerous occasions; cp. Josephus, *Ant.*, IX.14, 3; XI.8, 6; XII.5, 6.

24. For this style, cp. *Hymns* ii.15, 32; 'Zadokite' Document, i.18, etc.

25. Heb. *talmud*.

26. The traditional Hebrew text and the Ancient Versions read 'gazing-stock'. A transposition of two letters yields our author's reading.

27. Cp. Josephus, *Ant.*, IX.14, 3 (of the Samaritans): 'When they see the Jews in prosperity, they pretend that they are changed, and allied to them, and call themselves kinsmen, as though they were derived from Joseph and had by that means an original alliance with them; but when they see them falling into a low condition, they say they are in no way related to them' (trans. Whiston).

28. Heb. *keneseth* (from *k-n-s*, 'gather'); hence the antithesis of 'be dispersed'.

29. Heb. *by the streams of the Nile*. Nô Amon was Egyptian Thebes.

30. The commentator obviously took the prophet's words to mean that the city's ramparts had dissolved like water. For this imagery, cp. Jos. 7.5.

31. Properly, Somaliland and Libya.

32. Only the final letter *-h* remains. Perhaps restore: [Juda]h.

33. Heb. *house of Peleg*; cp. 'Zadokite' Document, viii.45. The identification was inspired by the initial letters of *Put* and *Lubim*.

34. For the imagery, cp. Hab. 2.16.

Habakkuk

1. The traditional (Masoretic) text reads, 'Look ye among the nations' (Heb. *BaGoYiM*). Our author read, by a slight change, *BoGeDiM*, 'traitors'—a reading also found in the ancient Greek (Septuagint) Version.

2. Cp. *'Zadokite' Document*, vi, 19; viii, 21; xx, 12–13; and see General Introduction, pp. 5, 23.

3. These words have been inserted to bring out the basis of the author's interpretation.

4. See Introduction to *The War of the Sons of Light and the Sons of Darkness*, below, p. 399.

5. The traditional (Masoretic) text reads, 'Its judgment and its dignity proceed from itself', i.e., 'it is a law to itself'. It is apparent, however, from his subsequent comment that our author construed the Hebrew word *se'tho*, usually rendered 'his dignity', as somehow connected with the verb *hishi'*, 'deceive'.

6. This is obviously intended as an interpretation of the words, 'His judgment [standard of justice] proceeds from himself'.

7. The traditional text reads, '[are turned] eastwards' [or, 'look straight ahead'].

8. All of the terms used in the Hebrew can refer either to temper or to tempest; and this is the basis of the interpretation.

9. This has been thought to refer to standard *Roman* methods of laying siege to a city.

10. Literally, 'this one', which the author construed as meaning 'so-and-so'.

11. The traditional text reads, 'and becomes guilty'—Heb. *ve-ashem*. Our author read *ve-yashem*, 'and devastates'.

12. This has been thought to allude to the Roman Senate.

13. The allusion may be general rather than specific. In any case, it would fit several different historical situations, so that, in the absence of further information,

attempts to precise it would seem both premature and futile.

14. The prophet's words are usually construed differently, viz. 'Thou hast set him, O Rock, for judgment, and established him, O Rock, for correction. [Thou art] purer of eyes than to behold evil, and canst not look on perverseness'.

15. The hebrew word [*bl'*] means both 'swallow up' and 'confound'. It is evident that our author understood it in the latter sense.

16. Not to be taken literally as referring to a particular person called Absalom. The expression means simply, 'conspirators like the associates of the Biblical Absalom'.

17. See General Introduction, p. 29.

18. The traditional text reads, 'Which have no ruler over them'.

19. This is thought to refer to the Roman practise of worshipping military standards. This, however, is not definitely attested before Imperial times.

20. Josephus tells us (*Ant.*, XIV, 4.5) that, until its capture by Pompey in 63 B.C., the city of Jerusalem had often to pay more than 2,000 talents annually in tribute to its foreign masters.

21. The traditional (Masoretic) text reads, 'His net' (Heb. *ḥermô*). Our author, by a change of one letter, read *ḥarbô*, 'his sword'.

22. The meaning of the Hebrew word is uncertain.

23. This seems the only way of reproducing the author's interpretation of the words, 'That he who runs may read' (literally, 'that he who reads may run').

24. The Hebrew word (*YAFIaH*) is usually rendered 'pants, hastens' or possibly 'depones'. But from his subsequent interpretation it seems that the author connected it with a like-sounding root, preserved in Syriac and Arabic, meaning 'be feeble, debilitated, laggard'.

25. Literally, 'for the mysteries of God are destined to be performed wondrously'.

26. King James Version: 'Behold, his soul [which] is lifted up is not upright in him'. American Jewish Version: 'Behold, his soul is puffed up, it is not upright in him'. The Revised Standard Version resorts to conjectural emendation and renders: 'Behold, he whose soul is not upright in him shall fall'. This, however, is patently wrong, because it misses the contrast between the two Hebrew words in question, the one of which means 'swollen, protuberant' and the other 'low-lying, level'.

27. The interpretation is based on a play on words: the term rendered 'swollen' is *'fl*, which the author fancifully identifies with the like-sounding *kfl*, 'be double', and this at once suggests to him Isa. 40.2.

28. Heb. *Judah*.

29. The Hebrew ('Masoretic') text has *hayayin*, 'wine'. By a slight change, our author read *hôn*, 'wealth'.

30. The Hebrew word *yahir* is usually derived from a root *yhr* which is assumed to mean 'be proud' and is therefore rendered 'grows insolent'. But our author may well have connected it with the Syriac and late Heb. *hrhr*, 'be prurient'.

31. The Hebrew word *ynvh* is usually connected with *naveh*, 'dwelling', and rendered 'and abides not at home'. But our author evidently identified it with an homophonous *nvh* (=*n'h*), 'be comely, seemly'.

32. I.e., the netherworld.

33. King James Version: 'Woe to him that increaseth [that which is] not his! how long? and to him that ladeth himself with thick clay!' (The 'thick clay' is here compounded out of ancient ignorance of what the relevant Hebrew word meant. We now know that it signifies 'pledge(s)'.)

34. Literally, 'who was called (renowned) for truth'. The assumption that this refers to his actual name, which he subsequently changed, is quite erroneous and overlooks a common Hebrew idiom.

35. See above, n. 13.

36. This colloquialism seems the only way of reproducing the effect of the Hebrew, which lies in the fact that

the word for 'creditor, usurer' derives from a verbal root meaning 'bite'!

37. The Hebrew word (*yakiṣu*), usually rendered 'awake', is fancifully construed by our author as if it were the very similar *ya'kiṣu*, 'sting'. Once again, an English colloquialism best conveys the point.

38. A. Dupont-Sommer has suggested that the reference is to the wicked priest Aristobulus II who was arrested and imprisoned and finally died of poison in prison at the hands of Pompey's supporters. But to die of poison is not to die of loathsome diseases, and what our author is trying specifically to interpret is Habakkuk's reference to 'bites' and 'stings'. Besides, this whole business of looking for precise historical allusions seems grossly overdone; the passages in question may have in mind *typical* rather than *actual* cases. The use of the perfect tense is not against this; we may render: 'This refers to the kind of wicked priest who, in the past, was invariably exposed to this and this suffering', etc.

39. Here again the reference may be typical rather than actual.

40. H. H. Rowley (*The Zadokite Fragments and the Dead Sea Scrolls*, [1952], p. 67) makes the ingenious suggestion that this refers to the rebuilding of the city of David in the time of Antiochus Epiphanes, mentioned in I Macc. 1.33. The wicked priest, he thinks, was Menelaus. But once again we may be chary of precise identifications.

41. Literally, 'making them weary themselves in'.

42. The traditional (Masoretic) text reads, 'in order to gaze on their nakedness' (*me'orêhem*). In the ancient Hebrew script, the letters *r* and *d* are often barely distinguishable, and our author evidently read *me'odê-hem*. However, he took this to mean 'their staggerings' (*rtm-'-d*) rather than 'their festivals' (*mo'ed*), as usually understood. Hence, he interpreted the Scriptural text as referring to an occasion when the congregation was made to totter (or stumble) in the observance of a holy day.

43. See General Introduction, p. 19. The Hebrew expression (*ABYT GLUTÔ*) has been read differently (viz. *ABÔT GLUTÔ*) and rendered 'desiring his exile', i.e., aiming to drive him into exile. Other considerations apart, however, it should be observed that the verb *A-B-H* (from which *ABÔT* would derive) means properly 'assent to, comply with', rather than 'desire, aspire to, aim at'.

44. Cp. Lev. 16.31; 23.32.

45. The Scriptural text says: *The violence of Lebanon* (i.e., which lurks in the forests of Lebanon) *and the assault of beasts shall crush* (or, *affright*) *you.* Our author, however, takes the words, *of Lebanon* and *of beasts,* as objective rather than subjective genitives (a construction paralleled in Joel 4.19). Substantially the same interpretation as is here given is to be found also in the Aramaic Targum *in loc.,* and is adopted in NEB.

46. The name Lebanon means 'white' (referring to the white cliffs). The point of the interpretation lies in the fact that the members of the Brotherhood wore white—as do the modern Samaritans and Mandaeans.

47. Heb. *Judah.*

Psalm 37

1. The received (Masoretic) text reads: 'Though thou look'.

2. A word (Heb. *'ôsê*) has dropped out.

3. In accordance with the common Jewish tradition that the 'Messianic' ministry will last for forty years and then be followed by the Golden Age.

4. The Hebrew word is *ebyônîm,* and this has inspired the theory that the Qumran Covenanters were really the Ebionites, rather than the Essenes. But the inference is unnecessary, for it is difficult to see what other word the writer could possibly have used in the normal sense of 'poor, needy'.

5. The interpretation is inspired by Ps. 78.9: 'The children of Ephraim were as archers handling the bow'. The reference is to the Samaritans; see note 10 to *The Commentary on Nahum*.

6. The Hebrew word is usually rendered 'be shamed', but in Aramaic (and in Arabic) it has the sense of 'suffer misfortune' or even 'be ill', and the subsequent comment shows that the writer so understood it. (The actual quotation from Scripture is missing in the manuscript; it was written at the foot of the preceding column, which is now lost.)

7. To be understood metaphorically as well as literally; see Introduction, pp. 4, 27.

8. Restoring *beyesh[a']* rather than *beyosh[er]*, which is suggested by Allegro. Cp. Jer. 23.6.

9. In fulfillment of the Scriptural promise, Deut. 7.9.

10. Cp. Gen. 12.7; 15.8; 17.7–8; 28.13; Deut. 1.8.

11. The received (Masoretic) text and all the Ancient Versions read 'But the enemies of the Lord'. In the Hebrew, there is a difference of only one letter.

12. RSV: 'The enemies of the Lord are as the glory of the pastures', i.e., as grass that quickly withers. But the Hebrew word rendered 'pastures' (viz. *karîm*), if derived from a different verbal root, can mean 'lambs', and this is how the ancient Jewish interpreters understood it. (The true meaning is in any case obscure, and various emendations of the text have been suggested.)

13. The text is defective, and reads simply, '[   ] sheep'; I supply 'bellwethers' (Heb. *êlê*) for the sense.

14. The traditional text reads, by a different vocalization of the same consonants, 'They shall vanish like smoke, yea vanish'.

15. See *Manual of Discipline*, i.11–12.

16. The expression is borrowed from Ezek. 17.23.

17. Usually rendered 'delighteth', but the word is also used in the sense of 'be preoccupied', and it is evident that the writer so understood it.

18. The expression usually rendered, 'Teacher of Righteousness'.

19. The word rendered 'congregation' came in Syriac to mean 'church'. It is extremely interesting to find it associated here with the verb 'build', for this usage—foreign to the Old Testament—at once recalls the New Testament's 'building the church'. Indeed, if one wishes to indulge fancy, one may even suppose that the imperfectly preserved phrase actually spoke of 'building a church [congregation] firmly on a rock', for the verb 'set firm', which is here employed, is actually used, in Ps. 40.3(2), of 'planting firmly on a rock'. In that case, we should have here a striking parallel to Jesus' famous words to Peter (Mat. 16.18).

20. Cp. *HabC.*, viii.8; ix.9; xi.4; xii.2, 8. An historical identification is at present premature.

21. The Hebrew word, *mith'areh*, is of uncertain meaning in this passage. Normally, the root *'-r-h* means 'be naked', and our author may so have understood it, albeit in a figurative sense.

22. The traditional (Masoretic) text has, *'he* passed by', but our author's reading agrees with that of the Greek (Septuagint), Latin (Vulgate), and Syriac (Peshitta) Versions.

23. Cp. *HabC.*, ii.2; v.11; *'Zadokite' Document,* xx.15. An historical identification is at present premature.

24. Restored *ad sensum.*

Psalm 45

1. The identification of the Ḳoraḥite choristers in the Temple (cp. I Chron. 6.22) with the sons of the Ḳoraḥ who led the revolt against Moses in the wilderness (Num. 16) is in accord with standard rabbinic tradition. Moreover, because it is said in Num. 26.11 that the 'sons of Ḳoraḥ did not die' when the earth swallowed up the rebels, tradition asserted that they repented their father's action and refused to make common cause with him when Moses called on him to desist; see L. Ginzberg, *The Legends of the Jews,* vi (1946), p. 104, nn. 389–90. They are therefore exemplars of penitence. In pseudo-Philo's *Biblical*

Antiquities (xvi.4) they are said to have been *seven* in number, and it is in line with that tradition that our author regards them as archetypes of seven varieties of penitents. As to their being styled l i l i e s (a symbol of purity), cp. *Midrash T^ehillîm, in loc.* (quoted also in Yalqūṭ *Shim^e'oni*, §747): 'Whenever a man repents his offenses, the Holy One, blessed be He, gives him an additional pet-name. Consider the case of the sons of Ḳoraḥ. . . . After they had repented, but not before, they were called l i l i e s . . . as in the title of Psalm 45'. See further on this metaphor, I. Löw, *Die Flora der Juden* (repr. 1967), ii.172ff. This fanciful interpretation is further supported by the fact that the Hebrew word for 'lilies', viz. *shôshānîm,* lends itself to a 'freak' identification with the similar *shônîm,* 'those that change, i.e., repent'—which is how the Greek (Septuagint) and Latin (Vulgate) Versions actually render it in our passage!

2. Our author's understanding of this clause accords more closely with the punctuation in the traditional (Masoretic) text than does the usual version. The deeds of the speaker complement his word (though the latter is here evidently taken to mean God's word). The king is, of course, identified with God.

3. On inspiration by the Holy Spirit, cp. Targum, Isa. 40.13; TB Sanhedrin, 99^b; *Sifrê,* §176, etc. Aristobulus, quoted by Eusebius, *Praeparatio evangelica,* viii.10, 4; W. Bacher, *Die aelteste Terminologie der juedischen Schriftauslegung* (1899), i.169ff.; ii.202–6.

4. *Vulgo,* 'the Teacher of Righteousness', but the author is evidently referring to any of the accredited expositors such as are prescribed in *Manual,* vi.6; '*Zadokite*' Document, vii.18. See Analytical Index, B. 2 (*u*). Our author interprets the Hebrew word for 'writer, scribe', viz., *sōpher,* in the later sense of 'scholar'.

5. Literally, 'utterance (response) of tongue'; cp. Prov. 16.1.

II. EVERYMAN'S BIBLE

Introduction.   Of a different order are two paraphrases of portions of the Pentateuch, both only partially preserved.

§1. The first, discovered in 1947, is composed not in Hebrew, the sacred tongue, but in Aramaic, the vernacular 'understanded of the people'. Neither a formal commentary on Scripture, nor a mere set of sermon notes, it is a fanciful elaboration of narratives about the patriarchs related in the Book of Genesis. It belongs to a genre of literature (modelled, no doubt, on such romantic embellishments of Homeric and early Greek legends as are exemplified by the *Argonautica* of Apollonius of Rhodes and the *Heracleid* of Rhianus of Crete) which seems to have developed and enjoyed popularity in Jewish circles during the Hellenistic age[1] and which is best represented by the *Book of Jubilees* (alias *The Little Genesis*)—with which our text in fact shares several legends—the apocryphal additions to Daniel and Esther, the *Biblical Antiquities* falsely ascribed to Philo, and the compositions (preserved only in quotations) of such writers as Artapanus and the poetaster Ezekiel.[2] Medieval examples of the same genre are the *Book of Jashar*, the *Chronicles of Josippon*, the Samaritan *Asāṭîr* (Legends) *of Moses*, the Anglo-Saxon paraphrases of Genesis and Exodus attributed to Caedmon, and the English poem *Cleanness*.

The work has come to be known as *The Genesis Apocryphon*, but that title is misleading. For modern readers, the term *apocryphon* suggests a work which originally purported to be divinely inspired but which, however popular it may have been, was not eventually accepted into the

canon of Holy Writ. There is no evidence, however, that
the present composition ever claimed or enjoyed any more
exalted status than might have been accorded to the
Targums (which no one would call apocrypha) or, in our
own day, to any popular volume of Bible stories.

§2. Not the least interesting feature of the work is that
in its fanciful elaborations of the Scriptural narrative it incorporates several motifs well attested elsewhere in world
folklore.

(i) *The birth of Noah is accompanied by a sudden
blaze of light.* This is likewise a feature of nativity-stories
associated with Abraham,[3] Moses,[4] Buddha, the Greek
god Asklepios and the early Roman king Servius Tullius,
as well as with several Christian saints.[5] It is told also of
the baptism of Jesus,[6] and is in turn bound up with the ancient notions that (*a*) human children begotten by gods or
other supernatural beings reveal their parentage by having
radiant faces,[7] and that (*b*) the 'genius' of a hero, situated
in his head, emits rays.[8]

(ii) Lamech seeks explanation of this phenomenon by
appealing to his father Methuselah to repair to his father,
Enoch, which Methuselah does. Here we have but a Hebraic version of the familiar folktale motif of 'Old, older,
oldest', the theme of which is that a quest for information
'moves back by progressive stages to the hoary Nestor who
possesses the knowledge sought'.[9]

(iii) In order to reach Enoch, Methuselah travels to a
land (or place) named Parvaim. This land or place, the
location of which is still unknown, is mentioned in II
Chronicles 3.6 as that from which Solomon obtained gold
for coating the woodwork of the Temple. Now, since in
Enoch 65.2 the ancient patriarch is said to have been translated to 'the ends of the earth', it is apparent that Parvaim
is regarded by our author as a semi-mythical land in the
far distance.[10] It is thus the equivalent of the Earthly Paradise or Isles of the Blest, a characteristic of which in popular lore is their abundance of gold.[11] A particularly arresting parallel is furnished in classical literature by the sands
of the River Pactolus, in Lydia, which are said similarly

to have yielded the gold for the bricks presented by Croesus to the shrine at Delphi, and which, even after that gold had in fact been exhausted, continued to be spoken of in proverbial lore.[12]

(iv) Abram is forewarned of the danger which awaits him and Sarai at the hands of Pharaoh by dreaming of a threatened cedar and palm, which symbolize their lives. Here, again, we have a familiar motif of popular lore—namely, that the life (or soul) of a person is bound up with that of a tree.[13] To cite but a few examples from classical sources: Domitian's death was thought to have been presaged by the falling of a tree (Suetonius, *Domit.*, 15), and that of Severus Alexander by the felling of an ancient laurel and fig tree (Alex. Lampridius, *Alex. Sev.*, 60.4–5). The grove of triumphal trees planted by the Caesars finally died in Nero's last year (Suetonius, *Galba*, i; Tacitus, *Ann.*, xiii.58). Moreover, a story almost identical with that in our text is related in the Second Lay of Gudrun in the Poetic Edda. In similar vein, it is (or was) a Jewish custom to plant a cedar at the birth of a boy and a pine at that of a girl and later to fell them in order to build the nuptial canopy (*ḥuppah*) at their wedding (Bab. Talmud, *Giṭṭîn*, 57a; Pal. Talmud, *Erubîn*, iv.27b). Goethe's father is said to have planted a tree in his garden on the day the poet was born.

(v) The description of Sarai's beauty is couched in a series of clichés virtually identical with those applied to the Virgin Mary in various apocryphal infancy gospels.

(vi) The 'plague' with which Pharaoh is afflicted—usually identified in rabbinical legend as leprosy[14]—here appears to involve a sexual malfunction. This probably reflects the widespread notion, attested alike in accounts of witchcraft and in Graeco-Roman spells, that impotence and similar disorders can be induced by sorcery.[15] Moreover, the disorder is inflicted by a demon (spirit),[16] and is cured by the laying-on of hands, both of which ideas are, of course, staples of folklore everywhere.[17]

(vii) Commanded by God, Abram ascends to the 'height of Hazor' and thence surveys the land promised to his offspring. Although, to be sure, this derives substantially from the Scriptural narrative (Gen. 13.14–16) and is paralleled by what Moses does from Mount Nebo (Deut. 33.49f.; 34.1–4), it may perhaps be suggested that it is here inspired also by legal usage in the writer's own day, for, as David Daube has acutely pointed out in discussing the Biblical passages, such pointing-out of boundaries (*fines demonstrare*), accompanied by a promise of assignment, was a recognized method of conveyance in Roman law.[18]

(viii) Abram makes a tour of the Promised Land. Here we have the common motif, attested alike in practise and in story, that circumambulation of territory is a method of registering title to it. Parish bounds are periodically circuited, for instance, in British and German calendar customs even at the present day, and this procedure was likewise a regular feature of coronation ceremonies in Malaya and among several African peoples.[19]

§3. It is not yet possible to determine with certainty when our text was composed. Clues may perhaps be found in: (*a*) the name Ḥ-r-q-n-s (Hyrcanus?) given to Pharaoh's counsellor;[20] (*b*) the use of such Hellenistic and Roman geographical names as *Gebalene* [G-b-l] for the mountainous region south of the Dead Sea;[21] 'Red Sea' for the Persian Gulf;[22] Coele-Syria [Ḥ-w-l-î-t-â, in the later sense of the term],[23] and 'Mount of the Ox' for the Taurus range; (*c*) the divine titles, 'Lord of all Worlds', 'Lord of Heaven',[24] and 'the Holy and Great'; and (*d*) the employment of the word *'spr*, if the latter be correctly identified with the Latin *sparus*, 'curved hunting-spear'. But I do not dare to speculate.

It should be added that the manuscript is in a sorry state. Both the beginning and end are missing, whole columns have perished, and much has been obliterated. The following translation, however, includes everything that is legible.

§4. The second of the Biblical paraphrases, now in the possession of the Government of Jordan, has been called by its first editors, D. Barthélemy and J. T. Milik, *The Speeches of Moses*. Pieced together with phenomenal skill out of some forty-nine tiny fragments, this is a paraphrase of Moses' farewell address to Israel as recorded in the Book of Deuteronomy. The extant portion covers the exordium, the law about the Year of Release (Deut. 15.1ff.), and the ritual of the Day of Atonement. The author hews close to the Scriptural text, tricking it out from parallel passages in Leviticus. In one passage, however, he spices the narrative with the legend (apparently unknown to rabbinic sources) that the calendar date of the Day of Atonement coincides with that on which the Children of Israel ended their wanderings in the wilderness.

In connection with this text it is not without interest that a Testament of Moses (the nature of which has long been a matter of scholarly speculation) is indeed mentioned in the list of pseudepigraphic books appended to the Chronography of Nicephorus, Patriarch of Constantinople in the early part of the ninth century, as well as in the so-called Catalogue of the Sixty Books sometimes tacked on to manuscripts of the *Quaestiones* of Anastasius of Sinai—a catalogue which may date from the sixth or seventh century. Whether or not this is our present work there is at present no way of determining.

NOTES

1. Cf. R. Pfeiffer, *History of New Testament Times* (1949), p. 102.
2. Cf. W. N. Stearns, *Fragments from Graeco-Jewish Writers* (1908).
3. Cf. L. Ginzberg, *The Legends of the Jews* (1909ff.), v.213; cf. also *ib.*, 167, 245, 397.
4. Babylonian Talmud, *Sôtah* 12^a.
5. Cf. H. Günter, *Die christliche Legende des Abendlandes* (1910), p. 89; P. Toldo, 'Leben und Wunder der Heiligen im Mittelalter', in *Studien zur vergl. Literaturgeschichte*, 14 (1901), 320–45.
6. *Protevangelium*, xviii.2; Justin Martyr, *Trypho*, 88; Codex Sangermanensis = M. R. James, *The Apocryphal New Testament* (1924), p. 33.
7. For stories involving this motif cf. A. B. Cook, *Zeus*, ii (1925), pp. 1003ff.; cf. also T. H. Gaster, *Thespis*^{2} (1961), p. 431.
8. Cf. L. Stephani, 'Nimbus and Strahlenkranz', in *Mémoires de l'Académie des Sciences de St. Petersbourg*, VI Série, Sc. pol. hist. philol., 9 (1859); R. B. Onians, *The Origin of European Thought About the Body*, etc. (1951), pp. 165ff.
9. This is F.571.2 in Stith Thompson's standard *Motif-Index of Folk Literature*. Examples from modern folk tales are cited in J. Bolte and G. Polivka, *Anmerkungen zu den Kinder-und Hausmärchen der Brüder Grimm*, ii (repr. 1963), p. 400.
10. This inference would be further supported if (despite a slight grammatical anomaly) the words immediately preceding mention of Parvaim be read, with several

scholars, *l'rk mt*, implying that Methuselah traversed the length of the land (earth). Another reading, however, is *lqdmt*, 'eastwards', which would tie in with the widespread notion that the Earthly Paradise lies where the sun rises; cf. T. H. Gaster, *Myth, Legend, and Custom in the Old Testament* (1969), §13(a).

11. This is F.163.1.2; 3.1 in Stith Thompson's *Index*. See also T. H. Gaster, *Myth, Legend, and Custom in the Old Testament* (1969), §15. A late Midrash says that angels set crowns made of 'gold of Parvaim' on the heads of the righteous in Paradise: *Massecheth Gan 'Eden*, in J. D. Eisenstein, ed., *Oṣar Midrashîm* (1915), i.84a.

12. See fully J. E. B. Mayor, *Juvenalis Satirae* (1872–78) ii.343 (on xiv.299).

13. Cf. I. Scheftelowitz, *Altpalästinensicher Bauernglaube* (1925), 25ff.; H. Ploss, *Das Kind*[2] (1884), i.71ff.; extensive bibliography in Frazer-Gaster, *The New Golden Bough* (1959), p. 758.

14. Cf. Ginzberg, *op. cit.*, ii.297, 355. The Samaritan version, in *Asāṭîr*, vi.15, says that the princes began to be plagued both privily and openly, and Pharaoh became like a stone, as though he had been smitten by sorcery. This reflects the motif of magical paralysis (Stith Thompson, D.2072).

15. Cf. G. L. Kittredge, *Witchcraft in Old and New England* (1929), pp. 113, 444, n. 78.

16. The demon appears (according to Fitzmyer's reading of the blurred text) to be called 'the spirit of *š-ḥ-l-î-t*', which word seemingly derives from a root *š-ḥ-l*, known from Syriac and post-Biblical Hebrew, meaning 'suppurate, discharge', i.e., here 'gleet, gonorrhea'.

17. On the laying-on of hands, cf. J. A. MacCulloch, in *The Encyclopaedia of Religion and Ethics*, vi.494; O. Weinreich, *Antike Heilungswunder* (1910), p. 51; Frazer-Gaster, *The New Golden Bough* (1956), §76 and Add. Note, p. 181; J. Behm, *Die Handauflegung im Urchristentum* (Diss. Leipzig, 1911).

18. D. Daube, *Studies in Biblical Law* (1967), p. 27, citing Justinian, *Digest*, xii.2.1.2; xii.2.18.2.

19. See fully T. H. Gaster, *Thespis*[2] (1961), pp. 193f.; *id., Myth, Legend, and Custom in the Old Testament* (1969), §104.

20. See n. 24 to the translation.

21. To be sure, this designation occurs once in the Bible (Psalm 83.8), but it became popular in Graeco-Roman times. The Palestinian Targum so renders 'Se'ir' in Deut. 33.2, and the Samaritan Targum in Gen. 33.14, 16; 36.8, 9. This is the Gebalitis of Josephus, *Ant.*, II, i, 2; iii.3, 7.

22. According to Pliny, *H.N.*, vi.167, it was so named from the glow of the rising sun.

23. The name means properly 'sandy tract', and is in fact applied to several areas. Here it is most probably Coele-Syria, in the later sense of the term, as in Josephus, *Ant.*, xiv, 4, 5, 'Coele-Syria as far as the River Euphrates'.

24. On these titles see A. Marmorstein, *The Old Rabbinic Doctrine of God*, i (1927), pp. 62f., 93f., 99; R. Marcus, 'Divine Names and Attributes in Hellenistic Jewish Literature', in *Proceedings of the American Academy for Jewish Research*, 1931–32, p. 83, s.v. *Kosmos*.

MEMOIRS OF THE PATRIARCHS

A. LAMECH

The Birth of Noah

Cp. Enoch 106.1–2   ii, 1–26

In the Bible, the story of Noah is preceded immediately
by that of the dalliance of the 'sons of God' with the daughters of men and the consequent peopling of the earth with
a race of giants (Gen. 6.1–8). This gave rise to the legend
that when the hero of the Flood was born, the house was
filled with a sudden and wondrous light; whereupon his
father Lamech suspected that the child was of supernatural
origin and sought to discover the truth from his grandfa-
ther Enoch who, in reward for his piety, had been translated to heaven (or to the ends of the earth) and made
privy to celestial lore (cp. Gen. 5.24).

The legend has hitherto been known to us only from
the Ethiopic *Book of Enoch* (ch. 106), written in the second or first century B.C., from a Latin fragment now in
the British Museum, and from a partial allusion in the medieval Samaritan *Legends* [*Asāṭir*] *of Moses* (ii.6).

A fragment discovered at Qumran describes, albeit ob-
scurely, how Lamech saw 'in the chambers of his house
a light like the rays of the sun'. Our present text takes up
the narrative from that point.

Suspecting then that the child had been conceived of
one of the (Heavenly) Watchers[1] or Holy Beings[2] and
[that it really belonged] to the giants,[3] I, Lamech, was disturbed at heart. In my confusion I went to my wife Bath-
Enosh.[4]

'[I want you,' I said,] 'to take an oath by the Most High, the Lord Supreme,* the Sovereign of all worlds,[5] [the Ruler of all] the heavenly beings, to the end that you will disclose everything to me in truth. For if [you swear by the Most High, the Lord Supreme], the Sovereign of all worlds to speak with me in truth and not with lies, this too will you have to disclose to me in truth and not with lies.'

At this my wife Bath-Enosh spoke to me with considerable vehemence and [heat].

'Sir cousin,'[6] said she, 'remember my delicate feelings. How[ever], the occasion is indeed alarming, and my soul [is writhing] in its sheath.[7] I will tell you everything truly.'

[Hearing this, I grew] very [excited] and perturbed at heart. But when my wife Bath-Enosh saw from my expression how perturbed I was, she repressed her indignation and proceeded to address me.

'Sir cousin,' said she, '[I will ignore] my delicate feelings, and swear to you by the Holy (and) Great One,[8] the Sovereign of hea[ven and earth] that this seed came from you, this conception was by you, and this fruit was planted by you and not by some stranger or by any of the Watchers or heavenly beings. Why, then, this troubled and marred expression and this gloomy mood? I am telling you the truth.'

Thereupon I, Lamech, rushed to my father Methuselah and [told] him the whole story, [begging him go in turn] to *his* father and find out definitely what the whole matter portended, since he (i.e., his father) was the favorite (of God) and [the gossip of the angels] to whom this role had been assigned and to whom they communicated all things.[9]

*   *   *

When Methuselah heard [my words, he in turn rushed] to his father Enoch to learn the whole truth from him and [to bespeak] his goodwill. He set out . . . for Parvaim[10] and came upon him there.

'Sir and sire', said he to his father Enoch, '[Pray explain] to [me] what I am going to [tell you]. I would ask you,

* Heb. 'Lord of greatness'.

however, not to be angry at my coming hither. . . . The
fact is that I have been alarmed by [   ]'.

. . . .

Cf. Gen. 6.1–3
Jubilees 4.15
Enoch 6.6   iii, 3
[Then answered Enoch:] 'To be sure, in the days of my
father Jared [heavenly beings did indeed come down to
earth and seduce mortal women].

*   *   *

Cf. Enoch 106.3   v, 3–4
   '(Howbeit,) I, Enoch, [have words of reassurance for
you. This child does not come from any of] the heavenly
beings but from [your] son, Lamech.

*   *   *

Enoch 106.18   v, 9–10
      107.2
   '(Moreover,) I have on this occasion [something else]
to tell and disclose to you [   ]. Depart and inform
your son Lamech [that   ]'.

*   *   *

Enoch 107.3   v, 24–27
   When Methuselah heard [these words . . . he rushed
home] and spoke [   ] with his son Lamech. And
when I, Lamech, [learned that God] had caused [the
child] to issue from *me,* [I was indeed reassured].

B. NOAH

The Character of Noah   vi, 2

*   *   *

. . . and all my days I behaved uprightly.

*   *   *

Gen. 6.9   vi, 6
. . . I, Noah, was a [righteous] man, [the one blameless
man in my generation].

*   *   *

God warns Noah of the Flood   vii, 1

"[The waters of the Flood will overwhelm] the earth and all that is upon it, the seas [and all that is therein]."

*   *   *

God assures Noah of deliverance   vii, 7

. . . ., and I rejoiced at the words of the Lord of Heaven.

The emergence from the Ark   x, 12–15

Gen. 8.4
Jubilees 5.28
The ark came to rest <on> one of the mountains of Ararat (i.e., Armenia).

Gen. 8.20
Jubilees 6.2
(Thereupon) I made expiation for the whole earth [   ].

Jubilees 6.3
I made smoke/burned incense on the altar.[11]

*   *   *

Noah's descendants are forbidden to eat blood
xi, 17

Gen. 9.4
Jubilees 6.7, 13
". . . You are to eat no blood

*   *   *

Noah's progeny   xii, 10–11

Gen. 11.10
Jubilees 7.18
Arphachshad [was born] two years after the Flood. [   ].
Such, then, were all the sons of Shem in their entirety.

Gen. 10.6

[And the sons of Ham were Cush (Ethiopia) and Egypt and] Put (Somaliland?) and Canaan.

[In *Enoch* 7.20–39 it is related that Noah commanded his sons to act uprightly and specifically to observe the rule (subsequently elaborated in Lev. 19.23–25) not to taste any produce of the earth until four years after planting. It is probable that something of the same kind filled the gap between the preceding and following sections of our text.]

Noah plants the first vine

xii, 13–17

Gen. 9.20

Jubilees 7.1

I and all my sons then began to work the land;[12] and I planted [   ] a vineyard on Mount Lubar.[13] After four years it yielded me wine [for my consumption].

Jubilees 7.2

On the first day of the fifth month I began to drink thereof.[14] (Thereupon) I summoned my sons and grandsons and all their wives and daughters.

Jubilees 7.6

We gathered together and went [and gave thanks] to the Lord of Heaven, the Holy and Great, Who had rescued us from destruction.

*   *   *

*Noah parcels out the earth among his sons
and they in turn among theirs*[15]

xvi, 11–12, 16

Jubilees 8.11–9.15

. . . all the land in the north, reaching as far as [   ].

Jubilees 8.23
The boundary on this side is the Great (i.e., Mediterra-
nean) Sea.

Jubilees 8.25
. . . [reaching as far as] the River Tînâ (i.e., Don).

* * *

xvii, 8–11, 16
To ASHUR (i.e., Assyria) [fell the land which lies] westwards, reaching as far as [the River] Tigris.
To ARAM (i.e., Syria) fell the land which lies [   ]
reaching as far as the crest (or, headwaters?)[16] of
[. The boundary] on this side is the Taurus range
(lit. the Mountain of the Ox). Thence this portion turns
westwards, reaching as far as [   ].
Over and above (these) three portions [there was as-
signed] to ARPHACHSHAD [the land which lies . . . . .
. . . . . , reaching as far as . . . .].

Jubilees 9.7–8
To GOMER (i.e., the Cimmerians) he gave what lies in
the northeast, reaching as far as the River Tînâ (Don)
and the point where it turns.
To MA[GO]G (i.e., Scythia?) [he gave   ].

* * *

C. ABRAHAM

Abraham builds an altar near Bethel
xix, 7–xxii, 32

Gen. 12.8
[I was on my way from Shechem heading toward the
mountain east of Bethel. I eventually pitched tent there,
with Bethel on the west and 'Ai on the east] and I built an
altar there [and called] there on [the name of G]O[D].
And I said: 'Thou art for [me] the God [ever]las[ting]
(*or*, [of the wo]rl[d]). . . . .'

* * *

Abram and Sarai in Egypt

Cp. Gen. 12.10–20

I had not yet reached the Holy Mountain[17] but I pursued my course and went on southwards [   ] till I reached Hebron (which was built [around that time]).[18] There I stayed for [two] years. Then, however, a famine swept the entire country. Hearing that there was produce in Egypt, I made my way th[ither]—that is, to the land of Egypt [   ]. Eventually I reached the C-r-m-o-n,[19] one of the arms† of the River (of Egypt) [   ]. I then crossed the seven arms of that river[20] [   ] and, leaving our own land behind, entered the land of Egypt, which belonged to the children of Ham.

In the night when I entered Egypt I dreamed a dream. And behold, in my dream I saw a cedar and a palm [   ]. (Suddenly,) some men came along, seeking to cut down the cedar and leave the palm to stand by itself. Thereupon the palm restrained (them). 'Do not cut down the cedar', it said, 'for we are two of a kind'. So the cedar was spared for the sake of the palm and was not [cut down].[21]

Awaking at night from my sleep, I said to my wife Sarai: 'I have had a terrifying dream'.

'Tell it me', said she, 'that I may know what it was'.

So I proceeded to tell it to her. 'That dream', [I added, 'was a portent. The men I saw in it are men] who are seeking to kill me but spare you. Do me, then, this favor [When these men enquire of you, Who is this fellow? Tell them simply:] "He is my kinsman".[22] In that way I shall live on account of you, and my life will be spared for your sake. [Abduct you they may, but they will] not kill me'.

For the rest of the night‡ Sarai kept weeping on account of my words [   ].

Then Sarai [and I journeyed on] towards Zoan, [but all

† Heb. 'heads'.
‡ Heb. simply, 'that night'.

the while I was] fearful for her§ lest anyone should set eyes on her [   ].

Well, after those five years, three Egyptian dignitaries [indeed came under orders] of the Pharaoh of Zoan [and confronted me] and my wife. And they kept bestowing [compliments upon her for her] goodly [grace] and wisdom and [   ]. I entreated them** [to listen] to what I had to say,†† [explaining that it was] only [because we had been suffering] from the famine which [that we had come thither]. [Paying] no [attention, however,] they went to present themselves [to their master]. Eventually, [reaching the palace, they reported to him].

[Pharaoh regaled them] with much eating and drinking, [and when they were full with meat and] wine, [they began to expatiate on the beauties of Sarai].‡‡

'[How   ,' they said]. 'How comely is the shape of her face, how [   ] and finespun are her tresses! How beautiful her eyes! How delicate is her nose and the whole lustre of her countenance! How fair are her breasts, and how comely withal is her complexion! How comely too are her arms, and how perfect her hands! How [delightful] are her hands to behold, how lovely her palms, how long and slender all her fingers! How comely are her feet! How well-rounded her thighs! No maiden or new-wed bride§§ is fairer than she! Her beauty is greater than all other women's, and she excels them all! What is more, along with all this beauty she has great wisdom, and whatever she does turns out well.[23]

When the king heard the words of Ḥ-r-q-n-o-s[24] and of his two companions, all three of them speaking with one accord, he fell violently in love with her, and sent forthwith to have her brought to him. As soon as he set eyes on her, he was dumfounded at all her beauty and took

§ Heb. 'for her person'.
** Heb. 'I called out in their presence'.
†† Heb. 'my words'.
‡‡ This is simply a restoration *ad sensum* and is not intended to represent the actual words of the original.
§§ Heb. 'None of the maidens and none of the brides that enter the marriage bower'.

her to wife; but me he sought to kill. Sarai, however (hoping that it might go well with me on her account), told him that I was (merely) her kinsman. So I, Abram, was spared for her sake and not killed. But throughout the night I and my nephew Lot fell to bitter weeping because Sarai had been abducted from me by force.

That night I offered prayers and supplications and entreaties[25] and said in (my) anguish, as the tears rolled down: 'Blessed art Thou, O God Most High, *Lord of all worlds*, for Thou art the Lord and Ruler of all things and Thou art the Ruler of all the kings of the earth, executing judgment upon them. Now do I complain before Thee concerning Pharaoh of Zoan, the king of Egypt, in that my wife has been violently abducted from me. Wreak justice upon him in my behalf, and let me behold Thy hand wax mighty against him and against all his household, and let him not be able this night to defile my wife (that she be put away) from me. Let them come to know, O Lord, that Thou art the Lord of all the kings of the earth!' And I wept in my perturbation.

That night God Most High indeed sent a noisome spirit —an evil demon*—to plague him and all the men of his household, and it so plagued him and all the men of his household that he could not come near her, far less know her,[26] although she stayed with him for two years.

When the two years were over, however, the plagues and afflictions had so overpowered him and all the men of his household that he sent and summoned all the [sages], sorcerers and physicians of Egypt to see if they could cure him and the men of his household of the plague. But none of the physicians, sorcerers or sages were able to effect a cure for him. Rather did the spirit plague them too, and they fled.

Thereupon Ḥ-r-q-n-o-s came to me and begged me to go and pray for the king and to lay my hands upon him so that he might recover, seeing that [I alone remained] in sound health. But Lot said to him: 'So long as his wife Sarai remains with the king, my uncle Abram will not be

* Heb. 'spirit'.

able to pray for him. Be off then and tell the king to send the man's wife back to her husband. Then he will pray for him and he will get well.'

No sooner had Ḥ-r-q-n-o-s heard Lot's words than off he went to the king.

'My lord king,' said he. 'All these plagues and afflictions have come on account of Sarai, the wife of Abram. Let Sarai be but restored to her husband Abram, and this plague and pox[27] will go from you'.

So (Pharaoh) summoned me and said to me: 'What have you done to me on account of Sarai? She told me she was (merely) your kinswoman, but she is really your wife! I took her to wife while she was really *your* wife! Yes, it is *your* wife who is with me! Depart and begone from the entire realm of Egypt, but now pray for me and my household that this evil spirit be exorcized from us'.

Thereupon I prayed (for him) that [he might be he]aled, and I placed my hand upon his [head], and the plague fell away from him, and the evil spirit was exorcized from him.

When he was recovered, the king arose and announced to me [   ] and swore an ir[revocable] oath to me that he had not [defiled her], and the king gave her silver and gold in abundance and much raiment of fine linen and purple [   ] in her presence,[28] and to Hagar[29] also [   ], and he commissioned men to escort me out [of the country].

Abram reaches Beth-el

Gen. 13.3   xx, 33–xxi, 4
Jubilees 13.15

So I Abram departed with exceeding much cattle and silver and gold and went up out of [Egypt] with my nephew [Lot]. Lot too received much cattle, and he took him a wife of the daughters of [   ].

Pitching camp now here now there, I eventually reached Beth-el, the place where I had originally built the altar. I built one a second time and offered upon it burnt offerings

and meal offering to God Most High, and I called there
on the name of the Lord of (all) worlds and offered praise
to the name of God and blessed God and gave thanks before God for all the possessions and prosperity which He
had bestowed upon me and for all the benevolence which
He had shown towards me and for having brought me back
safely to that land.

Lot parts from Abram

Gen. 13.7–11   xxi, 5–7
Jubilees 13.17–18

The following day, Lot parted company with me on account of what happened in connection with our grazing-
grounds,[30] and went and settled in the Valley of the Jordan. Although (he took) all his possessions with him, I
added lavishly to them. He went on pasturing his flocks
until eventually he reached Sodom. In Sodom he bought
himself a house and settled down, while I for my part settled in the mount of Beth-el. Nevertheless I was grieved
that my nephew Lot had parted company with me.

The Promised Land

Gen. 13.14–16   xxi, 8–22
Jubilees 13.20–21

One night God appeared to me in a vision.
'Go up', said He, 'to the height of Hazor,[31] which lies
left of Beth-el (the place where you are now settled), and
lift your eyes and gaze eastward and westward and southward and northward[32] and behold all this land which I
am going to give to you and to your seed for ever'.
So on the morrow I duly went up to the height of Hazor
and from that height I beheld the land, from the River of
Egypt as far as Lebanon and Senir, from the Great Sea
as far as the Hauran, the whole area of Gebal[33] as far as
Kadesh, the whole of the Great Wilderness which lies east
of the Hauran, and the region of Senir as far as the
Euphrates.

And God said to me: 'I am going to give this land to
your seed that they may possess it for ever, and I am going
to multiply that seed of yours like the dust of the earth.
Just as no man can count that dust, so will your seed be
countless. Up now, go, fare forth and see how long it is
and how wide. Behold, I am going to give it to you and to
your seed after you for ever'.[34]

So I, Abram, set out to tour and survey the land. I began the tour at the River Giḥon[35] and came to the shore
of the sea, beside which I travelled till I reached the Taurus
range.[36] Then I turned from the [shore] of that great
lake, i.e. the Dead Sea, and departed, alongside Mount
Taurus in an easterly direction across the breadth of the
land until I reached the River Euphrates. Then I journeyed
beside the Euphrates eastward until I reached the Persian
Gulf[37] and I proceeded along the Persian Gulf until I
reached the tongue of the Sea of Reeds which issues out
of it. I then pursued my course southward until I reached
the River Giḥon. At that point I turned back and came
safely to my family, where I found everyone well.

Thereupon I departed and settled in the plains[38] of
Mamre which lie close to Hebron, to the northeast, and
there I built an altar and offered upon it burnt offering
and meal offering unto God Most High. And I ate and
drank there together with all the men of my household,
and I sent and invited my friends, the three Amorite
brothers, Mamre, Aneram[39] and Eshcol, and they ate and
drank together with me.

The rescue of Lot

Gen. 14.1ff.   xxi, 23–xxii, 26
Jubilees 13.22–29

Some time previously, Chedorlaomer, king of Elam,
Amraphel, king of Babylon,[40] Arioch, king of Cappado-
cia,[41] and Tid'al, king of Goyim (which is in Mesopota-
mia) came and waged war against Bera', king of Sodom,
Birsha', king of Gomorram,[42] Shinab, king of Admah, and
Shem-'-b-d,[43] king of Zeboiim, and the king of Bela'. They

assembled for combat in the vale of Siddim, and the king of Elam and his royal allies overpowered the king of Sodom and his confederates, and he imposed tribute upon them. For twelve years they paid their tribute to the king of Elam, but in the thirteenth year they revolted against him. In the fourteenth, however, the king of Elam led forth all his allies and they went up along the Way of the Wilderness[44] and proceeded to attack and plunder from the River Euphrates inwards. They attacked the Rephaim who lived at Ashteroth-Qarnaim, the Zamzummim who lived at Ammon,[45] the Emim who lived at Shaveh-haQeriyoth, and the Horites who lived in the Gebalene hills, until finally they reached El-Paran which is by the wilderness. Then they turned back [and came to   and attacked the Amorites] at Hazezon-tamar.

But the king of Sodom, the king of [Gomorram, the ki]ng of Admah, the king of Zeboiim, and the king of Bela' went out to challenge them [and joined] battle in the vale of [Siddim] with Chedorlao[mer, king of Elam and his royal] allies. However, the king of Sodom was beaten and fled, the king of Gomorram fell into some pits [   ]. Thereupon the king of Elam seized all the property that was in Sodom and Gomorram [   ], and they carried off with them also Abram's nephew Lot, who had settled in Sodom, together with all his possessions.

But one of the shepherds[46] whom Abram had given to Lot and who had escaped from captivity came to Abram, who was dwelling at the time in Hebron, and told him that his nephew Lot had been captured together with all his possessions, but not killed, and that the kings had taken the route through the Great Valley and were looting and plundering and attacking and killing, and that they were headed for the province of Damascus. Thereupon Abram wept for his nephew Lot. Bracing himself, however, he proceeded to pick out from among his servants some three hundred and eighteen doughty stalwarts who might engage in combat and, with Aneram, Eshcol and Mamre marching beside him, pursued after them until he reached Dan. He came upon them encamped in the valley of Dan and, attacking them by night from all four directions, kept wreaking slaughter among them and discomfiting them throughout the night, and subsequently chased after them. They all fled before him until they reached Helbon[47] which is situated to the left of Damascus. Howbeit, he stripped them of all that they had taken as plunder and loot and likewise of all their own goods, and he also rescued his nephew Lot, restoring to him all his possessions and all that they had taken from him as spoil.

When the king of Sodom heard that Abram had restored all the spoil and loot, he went up to challenge him, and came to Salem (that is, Jerusalem).[48] Now, Abram was encamped in the valley of Shaveh (the same is the Valley of the King in the dale of Beth-cerem).[49] And Melchizedek, the king of Salem, furnished food and drink for Abram and for all the men that were with him; and he was a priest of God Most High. And he blessed Abram, and said: 'Blessed be Abram of God Most High, Lord of heaven and earth; and blessed be God Most High Who hath delivered thine enemies into thine hand'. And he gave him a tenth part of all the possessions of the king of Elam and his allies.

Thereupon the king of Sodom approached and said to Abram: 'My lord Abram, give me the persons who are (properly) mine but who are with you only as spoil, whom you have rescued from the king of Elam, but let all the property be left with you'.

But Abram said to the king of Sodom: 'This day do I lift my hand (in oath) unto God Most High, Lord of heaven and earth, that I will not take even so much as a thread or a shoestring which is yours, lest you should say that all Abram's wealth comes really from my possessions. The only exception will be what my youths who are with me have already eaten and what the three stalwarts who went with me have received as their share. They must be left to control their own shares in the matter of surrendering any of them to you'.

And therewith Abram returned all the possessions and all the spoil and gave them to the king of Sodom. And he released all the captives and sent them all away.

Abram is promised a son

Gen. 15.1–4   xxii, 27–34
Jubilees 14.1–3

After these things God appeared to Abram in a vision and said to him: 'Behold, it is ten full years since you went up from Haran. Two years have you passed here, and seven in Egypt, and one since you came back from Egypt. Now review and compute all that you have and see how it has increased to double of what went out with you in the day that you left Haran. But now, fear not, I am with you and I will be a help to you and a source of strength. I will also be a shield about you, and your spear[50] against any that is stronger than you. Your wealth and possessions will increase exceedingly'.

'My Lord God', replied Abram, 'my wealth and possessions have indeed increased, but what good are all these to me, seeing that I shall die childless and go without sons, and one of the boys of my household will inherit me, even Eliezer of [Damascus   ]?'

'Nay', replied God. 'None shall inherit you save one that issues [from your loins]'.

*   *   *

THE ORATION OF MOSES

A PARAPHRASE OF THE LAW

Moses' farewell exhortation

¶And [God called] unto Moses in the [fortieth] year of
the going out of the [children] of Israel [from the land of]
Egypt, in the eleventh month, on the first day of the month,
saying:

[Gather together] all the congregation, and go up unto
[Mount Nebo] and stand there, thou and Eleazar, [the
son of] Aaron.

Interpret [the Law] [unto the heads of the fam]ilies,
unto the levites and all the [priests];

And enjoin upon the children of Israel the words of the
Law which I commanded [thee] on Mount Sinai to enjoin
upon [them].

Explain carefully in their hearing all that [I exact] of
them; [and call] heaven and [earth to witness] concerning
that which will befall them if they and their children [walk]
not in the way which I have commanded [them throughout their lives] on earth.

[For] I declare that if they renounce Me and choose
[the filthy ways of] the heathen and their abominations
and their idols, and if they [worship] their godlings, these
will prove but a trap and a snare.

And if they neglect [any] of the holy [convocations],
or the sabbath which is itself a Covenant, [or the festivals]
which I command them this day to observe, it shall redound
to their being [smitten] with a great [smiting] in the midst
of that land [for the possession of which] they are about to
cross the Jordan.

For all the curses [of the Covenant] will come upon

them and overtake them, to the end that they shall perish and be [destroyed]. Then shall they know [that] the truth has been evinced among them.

So Moses called Eleazar the son of [Aaron] and Joshua [the son of Nun and said unto] them: Rehearse [all the words of the Law] completely. . . .

¶[Give ear,] O Israel, and hearken! This [day art thou to become a people] unto GOD* [your God].

Thou shalt keep [My statutes] and Mine orders and My [commandments] which [I] command thee this day [to perform].

When thou crossest the [Jordan] to [possess thee] of great and goodly [cities], of houses filled with all [goodly things, of vineyards and olives] which thou didst not [plant], and of hewn wells which thou didst not hew; and when thou eatest and art satisfied,

[Beware] lest thy heart become haughty and thou [forget] that which I [command] thee this day. For it is [thy] life and the length of [thy] days.

¶Then Moses [summoned the children of] Israel and [said]:

This day it is forty [years] since we went out from the land of Egypt; and this [day] hath GOD our God [caused] all these words—[all] His judgments and commandments —[to issue] from His mouth.

How can [I myself alone bear] your cumbrance and your [burden and your strife? When I am done with imparting unto you] the Covenant and with enjoining the way in which ye are to walk, [take you wise men who] shall serve to explain [unto you] and your [children] all the words of the Law.

Take heed exceedingly unto your souls [that ye do them, lest] the wrath of [your God] be fanned into flame and blaze against you, and He shut up the heavens above that they rain no rain upon you, and the [waters] below, that [the earth] yield no [produce] for you.

* A pious substitute for YHWH, the ineffable name.

And Moses [went on to rehearse] unto the children of Israel all these commandments [which God] had commanded them to do. . . .

Of the Year of Release

¶[At the end of every seven] years [thou shalt observe] a sabbatical rest [of the land. The produce of] the earth [during that period of rest shall serve both thee and the domestic beasts and the wild animals] of the field [for food]; and what is left shall be for the [needy] among thy brethren, who are [in the land].

No man shall [then] sow [his field] or prune his [vineyard, neither shall anyone glean the aftermath of the harvest, nor] gather fruits for himself.

[Thou shalt observe] all these [words] of the Covenant, [to perform them].

If thou [attend carefully] to the performance of [this commandment], and if thou [truly] 'relax thy [hand]' in that year, it shall mean also that anyone who is [a creditor of another] and hath [a claim of any kind] upon him [in respect of a loan] shall [likewise] 'relax [his hand'.] [It shall be called the Release] ordained by GOD [your God.]

One may exact payment from an alien, but not from any of one's own brethren. For in that year God will bless you, and He [too] will absolve you—of your iniquities.

Of the Day of Atonement

¶[   ] on this day. . . .

For your [fathers] were wanderers [in the wilderness] until the tenth day of the [seventh] month. . . .

On the tenth [day] of the month, [all work] shall be forbidden; and on that tenth day, atonement shall be made. . . .

[   ] [day] of the month [   ] shall take [   ].

[   ] [On that day, judgment shall be passed] also upon the congregation of the angels and upon the company of the Holy Beings. . . .

[   ] [on behalf of the children of] Israel and on behalf of the land. He† shall [take of its blood] and pour [it] upon the ground [   ]. And [atonement] shall be made for them. (*The rest of the text is fragmentary. It describes the ritual of the Day of Atonement.*)

† I.e., the high priest.

NOTES

Memoirs of the Patriarchs

1. I.e., the fallen angels. The name derives from Dan. 4.13, 17, 23. Cp. *'Zadokite' Document,* ii.18; Enoch 1.51; 10.9; 12.2; 13.10, etc.
2. Cp. Zech. 14.5; Pss. 16.3; 89.8; Job 5.1; 15.15; Dan. 8.13; Enoch 1.9; 9.3; 12.2; 14.23; 39.5.
3. Heb. *nephilim* (cp. Gen. 6.4). The word was popularly derived from *n-ph-l,* 'fall' and taken to mean 'fallen angels'. Cp. Enoch 15.8: 'The giants . . . from the holy Watchers is their origin'.
4. Lamech's wife is so called also in Jubilees 41.28 (Eth.). The name means 'daughter of Enosh'.
5. For this form of adjuration, cp. Enoch 98.6; 103.1. The title 'God Most High' was especially popular in Hellenistic times; cp. Ecclus. 41.5; 47.5; II Macc. 3.31.
6. Literally, 'My lord and kinsman (brother)'.
7. I.e., 'I am all choked up, not in command of my faculties'. The expression derives from Dan. 7.15 (cp. also Talmud, *Sanhedrin* 108a) and harks back to the primitive notion that the body is the sheath or envelope of the soul. A similar expression occurs in Pliny, *H.N.,* vii, 52.
8. Throughout the Book of Enoch, God is regularly styled 'Holy and Great One', e.g., 1.3; 10.1; 14.1; 35.1.
9. Legend asserted that in reward for his piety Enoch had been made privy to heavenly secrets; cp. Enoch 1.2; 27.4; 72.1; 81.1. In Jewish folklore he was sometimes identified with the angel Metatron.
10. See above, Introduction, §2 (iii).
11. Fumigation is an element of atonement procedures; cf. Lev. 4.10, 19, etc.; 5.12; 7.5; 9.10; 16.25. On the

subject in general, cf. I. Scheftelowitz, *Altpalästin-ensicher Bauernglaube* (1925), pp. 82ff.; M. Haran, 'The Use of Incense in the Ancient Israelite Ritual', in *Vetus Testamentum*, 10 (1960), 113–29.

12. The traditional Jewish text of Gen. 9.20 runs simply, 'Then Noah the husbandman began and planted a vineyard', but the Latin (Vulgate) and Syriac (Peshiṭta) Versions indeed read, 'began to work the earth', as here.

13. Lubar is mentioned both in the Book of Jubilees and in later rabbinic legend as the mountain on which the ark came to rest; cf. Ginzberg, *The Legends of the Jews*, v.186, 188. The name remains unexplained.

14. Noah piously observes the Law of Lev. 19.23–25 forbidding the consumption of produce until four years after planting! On the particular application of this to *vines* (*kerem rebaʿî*), cf. *Mishnah Pe'ah*, vii.6; *Terūmôth*, iii.9; *Maʿᵃser Shenî*, v.1–3; *Parah*, i.1.

15. Identifications (successively modernized) of the territories allotted to the sons and grandsons of Noah are to be found in Jubilees 8.11–9.15; the *Biblical Antiquities* mistakenly ascribed to Philo, 4.4; the medieval *Chronicles of Jeraḥmeel*, ch. 31; and the Samaritan *Asāṭir* [Legends] *of Moses*, ii.24–31.

16. Literally, *on the heads of* (i.e., in addition to the main portions?). The translation is uncertain.

17. I.e., Bethel. The Samaritans identify the mountain with Gerizim; cf. Marqeh, 71ᵇ–72ᵃ (in M. Heidenheim, *Bibliotheca Samaritana*, iii [1896], 51); *Maʿlef*, §§97–98.

18. Cf. Jubilees 13.10.

19. Evidently the river K-r-m-ô-n (or K-r-m-y-ô-n) mentioned in Mishnah, *Parah*, vii.9, and in Babylonian Talmud, *Babâ Bathrâ*, 74ᵇ.

20. I.e., the seven mouths of the Delta; cf. Herodotus, ii.17; Pliny, *HN*, v.64. The Nile is often described in classical Literature as 'seven-branched'; e.g., Moschus, ii.51; Catullus, xi.7; Vergil, *Aeneid*, vi.801; Ovid, *Met.*, v.187; xv.753.

21. See above, Introduction, §2 (iv).

22. The Hebrew word *'ah* has a wider meaning than 'brother', as usually rendered. In urging Sarai to use this more neutral term, Abram was resorting to the diplomatic stratagem of ambiguity, rather than to downright deception.

23. Literally, 'what pertains to her hands'.

24. This name does not occur in parallel versions of the story, and is not yet satisfactorily explained. If it is indeed to be identified as *Hyrcanos*, the name may have reference to John Hyrcanus (135–105 B.C.) and be used in a typological and derogatory sense, inspired by that sense of 'Pharisaic', opposition to him which is reflected in Josephus, *Ant.*, xii.10.5–6 and in the Talmud, i.e., 'a veritable Hyrcanus'. This would then be an important clue to the dating of our text. In the corresponding Samaritan tradition, the courtier is called Ṭ-r-ṭ-s (*Asāṭîr*, vi.18) or Ṭ-r-s-s (*Meshalma*, fol.197f.)—evidently Hellenistic names.

25. The original employs the standard terms for the different types of prayer.

26. See above, Introduction, §2 (vi).

27. Literally, *spirit* (demon) *of gleet*, i.e., gonorrhea.

28. This evidently refers to a declaration of divorce made by Pharaoh in the presence of Sarai. Rabbinic legend asserts that Pharaoh had given Sarai a formal marriage contract, cf. Ginzberg, *Legends*, i, p. 223. A formal declaration of divorce would then have been required, by Jewish law, before her husband could reclaim her. The Samaritan version (*Asāṭîr*, vi.21) adds the picturesque detail that the whole palace was lit up by the lustre on Sarai's face.

29. There was an old legend that Hagar was the daughter of Pharaoh and that he presented her to Abram; cf. Ginzberg, *Legends*, v.221, n. 74.

30. Cf. Gen. 12.7ff.

31. This is the modern Jebel el-'Aṣur, reputedly the highest spot in central Palestine. On this episode, see above, Introduction, §2 (vii).

32. The author seems to muddle the directions, for in the subsequent specifications he presents a survey which proceeds *northwards, westwards,* and *eastwards,* agreeing more with the order in Jubilees.

33. See above, Introduction, §3.

34. See above, Introduction, §2 (viii).

35. The *Giḥon,* one of the four tributaries of the river of Eden (Gen. 2.15) was popularly identified with the Nile; cf. Josephus, *Ant.,* I.i.3.

36. I.e., more strictly, the Amanus section of the Taurus range.

37. Literally, the *Red Sea,* the Greek name for the Persian Gulf.

38. Heb. *'elônē Mamrê'.* This is usually rendered 'the oaks of Mamre', but it may be suggested that the author may have followed an ancient tradition (preserved in the Vulgate's rendering, *convallis*) which interpreted the name from the like-sounding Greek *aulōn,* 'valley'— a word which was indeed adopted into Syriac. John Mandeville similarly speaks of 'the plain of Mamre'.

39. For this form, instead of the Biblical 'Aner, cp. Gomorram for Gomorrah. Curiously enough, the Samaritan version (in the *Asāṭīr*) has Arenam.

40. In the Bible, Amraphel is identified as 'king of Sh-n-'-r'. This is probably the Shanḥar(a) mentioned in the Amarna Letter, 35.49, Amraphel being a semi-Ḥurrianized name, Amurru-pal, and having nothing whatsoever to do with the Babylonian Ḥammurabi, as was previously supposed. But Sh-n-'-r was commonly equated in antiquity with Shin͏eʿar, a name for Babylonia in Gen. 10.10; 11.2; Zech. 5.11, etc., and is so rendered in both the Palestinian and the Samaritan Targums.

41. In the Bible, Ellasar, still unidentified.

42. See above, n. 39.

43. The traditional Jewish text has ShemebeR. Our author's reading agrees with the Samaritan recension.

44. Literally, the *sandy tract.* See Introduction, §3.

45. The traditional Jewish text has, the *Zuzim in Ham* (variant: *Ḥam*), which some scholars would identify

with modern *Hām*, on the southwest shore of the Dead Sea. Comparison with Deut. 2.20 suggests, however, that *Zuzim* (i.e., Z-v-z-i-m?) and *Zamzumim* are simply alternative representations of the same name. It is this latter passage which justifies our author in locating them in 'Ammon.

46. The Bible identifies him only as 'a refugee'.

47. The Bible has *Ḥobah*—the *Ubê* of cuneiform texts. For Ḥelbon (modern Ḥalbun), cf. Ezek. 27.18 and Strabo, 735; Athenaeus, i.22.

48. Actually, this may have been the modern Salim, near Shechem, as maintained by the Samaritans. But the tradition that it was Jerusalem (called Shalem in Ps. 76.3) is attested also by Josephus (*Ant.*, I.10.2) and by the Targums.

49. Cf. Jer. 6.1; Neh. 3.14; Mishnah, *Middoth*, iii.4; *Niddah*, ii.7. It is the modern 'Ain Karim, about four and a half miles west of Jerusalem.

50. The text has the word '*spr*, not found elsewhere. This has been identified with an Iranian word (none too well authenticated, I am told), said to mean 'square shield, buckler', but—despite the previous mention of a shield—the preposition *against*, rather than *from*, would seem to indicate a weapon of *offense* rather than of *defense*. I would therefore tentatively suggest comparison with the Latin *sparus* (whence our own *spear*), 'a short, curved weapon like a hunting-spear or scimitar'.

THE TRIUMPH OF GOD

Descriptions of the Final Age

There shall be a time of trouble, such as never was since there was a nation even to that same time; and at that time thy people shall be delivered, every one that shall be found written in the book.

DANIEL 12.1.

Repent, for the Kingdom of God is at hand.

MATTHEW 3.2.

Cause us to rejoice, O Lord our God, in the coming of Thy servant Elijah the prophet, and in the kingdom of the house of David, Thine anointed. Soon may he come and gladden our hearts!

Let there no stranger sit upon his throne, nor to his glory alien men fall heir, for Thou hast sworn unto him by Thy holy name that his lamp shall never go out.

From the JEWISH SABBATH MORNING SERVICE

INTRODUCTION

I

From time immemorial, it has been the custom in many parts of the world to usher in the New Year or a new season by staging a pantomimic combat in which the New defeats the Old, Fertility discomfits Drought, Summer ousts Winter, or Life subdues Death. Traces of such primitive ritual survive to this day in the European Mummers' Plays, which are acted out on crucial calendar dates (e.g. Midsummer) and which portray the conflict of the seasons or the triumph of a valiant 'Saint George' over a grisly dragon which threatens to engulf the earth.

In ancient Babylon, an essential element of the New Year ritual was the recital (possibly also the enactment) of a time-honored myth relating the victory of Marduk, the patron god of the city, over Tiamat, a draconic marplot who sought to overthrow the authority of the gods. In Canaan, a similar story rehearsing the defeat of Yam, the god of the waters, and Mot, the god of death, by Baal, lord of fertility, is preserved on clay tablets of the fourteenth century B.C. discovered, since 1929, at Ras Shamra on the north coast of Syria; and it is probable that this was recited in connection with the New Year festival, celebrated at the time when the drought broke and the early rains began. Moreover, vestiges of a similar myth, in which Yahweh (Jehovah) is portrayed as having conquered the draconic Leviathan in a primordial battle-royal, may also be detected in sundry poetic passages of the Old Testament (Pss. 74.13–14; Job 9.13; 26.12–13).

What is deemed necessary to restore the world-order from year to year is deemed necessary *a fortiori* in order to bring in the New Age which will succeed the present

Era of Corruption. The seasonal battle thus becomes pro-
jected into eschatology—that is, into the standard picture
of the Last Things. In Jewish folklore, as represented by
numerous references in pseudepigraphic literature and in
the Talmud, the adversaries of God in this final conflict
were identified not so much with demonic or cosmic powers as with the unrighteous elements among men—the
heathen and the recalcitrant who served the Prince of
Darkness (Belial) and constituted his 'army'. In accordance with a celebrated prophecy in the Book of Ezekiel
(chaps. 38–39), these earthly antagonists were in turn
identified more especially with 'the children of Gog and
Magog'—originally, remote northern peoples from 'the back
of the beyond', but now regarded, in a purely metaphorical
sense, as symbolic of all who denied the God of Israel and
oppressed His chosen. Moreover, in line with what the
prophet Zechariah had foretold (14.3–5), it was held that
the Lord Himself would come with His heavenly legions
and fight on behalf of His people.

The war against Gog and Magog formed the more mili-
tant complement to that process of inner regeneration and
repentance that was to secure the advent of God's Kingdom
on earth. If Israel itself might ensure its continuance and
the restoration of its fortunes by a sincere return to the
Law and the Covenant, it was nevertheless essential that
the wicked should be finally and irretrievably put to rout.

1. To men who believed that the Final Age was indeed
at hand, preparations for this war were a matter of imminent and urgent concern. They had to have a detailed
Plan of Campaign. *The War of the Sons of Light and the
Sons of Darkness* (inscribed on one of the scrolls discovered by the bedouin boys in 1947) is such a plan—a kind
of G.H.Q. manual for the guidance of the Brotherhood at
'Armageddon'.

Not the least interesting feature of this document is that
it is far from being a mere fanciful lucubration, something
spun out of thin air. On the contrary, as General Yigael
Yadin has pointed out, it very largely conforms to standard
Roman patterns of military organization, procedure and

strategy. A few examples (drawn from the present writer's independent observations) must here suffice:

(1) The troops are to be drawn up in three lines [viii, 6]; this is the Roman *triplex acies* (Sallust, *Jugurtha*, 49). (2) The soldiers who initiate the attack are to hurl javelins *seven* times into the enemy ranks [vi, 1]; this recalls the fact that the front-line *velites* of the Roman army were armed with seven javelins (Livy, xxiv, 34). (3) The attack is to be launched to the accompaniment of a united war-cry destined to strike terror in the heart of the foe [viii, 9–10]; the same practise obtained among the Romans (Caesar, *Bell. Civ.*, iii, 92; Livy, vii, 36; Sallust, *Catiline*, 60). (4) The high priest exhorted the troops before they went into action, and addressed them as 'warriors' [xii, 10]; this is simply an adaptation of the *allocutio* delivered by a Roman general. He, too, was expected to call them *milites;* when Caesar once addressed them as *Quirites,* this aroused indignation (Suetonius, *Caes.*, 70; Dio, xlii, 53). (5) The 'trumpets of assembly' answer to the Roman *tuba concionis;* (6) the inscriptions on the standards are in accordance with Roman usage (Veget., ii, 13), though cleverly adapted in accordance with the Biblical phrase, 'In the name of our God will we set up our banners' (Ps. 20.6).

We cannot yet tell when this document was written. A clue to the date has been recognized by some scholars in the fact that two of the prime enemies of Israel are identified as 'the Kittians of Assyria' and 'the Kittians of Egypt'. Since the Biblical term 'Kittians'—originally denoting the inhabitants of Kition in Cyprus—was used in Hellenistic Jewish literature to denote the 'Macedonians' of the Alexandrian Empire, it has been supposed that this refers to the Seleucids of Syria and the Ptolemies of Egypt, which would mean—in the words of its original editor, the late Professor E. L. Sukenik—'that this scroll was composed after the partition of Alexander's empire among the Diadochi'. This, however, is not an absolutely necessary inference. Assyria and Egypt were, after all, the classic foes of Israel, and their ultimate downfall bulks very largely in Old Testament prophecies of the Final Age, while the

term 'Kittians' came in time to lose any precise signification
and to be used—like 'Hun' or 'Tartar'—to denote 'barbarians' in general. Hence, the reference to 'Kittians' of Assyria and Egypt may have been made, like that to Moab-
ites, Edomites, Ammonites, and Philistines [i.1–2], merely
out of deference to tradition.

2. Of different structure but of the same purport is the
text here entitled *The Rout of Belial*. Put together out of
thirty fragments (only fourteen of which, however, are sufficiently preserved to permit of translation), this is a
catena, or chain, of Scriptural passages which, on an eschatological interpretation, can be taken to predict the ultimate discomfiture of the partisans of Belial (the 'sons of
darkness') who are currently harassing and assailing the
'sons of light'. The author draws especially on verses of
Psalms 11–17 and on the twentieth chapter of the Book
of Ezekiel. At certain points his interpretation depends not
only on an over-all principle of eschatological exegesis but
also, more specifically, on reading secondary meanings into
the Biblical texts by means of ingenious but fanciful play
on words. The picture of the final struggle seems to reflect
in some measure the influence of Iranian ideas which percolated into Jewish circles during the periods of Persian
and subsequent Graeco-Roman domination.

3. A pendant to these longer texts is the fragment which
I have named *The Coming Doom*. This is best understood
as part of a sermon or discourse (Hebrew, *derashah*) based
on a string of similes relating to the Last Days.

II

Balancing the punishment of the unrighteous is the redemption of the faithful and the restoration of Israel. It
is, however, not merely by the defeat of His enemies that
the Kingdom of God will be re-established on earth. This
will depend also on the repentance of his sinful people and
its return to observance of the Law and fulfilment of the
obligations of the Covenant. The call to such change of
heart ('Repent, for the Kingdom of Heaven is at hand')

forms the subject of the exhortation here entitled *Weal and Woe.* As in the Biblical prophets and in such later writings as the Book of Enoch, the doom of the wicked and the triumph of the righteous are here described side by side.

III

1. The Golden Age which will follow these periods of visitation, trial, and testing is graphically portrayed in the text which I have called *The Last Jubilee.* Preserved only in a single copy, this is best regarded as a series of notes for a sermon, and was evidently compiled by one of those official 'expositors' mentioned expressly both in the *Manual of Discipline* and in the *'Zadokite' Document* as well as in Josephus' accounts of the Essenes.[1]

The purpose of the text is to depict the Golden Age as the fulfilment, in eschatological terms, of the Law of the Jubilee, in the twenty-fifth chapter of the Book of Leviticus. In a manner familiar from rabbinic literature, the expositor buttresses his interpretation by correlating crucial terms in the commandment with other passages of Scripture, in which they are used in a different and wider sense; and he enhances the cumulative effect of these comparisons by drawing alike on the Law, the Prophets, and the Holy Writings. The basis of his exegesis, however, is sometimes allusive rather than explicit, dependent on latent suggestion and association, which was evidently intended to be spelled out in the oral discourse. For the modern reader, therefore, the bare skeleton has, as it were, to be fleshed out, and this I have here attempted to do by having the text set in small capitals and the necessary amplifications in roman type and by explaining them in more detail in the accompanying notes. It cannot be guaranteed, of course—particularly since the manuscript is damaged and incomplete—that the resultant reconstruction of the sermon is one hundred percent certain, but a purely mechanical rendering of what are, after all, mere mnemonic jottings would leave the text a virtual torso, and I have been moved by a desire to help return the forgotten author to his patrimony.

A word should be added about the role played in our text by Melchizedek, the ancient 'king of Shalem and priest of God Most High', who is said, in Gen. 14.18–20, to have conferred upon Abraham (and, by implication, upon Abraham's descendants) the blessing of that deity. Melchizedek is introduced into our sermon as the future savior-king who will bring peace and salvation to the faithful and condign punishment to the wicked and who will also mediate divine forgiveness for the former on the Final Day of Atonement.

The reason why he is chosen for this role is really very simple. First: the eschatological doctrines of the Dead Sea Scriptures derive, in large measure, from Iranian lore which, during the period of Persian domination, the Jews picked up on a popular level.[2] A major feature of that lore was the ultimate triumph of Right (Asha) over Perversity (Druj). Accordingly, throughout the Scrolls, great stress is placed on Righteousness (*ṣedeq*); the Brotherhood styles itself 'the sons [or, elect] of righteousness',[3] and its opponents those 'of perversity' (*'awel*)[4]—corresponding to the Iranian *ashavanō* and *dregvatō*—and its spiritual mentor, the man who expounds the Torah aright, is 'the teacher of righteousness'.[5] Now, since the name Melchizedek lends itself readily to the interpretation 'king of righteousness' (*melech ṣedeq*),[6] and since—through a mistaken interpretation of Psalm 110.4 (*Thou art a priest for ever, after the order of Melchizedek*)—he himself, rather than the priesthood which he served, was popularly deemed to be eternal, he becomes at once an appropriate candidate for the role of the future messianic king who will establish the dominion of righteousness on earth.[7] Moreover, this notion could draw also on the widespread myth of the ancient hero *redivivus,* who would reappear eventually to save his people[8]—a myth associated in sundry passages of the Old Testament with David.[9]

Second: Melchizedek's title 'king of Shalem' lends itself, with equal facility, to a fanciful association with the Hebrew words, *shālôm,* 'peace',[10] and *shallem,* 'requite', so that he can at once be identified with the promised redeemer who will bring both peace to the faithful and requital to the wicked.

Third: Melchizedek combines the functions of king and priest, and therefore serves fittingly as a prefiguration of the future Messiah who will not only re-establish the dominion of God over that of Belial, but also mediate forgiveness for the faithful on the Final Day of Atonement, as did the high priest on the annual holy day (cf. Lev. 16.30–33).[11]

It has been suggested that the title, *melech shālem*, 'king of Shalem', in Gen. 14.18, is an historicization on the part of the Biblical writer (or his source) of an original *mal'ach shālôm*, 'angel of peace', and that the role assigned to Melchizedek in our sermon harks back to that earlier myth.[12] It has been suggested also that he is here regarded as an hypostasis of God Himself. In regard to such theories, however, we may perhaps be content, as was that ancient worthy himself, with but a tenth part. Although, by virtue especially of his assumed immortality, Melchizedek did indeed become the subject of divers legends in both Jewish and Christian lore,[13] it is not necessary to go beyond the simple midrashic interpretation of Scripture summarized above in order to account for his messianic role in our text.[14]

2. The text entitled *The New Covenant* is quite obviously part of a homiletic exposition of the famous prophecy in Jer. 31.31–33: 'Behold, days are coming' saith the Lord, 'when I will make a new covenant with the house of Israel and the house of Judah. . . . I will put my Law in their inward parts, and in their heart will I write it; and will be their God, and they will be My people.'

3. The war against Gog and Magog would mark the end of the present Era of Wickedness, but not the end of the world. It would last forty years—the period of so-called 'Messianic travail', and would pave the way for the 'Era of (Divine) Favor'. This too needed its blueprint, and a small portion of that blueprint is preserved in what has generally been called *The Two-Column Fragment*.

This tantalizing document, found in the same cave as

the main scrolls, is really a Manual of Discipline for the future Restored Congregation of Israel. It has excited especial interest because it describes the protocol for a banquet attended by 'the Messiah'. This has led to the belief that it deals with the Messianic Banquet (on the flesh of Leviathan) often described in rabbinic literature, and also that it prefigures, albeit in a limited degree, the Christian Eucharist.

The plain fact is, however, that the term 'Messiah'—or, more specifically, 'Messiah of Israel'—means no more than 'the duly anointed king'. This text, as we have said, is concerned with the administration of the future 'ideal community of Israel. After describing the rules that are to obtain regarding education, eligibility for public office, and military service, the author takes up the question of rank and precedence. The high priest, he affirms, is to occupy the supreme position and to be superior to any layman. He then gives a pertinent illustration. If, he says, the anointed king himself (expressly described as 'the Messiah [anointed] of Israel', in implied contrast with 'the Messiah of Aaron', i.e., the high priest) should attend a communal banquet, the high priest is nevertheless to be seated first, and it is to be the high priest's duty and privilege to pronounce the Grace before Meals. Moreover, in order to make the point even clearer, our author lays it down explicitly that this rule is to be observed even at smaller gatherings, when there may be no more than ten persons present—the minimum religious quorum [*minyan*] in traditional Jewish law!

The interpretation of this document as referring to a 'Lord's Supper' has been bolstered by a daring but unfortunate conjecture, whereby a faint and damaged passage of the text is made to read: 'When God begets the Messiah, he [i.e., the Messiah] is to enter with them'. It may therefore be pointed out that the crucial word 'God' is here simply an arbitrary restoration, and that the word read as 'begets' (viz. $YW[LI]D$) is more probably to be read 'is present' (viz. $YW[']D$), while that rendered 'he is to enter' means properly 'he is to come' and belongs to the next sentence. What is actually said, therefore, is that 'if the anointed (king, i.e., [*hmlk*] *hmšiḥ*) happens to be present (*yw*[*ʻ*]*d*) with them, the priest, as head of the entire Congregation of Israel is (nevertheless) to come . . . and take his seat (first)'.[15]

IV

Lastly come four texts attesting the 'messianic' expectations of the men who wrote the Scrolls and of the community at Qumran.

1. The first contains extracts (pitifully short, to be sure) from commentaries on relevant verses from the Last Blessing of Jacob (Gen. 49) and from the promise of God to David in the Book of Samuel.

2. The second is a *catena* of five Scriptural passages attesting the advent of the Future Prophet and the Anointed King and the final discomfiture of the impious. The first four are taken from the Pentateuch, and include an excerpt from the oracles of Balaam. The fifth is an interpretation of a verse from the Book of Joshua. An interesting feature of this document (not noticed by the original editor) is that precisely the same passages of the Pentateuch are used by the Samaritans as the stock testimonial to the coming of the Taheb, or future 'Restorer'.[16] They evidently constituted a standard set of such quotations, of the type that scholars have long supposed to have been in the hands of New Testament writers when they cited passages of the Hebrew Bible supposedly confirmed by incidents in the life and career of Jesus. The interest of this text is further enhanced by the comment on the passage from Joshua, for the curse which is there invoked upon re-builders of the city of Jericho is applied to two contemporaries, evidently brothers, who have been building a wall and towers in Jerusalem in order to turn it into a 'stronghold of wickedness' and who have also been perpetrating disgraceful excesses in Israel and Judah. Unfortunately, the identity of these impious men cannot yet be determined with certainty; one may think, perhaps, of Aristobulus II and Hyrcanus II (as suggested by Allegro) or, alternatively, even of

Herod and Phasael. In any case, however, we have in this allusion a highly important piece of evidence for the eventual definitive dating of the Scrolls.

3. The third, conventionally styled *A Messianic Florilegium*, is an exposition, in similar vein, of God's promise to Israel, in II Sam. 7.10–14, concerning the building of the Temple and the emergence of a scion of David, coupled with a warning against false teachers, fancifully derived from the words of Psalm 1.1, and a prediction of the attacks by heathen kings, deduced from Psalm 2.1–2.

4. The same theme is treated also, but in more discursive fashion, in the little piece which I have entitled *The Wondrous Child*.

This text, composed in Aramaic, is something of a teaser. It has been put together out of no less than twelve small fragments, which furnish the remains of two columns of writing.[17] Both the beginning and the end are missing; few lines or phrases are completely preserved; one of the 'joins' is doubtful; and several words are indistinct. The script seemingly indicates that the manuscript was penned at some time between about 30 B.C. and the collapse of the Qumran commune in A.D. 68, but it may, of course, have been copied from an older original.

All of this sounds, to be sure, pretty discouraging. Nevertheless the general drift of the text can still be made out. It is a prediction (one scholar has called it a horoscope)[18] of the birth of a Wondrous Child, characterized as 'the chosen of God' and of events which will ensue thereafter. The child will bear (like Krishna and Buddha)[19] special marks on his body, and will be distinguished by precocious wisdom and intelligence. He will be able to probe the secrets of all living creatures, and no schemes against him will succeed.

The problem is to identify this infant prodigy. According to the first editor of the text,[20] he is the Messiah—a view based mainly on the fact that in certain passages of the Book of Enoch the future savior and judge is indeed described as 'God's elect'.[21] To this, however, the objection has been raised that the passages in question come from later additions to the original Book of Enoch, apparently unknown to the men of Qumran since they do not appear among the portions of that book which have been discovered there. Moreover, it is urged, the title 'chosen of God' was not applied specifically to the Messiah—that is, to the salvific scion of David or Aaron—before the New Testament, however much such a general figure of myth may have existed previously. It has therefore been suggested that the Child is really Noah, whose birth was indeed believed in legend (e.g., in the Qumran *Memoirs of the Patriarchs*) to have been attended with miraculous signs, the references to impending general destruction and to 'waters' (ii.14) then being to the Flood rather than to events in the Last Days.[22]

There is at present no way of settling the question, and it should be borne in mind in any case that the myth of the Wondrous Child who will inaugurate a new age has a long history behind it,[23] so that this may be simply a Jewish adaptation of what was at the time a more widespread popular belief. We may recall, for instance, its Roman counterpart in the famous Fourth Eclogue of Vergil (virtually contemporary with our manuscript),[24] as well as the so-called Priene Inscription containing a decree promulgated in cities of Asia Minor in 9 B.C., which hails Augustus as the Savior who 'will end all strife and restore the world-order', and which signalizes his birthday as 'the beginning of all things'.[25]

NOTES

1. *Manual*, vi.6; '*Zadokite*' *Document*, vi.7; vii.18; *Florilegium*, i.11; Josephus, *Bellum Judaicum*, VIII.6.19; *Ant.*, XIII.5.9.
2. See above, General Introduction, pp. 24ff.
3. *Manual*, i.20, 22; ix.14; *Hymns* iii.13.
4. *Manual*, iii.21. Cf. also: *ib.*, iv.23, 24; v.2, 10; viii.13; ix.17; *Hymns* v.8. Cf. also: *Hymns* xi.22; xv.15, 25, etc.
5. *HabC*, i.13; v.10; vii.4; viii.3, etc.; *Ps̱. 37C* ii.15; '*Zadokite*' *Document*, i.11; vi.11; xx.32.
6. Cf. Heb. 7.2.
7. Righteousness is especially associated with the eschatological king in several passages of the Old Testament, e.g., Isa. 11.5; 16.5; Hos. 10.12; Pss. 96.1; 98.9; and with the Final Days in general, e.g., Isa. 51.5; 62.2; Jer. 33.16.
8. Standard examples are Arthur of Britain, Frederick Barbarossa; cf. Stith Thompson, *Motif-Index of Folk Literature*, A 530; T. H. Gaster, *Myth, Legend, and Custom in the Old Testament* (1969), §205a.
9. Jer. 34.23–24; Ezek. 37.24; Hos. 3.5. Cf. H. Schmidt, *Der Mythos vom wiederkehrenden König im Alten Testament* (1925). Cf. also TJ. *Ber.* 5a.
10. Cf. Heb. 7.2.
11. For the combination of royal and priestly factors in the future Messiah (as in Christ), cf. '*Zadokite*' *Document*, xix.10f.; xx.1; xii.23; John 6.14–15.
12. J. T. Milik, in *Journal of Jewish Studies* 23 (1972), 137.
13. For a resumé of these legends, cf. J. A. Fabricius,

Codex Pseudepigraphus Veteris Testamenti (1722), 311ff.; M. R. James, *The Lost Apocrypha of the Old Testament* (1920), pp. 17ff.; L. Ginzberg, *Legends of the Jews* (1909ff.), v.226; vi.325.

14. Nor is it really pertinent to adduce the reference to him in the *Epistle to the Hebrews* (chs. 5, 7) for there he is cited in a somewhat different context, namely, to furnish a precedent justifying the claim that Jesus is a spiritual high priest, superseding the levitical order, although not, in fact, a descendant of Aaron.

15. Some of the scholars working directly on the scrolls claim that infra-red photographs definitely establish the reading *YWLID*. I should like to see the photographs.

16. See J. A. Montgomery, *The Samaritans* (1907), pp. 247f.; M. Gaster, *The Samaritans* (1925), p. 92; *id.*, *Samaritan Eschatology* (1932), pp. 229f.

17. There is also a tiny scrap containing only five legible, but unintelligible letters.

18. J. Carmignac, 'Les horoscopes de Qumran', in *Revue Biblique* 18 (1965), 199–217. However, J. A. Fitzmyer has pertinently observed (in *Catholic Biblical Quarterly* 27 [1965], 348–72) that the text nowhere mentions stars or signs of the zodiac!

19. Krishna bore the sign of Śrivatsa, and Buddha the well-known thirty-two marks.

20. J. Starcky, 'Un texte messianique de la grotte 4 de Qumran', in *Mémorial du cinquantenaire de l'École des langues orientales anciennes de l'Institut Catholique de Paris* (1964), 51–66.

21. Cp. Enoch 45.3; 51.3, 5; 61.4, 8; 62.1.

22. J. A. Fitzmyer, *op. cit.* (reprinted in his *Essays on the Semitic Background of the New Testament* [SBL, Sources for Biblical Study, 5] (1974), pp. 127–60). This is the most thoroughgoing treatment of the text to date, though the author's suggestion that the Wondrous Child is Noah is open to debate, as he himself frankly concedes.

23. See on this especially, E. Norden, *Die Geburt des Kindes* (1924).

24. See: R. S. Conway, *Virgil's Messianic Eclogue* (1907); J. Carcopino, *Virgile et le mystère de la Vème eclogue* (1943).

25. See: F. H. Gaetringen, *Inschriften von Priene* (1906), No. 105; translated in F. C. Grant, *Ancient Roman Religion* (1957), pp. 173–74; cp. also: A. Harnack, *Reden und Aufsätze*[2] (1906), i.301; H. Lietzmann, *Der Weltheiland* (1909), pp. 14f.; O. S. Rankin, *The Origins of the Festival of Hanukkah* (1930), p. 243. This concept has been invoked by many scholars to explain the Immanuel and related prophecies in Isaiah, chs. 7 and 9; cp. T. H. Gaster, *Myth, Legend, and Custom in the Old Testament* (1969), §176.

THE WAR OF THE SONS OF LIGHT
AND THE SONS OF DARKNESS

· · · · · · · · · · · · · · · · · ·

The first engagement of the Sons of Light against the Sons of Darkness—that is, against the army of Belial—shall be an attack on the troop of Edom, Moab, the Ammonites and the Philistine area and upon that of the Kittians of Assyria, and of those violators of the Covenant who give them aid. When the Sons of Light who are now in exile return from the 'desert of the nations' to pitch camp in the desert of Jerusalem, the children of Levi, Judah and Benjamin, who are now among those exiles, shall wage war against these peoples—that is, against each and every one of their troops.

After that battle they shall advance upon the [king of] the Kittians of Egypt. In due time, he will sally forth in high fury to wage war against the kings of the north, being minded in his anger to destroy his enemies and cut down their power.[2] This, however, will be the time of salvation for the people of God, the critical moment when those that have cast their lot with Him will come to dominion, whereas those that have cast it with Belial shall be doomed to eternal extinction. [Great] havoc shall then beset the descendants of Japheth:[3] Assyria shall fall, with none to help her, and the dominion of the Kittians shall depart. Wickedness will thus be humbled and left without remnant, and no survivor shall remain of the Sons of Darkness.

[Streaks of lightn]ing will flash from one end of the

world to the other, growing ever brighter until the era of darkness is brought utterly to an end.[4] Then, in the era of God, His exalted grandeur will give light for [evermore,][5] shedding on all the Sons of Light peace and blessing, gladness and length of days.

On the day the Kittians fall, there shall be mighty combat and carnage in the presence of the God of Israel, for that is the day which He appointed of old for the final battle against the Sons of Darkness. Thereon the company of the divine and the congregation of the human shall engage side by side in combat and carnage, the Sons of Light doing battle against the Sons of Darkness with a show of godlike might, amid uproarious tumult, amid the war-cries of gods and men, in a veritable day of havoc. It will be, indeed, a 'time of [   ] tribulation'[6] for 'the people redeemed of God', but, unlike all their previous tribulations, this one will come to a speedy end in a redemption which shall last for ever.

When they engage the Kittians, [amid all the combat and car]nage of battle, the Sons of Light shall have luck three times in discomfiting the forces of wickedness; but three times the host of Belial shall brace themselves to turn back the tide. At this, the squadrons of the infantry shall become faint-hearted, but the power of God shall strengthen their hearts, and on the seventh occasion the great hand of God shall finally subdue [the army of Belial. For will He summon] all the angels of His dominion and all the humans [that are bound to His communion] [   ] [and amid] the Holy Beings He Himself will appear* to give aid [   ], [and He will make] the truth [to shine forth,] bringing doom upon the Sons of Darkness [   ] [and] they shall surrender. . . .

* Restored after Zech. 14:3, 5: 'Then shall the Lord go forth and fight against those nations, as when He fighteth in a day of battle . . . And the Lord my God shall come, and all the Holy Ones with Him (LXX text)'.

[*Of religious offices during wartime*]

(ii, 1–6)

[   ] fathers of the community, fifty-two in number.[7]
After the high priest and his deputy they shall appoint
an order of major priests, twelve in number, to serve constantly before God. Furthermore, twenty-six major officials
duly assigned to service shall serve in their appointed offices;[8] and after them there shall be twelve major levites,
one for each tribe, to serve constantly. The major officials
charged with service shall serve in rotation, but subordinate
to them shall be the chiefs of the tribes and the fathers
of the community stationed constantly at the gates of the
sanctuary.

The major officials assigned to service shall take up their
positions, in discharge of their duties, on the festivals, new
moons, sabbaths or weekdays duly assigned to them.
They shall be fifty years of age and upwards.[9] Their function shall be to attend to the burnt-offerings and the sacrifices, to set out the incense of 'pleasant savor' for God's
acceptance, to perform rites of atonement in behalf of all
His congregation, and constantly to clear away the fat
ashes which lie before Him on the 'table of glory'.

[*Of recruitment*]

(ii, 6–9)

All of these dispositions, however, are to apply only to
the year of release. For the remaining thirty-three years
of the War,[10] the dignitaries appointed to the Assembly
and all the chiefs of families in the community are to select
the soldiers for service in the various foreign countries.
They are to draft them annually out of all the tribes of
Israel in accordance with the established conventions of
warfare.[11] Only in the year of release is there to be no
draft, for that is a year of sabbatical rest for Israel.

[Of the sequence of campaigns]

(ii, 9–14)

Of the thirty-five working years, the first six are to be devoted to mobilization, the entire community collectively taking part in it. During the remaining twenty-nine years, the war is to be conducted in a series of separate campaigns. In the first year, they are to fight in Mesopotamia; in the second, against the Lydians; in the third, against the rest of the Syrians, against Uz, Ḥul, Togar and Masha,[12] which are across the Euphrates; in the fourth and fifth, against Arpachshad;[13] in the sixth and seventh, against all the Assyrians, Persians and Easterners as far as the Great Desert; in the eighth, against the Elamites; in the ninth, against the descendants of Ishmael and Keturah.[14] For the next ten years the campaign shall be concentrated against all the Hamites,[15] wherever they dwell; and for the remaining decade against all the [   ] throughout their habitations.

*   *   *   *

Concerning the Battle Dispositions and the Trumpets of Assembly at the time when the gates of war are opened for the infantry to go forth, and concerning the trumpets for signaling the first onslaught, the ambush, the pursuit after the defeat of the enemy, and the recall

(iii, 1–11)

On the trumpets of assembly for the entire community, they shall write: *The Enlisted of God.*[16]

On the trumpets of assembly for officers, they shall write: *The Princes of God.*

On the trumpets of enrollment they shall write: *The Rank of God.*

On the trumpets of the dignitaries they shall write: *The Heads of the Families of the Community.*

When they assemble at the general meeting-house, they

shall write: *Enactments*[17] *of God for the Sacred Council.*

On the trumpets of the camps they shall write: *The peace of God be in the camps of His saints.*

On the trumpets of advance they shall write: *The Power of God is able to scatter the enemy and to put to flight all who hate righteousness. And he recompenses the loyalty [of them that love God, but requites]*[18] *them that hate Him.*

On the trumpets for marshalling the battle they shall write: *The marshalled squadrons of God are able to wreak His angry vengeance upon all the Sons of Darkness.*

On the trumpets of assembly for the infantry, when the gates of war are opened for them to go out to the enemy line, they shall write: *A reminder*[19] *of the vengeance to be exacted in the Era of God.*

On the trumpets of carnage[20] they shall write: *The force of God's power in battle is able to fell all the perfidious as slain men.*

On the trumpets of ambush they shall write: *The hidden powers*[21] *of God are able to destroy wickedness.*

On the trumpets of pursuit they shall write: *God has smitten all the children of Darkness. He will not turn back His anger until He has consumed them.*

And when they return from the battle to rejoin the ranks they shall write on the trumpets of recall: *God hath taken back* (gathered in).[22]

And on the trumpets which signal the route of return from the war against the enemy and the way back to the community in Jerusalem, they shall write: *Joy of God at the return of peace.*†[23]

*This is the order
of the standards for the entire community
when they are enrolled*

(iii.12–iv, 2)

On the great standard which precedes the entire army [lit. 'people'] they are to write *People of God* together with

† Or, 'at a safe return'.

the names Aaron and Israel and those of the twelve tribes of Israel according to their pedigrees.

On the standard of the camp commanders of the three tribes (of Levi, Judah and Benjamin) they are to write [   ].

On the standard of each separate tribe they are to write: *Banner of God*, together with the name of the chieftain of the [   ], the name of the chieftain of the ten thousand and those of the [   ].

On the standard of Merari[24] they are to write: *Offering unto God*,[25] together with the names of the chiefs of the Merarites and those of the commanders of its thousands.

On the standard of the thousand they are to write: *God's anger is vented*[26] *in fury against Belial and against all that cast their lot with him, that they have no remnant;* together with the name of the commander of the thousand and of its hundreds.

On the standard of the hundred they shall write: *From God*[27] *comes the power of battle against all sinful flesh,* together with the names of the commander of the hundred and of its tens.

On the standard of fifty they shall write: *Finished is the stand of the froward through the mighty acts of God,*[28] together with the names of the commanders of the fifty and of its tens.

And on the standard of ten they shall write: *Paeans of God on the ten-stringed harp,* together with the names of the commander of the ten, and of the nine men under his command.

When they go out to battle, they shall write upon their several standards: *Truth of God, Righteousness of God, Glory of God, Justice of God,* and thereafter the specific name of each division. And when they draw near the battle, they shall write upon their standards: *Right Hand of God, Battle-Array of God, Tumult of God, Slain of God,* and thereafter their specific names.[29]

And when they come back from the battle, they shall write upon their standards: *Grandeur of God, Greatness of God, Praises of God, Glory of God,* together with their specific names.

Order of the standards of the community

When they go out to battle, they shall write on the first standard: *Community of God;* on the second, *Camps of God;* on the third, *Tribes of God;* on the fourth, *Families of God;* on the fifth, *Squadrons of God;* on the sixth, *Assembly of God;* on the seventh, *Recruits of God;* on the eighth, *Armies of God;* and they shall write also the specific names, with all their ranks.

And when they draw near to the battle, they shall write upon their standards: *War of God, Vengeance of God, Feud of God, Requital of God; Strength of God; Recompense of God; Might of God; Annihilation by God of all vain nations;* together with all their specific names.

And when they return from the battle, they shall write on their standards: *Salvation of God, Triumph of God, Help of God, Support of God, Praise of God, Thanksgiving to God, Acclaim of God, Peace of God.*

(*A fragmentary passage follows, giving the measurements of the standards.*)

[.] On the [standard?] of the leader of the entire community they are to write his name and the names of Israel and Levi and Aaron, and the name of the twelve tribes of Israel according to their pedigrees, and the names of the twelve commanders of those tribes.

Order of deploying the battle-squadrons when their full force is mustered

(iv.3–vi, 6)

To form a complete front. The line is to consist of a thousand men. Each front-line is to be seven deep, one man standing behind the other. All of them are to hold shields of polished bronze, resembling mirrors. These shields are to be bordered by a wreath-like rim wrought artistically by a skilled smith out of [   ][30] gold, silver, bronze, and precious stones, blended in a variegated arrangement as on a woman's breastplate.

Each shield is to be two and one half cubits long and two and one half cubits wide. The men are to hold in their hands a spear and a lance. The length of the spear is to be seven cubits, of which one half-cubit is to consist of the blade and the point. (*There follows a highly technical description of the spears. Since, however, we do not yet know the precise meaning of many of the terms employed, it is impossible to translate the passage with confidence.*)

* * * *

[   ] seven times and then return to their positions. After them three squadrons of the infantry shall go forth and take up positions between the lines. The first squadron shall fling seven war-darts into the enemy line. On the blade of each dart they shall write: *The flash of the spear*[31] *evinces the Power of God.* And on the second javelin they shall write: *Spurtings*[32] *of blood, causing men to fall slain through the anger of God.* And on the third dart they shall write: *Flame of the sword devouring the evil-doing slain by the judgment of God.* They shall hurl such darts seven times in all, and then return to their positions. After them shall go forth the two other squadrons of the infantry and take up positions between the two lines. The one shall hold spear and shield and the other spear and lance, to fell the slain in the judgment of God and to subdue the enemy line by the might of God, to the end that every vain nation may reap the fruit of its evil. Then shall the sovereignty belong to the God of Israel, and He will evince His power among the sacred hosts[33] of His people.

[*Of the cavalry*]

(vi, 7–17)

The seven battle lines shall be flanked in turn, on the left and on the right, by cavalry. Each line shall be accompanied by two hundred light horsemen, so that there will be in all seven hundred of the latter on the one side and seven hundred on the other.

These horsemen shall occupy a similar position in the camp, though in that case they shall be disposed on all (four) sides.

There shall be four thousand and six hundred of them, all told. In addition, there shall be fourteen hundred heavy horse accompanying the general ranks—fifty for each line of troops.[34] The light and heavy horse that accompany the troops shall therefore amount in all to six thousand.

All the cavalry that go out to battle with the infantry shall consist of stallions swift of foot, non-biters,[35] long in the wind, full-grown and mature, trained for battle and used to hearing all kinds of sounds and facing all kinds of sights. Their riders shall be stout-hearted warriors, trained in horsemanship; and their ages shall range between thirty and forty-five.[36] Those, however, who are assigned to line duty shall be from forty to fifty years old. They shall [be equipped with] [   ] and helmets and greaves, and shall hold in their hands round shields and spears [   ], long [   ] and a bow and arrows and war-darts. And all of them shall be primed in [   ]. [It shall be their duty to] [   ] and to shed the blood of those who are destined to be slain in consequence of their guilt.

*   *   *   *

[*Of age and health requirements*]

(vii, 1–7)

The line troops are to be forty to fifty years of age.[37] Those who arrange the camps are to be from fifty to sixty.[38] The officers too are to be from forty to fifty years of age; and all who strip the dead and collect the spoil and clean up the terrain and keep the weapons and prepare the food are to be between twenty-five and thirty. No toddling child or woman is to enter their camps from the moment they leave Jerusalem to go to war until they return; neither is anyone that is lame or blind or halt, or that has a long-standing blemish in his flesh or that is afflicted with any manner of bodily contagion, to go with them to war. All of them are to be men willing to face the hazards of battle, unimpaired in spirit and flesh and ready for the day of vengeance. Moreover, any man who is not yet cleansed from a bodily discharge on the day of battle is not to go down with them; for holy angels march with their hosts.

A distance of about two thousand cubits is to be set in every case between the camp and the latrine, and no uncleanliness is ever to be in evidence in the precincts of the camp.

[*Of the battle signals*]

(vii, 8–ix, 9)

When the lines of battle are drawn up to face the foe, line in front of line, then out of the center gap in the ranks[39] there shall come into the lines seven priests of the descendants of Aaron, clothed in robes of white silk, wearing the linen tunic and the linen breeches, girt with the linen girdle of silk twined artistically with blue and purple and deep scarlet thread, after the model of broidery, and with mitred turbans on their heads—garments of war which they are not to bring into the sanctuary. The one priest shall walk about before all the troops of the line to encourage them in the battle, while in the hands of the other six shall be the trumpets for calling to arms, and the trumpets for sounding the charge, and the trumpets for recall. And when these priests go out between the lines, seven levites shall go out with them, and in their hands shall be seven trumpets made out of rams' horns. And three officers selected from the levites shall walk ahead of these priests and levites. And the priests shall sound a blast on the two [*or:* two of the] trumpets used for call[ing to arms].
[   ] fifty shield-men,[40] and fifty infantrymen shall go out from the one gap, [and fifty from the other,] and the levitical officers [shall go out with them.] And they shall go out with every line in this manner. [   ]. The men of the infantry shall go out from the gaps and [take up posi]tion between the two [lines.]

*   *   *   *

The trumpets shall keep sounding for the slingers until they have hurled a full seven times. Then the priests shall blow the recall for them, and they shall return (lit. come) to the first line to take their stand in their assigned position. Thereupon the priests shall sound a blast on the trumpets of assembly, and the squadron of infantry shall go forth from the gaps and take up position between the lines, and on their flanks shall be horsemen to the right and to the left. The priests shall then sound upon the trumpets a quavering (?) blast for the drawing up of the line of the battle. The columns shall disperse to their several ranks, each to his assigned position. And when they have taken up position in three lines, the priests shall sound a second blast—a low, subdued note for advance to the enemy line. Thereupon they are to grasp their weapons. Then the priests are to sound blasts on the six trumpets used for rousing to the slaughter—a sharp insistent note for directing the battle. And the levites and all the people with rams' horns are to sound a single blast—a great war-like trump to melt the heart of the enemy. At the sound of that blast, the war-darts are to issue forth to fell the slain. Then they are to accelerate the notes of the rams' horns, and the priests are to blow upon the trumpets a sharp, insistent sound to direct the wings of the battle, until they have hurled their darts into the enemy line seven times. Thereupon the priests are to sound upon the trumpets the signal of recall—a low, quavering (?) subdued note.

In such fashion are the priests to blow the signals for the three squadrons. And when the first squadron begins to hurl its darts, the [priests] are to blow [   ] [on the trump]et a great blast to direct the bat[tle] [   ]; the priests are to sound a blast for them on the trumpets [   ] their assigned positions in the ranks [   ], and [   ] shall take up position.

*   *   *   *

[   ] they shall engage in felling the slain. And all the people shall silence their war-cries, while the priests keep blowing the trumpets for carnage, to direct the battle, until the enemy are discomfited and turn tail. The priests

shall go on blowing to direct the battle, and when the enemy are being discomfited before them, the priests shall sound on the trumpets of assembly, and all the infantry troops stationed between the front lines shall go out to them, and six squadrons shall take up positions. The force of the total squadrons then entering the combat shall consist of seven lines comprising in all twenty-eight thousand troops, and the cavalry shall number six thousand. All of these shall pursue the enemy to annihilate him in the battle of God unto his eternal extinction. And the priests shall blow for them on the trumpets of pursuit, and they shall fall upon the enemy to pursue him unto destruction. And the horsemen shall keep chasing them back into the thick of the battle until utter destruction is achieved. And while the enemy are falling slain, the priests shall go sounding the signals from a distance; they shall not go into the midst of the slain lest they be defiled by their impure blood; for the priests are holy and they are not to defile the oil of their priestly anointment with the blood of vain heathen.[41]

*Order of disposing the troops
in various battle-formations:*[42]

(a) in a straight line[43] *flanked by so-called '(human) towers';*[44]
(b) in a curved line resembling the lower half of a circle,[45] *similarly protected;*
(c) in a curved line resembling the upper half of a circle,[46] *similarly protected;*
(d) in a slight curve with center foremost, protected by spearhead columns advancing from the flanks;[47]
(e) in a slight curve with ends foremost, protected by wings (of cavalry)[48] *advancing on both flanks, in order to strike terror in the enemy.*

(ix, 10–15)

(In all such cases,) the shields of the men constituting the '(human) towers' are to be three cubits long, and their spears eight cubits. The 'tower' is to consist of two side-

lines each made up of a hundred men carrying shields, and
of a front line similarly composed. It is to be a three-sided
affair, and thus to comprise three hundred shields in all.
It is to have two gaps, one on the [right and] one on the
left. All of the shields of the 'towers' are to bear inscriptions. Those of the first 'tower' are to carry the legend, MI-
CHAEL; [those of the second, GABRIEL; those of the third,]
SARIEL; and those of the fourth, RAPHAEL[49] . . .

*   *   *   *

[*Of the exhortation
of the troops*]

(x, 1–xii, 18)

[   ] our[50] camp, and to guard ourselves from all
unclean things, and Thou art He who told us aforetime
that Thou wouldst be in our midst, a great and awful God,
to make spoil of our enemies before us. Thou also art He
who taught us from of old for all our generations saying:
When ye draw near unto the battle, the priest is to stand
and speak to the people saying: 'Hear, O Israel, ye are
drawing near this day unto battle against your enemies.
Fear not, neither let your hearts grow soft, neither be dismayed nor affrighted before them, for your God is marching with you to do battle for you against your foemen to
the end that He may save you'.[51]
Then shall the officers thus address all that are ready
for the battle, stout-hearted men, to encourage [them] with
the power of God and to restore all whose hearts melt and
to encourage altogether all the soldiers of the army: 'To
this didst Thou refer when Thou spakest through Moses
saying: "When thou goest to war in your land against a
foeman that assails you, sound ye the trumpets [Num.
10.9]. Then shall ye be called to remembrance before your
God and ye shall be saved from your enemies." Who is
like Thee, O God of Israel, in heaven or on earth, that
can do the like of Thy great deeds and of Thy mighty
power? And who is like Thy people Israel whom Thou
didst choose for Thyself out of all the nations of the lands,
a people of men hallowed by the covenant and schooled

in the Law, men enlightened with un[derstanding], men who [   ], who heard the glorious voice and saw the holy angels, men whose ears are opened and who hear deep things. [Thou art He who ordained] the outspreading of the heavens; the host of the luminaries; the several duties of spirits and the spheres of dominion of holy beings; the treasuries of ha[il and snow; and the balance of] the clouds.

'Thou art He who created the earth and the rules whereby parts thereof are assigned to desert and wasteland; likewise all that issues from it and all the fruits of its [yield]; the bounds of the seas also and the reservoirs of the rivers; the cleavage of the deeps; all manner of beasts and fowl; the fabric of man and his offspring; the confusion of tongues and division of peoples; the settlements of [all] the families [of men], and the apportionment of the earth as inheritances [among them].

'[Thou art He who decreed the day of sabbath rest and] the holy festivals, and the turning-points of the years[52] and [all] the appointed seasons. [   ].

'These things have we come to know through Thine understanding which [Thou hast planted within us].

'[Thou hast bent] Thine [ear] to our cry; for [   ]'

*   *   *   *

'[To none] but Thee belong the [issues of] war, and it is by the strength of Thy hand that their corpses have been flung forth, with none to bury them.

'Goliath the Gittite, a man of mighty strength, didst Thou deliver into the hand of thy servant David, because David trusted in Thy great name and not in sword or spear.[53] For Thine is the battle. The Philistines also didst Thou humble time after time by Thy holy name; and Thou didst also deliver us many times through the hands of our kings by virtue of Thy mercies and not of our deeds which we did evilly commit, nor of our acts of transgression.

'Thine is the battle; from Thee comes the power; and it is not ours. It is not our strength nor the might of our hands that achieveth this valor, but it cometh through Thy strength and through Thy great valorous might. So didst

Thou tell us of old, saying: "There shall step a star out of Jacob; there shall rise a rod out of Israel, and it shall smite the brow of Moab and undermine all the children of pride. And it shall proceed from Jacob and destroy every remnant from the city; and the enemy shall be dispossessed, but Israel shall triumph" [Num. 24.17–19]. Moreover, by the hands of Thine anointed, the men who had vision of things foreordained, Thou hast related unto us the warlike triumphs of Thy hand—how Thou hast waged battle against our foes and caused the troops of Belial—the seven vain nations[54]—to fall into the hands of the pauper folk whom Thou didst redeem by wondrous might [and set] in [safe]ty and peace.

'Now is the heart that was melting turned to a wellspring of hope. Thou hast done unto these as Thou didst unto Pharaoh and the captains of his chariots at the Red Sea. The base[55] of spirit wilt Thou burn up like a flaming brand in a hayrick, a brand that devours wickedness and that will not turn back until guilt is destroyed.

'Of old didst Thou tell us of the time when Thy mighty hand would prevail against the Kittians, in that Thou didst declare: "Assyria shall fall by the sword of no human, and the sword of no man shall devour him".

'Into the hands of the needy hast Thou delivered the foemen in all lands, and into the hands of them that were bowed to the dust. So hast Thou humbled the mighty of the peoples; brought their deserts upon the wicked; vindicated among all men the truthfulness of Thy judgments; won for Thyself eternal fame among the people [whom Thou hast redeemed; revealed to those whom Thou hast worsted that Thou art indeed the Lord] of Battles;[56] shown forth Thy great and holy Being[57] in the sight of the rest of the nations, that [   ] may know [   ], when Thou wreakest judgment upon Gog[58] and upon all his throng and takest vengeance upon [   ], that Thou wilt wage battle against them from heaven [   ]'.

* * * *

'For [with Thee] in heaven are a multitude of holy beings,[59] and armies of angels are in Thy holy abode, to [serve as] Thy [legionaries];[60] and down on earth Thou hast [likewise] placed at Thy service the elect of an holy people.[61] The roster of all their host is with Thee in Thy holy habitation, and the [   ] in Thy glorious abode. And the benefits[62] of Thy blessings and Thy covenant of peace hast thou inscribed for them in a charter[63] of [Eternal] Life—an assurance that through all the epochs of time Thou wilt be their king, and that when Thou contendest in judgment Thou wilt muster an army of (these) Thine elect, in their thousands and tens of thousands, side by side with Thine holy beings and Thine angels, and that they shall prevail in battle and, along with the heavenly elect [be triumphant.]

'O God, Thou, resplendent in Thy sovran glory, and the congregation of Thy holy beings are indeed in our midst as a perpetual help. We have [poured] contempt upon kings, scorn and contumely upon mighty men. For the Lord [*Adonai*] is holy, and the King of Glory is with us, along with the holy beings.[64] Warrior angels are in our muster, and He that is Mighty in War[65] is in our throng. The army of His spirits marches beside us. Our horsemen come like clouds or like banks of dew, to cover the earth, or like torrential showers, to rain judgment on all that grows in it.'

'Arise, O warrior![66]
Take thy captives, thou man of glory;
and reap thy spoil,[67] O valiant![68]
Set thy hand upon the neck of thy foemen,[69]
and thy foot upon mounds of the slain.[70]
Smite the nations that assail thee,[71]
and let thy sword devour guilty flesh.[72]
Fill thy land with glory
and thine inheritance with blessing.[73]
Be a multitude of possessions[74] in thy fields,
silver and gold and precious stones in thy palaces.
Zion, rejoice exceedingly,[75]
and shine forth, O Jerusalem, with songs of joy,
and let all the cities of Judah exult![76]
Let thy gates be continually open,

that the wealth of the nations may be brought unto
    thee;[77]
and let their kings minister unto thee,
and all that oppressed thee make obeisance to thee,
and lick the dust of thy feet![78]
   O daughter of my people,
ring out your songs of joy![79]
Put on your finery,[80]
step forth [   ]
[   ] Israel, to rule for evermore!
[   ] the warriors, O Jerusalem!
Be exalted, O Lord, above the heavens!'[81]

*   *   *   *

[Of the priestly benediction]

(xiii, 1–xiv, 1)

And his brethren the priests and the levites and all the
elders of the ranks that are with him, standing each in his
assigned position, shall bless the God of Israel and all His
unerring works, and shall curse the name of Belial and all
the spirits associated with him. And they shall take up
word and say:

'Blessed be the God of Israel for all His holy plan and
for His unerring works; and blessed be all that serve Him
in righteousness and acknowledge Him in faithfulness. But
cursed be Belial for his invidious schemes, and damned
be he for his guilty dominion; and cursed be all the spirits
of his ilk for their wicked designs, and damned be they
for all their filthy acts and unclean. For they are of the
portion of darkness, while the portion of God is everlasting
light.

'And now, O God of our fathers, we will bless Thy name
for ever. For we are the people [of Thine inheritance.]
With our fathers didst Thou make a covenant, and Thou
hast confirmed it with their seed throughout the epochs of
time. In all the evidences of Thy glory among us there
hath always been the memory of Thy covenant. Therefore
hast Thou granted help to the remnant and ever renewed
that covenant, and therefore hast Thou ever vouchsafed

unto us Thy deeds of truth and Thy wondrous acts of justice. Thou hast made us unto Thee an eternal people, and
hast cast our lot in the portion of light, that we may evince
Thy truth; and from of old hast Thou charged the Angel
of Light[82] to help us. In his hand are all works of righteousness, and all spirits of truth are under his sway. But
for corruption thou hast made Belial, an angel of hostility.
All his dominion is in darkness, and his purpose is to bring
about wickedness and guilt. All the spirits that are associated with him are but angels of destruction. They follow
only the laws of darkness, and all their craving is directed
toward it. But we—we are in the portion of Thy truth.[88]
We will rejoice in the might of Thy hand and be glad in
Thy salvation and exult in the strength of [Thy right hand
and in the gift] of Thy peace.

'Who is like Thee in strength, O God of Israel? Thy right
hand is with the needy.

'And what angel or [prince of heaven] can give such
help as Thou givest with Thy redemption?

'Of old hast Thou set for Thyself a day of warfare against
wic[kedness], to triumph in truth and to destroy guilt; to
bring darkness low and raise light on high;[84] [   ] [to
ensure that the Sons of Light] stand for ever, and to destroy all the Sons of Darkness; to bring joy to [all   ].
Hast Thou not appointed us for [that time?].'

*   *   *   *

'[   ] as when the fire of His fury was kindled
against the idols of Egypt'.

[*Of the hymn of victory*]

(xiv, 2–17)

When they come up from gathering in the fallen and
return to the camps, they shall all of them sing the hymn
of return. Next morning, they shall launder their garments
and wash themselves clean of the blood of the guilty
corpses and return to their assigned positions at the place
where the line was drawn up before the slain of the enemy

fell. And there they shall all of them bless the God of Israel and extol His name together in joy and take up word
and say:

'Blessed be the God of Israel
Who keeps the loyalty of His covenant
and constantly evinces salvation
to the people whom He redeemed.
He   has   summoned   those   that   were   stumbling
      [   ],85
but has gathered the horde of the heathen for extermina-
      tion without survival,
exalting the melting heart by [His] justice,
opening the mouth of the dumb for joyful song,
endowing with strength hands that were slack,
teaching them arts of war;
giving firm stance to tottering knees
and vigor to the shoulders of the bowed;
and [   ] to the lowly spirits;
firmness to the melting heart,
and [   ] to those whose way is blameless.
All wicked nations are come to an end
and all their heroes have no standing.
But we— [Thou hast granted us] a remnant;
[therefore will we bless] Thy name.

'O God of mercies,
Who keepest the covenant sworn unto our fathers,
and Who, throughout all our generations,
hast wondrously shown forth Thy mercies unto our rem-
      nant,
[Thou hast caused us to prevail] against the dominion
      of Belial
that, for all His covert hostility,
he has not thrust us away from Thy covenant.
Thou hast rebuked the spirits of His lot
[   ] the [   ] of his sway.
Thou hast preserved the life
of [the people] whom Thou didst redeem;

hast upholden the falling by Thy strength,
but cut down all the proud of stature.
Their warriors have none to deliver them;
their fleet men[86] have no escape;
their honored men Thou turnest to contempt;
and every creature of vanity [thou reduces to nau]ght.
But we—we are Thy holy people;
For Thy holy works we will praise Thy name,
and for Thy deeds of power we will extol [Thy]
        [   ]
at all the stated times, and at all the foreordained mo-
        ments of nature:
at the coming of day and night,
and the outgoing of evening and morning;[87]
for great is [   ] of Thy [   ]
and Thy mysterious wonders in the heights.
For Thou raisest up unto Thee out of the dust,
and castest down from the angels.
Be exalted, be exalted, O God of gods,[88] and lift Thyself
        up in Thy wrath! [   ]
[Let destruction befall] the Sons of Darkness,
but let Thy great light shine [for the Sons of
        Light   ]'.

*   *   *   *

B[89]
[*Preparations for battle*]

(xv, 1–2)

*   *   *   *

[For it is a 'time of trouble for Israel',][90] and of the
[visita]tion of war upon all the nations. They that have
cast their lot with God shall [be blessed] with everlasting
redemption, but annihilation shall overtake all the wicked
nations. All who have been making preparations for the
war shall go and pitch camp against the king of the Kittians and against all the army of Belial that are destined
along with him [for the day of vengeance] by God's sword.

[*Of the exhortation
of the troops*]

(xv, 3–xvi, 1)

The high priest shall stand up with his brethren the
priests and the levites and all the men of the ranks beside
him, and shall recite in their hearing the prayer of the battle line and shall rehearse to them the full order of regulations for the occasion together with all the words of their
thanksgivings, and he shall there marshal all the lines according to [   ]; and the priest that is chosen by the
unanimous decision of his brethren to officiate at the moment of vengeance[91] shall walk about and encourage all
the troops and say:

'Be strong and stout-hearted and acquit ye as men of
valor. Be not afeared neither dismayed [neither terrified
before] them; and be not a-quail neither awe-struck before them, and turn not back, neither [   ], for they
are a wicked horde, and all their deeds are in darkness,
and for darkness is all their craving. But all their refuges
and strength shall be as smoke that dissolves, and all their
multitudinous throng [   ]. None of their [   ]
shall be found any more, and all their ruinous structure[92]
shall be speedily cut down [   ]. Be of good courage
for the battle of God; for this day has been determined as
the day of battle [   ] against all [   ] and as the
day of combat against all flesh. The God of Israel lifts up
His hand with wondrous power [against] all the spirits
of wickedness [   ]. And the warrior angels gird themselves for battle; they are marshalled in serried ranks and
[mustered] for the day [of combat] [   ], to remove
[   ] in his destruction'.

*   *   *   *

'The God of Israel has [summoned] a sword against all
the nations,[93] but with the saints of His people He will do
a work of power'.

[*Of the order of battle*]

(xvi, 2–9)

This is the order of their operations [   ] when they stand over against the camps of the Kittians. After the priests have sounded a blast for them on the trumpets of [memorial,][94] they shall open gaps [in the ranks], and the infantry shall go forth, and their columns shall stand between the lines; and the priests shall sound for them the signal for drawing up the lines, and at the sound of the trumpets the chiefs shall disperse and each take up his position at his assigned place. Then the priests shall blow a second time, and when they stand over against the line of the Kittians, within hurling distance, each man shall raise his hand with the weapon in it. Six [times] shall the priests sound on the trumpets the signal for carnage—a sharp, insistent sound, to direct the battle. And the levites and all the people with rams' horns shall sound a loud blast. And as the sound goes forth, they shall start lashing out and felling the Kittians. All the people shall silence their war-cries while the priests are sounding on the trumpets the signal for carnage. And the battle shall be waged victoriously against the Kittians.

[*Of encouragement
in moments of reverse*]

(xvi, 11–xvii, 15)

In the event that Belial girds himself to help the Children of Darkness, so that through God's inscrutable will and as a means whereby he may 'put the gold to the test',[95] the corpses of the infantry begin to fall, the priests shall sound the signal of assembly for the second line to go out as a relief to the battle. They shall stand between the lines, and as the relief approaches the original line, they shall sound the signal for the former to retire. Then the high priests shall come near and stand before the second line and encourage them [   ] in God's war. And he shall take up word and say:

'[Blessed be He who] strengthens the heart of His people; who "tests [the gold"]. He will not suffer your slain [to be many]. For ye have heard of old of the mysterious ways of God'.

* * * *

'[   ] and He hath appointed their retribution, hotly pursuing them; and [He will come to the rescue] of those tested in the trial, [   ]. And He hath sharpened His weapons, and they shall not be [blunted] until the wicked is [consumed.] And as for you, remember the judgment passed upon Nadab and [Abih]u, the sons of Aaron. By passing judgment upon them God also shewed His holiness before the sight of the people, in that he [at once] chose [Eleazar] and Ithamar to confirm the covenant of eternal [priesthood].[96]

'And ye—be of good courage and fear them not. For they are but vanity. All their craving is for emptiness and futility, and that in which they rely shall be as though it had never been. But as for the God of Israel, all that has been and is and shall be throughout the vicissitudes of all time are in His hand.

'This is the day which He hath appointed for abasing and humbling the [Prince] of the Dominion of Wickedness. But He will send perpetual help to those who have a share in His redemption through the power of Michael,[97] the mighty, ministering angel; and He will send also an eternal light to light up the children of Israel with joy.[98] They that have cast their lot with God shall enjoy peace and blessing. In this way, the rule of Michael will be exalted among the angels, and the dominion of Israel among all flesh. Righteousness shall flourish in heaven, and all who espouse God's truth shall rejoice in the knowledge of eternal things. And ye, the sons of His covenant, be of good courage in the trial which God visits upon you, until He gives the sign[99] that He has completed His test. His secret powers will always support you'.

After these words, the priests shall blow a blast to deploy the various divisions of the line; and at the sound of

the trumpets, the columns shall break up and take up positions in their assigned places. Then the priests shall sound
a second blast on the trumpets to bid them draw near. And
when the men of the line draw near the lines of the Kittians, and are within hurling distance, everyone shall raise
his hand with his weapons in it, and the priests shall sound
on the trumpets the signal for carnage, and all the people
with rams' horns shall sound a blast, and the infantry shall
start to launch out against the army of the Kittians, and to
fell them. Then all the people shall silence the sound of
the blast, while the priests keep on blowing [   ] to
attacks before them.

*   *   *   *

[*Of thanksgiving for victory*]

(xviii, 1–15)

When the great hand of God is raised against Belial
and against all the forces under his dominion, inflicting on
them an eternal discomfiture, and when the war-cry of
Israel and of the holy beings rings out, as they pursue
Assyria; and when the sons of Japhet fall never to rise,
and when the Kittians are cut off without [survivor]; then,
[   ] when the hand of the God of Israel has indeed
prevailed against all the multitude of Belial, the priests
shall sound the blasts of memorial, and all the lines of
battle shall rally unto them, and all shall receive their portion of the spoil [   ] to 'devote' it.[100] And when
the sun is hasting to set on that day, the high priest shall
stand up, and the priests and the levites that are with him,
and he shall look upon the [   ] battle array and
there bless the God of Israel. And they shall take up word
and say:

'Blessed be Thy name, O God [of merci]es, for Thou
hast done great and wondrous things. From of old hast
Thou kept Thy covenant unto us; and because of that
[cov]enant of Thine (and) in accordance with Thy goodness towards us, Thou hast ofttimes opened for us gates of

salvation, when we were oppressed. So hast Thou done, O God of righteousness, for Thy name's sake.

'[Verily, Thou hast wrought] wondrously, and the like of this hath not been from of old. Thou it is who determined [this] time for us, and this day [Thy glory] hath shone upon us, [   ] and Thy [   ] is with us, ensuring perpetual redemption, removing the enemy from us, that he be no more. And Thy mighty hand [   ] felleth our foemen until final discomfiture. And now the day is pressing upon us to chase after their horde, for Thou [hast] [   ] and chilled the hearts of [their] mighty men, that they cannot stand. Thine is the power,[101] and in Thy hand lies [the issue of] war, and there is none [can withstand Thee]'.

* * * *

(*Column 19, the concluding column, is largely a duplicate of the high priest's exhortation in Column 12. It is preserved in fragmentary fashion.*)

THE ROUT OF BELIAL:
SCRIPTURAL PREDICTIONS

. . . *the LORD will take away from you all sickness*
[Deut. 7.5]

. . . [And as for the text which has them saying,] *Let us
be like the tribes of (other) countries* [Ezek. 20.32], . . .
in an eschatological sense[1] this refers to the time when
[Belial] will seek [to seduce them].[2] . . . Specifically, it
refers to the fact that a man will arise . . . ; from him
[will come a very fla]me (?), and [his partisans (?)] will
be like a fire to the entire world.[3] It is concerning them that
it is writ that in the Last Days [there will arise] intemperate
men[4] who will operate with the spirits [of Darkness] and
attack the partisans of Light[5] who will be in a state of
mourning through the domination of Belial.[6] . . . [How-
beit, those who feel this sense of] mourning are [everyone
of them registered and spelled out] by name [in God's record[7]. . . , and He,] being a god of mercy[8] and the God
of Israel, [will, when He] deals retribution, [show mercy
to] those prophets of Judah whom Belial [seduced],[9] and
they will be forgiven[10] for all time, and He will bless them,
forasmuch as He has said that He would bless them for
ever [II Sam. 7.29].

. . . The several epochs which are to be completed, [the
nam]es of their leading men (lit. fathers), [the number
of] their years and the periods of their office, [together
with their] . . . and language, are all spelled out, man for
man . . . ; [and] behold, [the names of their] progeny
are all inscribed on the (heavenly) tablets[11] which God
[communicated to] . . . ,[12] apprising him of the number

of the (successive) generations, and which he gave as an inheritance . . . to him and his seed for ever. *And he proceeded to go thence.*[13] . . .

Blow the ram's horn in Gibeah [Hos. 5.8]. The ram's horn is (symbolic of) the Book of . . . The reference is to a second (giving of) the Book of the Law (Torah),[14] which the men of His council [have spurned]. They have spoken rebelliously against it (or, Him),[15] and for[get (?)] . . . the great signs[16] [which He is displaying] over . . . and Jacob, as He stands upon the winepress and makes merry over the flow of [the juice].[17] And as for the saying that *He will cut off their enemies by the sword,*[18] the reference in the word *sword* is to His own partisans (lit. the men of His counsel).

And as to the statement, . . .

v–vi

. . . [As to] the prophet [Isaiah's statement], *This year you shall feed on casual grains* [Isa. 37.30], the casual grains denote the [Wr]ath[19] which will endure until the Time of Testing.[20] Thereafter there will arise [a Teacher of Righteousness (?)],[21] for they are all of them (mere) children;[22] they have bartered [their (finer) instincts for foolish delusion].[23] These 'foolish men' are those who [disdain(?)] the Book [of Study(?)].[24] The Torah of these fools is [   ], wherefore (Scripture) has called them [*Pursuers of infamy* (Ps. 119, 150)],[25] in conformity with the statement, *He devises infamous plans, to ruin the poor by falsehoods* [Isa. 32.7], thereby poisoning(?)[26] Israel.

For the Chief Musician; attributed to David. In the LORD have I taken refuge. How then can you go saying to me: Flee to the mountains like a bird! See how the wicked are bending their bows, are fitting the arrow to the string [Psalm 11.1–2]. The word *flee* here connotes that God-minded men [are being made to flee] like a bird from His place and are being driven into exile.[27] Allusion is made to them in the Book of . . .[28]

For the Chief Musician: on the octave[29] [Psalm 12.1]. The reference is to the Eighth (world-) period,[30] [when . . . , and the wicked will have] no peace because they are 'seekers after smooth things'.[31]

(As to the words:) *Butchering of bullocks and slaughtering of sheep; wining and dining* [Isa. 22.13], the reference is to the behavior of the partisans of Belial who [savage[32] the men that have been observing] the Law—that is, the men who form (this) commune (of ours),[33] the men who be[ar the] yo[ke of God's service].[34]

vii

[And as to the text which says . . . , this refers to the fact that He will destr]oy [the partisans of Belial] who seek to harm [   ]. It is to them that Scripture refers when it speaks in the Book of the pro[phet] Ezekiel of men against whom there will be assembled[35] [. . . . and upon whom there will be visited His plag]ues (?)[36]—men who have been worshipping [other] go[ds, and directing their lusts (?)] towards that which is (really) impure to them and to that which . . . . [cp. Ezek. 30.34–36].

viii

[*fragmentary*]

ix

. . . upon them at the end [of days]. . . . [Retribution will befall] them amid the multitude of those who will be purged away.[37] . . . These are the congregation of them that 'seek after [smooth things]'[38] . . . through their frenzy and hostility. . . . [When God purges them] from Judah [He will at the same time wreak vengeance] on all the peoples, [entering into judgment] with righteous and wicked (alike),[39] with the foolish and the naïve, [and with those who have not rem]oved (their) moral uncleanliness,[40] so that, in the la[st] generation,[41] He might set them aright.

x–xi

The words of the LORD are words as good as pure metals,
silver purified by smelting (here) on earth, gold seven times
refined [Psalm 12.7].[42] This chimes with the text which
says: *Look at this (precious) stone which I set before*
Joshua, one stone with seven facets. . . . [Look, 'It is I']
quoth the LORD, '[that will make] the engraving upon it'
[Zech. 3.9]. . . .

. . . It is to them that Scripture alludes when it says, *I will*
heal the[43] . . . [   ]. [The slag represents a]ll the
men of Belial and all the rabble that follows in their
wake,[44] [while the purified silver and the refined gold]
stand for the (authentic) exponent of the Law, for [in
him] there is no [alloy].[45] . . . ; no man will desert his
post.[46] When [these men] arise (or, hold office), [the baser
metal will indeed be purged away—that is, the sons of darkness (?)] who have been causing the sons of light to
stumble.[47] . . .

[*How long, O LORD,*] *wilt Thou forget* [*me? (Will it be)*
for ever? How long wilt Thou hi]*de Thy face from me?*
How long must I suffer [*anguish in my soul, grief in my*
heart day by day]*? How long* [*is my enemy to triumph over*
*me? (*Psalm 13.2–3)]. The meaning of the words *for ever*
is that the heart of men of[48] . . . . to test them and refine
them.[49] The enemy (of whom the text speaks) has been
saying, ...

xii–xiii

. . . . [As to the text which says,] *Guidance (torah)*
[*shall not perish*] *from the pri*[*est, nor counsel from the*
sage, nor the word] *from the prophet* [Jer. 18.18], in an
eschatological sense [this refers to] the same situation as
is described by David when he says, *Con*[*demn me*] *not,*
LORD, in Thine anger, [*neither chasten me in Thy wrath.*
Be gracious to me, LORD,] *for I am weak;* [*heal me, O*
LORD, for my bones are perturbed; yea,] *my very soul is*
greatly perturbed; and now, LORD, how long more? Be
gracious to me, rescue [*my*] *soul!* [Psalm 6.2–3.] [The ref-

erence is to those who are being crushed (?) and exposed
to oblo]quy[50] on account of [the machinations of] Belial
to destroy them in his fury, not leaving th[em . . . .][51]
so that in the (whole) city there be not more than but
ten[52] righteous men, inasmuch as he has caused the spirit
of truth [to depart from them(?), and they are indeed
greatly perturbed(?)], for, through the machinations of
Belial,[53] both they themselves and their brethren (in general) have no [peace], and (Belial) keeps strengthening
[his snares(?)][54] against th[em]. . . . (Howbeit), [God
and] the angel of His truth will bring aid to all the sons of
light. [He will snatch them] out of the hand of Belial[55]
[who now plans to scatter] and disperse them in a dry and
desolate land.[56] This is indeed the time of affliction.[57] . . .
The righteous is in flight, but the great hand of God will
be with them to help them.

[He will deliver them] from all the spirits of [perversity
because] they have placed [their reliance (or, refuge) in
the wond]rous acts of God and of His holy beings.[58]
They will (yet) come to Zion in joy and to Jerusalem [in
jubilation. . . . .]. [Be]lial and all his partisans [will be
routed] and [destroyed] for ever, while all the sons of
li[ght] will be ingathered.[59]

xiv

. . . . [This is what is meant by Scripture] when it says,
*As for the saints that are on ear[th], and the worthy among
the general, it is [in them] that I take delight* [Psalm
16.3],[60] [even though now there be (?) *melting of heart
and*] *quaking of knees and writhing in every limb*
[Nahum 2.11]. [This is the situation implied in the verse,]
Pay heed unto my plaint, give ear unto [my prayer] (Psalm
17.1). . . . the council of the commune,[61] and
He/it. . . .

xv–xxx

*(There are sixteen further fragments containing only
isolated words and parts of words.)*

THE COMING DOOM

*   *   *   *

[They pay no heed to the] real hidden [meaning of things, but divert themselves instead with all] kinds of iniquitous arcane lore. [   ] They do not know the hidden meaning of what is actually taking place, nor have they ever understood the lessons of the past. Consequently, they have no knowledge of what is coming upon them and have done nothing to save their souls from the deeper implications of present events.

This, however, will symbolize things for you. What is going to happen is, as it were, that all iniquity is going to be shut up in the womb and prevented from coming to birth. Wrong is going to depart before Right, as darkness departs before light. As smoke disappears and is no more, so will Wrong disappear for ever. But Right will be revealed like the sun. The world will rest on a sound foundation. All who cling to rarefied arcane lore will cease to exist. The world will be filled with knowledge, and ignorance exist no more.

The thing is certain to come. The prophecy is true, and by this you may know that it will not be revoked:

Do not all peoples hate wrongdoing? Yet, is it not rampant among them all? Are not the praises of truth sung by'all nations? Yet is there a single race or tribe that really adheres to it? What nation likes to be oppressed by a stronger power? Or who wants his property plundered unjustly? Yet, is there a single nation that has not oppressed its neighbor? Or where in the world will you find a people that has not plundered the property of another?

*   *   *   *

WEAL AND WOE: AN EXHORTATION

(I, i 5–15)

(The opening lines are fragmentary, but seem to say that God is pure and holy and will champion [those that espouse] His tr[uth], but will [call evildoers to accou]nt[1] and exact punishment from them, even if they go on sinning ten times over,[2] i.e., incessantly.)

. . . . and there will be no strength to withstand it[3] (i.e., the punishment), neither any hope[4] for [the guilty].[5] Who will be able to withstand God's* angels, for like a blazing fire will they execute judgment, and His spirits will [wreak vengeance]?[6] Mere mortals that ye be, h[ow will ye escape]? For behold, man is like grass which sprouts from its ground, and his glory blossoms like a flower; when once God's* breath has blown [upon it, its root] withers,[7] and the wind carries off its flower, so that it has no continuance, (but) [peri]shes for ev[er], and in consequence of (a single) gust of wind, is no more to be found. (So) will men seek him, but find him not;[8] and there will be no hope. He—[his] da[ys] are like a shadow on the grou[nd].[9]

(Wherefore,) my people, now hearken to me, and ye fools give mind to me, and grow wise[10] through (awareness of) God's* [po]wer. Recall the wonders He wrought in Egypt and His portents [in the Land of Ham,[11] and so] let your hearts take fright at the terror He wields.[12]

(I, ii)

Do, then, [His] wi[ll with a perfect heart,[13] for so will

* Heb. 'His'.

He spare] your lives,† in accordance with His goodly mercies. Seek out for yourselves a way to life;[14] [make ye a straight] highroad[15] to [deliverance] and survival for your children after you. Wherefore should ye yield your [souls] to She[ol,‡ and your bodies to the scourges of that Ju]dgment which—so I have heard—(is coming) upon us?[16]

Defy not the words of the LORD.[17] Take not a (single) step [away from the holy Law][18] which was writ[19] [for the offspring of Ja]cob (and) which God§ decreed[20] for (that of) Isaac.

Is not a single day [in His courts] better than ten (outside them)?[21] [Let] the fear of Him [be with you day by day,][22] and not (merely) from time to time. [So will ye be delivered] alike from the Terror and 'the fowler's snare';[23] [salvation will be yours and re]demption, [and ye will be spared] from His angels (of judgment). For there is no darkness [where wrongdoers and frowa]rd (men) can be [hid].[24] (Nay,) God§ [will visit] His [sc]ourge [upon them].[25] I, for my part, am conscious (of this),[26] but ye—what will ye [do on the day of Inquisition,[27] at the time when] woe proceeds [from] Him unto every people?

Happy is the man to whom there has been given out of [His] tr[easury the reward reserved for them that fear Him and the glo]ry which they have earned!**[28]

Let not the wicked vaunt themselves,[29] saying: 'He will not take count of [my wrongdoing, neither compute it] against me, for He [always shows mercy] to Israel, so that when He takes measure thereof, it will be with the measure of [kind]ness,†† and the *whole* of His people will it be that He will redeem. (Only) them that h[ate Him] will He slay,

† Heb. 'souls'.
‡ That is, the netherworld.
§ Heb. 'He'.
** Heb. simply, 'their glory'.
†† Heb. '[good]ness'.

[and (only) the heathen will He de]str[oy]? 'Nay,' says
He, 'it is (only) the man that [dispenses (?) good]ness (?)
that will receive it; [(only) the man who se]eks it[30] that
will find it; and [(only) the man who . . . es] it that will
fall heir(?) to it.[31] Along with it also will go . . . and joy
of heart together with [abundance] of God's mercies, . . .
and salvation [everlasting].[32] Happy is the man who practises it and does not . . . ;[33] who does not go trying to
acquire it‡‡ with disingenuous [heart],[34] nor lay claim[35]
to it by dissimulation.[36] So will he too possess it, even as
it <was> bestow<ed>[37] upon his forebears, [and if he but
cling to it] with all his might and main,§§ interminably
with all his [power], he (too) will leave it as a heritage to
his offspring.[38] I know,[39] indeed, that God will mete out
to [His] people their [deserts].[40] . . .

*   *   *

(III, 11–15)

. . . . [God will probe] into the inner recesses of man's
being, and search out his reins.[41]

. . . . It is the tongue of one who has knowledge that has
been speaking.[42] God has made hands [to carry out His
purpose(?)]. . . .

‡‡ Heb. 'who does not seek it'.
§§ Heb. 'with all the might of his strength'.

THE LAST JUBILEE: A SERMON
('MELCHIZEDEK TEXTS')

(Reconstruction)

1 I take my text from the law of the jubilee. *In this year of the jubilee,* we read, *you shall return, everyone of you, to his patrimony* (Lev. 25.13).

2–3 THIS IS OF A PIECE WITH the commandment concerning the Period of Remission. WHAT IS MEANT BY THE PERIOD OF REMISSION, SAYS THE SCRIPTURE, IS THAT ANYONE WHO HAS MADE A LOAN TO HIS NEIGHBOR IS THEN NOT TO EXACT PAYMENT OF IT FROM THAT NEIGHBOR OR KINSMAN, SEEING THAT A PERIOD OF

4 REMISSION HAS BEEN DECLARED BY 𝕲𝖔𝖉[1] (Deut. 15.2).

AS APPLIED TO THE LAST DAYS,[2] THIS REFERS TO THE Liberation[3] of those IN CAPTIVITY, CONSONANT WITH THE WORDS of Isaiah: (*The Lord has sent me*) *to proclaim liberation to captives* (Isa. 61.1). Since the (Hebrew) word for 'liberation' is homonymous with one meaning 'swallow'[4]—which is, of course, a

5 celestial creature—THIS SIGNIFIES THAT THEY WILL BECOME ONE WITH THE SONS OF HEAVEN.[5]

The same may be expressed ALSO by saying that [THEY WILL PARTAKE] [OF THE INHERIT]ANCE OF [MELCHIZ]EDEK. Melchizedek, you will recall, was 'a priest of God Most High' who pronounced the blessing of that God over our father Abraham (Gen. 14.18–20). Now, the 'inheritance' of a priest is, as we learn from the Scriptures, the Lord God Himself,[6] and since the God of Melchizedek is expressly described as 'owner of heaven and earth', the meaning is that Abraham will thenceforth have a stake in the things

both of heaven on high and of the earth below.[7]
Moreover, since the priesthood in Israel and that of
Melchizedek himself are said in Scripture to be eter-
nal (cf. Num. 25.13; Ps. 110.4), it is not only to
Abraham but also to his offspring that this privilege is
vouchsafed; they will be linked to God in an everlast-
ing covenant (cf. Gen. 17.7, 19, etc.) and the Lord
Himself will be their inheritance and patrimony (cf.
Ezek. 44.28).

6   At the final jubilee, therefore, GOD WILL IN FACT
BE RESTORING THEM TO what is rightfully theirs; they
will indeed 'return, every one, to his patrimony'.

As FOR THE ALLUSION in the law of the jubilee
(Lev.25.10) TO *proclaiming liberation to them*, THIS
IS TO BE UNDERSTOOD ALSO IN THE SENSE THAT HE
WILL THEN REMIT [THE FULL TERM OF] THE PUNISH-
MENT FOR THEIR MISDEEDS, for the (Hebrew) word
rendered 'liberation' is also a technical term for the
remission of debts.[8]

7   ALL THIS WILL HAPPEN IN THE FINAL 'WEEK' OF A
SERIES OF YEARS INVOLVING NINE PRECEDING JUBI-
LEES.[9] WHEN, THEREFORE, THE SCRIPTURE SPEAKS OF
A DAY OF ATONEMENT to be observed in the seventh
month, on the tenth day of that month (Lev. 25.9),
WHAT IS MEANT, in an eschatological sense, IS THAT
this final jubilee will be marked BY A DAY ON WHICH

8   ALL THE CHILDREN OF LIGHT[10] AND ALL WHO HAVE
CAST THEIR LOT WITH (THE CAUSE OF) RIGHTEOUS-
NESS[11] WILL ACHIEVE FORGIVENESS OF THEIR SINS,
[WHEREAS THE WICKED WILL REAP THEIR DESERTS AND
BE BROUGHT TO AN E]ND.

9   THIS IS THE ERA which Isaiah terms *the Year of
Favor* (Isa. 61.2)[12]—that is, the one designed, by
God's favor, for the King of Righteousness—which is
what, by his very name, MELCHIZEDEK prefigures—to
come into his dominion. [HE WILL TAKE THE LEAD
AMONG] GOD'S (HEAVENLY) SAINTS[13] IN EXECUTING

10   THE VARIOUS SENTENCES OF JUDGMENT,[14] EVEN AS IT
IS SAID IN THE SONGS[15] OF DAVID: *God has taken His*

stand in the council divine, among the beings divine,[16]
to render judgment (Ps. 82.1). OR AGAIN, in another
11 place, IT SAYS: (*Though a very congregation of*
(*heathen*) *peoples now surround you*), rise *above it,*
O Israel, *and return to your eminence,*[17] (*for*) *God
will judge the peoples* (Ps. 7.8–9). The return in question is, of course, that which is prefigured in the rule
of the jubilee that everyone is then to return to his
patrimony (Lev. 25.13).

Moreover, it should be observed that the (Hebrew)
word for Favor can also be understood, by a different
derivation,[18] to mean the expiration of a term of punishment, so that this too is implied in the prophet's expression.

THERE IS A FURTHER REFERENCE TO THIS FINAL
JUDGMENT IN THE CONTINUATION OF THE VERSE FROM
THE PSALTER. *How long,* we read, *will you go judging
unjustly and showing partiality to the wicked? Selah.*
12 (Ps. 7.9). THE ALLUSION IS TO BELIAL AND THE SPIR-
ITS OF HIS ILK[19]—THAT IS, TO (elders who sit in assizes
but) DEFY GOD'S STATUTES IN ORDER TO PER[VERT
13 JUSTICE].[20] The future King of Righteousness—that
is, MELCHIZEDEK redivivus—WILL EXECUTE [UPON
THEM] GOD'S AVENGING JUDGMENTS, AND at the same
14 time DELIVER [THE JUST] FROM THE HANDS OF BELIAL
AND ALL (THOSE) SPIRITS OF HIS ILK. WITH ALL 'THE
ANGELS [OF RIGHTEOUSNESS]'[21] AT HIS AID, HE WILL
[BLA]ST [THE COUNCIL OF] BELIAL [TO DESTRUC-
TION].[22] But the faithful, as the Psalmist says, will
return to (their) eminence (*ibid.*), THE EMINENCE IN
QUESTION BEING THE [DESTINATION] OF ALL WHO ARE
INDEED CHILDREN OF GOD.
15 THE VISI[TATION][23] OF WHICH I HAVE BEEN SPEAK-
ING IS THE SAME AS THE DAY OF [RETRIBUTION][24] OF
WHICH THE PROPHET [ISA]IAH SPEAKS IN THE WORDS:
16 *How fair upon the mountains are the feet of the
herald who proclaims 'Shalom! (peace)', the herald
of good tidings who proclaims 'Salvation'! who says to
Zion, 'Your God has now claimed His kingdom!'* (Isa.
52.7), for the word *shalom* may also be read *shillum,*

'retribution', as who should say, 'All is hell!' rather than 'All is well!'

17 THE MOUNTAINS in that passage STAND FOR THE PROPHETS, [AND THE FEET FOR THEIR WORDS, WHEREBY] THEY BR[ING THEIR MESSAGE] TO ALL [WHO ARE WILLING TO LISTEN];[25] WHILE THE HERALD IS he who is elsewhere described AS THE ONE ANOINTED

18 WITH THE SPIRIT (Isa. 61.1)—THE SAME WHOM DAN-[IEL] CALLS THE [ANOINTED LEADER WHO WILL MAKE HIS APPEARANCE AT THE END OF SEVEN WEEKS (OF

19 YEARS)[26]—THAT IS, AT THE FINAL JUBILEE.] Similarly, THE HERALD OF GOOD TIDINGS, THE SAME WHO PRO-CLAIMS ['SHALOM'] IS HE OF WHOM IT IS WRITTEN: [(The Lord has sent me) to comfort all who mourn,

20-22 etc.] (Isa. 61.3), for the word shalom suggests also the expression shallem niḥumîm,[27] which is used of comforting mourners (Isa. 57.18). THE COMFORT IN QUESTION WILL CONSIST IN GIVING THEM A TRUE OVER-ALL VIEW OF THE SUCCESSIVE ERAS OF HISTORY (LIT. THE WORLD), IN THEIR RESPECTIVE TIMES.[28]

22 At that time, IT WILL BE FROM BELIAL, not from God, THAT MEN WILL TURN AWAY IN REBELLION,[29] AND THERE WILL [BE A RE-ESTABLISHMENT OF THE REIGN OF RIGHTEOUSNESS, PERVERSITY BEING CON-

23 FOUNDED] BY THE JUDGMENTS OF GOD. THIS IS WHAT SCRIPTURE IMPLIES IN THE WORDS, Who says to Zion, Your God has now claimed His kingdom! (Isa. 52.7), THE TERM ZION THERE DENOTING THE TOTAL CONGRE-

24 GATION OF THE 'SONS OF RIGHTEOUSNESS'[30]—THAT IS, THOSE WHO MAINTAIN THE COVENANT[31] AND TURN AWAY FROM THE POPULAR TREND,[32] AND YOUR GOD

25 SIGNIFYING [THE KING OF RIGHTEOUSNESS, ALIAS MEL-CHIZEDEK REDIVIVUS, WHO WILL DEST]ROY(?) BELIAL.

OUR TEXT SPEAKS ALSO OF SOUNDING A LOUD TRUMPET BLAST THROUGHOUT THE LAND ON THE TENTH DAY OF THE SEVENTH MONTH (Lev. 25.9). [AS APPLIED TO THE LAST DAYS, THIS REFERS TO THE FAN-FARE WHICH WILL THEN BE SOUNDED BEFORE THE MESSIANIC KING.][33]

(The rest is lost)

THE NEW COVENANT

. . . .
[but   wilt Thou] allot unto the righteous.

The portion of the wicked shall be [to be afflicted with
pain]s in their bones and to be a reproach to all flesh;
but the righteous [shall be destined to en]joy the rich delights[1] of heaven and to be [glut]ted[2] on the yield of the
earth.

[Thou wilt distinguish between the right]eous and the
wicked.
Thou wilt give the wicked as our [ran]som, and the faith-
less [in exchange for us].[3]

[Thou wilt make] an end of all that oppress us;
and we shall give thanks unto Thy name for ever, [and
bless Thee alway;]
for this it is for which Thou hast created us,
and that it is that [beseemeth] Thee.
     BLESSED . . .

(Col. 2)

[and Thou hast appointed] the greater luminary for the
season of [day and the lesser luminary for the season of
night],[4] and there is no overstepping their bounds.
They all [minister unto Thee, and defy not Thy word],[5]
and their sway is over all the world.

But the seed of man hath not understood all of which
Thou hast made it heir, neither have men known Thee
whensoever Thou hast spoken;
but they have done more wickedly than all things else,
and have not perceived[6] Thy great power.
And Thou hast rejected them, because Thou delightest
not in wrongdoing, and wickedness hath no standing in
Thy presence.

Howbeit, in the time of Thy good pleasure,[7] Thou wilt
(again) choose unto Thyself a people, for Thou hast remembered Thy covenant; and Thou wilt make them to
be set apart unto Thee as an holy thing distinct from all
the peoples; and Thou wilt renew Thy Covenant unto them
with a show of glory[8] and with words of Thy holy [spirit,]
with works of Thy hand and with a script of Thy right
hand, revealing unto them both the basic roots[9] of glory
and the heights of eternity; [; and Thou wilt ap-
point] for them a faithful shepherd,[10] one who will
[   ] the lowly and [   ] the [   ].

MANUAL OF DISCIPLINE FOR THE FUTURE CONGREGATION OF ISRAEL

This is the rule for the whole body of Israel when, in the future, they lead their lives in the manner of the sons of Zadok, the priests, and of those associated with them—the men who declined to follow the popular trend, who constituted the true community of God, who went on keeping the Covenant in the midst of general wickedness and so made atonement for the land:

All that present themselves are to be assembled together, women and children included. Then, all the provisions of the Covenant are to be read out aloud to them, and they are to be instructed about all its injunctions, so that no one may fall into error through ignorance.

And this is the rule for all that make up the complement of that body—that is, for every individual who is an Israelite by birth:

Every person is to be trained from childhood in the Book of Study, to be enlightened (so far as his age permits) in the various provisions of the Covenant and to be schooled in its various injunctions for a period of ten years; after which he is to be liable to the regulations regarding the several degrees of purity.

At twenty, he is to undergo an examination preparatory to his admission by vote, as a constituent member of his family, to the council of the holy community. He is not to have carnal knowledge of woman until he is twenty years old and has reached the age of discretion. Furthermore, it is only then that he is to be eligible to give testimony in matters involving the laws of the *Torah* or to attend judicial hearings.

At twenty-five, he is to take his place in the formal structure of the holy community and be eligible for communal office.

At thirty, he may take part in litigation and in rendering judgments and may occupy a position on the staff of the militia—that is, as the captain of a battalion, company, squadron or platoon or as one of the tribal commissioners or officers selected from the various families by the Aaronid priests.

All heads of families within the community who are chosen by lot for communal service, 'to go in and come out before the congregation', are to receive their assignments in accordance with their intellectual ability and their moral integrity. Everyone is to respect the rank of his fellow, and in case of dispute between any two men, each is to be given his commission according to his capacity.

No one who is feeble-minded is to take part in litigation or in rendering judgments in any matter affecting the community as a whole, or is he to occupy any communal office or to serve in the armed forces in wars against the heathen. His family, however, is to be duly registered in the military roster, and he is to be drafted [instead] for compulsory labor in the line of his usual occupation.

The levites are to serve as local adjutants to the Aaronid priests in formally admitting to the armed forces all members of the community selected for service as commissioners or officers in accordance with the total military requirements to be laid down by the sons of Zadok, the priests and the heads of the various families. Ditto in the matter of granting releases. The draft status of every man is to be determined by the heads of the families.

If public notice is posted for a juridical or consultative assembly, or if notice of war be posted, everyone is to observe a three-day period of personal sanctification, so that any one who presents himself on any of these occasions may come duly prepared. This refers to men over twenty who are eligible for summons to the council and likewise to all the sages, scholars and learned men of the community—the so-called 'irreproachables'—and again to all men serving in the armed forces, including the commissioners and officers and the captains of battalions, companies, squadrons and platoons, as well as to the levites in the several departments of their office. These together constitute the so-called 'dignitaries'—that is, the laymen who sit in the presence of the sons of Zadok, the priests, at all deliberative assemblies.

No one who is afflicted by any form of human uncleanness is to be admitted to the community, nor is anyone who becomes so afflicted to maintain his position within it. Similarly, no one who is afflicted with a bodily defect, who is stricken in hands or feet, who is lame or blind or deaf or dumb, or who has any visible bodily defect, is to be admitted to a place among the 'dignitaries' for 'holy angels are in the congregation'.

If any such person has something to say to the sacred council, an oral deposition is to be taken from him, but he himself is not to come, seeing that he is afflicted.

This is the protocol for a session of the dignitaries, the men eligible for summons to the consultative council, in the event that the anointed (king) should be present among them:

The (high) priest, as head of the entire community of Israel, is to come first, and the heads of the Aaronid priestly families and the dignitaries—that is, the men eligible for summons to meetings of the general council—are to take their seats before him in order of rank. After that, the anointed (king), being a layman, is to come, and the chiefs of the armed forces are to take their seats before him in order of rank, each occupying the same position as he does in camp or on the march. Then, in turn, the heads of the families of the community, together with the sages, [scholars and learned men], are to take their seats before them.

If they happen to be foregathering for a common meal or to drink wine together, when the common board has been spread or the wine mixed for drinking, no one is to stretch out his hand for the first portion of the bread or wine prior to the priest. It is he who is to pronounce the blessing over the first portion of the bread or wine, and it is he that is first to stretch out his hand to the bread. After that, the anointed (king), a layman, is to stretch out his hand to the bread; and after that the members of the community in general are to pronounce the blessing, in order of rank.

This rule is to obtain at all meals where there are ten or more men present.

'THY KINGDOM COME'

I. THE MESSIANIC KING

GENESIS 49.10

> [*Ne'er shall the sceptre from Judah depart, nor the ruler's staff from between his feet, until (in the end) one who owns them*[1] *shall come and claim the subservience of peoples.*]

(This means that) the wielding of sovereignty[2] will [never] be diverted from the tribe of Judah. So long as Israel possesses a government of its own, occupancy[3] of the throne shall [not] be dissociated from (the line of) David. For the word *meḥôqeq* (commonly rendered 'ruler's staff', is connected with *ḥôq*, 'statute, stipulation', and thus)[4] refers to the covenant (sworn by God) regarding the kingship,[5] while the 'feet' denote the clans of Israel.[6]

(The words, *Until one who owns them shall come* mean:) Until the coming of the legitimately anointed (king), the Scion of David.[7] For it was to David and his seed that the covenant was given regarding kingship over his people for eternal generations—(that covenant) which [the Lord] has indeed kept [and maintained and now consum]mated[8] with the members of (this) Community, [the expression, *The subservience of peoples*] referring to the church[9] of the members of [(this) Community].

II. TESTIMONIA: PROOF-TEXTS OF THE MESSIANIC ERA

A. The Commitment and the Promise

DEUTERONOMY 5.25–26 (28–29)   (1–4)

And the 𝔏𝔬𝔯𝔡[1] spake unto Moses, saying: *Thou hast heard[2] the voice of the words of this people, which they have spoken unto thee. They have well said all that they have spoken. Would only that they be so minded alway, to hold Me in awe and keep My commandments, that it may go well with them and their children for ever!*

B. The Coming Prophet

DEUTERONOMY 18.18–19   (5–8)

I will raise them up a prophet from among their brethren, one like unto thee; and I will put My words in his mouth, and he shall speak unto them all that I command Him. And it shall be that if any man hearken not unto My words which the prophet speaketh in My name, I shall require it of him.

C. The Star of Jacob

NUMBERS 24.15–17   (9–13)

And he took up his parable and said:
The rede of Balaam, son of Beor,
the rede of the man whose sight is undimmed,[3]
the rede of him who hears God's words,
who knows the mind[4] of Him on High,
who, though a-swoon, yet with open eyes
sees the Almighty in vision:
I see it, though not of this time,
descry it, though yet it be far:
A star out of Jacob is heading,[5]

out of Israel is rising a rod;
it shall smite the brow of Moab,
and batter all that work havoc![6]

D. *The Role of the Priest*

DEUTERONOMY 33.8–11 (14–20)

And of Levi he said:
Bestow[7] *on the Levites*[8] *the gift of Thy light,*
Thy perfection[9] *on them that are loyal to Thee*
—whom Thou has put to the test,[10]
challenged as by waters of ordeal;[11]
who, saying to their fathers and mothers,
'We ignore you',
disregarding their kinsmen,
acknowledging not their own sons,
have stood sentinel over Thy word,
safeguarded Thy covenant—
that they may bring the light of Thy judgments to
  Jacob[12]
and of Thy teaching (Torah) to Israel,
so setting (as it were) incense in Thy nostril
and a whole burnt-offering upon Thine altar.[13]
Endow them, ꕯꝏꝛꝺ,[14] *with the blessing of strength,*
and favour the work of their hands;
smite the loins of them that rise up against them
and of them that hate them, that they rise not again!

E. *The Discomfiture of the Impious*

JOSHUA 6.26 (21–30)

Said Joshua when he had finished giving praise and
rendering thanks in his praises:[15]

> *Cursed be the man that rebuildeth this city.*[16]
> *With his firstborn shall he lay the foundation*
> *thereof, and with his lastborn set up its gates!*

The 'cursed one' in question is that man of Belial who is
even now standing up to serve as a fowler's snare[17] unto

his people and a source of ruin to all its neighbours. He has stood up [to incite the two   so that] both of them are become as instruments of violence. They have proceeded to rebuild [the city and have ere]cted for it a wall and towers that it may serve as a stronghold of wickedness.[18] [They have done a shocking thing] in Israel and an appalling thing in Ephraim and Judah.[19] They have wrought defilement in the land and great filthiness among [their] com[patriots, spilling blo]od like water over the rampart of the daughter of Zion and in the bounds of Jerusalem.

*   *   *   *

III. A 'MESSIANIC' FLORILEGIUM

II SAMUEL, 7.10–14

[The Human Temple]

(10–11[a]) [*I will appoint a place for My people Israel, and will plant them, that they may be settled there undisturbed;*] *and no son of perversity*[1] *shall oppress them any more, as has happened throughout the past, ever since that day when I commanded judges to be over My people Israel.*

The reference here is to the House [which God will cause to be built for His abiding] in the Last Days, even as it is written in the Book of the Law: *A sanctuary, O LORD, have Thy hands established, (whence) the LORD shall reign for ever and ever* [Ex. 15, 17–18]. It will be a house in which (as the Scripture puts it) *neither Ammonite nor Moabite nor half-breed nor alien nor stranger shall ever enter* [Deut. 23.3–4; Ezek. 44.9], but where (only) those shall be that are God's saints. [Moreover, the words, *(whence) the LORD shall reign for ever*] *and ever* (mean that) God will be manifest over it at all times, and that never again, as in the past, will aliens lay waste the sanctuary of Israel on account of his sins.

What (in fact) God here declares is that (in the future) there shall be built for Him a sanctuary constituted out of mankind itself[2]—a sanctuary in which performance of the things laid down in the Law shall rank as the equivalent of the (erstwhile) burning of incense in His presence.

[*Freedom from Belial*]

(11^b) And as for His saying to David, *I will give thee rest from all thine enemies,* this means that God will (then) give them rest from all those 'sons of Belial' who put stumbling blocks in their way in order to compass their rack [and ruin],[3] *i.e.,* from all who will (then) enter into the conspiracy* of Belial and lay stumbling blocks for [the Children of] Light, devising devilish devices† against them, so as to make them yield to Belial because [their hearts] have been led astray.[4]

[*The Scion of David*]

(11^c) *Also the LORD telleth thee that He will build[5] thee an house . . .*

(12^b) *'I will raise up thy seed after thee' . . .*

(13^b) *'I will stablish the throne of his kingdom [for ever]'.*

(14^a) *'I will be unto him a father, and he shall be unto Me a son'.*[6]

The 'he' in question is that Scion of David who shall function [and reign] in Zion in the Last Days, alongside the Expounder of the Law,[7] even as the Scripture says: *I will raise up the booth of David that is fallen down* [Amos 9.11]. These words refer to him who will (then) arise to bring salvation to Israel.[8]

PSALM 1.1

[*Know your Enemies*]

Signification of the words, *Happy is the man that hath not walked in the counsel of the wicked.* The reference here is to those who have turned aside from the ways (*i.e.,* practices) of the people. A similar expression occurs in the Book of the prophet Isaiah, in reference to the Last Days, viz. *Then, with a grasp of (His) hand, the LORD caused*

---

* Heb. *counsel;* cp. Nah., 1.11.
† Heb. *devices of Belial.*

me to turn aside[9] *from walking in the way of this people*
[Isa. 8.11]. The 'people' in question are the levites who,
as it is written in the Book of the prophet Ezekiel, *are gone
far away from Me, straying after their idols, in common
with the (general) straying of Israel.*[10] They are those of
the descendants of Zadok[11] who expound the Law to suit
their policies[12] and who follow [their own inclinations],
apart from the consensus of the Communal Council.

PSALM 2.1–2

[The Time of Testing]

Why do the heathen rage,
and the peoples meditate a vain thing?
Kings of the earth set themselves up,
and rulers conspire
against the LORD and against His anointed.

The reference here is to those kings of the heathen (*lit.*
nations) who, in the Last Days, will [conspire] against the
Elect of Israel.[13] This will be the Time of Testing[14] which
is to come . . .

IV. THE WONDROUS CHILD

(Col. i 1–3)

*The first two lines are fragmentary. They seem to
refer to bodily marks which will characterize the
newborn child. Two of them will appear on the
flat (or palm) of his hand; others, resembling
lentils, elsewhere, and several very small spots on
his thigh.—The reference to 'lentils' is particularly
interesting (though it has somewhat puzzled previous editors) because 'lentils' is the common
term in Greek, Latin, and Italian for freckles.*[1]

(3–11)

[After tw]o years[2] he will know this from that[3]. . . .
When he reaches puberty, he will be like . . . . [and will

not be like (the average) m]an who knows nothing until he has mastered[4] the (usual) couple of (lit. three) (text) books.[5]

He will then acquire shrewdness and commonsense. (Even) professional seers [will foreg]ather[6] to come to him on [their] knees. [For all their long]evity and age, he will [surpass] both his father and his forebears.[7]

He will be possessed of counsel and shrewdness [and] will know what men keep secret. Moreover, his wisdom will go (forth) to all the peoples.[8] He will know the secrets of all the living, and all their schemes against him will be brought to an end. The turpitude (or, defection)[9] of all the living will be great, but it is his plans [that will prevail], inasmuch as he is the chosen of God. His birth and the (very) breath which he draws[10] [have been ordained by One] whose plans endure for ever[11]. . . .

*   *   *

(Col. ii 1–13)

The first twelve lines are fragmentary. There is a reference to something which befell men of old, children of corruption;[12] *then to something* bad; *and then an obscure reference to* (the) lentil. *Just possibly, what is here stated is that a worse disaster awaits mankind than that which befell their corrupt ancestors in ancient times (i.e., at the Deluge); that all produce of the earth will go rank and bad, and that there will not be even a mess of lentils—one of the most common dishes in the Near East[13]—to eat. But this is, of course, simply a stab in the dark. There is then an allusion to something, evidently calamitous, which is* yet to come, *and this is followed, probably by way of contrast, by a repetition of the statement that the Wondrous Child* draws his (very) breath [by the will of One whose plans endure] for ever, *the implication being, of course, that he himself will be exempt from the doom which awaits the rest of mankind.*

450 THE TRIUMPH OF GOD

[Lacuna of three lines]
Next, we find the isolated word, and cities. *Since the ensuing clause begins,* and they will be destroyed *(the form of the verb indicating a masculine subject) and proceeds to a reference to* the inhabitants [there]of,[14] *what is here predicted is, in all likelihood, the imminent destruction of lands and cities and of those who dwell in them. In between comes a fragmentary clause ending,* and by words. *A tentative restoration of the whole passage might therefore be:* [Kingdoms] and cities [will go down to their doom . . . . , and] the inhabitants [there]of [who have transgressed by deeds] and by words[15] will be destroyed.

(14–21)

We now come to the most obscure portion of the entire text. The following is a literal translation of the words that remain:

Waters will come to an end; . . . . will be destroyed; all these[16] will come . . . . will . . . . and all of [th]em will have understanding like (that of) the (heavenly) Watchers.[17] 'His deed instead of his voice'[18]—on that basis will [every one of them] lay his foundation. His sin and his guilt[19] . . . . his breast . . . . holy beings and (heavenly) Watchers[20] . . . . a saying . . . . have they said about him. . . .

The purport of these lines is anyone's guess. The statement that waters will come to an end *(i.e., fail) accords with eschatological prophecies found elsewhere, so that there is a presumption that what are here being described are further features of the impending doom. The rest of the text will then depict the eventual regeneration of mankind, or the reward of the righteous. On the other hand, if—as has been suggested—the Won-*

drous Child is Noah rather than any messianic figure, these words may refer to the end of the Flood. (The rest would still depict the eventual regeneration of men.)

NOTES

The War of the Sons of Light and the Sons of Darkness

1. Since Cols. xv–xix largely repeat what has been said previously, it is apparent that our present text of this document really represents a compilation out of two different recensions. They are here distinguished as A and B respectively.
2. Literally, 'cut off the horn'. For a similar idiom, cp. Lam. 2.3.
3. I.e., the Greeks and their associates; cp. Gen. 10.2–5.
4. *The Third Book of the Sibylline Oracles* (334–40) — a basically Jewish work written around 140 B.C.—predicts a comet before the final disaster.
5. Cp. Isa. 60.20.
6. Jer. 30.7.
7. I.e., for the weeks in the year.
8. This diverges from normal Jewish usage, which recognized only 24 courses.
9. According to Num. 1.3, the minimum age for military service was 20 years; in Roman usage, it was 17. In *The Manual of Discipline for the Future Congregation of Israel,* twenty is regarded as the age of majority.
10. The war is to last forty years. The release occurs at the end of every seventh year, and lasts for one year.
11. Cp. Num. 1.3–4.
12. I.e., the children of Aram (Syria), mentioned in Gen. 10.23. (*Togar* is an error for *Gether* of the Scriptural text.)
13. Cp. Gen. 10.23.
14. I.e., the South Arabians; cp. Gen. 25.1–5.
15. Cp. Gen. 10.6–20.

16. The Heb. word for 'enlisted' comes from the same root as that for 'assembly'. For the military sense, cp. Isa. 13.3, etc.

17. In Hebrew, the word rendered 'enactments' (viz. *te'udoth*) resembles that for 'meeting' (viz. *mo'ed*).

18. These words have evidently fallen out of the text.

19. A play on the Biblical expression, 'memorial of the trumpet'; Lev. 23.24. Cp. also Num. 10.10.

20. Literally, 'of the slain', i.e., for giving the signal for slaughter.

21. Literally, 'the mysteries'. The idea is suggested, of course, by the mention of *ambush*.

22. I.e., withdraws (His troops).

23. A pun on the name Jeru*salem*, the Hebrew for 'peace' being *shalom*.

24. Merari was a son of Levi (Ex. 6.16, 19). According to rabbinic legend, the sons of Merari were entrusted with the transportation of the heavy portions of the Tabernacle, when Israel was wandering through the wilderness (cp. L. Ginzberg, *Legends of the Jews*, vol. iv [1911], p. 194). In line with this tradition 'Merari' may here denote the ordnance corps.

25. A crude pun on the name Merari, the Heb. for 'offering' being *terumah*. If the last two syllables are read backwards (in Hebrew) they somewhat resemble the first two of Merari!

26. Again a crude pun: 'thousand' is *elef;* 'God's wrath' is *af el.*

27. Another pun: 'hundred' is *me'ah;* 'from' is *me'eth.*

28. Certain letters of the motto, when combined, spell out the Hebrew word for 'fifty'. I have tried to reproduce this in the translation.

29. The ensign of a Roman manipulus included a shield, usually of silver, on which were represented the images of such warlike deities as Mars or Minerva; and, in Imperial times, of the emperors (Tacitus, *Annals*, i.43; *Hist.*, i.41; iv.62) or of their favorites (Suetonius, *Tiberius*, 48; *Caligula*, 14). The specification in our text may have the earlier Roman usage in mind, but

it is clearly influenced also by Ps. 20.6: 'In the name of our God will we set up our banner(s)'.

30. We do not yet know what the Heb. term employed here really means.

31. The word for 'blade' also means 'flash'.

32. The Heb. for 'javelin' comes from a root which also means 'spurt'.

33. Literally, 'the holy ones'. But the point is that this was also a term for 'warriors', who were consecrated for war; cp. Jer. 22.7; 51.27f.

34. Note that later (ix.4) the total attacking force is said to comprise 28,000 men.

35. Literally, 'mild-mouthed'.

36. In the Roman army, service in the cavalry was the privilege of the upper class.

37. In Num. 4.3, fifty is the maximum age for military service; in Roman usage, it was 46.

38. These would correspond to the *fabri* and similar technicians of the Roman army.

39. Literally, 'gates', but what are meant are the spaces (*intervalla*) between the massed lines—a regular feature of Roman military formations.

40. These would correspond to the Roman *scutati*, opposed to the cavalry (*equites*); cp. Livy, xxviii, 2.

41. It has been contended that in the days of the Second Temple, priests were not in fact anointed. But no deductions as to the date of our document should be drawn from that fact, for the expression is purely metaphorical and may therefore be a survival in language from earlier usage. Exactly comparable is our own expression, 'a blot on the scutcheon'; no one carries a scutcheon today.

42. In this section, the author employs a number of technical terms derived from Roman military strategy. Since these would be unintelligible to the layman, I have reproduced them by paraphrase. In identifying them, I have leaned heavily on Yigael Yadin's masterly interpretation.

43. Literally, 'rectangle', i.e., the Roman *agmen quadratum*.

44. I.e., the Roman *testudo*, a compact mass of troops advancing under cover of their uplifted shields joined together in the form of a *testudo*, or tortoise, to protect themselves from the shafts of the enemy. This formation was also called 'tower' (*turris*).

45. I.e., the Roman *forfex*, or 'scissors-formation'.

46. I.e., the Roman *cuneus*, or 'wedge-formation'.

47. Literally, 'slight flexing of the bow'.

48. I.e., the Roman *alae* (*equitum*).

49. Cp. Enoch 40.9–10.

50. This is part of the exhortation ('pep-talk') delivered to the troops before battle, i.e., the Roman *allocutio*.

51. Deut. 20.3–4.

52. I.e., solstices and equinoxes.

53. Cp. I Sam. 17.

54. I.e., the seven nations dispossessed by the Israelites when they conquered Canaan.

55. The Hebrew words (*necha'e ruah*) are usually rendered 'crushed in spirit' (cp. Isa. 66.2). But it is apparent that our author interpreted them rather from a like-sounding word (*nechim*) which occurs in Psalm 35.15 and which the ancient Aramaic version (*Targum*) indeed understood to mean 'base, impious'. (The expression is similarly employed in the *Hymn of the Initiants*.)

56. The restoration is based on Isa. 42.13. Cp. also Ex. 15.3.

57. Literally, 'Thou magnifiest and hallowest Thyself'. The phrase is especially significant because it echoes the opening words of the famous *Kaddish*-doxology, one of the earliest elements of the Jewish liturgy. It derives from Ezek. 38.23.

58. Ezek. 38. See the *General Introduction*, p. 27.

59. The point lies in the double meaning of the word rendered 'holy beings', viz. (a) angels, (b) warriors; cp. above, note 33.

60. The restoration is based on the necessity of finding a heavenly counterpart to the earthly election of God's people as His fighting army.

61. The word rendered 'elect' also means 'picked troops' —a usage which occurs already in documents of the eighteenth century B.C. from Mari, on the Upper Euphrates.
62. Literally, 'lovingkindnesses'. What the writer has in mind, I think, is something like a Roman Imperial decree imposing peace and promising prosperity.
63. The writer uses the rare Hebrew word *ḥereṭ*, which occurs only in Ex. 32.4 with the here inappropriate sense of 'graving tool'. Perhaps he chose this recondite term to suggest the Latin *charta*, somewhat in the sense of 'charter'.
64. Ps. 24.7f.; Zech. 14.5.
65. *Ibidem;* in both passages God is called 'the Mighty One'.
66. Judges 5.12.
67. Ezek. 39.10.
68. Num. 24.18.
69. Gen. 49.8.
70. II Sam. 1.19, 25.
71. Cp. Num. 24.8.
72. Deut. 32.42.
73. Ecclus. 36.14.
74. Jer. 49.32.
75. Cp. Zech. 2.14(10).
76. Ps. 48.12.
77. Isa. 60.11.
78. Isa. 49.23.
79. Isa. 42.11 (read as in the Qumran Scroll of Isaiah, with a slight variation from the standard [Masoretic] text).
80. Isa. 52.1; Psalms of Solomon, 11.8.
81. Pss. 57.6, 12; 108.6.
82. Cp. *Manual of Discipline*, iii.13ff.
83. I.e., Thy Law.
84. For the word *u-lehagbir* in the manuscript, I emend *u-lehagbiᵃh*.
85. E.g., to renewed vigor. (There is a small gap in the text.)

86. The word is perhaps an imitation of the Latin *velites* (as if from *velox*, 'swift'), the light-armed front-line troops.
87. Cp. the beginning of the *Hymn of the Initiants*.
88. Cp. Ps. 7.7.
89. See above, n. 1.
90. Cp. Jer. 30.7.
91. This is 'the priest anointed for leading in war'. The office is mentioned in Mishnah, *Soṭah*, VIII, 2, where he is described as addressing the troops in Hebrew (rather than Aramaic or any other vernacular). Cp. also Talmud, *Yomâ*, 72b, 73a.
92. Or, 'all the structure *of their being*'.
93. Cp. Jer. 25.29.
94. Cp. Num. 10.10.
95. There is perhaps a pun in the original, for the word rendered 'gold' could also mean 'diligent'. The sense will thus be that the truly adept are tested like gold against dross.
96. Cp. Lev. 10.1ff.
97. Michael guards Israel; cp. Dan. 12.1ff.
98. Cp. Isa. 60.19.
99. Literally, 'wave his hand'.
100. I.e., to destroy everything unacceptable and offensive to the God of Israel.
101. Cp. I Chron. 29.11.

The Rout of Belial

1. Literally, 'its interpretation at the end of days'—a regular formula when a Scriptural text is explicated in an eschatological sense.
2. Restored *ad sensum;* cp. *Florilegium*, iv.3–4; Analytical Index, D. 1.
3. If this refers to God's consuming fire, cp. Isa. 26.11; 29.9; 30.30; 66.13, etc. Luke 12.49; II Peter 3.10–13; Gospel of Thomas, §9; *Pistis Sophia*, ch. 141. But it could equally well refer to the inflammatory teachings of the 'men of Belial'.

4. Probably an allusion to the description of false prophets in Jer. 23.32; Zeph. 3.4.

5. Literally, 'the Lot of Righteousness'; cp. *War*, xiii.9.

6. Cp. *Consolation*, 9.

7. Cp. *'Zadokite' Document*, ii.9, 13; ix.4–5.

8. Cp. *Hymns* x.14; xi.29.

9. Restored *ad sensum*.

10. What Allegro reads tortuously as *wnslw* (?)—a word barely intelligible—is surely *wnslḥ*, 'and it shall be forgiven'.

11. Cp. *'Zadokite' Document*, ii.9; iv.5.

12. The obvious restoration is [*ḥqq*], 'engraved', as in *Manual*, x.1; *Hymns* i.24. The text must here have named the mortal to whom the contents of the tablets were imparted for transmission. The obvious candidate is E n o c h; cp. Enoch 68.1; *Testament of Simeon*, 5.4, etc. But there are also traditions that the book was originally given to Adam, who gave it to Enoch, who gave it to Noah: Samaritan *Asāṭîr* ii. 7, 44; L. Zunz, *Ges. Schriften* (1885), i.13.

13. This probably refers to Enoch's translation to the far ends of the earth; cp. Enoch 12.1; 56.2; 65.2; *Memoirs of the Patriarchs*, i.24.

14. The interpretation is suggested, of course, by the sounding of the ram's horn at the original giving of the Law on Sinai; cp. Exod. 20.13, 16, 19.

15. I.e., repeating the apostasy (in the worship of the Golden Calf) at Sinai.

16. Again with reference to the events at Sinai. The imperfectly preserved verb may perhaps have been *yish-*[*kᵉḥū*], 'they will forget'.

17. Allegro takes 'Jacob' to be the subject of the sentence, but this makes no sense, for it is obviously G o d who, in the last days, will be 'treading out the winepress where the grapes of wrath are stored'—an eschatological interpretation of Isa. 63.2. 'Jacob' must therefore be the end of the preceding clause. 'Their juice' (Heb. *nišḥam*) is restored from Isa. 63.3, 6.

18. Cp. Dan. 11.34. This is, of course, 'the terrible swift

sword'; cp. especially Ezek. 21.8, 9, 13; Enoch 50.2; 90.19; 91.12; 95.7.

19. Tentatively I restore: [ṣa]rah; cp. Dan. 12.1; *War*, i.12; xv.1—the standard precursor of the final judgment; cp. especially *Manual*, viii.1. Not impossibly, our author fancifully connected the Hebrew word *śapîᵃḥ*, 'casual grain, leavings', with *miśpaḥ* in Isa. 5.7, usually interpreted as 'bloodshed' or 'lawlessness'.

20. For this eschatological *terminus technicus* (derived from Dan. 11.35; 12.10), cp. *Commentary on Psalm* 37.15; *Florilegium*, ii.1; cp. also *Manual*, xvi.15; xvii.1.

21. Restored on the basis of *'Zadokite' Document*, vi.10. Reference to the 'teacher' is peculiarly appropriate in view of the comparison of the broad masses to children.

22. For the sentiment, cp. Jer. 4.22.

23. For Allegro's [ʾa]mᵉrû, i.e., '[they s]aid', I read: [yiṣram he]mērû, 'they altered their nature, changed character, bartered their instincts', after *Hymns* ii.36: 'They change for wild delusion/folly the sound nature/ spirit which Thou hast vouchsafed'.

24. In the *Manual for the Future Congregation*, i.7, the 'Book of Study' (Hgû, or Hgy) is prescribed as required reading; cp. also *'Zadokite' Document*, x.6; xii.2. (The missing verb would have been *ma'asû*.)

25. This is a tentative supplement, based on the ensuing quotation.

26. The manuscript is here indistinct. Allegro reads [l]hl'yn, which certainly seems to be warranted by the photograph, but which introduces a word unparalleled elsewhere in this form. He connects it with the Arabic and Nabatean l-'-n, 'curse', i.e., 'in order to bring a curse upon Israel'. It seems to me, however, that if the reading is indeed correct, the word might rather be regarded as an artificial coinage from Heb. la'ᵃnah, 'wormwood', in the sense of 'poison'. In the Bible that word is used metaphorically of the perversion of justice and righteousness (Jer. 9.4; 23.15). We might then compare the words attributed to Jesus in the apocryphal Gospel of the Egyptians (quoted by

Clement of Alexandria, *Stromat.*, iii, 6.1–2); 'Eat every plant, but do not eat the one which contains bitterness'.

27. Cp. *Psalms of Solomon*, 17.15–16: 'They that loved the synagogues of the pious [i.e., Hasîdîm] fled from them like sparrows that fly from their nest. They wandered in deserts, that their lives might be saved from harm'.

28. The reference is perhaps to Hos. 9.11—but this is simply a guess.

29. The meaning of this musical notation is disputed. Some think it means on an eight-stringed instrument.

30. I.e., the period which will follow the eschatological 'seventh week (of years)' and which will be characterized by the reassertion of righteousness and vengeance on the wicked; cp. Enoch 91.12f.; *Testament of Levi*, ch. 18.

31. Cp. *'Zadokite' Document*, i.18; *Hymns* ii.15, 32; *Commentary on Nahum*, ii.7.

32. Restored *ad sensum*.

33. The Hebrew expression, *'ôśê ha-yahad*, lit. 'who make the commune', sounds a little unusual, but the photograph seems to warrant this reading, and it is not more odd than the words, *we-ye'aśû kullam 'agūddah 'ahat*, 'and they shall all of them make (i.e., form) one band', in the Standing Prayer (*'Amîdah*) for the High Holydays (S. Singer, ed., *Authorized Daily Prayerbook* [1890], p. 239)—a prayer believed to be ancient.

34. I restore [*sabelû*] to vindicate the identification of the pious with the bullocks which the partisans of Belial have been slaughtering.

35. Cp. Ezek. 20.34f.

36. Restoring: [*neg*]*'iê*; cp. *Manual*, iii.14; *Commentary on Habakkuk*, ix.11; *Hymns* xi.8; frag. iii.16, etc.

37. Cp. Ezek. 20.38; Dan. 11.35; 12.10.

38. See above, n. 31.

39. Restored *ad sensum*.

40. Cp. Ezek. 21.8. The concluding phrase is perhaps to be restored [*wa-'asher lô' hēsî*]*rû 'orlôt* 'and who have

not removed the foreskins'—the expression being understood metaphorically, as in Jer. 4.4.

41. See Analytical Index, E. 2 (*a*).

42. The meaning of the Scriptural verse is disputed; the text may even be corrupt. (NEB resorts to an ingenious emendation.) Since the word *qᵉdôshîm*, 'holy ones (saints)', is a technical term for celestial beings (see Analytical Index F. 1 [b]), our author may have taken the words, *the qᵉdôshîm which are on earth*, in a very pointed sense, to mean 'the earthly counterparts of the heavenly beings'. In the succeeding clause, *wᵉ'addîrê kôl ḥefṣî bām*, I think our author took *kôl* absolutely, i.e., 'the general, all men', and joined it to *'addîrê* rather than to *ḥefṣî* (i.e., 'all my delight'). In the Biblical context, this was a protest against the worship of heathen gods, and the verse meant properly, *As for those deities (recognized) in the land, and those who are deemed majestic by all with whom I consort* (cp. Arabic *ḥafaẓa*).

43. Cp. Jer. 33.6.

44. Heb. *'aṣafṣûf* means properly, 'camp-followers'; cp. Num. 11.4.

45. Restored from the context. For 'the exponent of the Law', see Analytical Index, B. 2 (*a*).

46. Literally, 'every man will be at his post'; cp. *'Zadokite' Document*, iv.12.

47. The metaphor is taken from the process of refining silver. For the general idea, cp. *Manual*, iii.24; *Florilegium*, i.8. This reflects the Iranian doctrine of the eschatological struggle between the *ashavanō*, or partisans of Right (Asha) and the *dregvatō*, those of the Lie (Druj); see above, p. 24.

48. Not impossibly, our author fancifully took the Heb. word *la-neṣaḥ*, 'for ever', in the alternative sense of 'for victory', his interpretation thus conveying the general sense that depressed hearts were awaiting their eventual triumph.

49. Cp. Dan. 11.35; 12.10; *War*, xvi.15; xvii.1.

50. If the reading,]*lmîm* is right, the only possible restora-

tion would seem to be [*nich*]*lāmîm*. This is based on Ps. 74.21.

51. A possible, but speculative, restoration might be: ['*asher lô' yistape*]*aḥ li-Beli'al*, 'anyone who has not attached himself to Belial'. For the verb, cp. '*Zadokite*' *Document*, iv.11; Isa. 14.1 (though with the preposition '*al*, not *l*-); I Sam. 26.19 (with *b*-). But the repetition of 'Belial' seems clumsy.

52. For the sense, cp. Isa. 6.13.

53. Cp. *Hymns* iv.12; *Florilegium*, i.8. Cp. also *Hymns* ii.17.

54. Cp. Job 18.9.

55. Cp. *Manual*, iii.24–25. The Angel of Truth is the Hebrew equivalent of the Iranian Asha, who will aid Ahura Mazdāh in the final discomfiture of Angra Mainyu (Ahriman).

56. Cp. Joel 2.20.

57. Cp. *Ps. 37C*, i.9.

58. See Analytical Index, F. 1 (*b, d*); 7. Tentatively, I restore [*kî' mibtaḥamoh* (cp. Ps. 40.5) or *ma'uzzamoh* (cp. *Hymns* x.23) *bi-fel*]'*āê El u-qedôshāw śāmû*.

59. Cp. Isa. 11.12; 56.8; Ezek. 11.17; Micah 2.12.

60. The translation of this Scriptural verse is a notorious problem; the text is probably corrupt. This, however, is how our author evidently understood it.

61. See Analytical Index, B. 1.

Weal and Woe: An Exhortation

1. The restoration is, to be sure, but one of several possibilities. At the beginning of line 5 I read ['*a*]*mitô* (i.e., *benê 'amitô*), and regard the enigmatic]*sh* of line 6 as the remnant of some such phrase as [*we'-awônam mi-yadam yebaqqe*]*sh*.

2. Cp. Num. 14.22; Job 19.3; Neh. 4.6.

3. Cp. Dan. 11.15.

4. Cp. I Chron. 29.15; Enoch 46.6.

5. Restoring provisionally, *li-*[*benê 'ashama*]*h;* cp. *Hymns* v.7; vi.30, viii.11.

6. Cp. Enoch 100.9–10; 102.1. See Analytical Index, F. 7, 8.

7. Cp. Isa. 40.6–8. For the sentiment, cp. also *ib.*, 51.12; Job 8.12, Ps. 103.15.

8. Cp. I Sam. 16.21; II Sam. 17.20; Isa. 41.12; Ezek. 26.21.

9. Restored after I Chron. 29.18; Job 8.7.

10. I read the traces as *ḥkmû;* cp. *Hymns* i.35.

11. Restored from Pss. 105.27; 106.22.

12. Literally, 'His terror'; cp. Isa. 2.19, 21.

13. This expression is common in the Jewish prayer book, e.g., Singer, *Authorized Daily Prayerbook* (ed. 1890), pp. 74, 239.

14. Cp. Lam. 3.40.

15. For 'the way to life' cp. Jer. 21.8.

16. Allegro's reading, *shama'tî banay yaṣṣel*, 'I have heard, my children, Let Him deliver', seems too abrupt to be plausible, and also to be unwarranted by the traces in the manuscript. I read the entire passage thus: *wᵉ-lammah tittᵉnū [nafshᵉ]kem li-shᵉ'o[l u-bᵉśarᵉ]kem [li-nᵉgā'ê mish]paṭ shama'tî banû* etc. Cp. *Hymns* x.34. The 'hearing' evidently refers to a revelation; for an exact parallel, cp. Enoch 92.18, 19; 94.1.

17. Cp. Pss. 105.28; 107.11.

18. Cp. *Manual*, i.13; iii.11.

19. I read the traces as *kᵉtūbah*, rather than, with Allegro, *ḥ(?)at(?)îmah.*

20. Cp. Isa. 30.7–8. The Heb. word could also mean 'engraved', sc. on the Tablets.

21. Restored after Ps. 84.11.

22. Restoring, purely *exempli gratia*, [*ba—boqer'ba-boqer tᵉhî*] *yir'ātô* as a contrast to *l'tt*, which I interpret as *lᵉ-'ittôt.*

23. Cp. Ps. 91.3. The 'fowler's snare' is here the false doctrine of apostatic preachers; cp. *Testimonia*, 14.

24. For the sentiment, cp. Ps. 139.12; Job 34.22. I restore *ad sensum: wᵉ-'ên ḥoshek yi[ssatᵉ]rû sham bᵉnê' ashamah.*

25. Restoring provisionally *hū* [*yābî* (or similar verb) *nᵉg*]*î'ô* (common spelling in the Scrolls for *nigᵉᵉô*).
26. For this claim to special knowledge as the basis of an admonition, cp. Enoch 91.5, 93.2; 103.2; 104.10.
27. Restored after Isa. 10.3. Cp. also Enoch 97.3; 102.1.
28. For the sentiment, cp. Ps. 31.20.
29. For this warning against the complacent belief of the wicked that they will be immune from final judgment, cp. Enoch 106.7.
30. Restoring, [*mᵉbaqqᵉ*]*shah*.
31. Restoring tentatively, *yanḥîlah*. (Allegro's *yᵉkîlah*, 'will sustain her (!)', makes little sense, and seems unwarranted by the manuscript.)
32. Cp. similarly, Isa. 45.17.
33. The manuscript is here indistinct. (Allegro's *y'al* introduces an unparalleled form. I have thought of *ybṭl*, 'cease, desist', but the traces seem to preclude it.)
34. Literally, '[with heart of] guile', restoring [*bᵉ-leb*] *mirmah*.
35. Heb. *yaḥzîkēnah* is here used in the post-Biblical sense of the word.
36. The Heb. word can also mean 'blandishments', but, as a parallel to 'guile', better sense is obtained by deriving it from *ḥ-l-q* II, 'divide', i.e., 'double-mindedness', than from *ḥ-l-q* I, 'be smooth'.
37. The manuscript's *ttn* seems a scribal error for *tntn*.
38. What we have here is the famous rabbinic doctrine of *Zekûth Abôth*, the 'merit of the fathers' (especially the Biblical patriarchs), which constitutes a kind of moral credit with God on which their descendants can draw; cf. Mishnah, *'Eduyôth*, ii.9; *Aggadath Bᵉreshîth*, ch. 10. See fully, S. Schechter, *Aspects of Rabbinic Theology* (1909; reprinted 1961), pp. 170–85; S. Levy, *Original Virtue* (1907).
39. See above, n. 26.
40. Cp. Gen. 50.15; Hos. 12.15; Ps. 28.4. (I read [*yāsh*]*îb* for the [*yash*]*ūb* of the *editio princeps*.)
41. Cp. Prov. 20.27.
42. See above, n. 26.

The Last Jubilee

1. As elsewhere in the Scrolls, a pious substitute for the ineffable name YHWH in the Scriptural text.

2. For such eschatological interpretations—a leading feature of the 'commentaries' from Qumran—cf. *Comm. on Isaiah*, on 5.10; 10.28–32; 30.18; *Comm. on Habakkuk*, on 2.8, etc.

3. For this sense of Heb. *deꝛôr* cf. Lev. 26.10; Jer. 34.15, 17; Ezek. 46.17. Cp. also Akkadian *durāru*, which refers especially to manumission, being written with an ideogram which means properly, 'go home to mother'.

4. Ps. 84.4; Prov. 26.2. In rabbinic literature the word sometimes denotes a free-flying bird in general, e.g., TB, *Shab.* 106ᵃ; Toseftâ, *Nega'im*, viii.3.

5. For this concept, cf. *Manual*, iii.25; xi.7–8; *Hymns* iii.21; xi.11–12; frag. ii.10; Enoch 6.2; 13.8; 14.3; 101.1. The expression, 'sons of heaven', recurs in *Hymns* iii.22; frag. ii.10; *War*, iv.22; xi.8. Note also that in OT, 'of heaven, celestial' sometimes means 'eternal': A. B. Ehrlich, *Mikrâ ki-feshuṭô* (repr., New York, 1969), i.378 (on Deut. 33.40).

6. Cf. Deut. 10.9; 18.2; Jos. 13.33; Ezek. 44.28.

7. The same interpretation was given by R. Alexandr(a)i (third cent. C.E.), as quoted by R. Samuel b. Naḥman; cf. Midrash Tanḥumâ, *Be-Har*, §1 (on the Law of the Jubilee). Not impossibly, our author referred the words, 'owner of heaven and earth' (prospectively), to Abraham rather than (actually) to God.

8. Correspondingly, Heb. *ḥôb*, 'debt', comes to mean 'sin' (as similarly in the familiar 'forgive us our debts' in the Lord's Prayer).

9. The concept of the ten 'weeks' of years is developed in Enoch 93; 91.12–17.

10. For this expression, cf. *Manual*, i.9; ii.16; iii.13, 24, 25; *War*, passim.

11. J. T. Milik reads: *who are in the lot of Mel(?)-[chi]zedek*, but the manuscript is indistinct.

12. 'Era (Heb. *qeṣ*)' or 'Season (Heb. *mô'ed*) of Favor'
is a technical term in the eschatology of the Scrolls;
cf. *Hymns* xv.15; frag. ix.15; *DJD* I, 34, iii.4–5.

13. Literally, 'holy ones'. For this as a term for *celestial*
beings, cf. Dan. 4, 10, 14, 20, etc.; *'Zadokite' Docu-*
ment, xx.8; *Hymns* iii.22; iv.25; x.35; xi.12; *War*,
xii.4, 7, 8; xviii.2; *Oration*, iv.1; Enoch 39.5; 45.1;
61.12.

14. For the concept that angels execute the final judgment,
cf. *Manual*, iv.12; *'Zadokite' Document*, ii.6; *War*,
xiii.12; xiv.10; *Hymns* iii.35; Enoch 53.3; 56.1; 62.11;
100.4; TB *Shab*, 88[a], etc.

15. Cp. Heb. 4.7 ('saying in David'). For the designation
of the Psalter as 'the songs of David', cf. the conclusion of the *Qedushah* in the Sabbath Morning Service
of the Synagogue: Singer (ed. 1890), p. 138. (In point
of fact, the psalm here quoted is not ascribed to
David.)

16. Literally, gods. For 'gods' = 'celestial beings, angels',
cf. *Liturgy of the Angels* (b), 5, 7; *Hymns* x.8; frag.
iii.3, 10; *War*, i.10, 11; xiv.15, 16; xv.14; xvii.7; *Ora-*
tion, iv.1.

17. The words, 'return thou on high', are usually referred
to God; our author refers them to Israel, which is bid-
den to return to its patrimony, as men did at the periodic jubilee. (Although the point is irrelevant to our
author's exegesis, it may be suggested that the words,
Wᵉ-'ālêhā la-mārôm šûbah, in the traditional text are
really a misvocalization of the original *Wᵉ-'ᵃleh la-*
mārôm šᵃbeh, 'go up in triumph [lit. to the height]
with captives in Thy train'—for which expression cf.
Ps. 68.19).

18. I.e., from *r-ṣ-h* II (Lev. 26.41; Isa. 40.2).

19. For this expression, cf. *War*, i.5; iv.2; xii.4.

20. In the context of a judicial tribunal, the word 'show
defiance' (viz. *ha-mamᵉrîm*) immediately suggests the
technical expression, 'defiant elder (*zāqen mamreh*)'
applied in Mishnah, *Sanhedrin* 11.1 to one such who
refuses to abide by the rulings of the supreme court
and is therefore sentenced to execution. The words

may therefore be read as a polemic against what were deemed the apostatic priests in Jerusalem. At the end of the sentence I restore *l^e-'a[wweth mišpaṭ]*, after Ps. 146.9, Job 34.12, rather than *la-'a[śôth riš'ah]*, 'to commit wickedness', as proposed by Milik.

21. The expression derives from Isa. 61.3, but the words *'êlê ṣedeq*, which in the Scriptural context mean 'terebinths (sturdy oaks) of righteousness', are fancifully interpreted as 'angels [lit. gods] of righteousness'. The Targum *in loc.* renders similarly, 'chieftains'.

22. The text is indistinct. It seems, to my eyes, to read: [   ]*îd '*[   ] *Beli'al*, which I would tentatively restore: [*yašm]îd 'E[l 'adat(?)] Belial*, after *Manual*, iv.19; v.19; *Hymns* xiv.16. On the ultimate defeat of Belial, see Analytical Index, E. 2 (*i*).

23. The text is again indistinct. Accepting Milik's reading, *whp*[   ], I would restore *w^e-hap^e[qûddah]*. This too is a technical term in the eschatology of the Scrolls; cf. *Manual*, iii.18; iv.19; *'Zadokite' Document*, vii.21; xix.10, etc.; *Comm. on Isa.* 5.10. The expression derives from Isa. 10.3; Hos. 9.7; Micah 7.4. Here it would also echo the employment of the corresponding verb in Lev. 26.16—part of the commination which follows on the Law of the Jubilee.

24. The subsequent quotation from Isa. 52.7, where the similar word *šālôm* (peace) is interpreted in this sense, shows that we must here restore *ha-[šillûm]*, rather than *ha-[haregah]*, 'of slaughter', as proposed by Fitzmyer and others, on the basis of *Hymns* xv.17 (derived from Jer. 12.3). For the expression, 'Day of Retribution', cf. Deut. 32.33 (according to LXX, Samaritan and a fragment from Qumran itself); Hos. 9.7. In the latter passage the term stands parallel to 'days of visitation' (*p^eqûdah*), thus supporting my restoration of that word at the beginning of the sentence.

25. Provisionally, I follow Milik's restoration.

26. The text reads, indistinctly and defectively, *Dn*[   ]. Milik ingeniously restores this to read *Dan[iel]*, and then finds the appropriate quotation in Dan. 9.26. This has the added advantage of providing

another 'support' (*'asmaktâ*) from the Holy Writings, among which the Book of Daniel is reckoned in the Hebrew Bible. Not impossibly, however, the initial letter which Milik reads as *D* is really the vestige of *Ḥ*, in which case we may restore *Ḥn*[*wk*], i.e., Enoch, and find the relevant passage in Enoch 91.15; '. . . in the tenth week (of years), in the seventh part thereof, there will occur the great eternal judgment, when He will execute judgment in company with (or, upon) the angels'. Enoch, it may be added, is similarly cited in the pseudepigraphic *Testaments of the Twelve Patriarchs;* Simeon, 5.4; Levi, 10.5; Dan., 5.6; Naphtali, 4.1; Benjamin, 9.1.

27. Cf. Isa. 37.18.

28. For this concept, cf. Analytical Index, E. 1–2. (I read here: *bᵉ-ḵôl qiṣṣê ha-'o*[*lam*] *bᵉ-'emeth lᵉ-'i*[*ttîm,* or *la'eth* (*ba'-eth;* cf. *Manual,* viii.19)]).

29. The word *sarah* is here a noun, meaning 'defection', as in Isa. 1.5; 31.6. It counterbalances the previous reference to 'turning away (defecting) from God's statutes'. The sequel shows that the subsequent clause, which is torn away in the manuscript, must have said, *en revanche,* something about the restitution of the reign of righteousness (or, of God). These two contrasting statements are made in exposition of a Scriptural text the words of which are no longer preserved in our tattered fragment. It may perhaps be suggested —though admittedly, as no more than a shot in the dark—that, since our author has been drawing heavily on Isaiah, ch. 61, the words in question were those of v.3: '(The Lord has sent me) . . . to give them sashes [lit. garlands; Heb. *pᵉ'ēr*] in place of ashes (Heb. *'epher*)'.

30. For this expression (corresponding to the Iranian *ashavanō*), cf. *Manual,* iii.20, 22; ix.4.

31. Cf. Jer. 34.18; *Manual,* v.21f.; viii.10; *'Zadokite' Document,* xv.6. In Lev. 26.15f., part of the commination which follows on the Law of the Jubilee, the visitation of God is threatened on those who *abrogate* the Covenant.

32. The expression derives from Isa. 8.11. It recurs in *'Zadokite' Document*, viii.16; xix.29.

33. This interpretation can only be inferred, since the text is incomplete. For the royal fanfare, cf. Ps. 47.8 (still recited in the service of the synagogue before the first blowing of the ram's horn at New Year); Num. 23.21; Ps. 98.6.

The New Covenant

1. The word *b'dy* of the original text is clearly an error for *b'dny* (or *b'dn*).
2. Restoring *le-he[rawô]th*; cf. Isa. 34.7; Ps. 23.5.
3. Cp. Isa. 43.3.
4. Cp. Gen. 1.14–18.
5. Cp. Ecclus. 42.23; 43.10.
6. Literally, 'understood'.
7. A technical expression for the future age; cp. *War*, xv.15; frag. ix.8.
8. Cp. Ex. 24.16–17.
9. Literally, 'fundaments, rudiments'. The word is used in Samaritan to denote the elemental hosts that were believed to be present at the revelation on Mount Sinai. Our author, however, employs the term in a somewhat different sense, implying that the essence of God's glory and the lofty eminences of eternity were then made manifest to Israel. (We must read *YeSODê*, not *YiSSuRê*, since the word is contrasted with *Ma'aLê*, i.e., 'foundations' with 'heights'.)
10. I.e., a new Moses. The lawgiver was known in later Jewish literature as 'the faithful shepherd'; cp. Ex. 3.1. Cp. also John 10.14.

I. The Messianic King

1. This was the way in which many of the ancient interpreters explained the baffling Hebrew word *Shiloh*, which can here scarcely denote the place of that name. They took it as the equivalent of *shelô*, 'whose', i.e., he whose it is.

2. Literally, 'sovereign, wielder of sovereignty'.
3. Literally, 'the occupant'.
4. These words have been inserted in order to clarify the sense for English readers. The Hebrew word, *ḥôq*, 'statute', is frequently conjoined in the Old Testament with *berîth*, 'covenant', e.g., II Kings 17.15; Pss. 50.16; 105.10. For a similar interpretation of the Scriptural verse, cp. *'Zadokite' Document*, vi, 3 (above, p. 73).
5. Cp. II Sam. 7.11–16; Ps. 89.3–4, 29, 36.
6. This interpretation is based on the fact that the expression, 'that which issues from between the feet' is used in Deut. 28.57 as a euphemism for 'progeny'. The ancient Greek and Aramaic versions understood our passage in the same way.
7. Cp. Jer. 23.5; 33.15; Zech. 3.8; 6.12.
8. There is a small gap in the text. As an approximate restoration, I read: *shmrh [YHWH bkôl hdôrôt wg]mrh* (or, *[wn]ṣrh?*) *'m anshê hyḥd*. Cp. II Sam. 23.5. For the general sense, cp. Luke 1.69, 72.
9. It is interesting to find in the Hebrew the same word (*knst*), the Syriac cognate of which was later adopted by the Christians to designate their own communion.

II. Testimonia: Proof-texts of the Messianic Era

A. THE COMMITMENT AND THE PROMISE

1. Written in archaic script.
2. The received (Masoretic) text reads, *'I have* heard'.

C. THE STAR OF JACOB

3. Literally, 'he whose eye is perfect'. The received (Masoretic) text contains the unique Hebrew word *satam*, of uncertain meaning. Our author substituted for it the 'correction', *shehatem*, in line with several ancient interpreters.
4. Literally, 'knowledge, lore'.
5. The passage is cited again in a Messianic sense in *'Zadokite' Document*, vii, 19 (above, p. 76) and in *War*, xi, 6–7 (p. 413). The same interpretation appears

also in the ancient Aramaic Versions (Targumim) and was adopted by many Jewish expositors.

6. The Scriptural text reads: 'It shall smite the brow of Moab and batter all the children of Sheth'. The latter term properly denoted the Shûtu, an early nomadic tribe. But our author evidently identified it with the Hebrew word *sh'eth*, 'uproar', thus giving the verse a wider sense. The same interpretation was adopted by Jeremiah (48.45); see above, p. 110, n. 33. Not impossibly, the same Moab was likewise interpreted in a larger sense by being connected with the word *'oyeb*, 'enemy'—a fanciful interpretation suggested also by several ancient Jewish commentators.

D. THE ROLE OF THE PRIEST

7. This follows the text of the Greek (Septuagint) Version. The word is missing in the received Jewish (Masoretic) recension.

8. Heb. singular, i.e., 'Levi', and so throughout.

9. Heb. 'Thine Urim and Thy Thummim'—emblems of the high priest. But the words were anciently interpreted as plurals of *'ôr*, 'light' and *tôm*, 'perfection', and it is in this extended sense that our author evidently understood them. Indeed, the compound term, *Ôr-Tôm* was coined by the Brotherhood to denote the peculiar 'illumination' which they claimed; see above, p. 21.

10. Heb. 'whom Thou didst test at Massah'. It has long been pointed out by commentators that there is in fact nothing about the incident at Massah recorded in Ex. 17.5–7 to connect it specifically with a testing of the levites. The word, however, itself means 'testing', and it is therefore probable that our author—and perhaps even the original writer—intended it only as a common noun and not as a place-name.

11. Heb. 'with whom Thou didst contend (enter suit) by the waters of Meribah'. Here, again, there is no ostensible relationship between the incidents at Meribah recorded in Ex. 17.5–7 or Num. 20.3, 13, 24 and any trial of the levites. The word, however, means simply

'contention, suit', so that here too it is probable that the author intended it only as a common noun, in which case he would be referring figuratively to trial by waters of ordeal (cp. Num. 5.17).

12. The Masoretic text and the Ancient Versions read, 'They shall teach (Heb. *yôrû*) Thy judgments to Jacob'. But in changing this to the very similar Hebrew word (*ya'irû*) meaning 'they shall bring the light', our author is not merely blundering; he is harking back to the allegorical interpretation of 'Thine Urim' in the preceding lines; see above, n. 9.

13. In the Scriptural context, these lines refer to the sacrificial functions of the levites. Here, however, they are understood in a figurative sense: obedience to the Torah (Law) is equivalent to setting a pleasant savour in the nostrils of God, and *wholehearted* devotion to the presentation of a whole burnt offering upon His altar.

14. Written in archaic script.

E. THE DISCOMFITURE OF THE IMPIOUS

15. A Jewish tradition, hitherto known only from later sources, says that the *'Alenû*-prayer, one of the most prominent elements of the liturgy (S. Singer, *Authorized Daily Prayerbook*, p. 76), was composed by Joshua upon entering the Holy Land, and the *'Al ken nekavveh*, which now serves as its continuation, after Achan had confessed his guilt respecting the appropriation of forbidden booty after the sack of Jericho (Jos. 7.1–26). Joshua is said also to have intoned a lengthy hymn of praise after defending the Gibeonites (*Sepher ha-Yashar*, 135b–136a), and is likewise credited with the authorship of the Second Benediction in the traditional Grace after Meals (Talmud, *Berachoth*, 48b). Samaritan tradition similarly attributes to him one of the cardinal prayers of the *Defter* (i.e., Greek *diphthera*, 'codex'), the earliest element of the liturgy (A. E. Cowley, *The Samaritan Liturgy* [1909], pp. 4f.); while in the mediaeval Samaritan-Arabic *Book of Joshua*, several prayers by that hero are in-

terspersed in the narrative. Fragments of hymns (or
psalms) attributed to Joshua have indeed been found
at Qumran.

16. The Masoretic text adds, 'even Jericho'. Our author
omits the words in order to accommodate the Scriptural passage to the rebuilding of *Jerusalem!*

17. Cp. Hos. 9.8; Ps. 91.3.

18. In Gen. 49.5 the expression, 'instruments of violence'
is used in connection with the brothers Simeon and
Levi. Hence, the reference here would most naturally
be to *a pair of brothers,* but precisely who cannot yet
be determined with certainty. Allegro ingeniously suggests that the reference is to Aristobulus II and
Hyrcanus II, the two sons of Alexander Jannaeus, to
the latter of whom Caesar indeed gave permission, in
47 B.C., to rebuild the walls of Jerusalem (Josephus,
Ant., XIV, 8.5; 10.5; *War,* I, 10.3). Alternatively, we
may perhaps think of Phasael and Herod, sons of
Antipater, who were appointed by their father gover-
nors of Jerusalem and Galilee respectively (Josephus,
Ant., XIV, 9.2) and later (43 B.C.) by Mark Antony
as tetrarchs in charge of the public affairs of the Jews
(*ib.,* XIV, 13.1). The reference to the building of the
walls and towers of Jerusalem might then allude more
specifically to Herod's repair of the walls and erection
of the towers of Hippicus, Phasael and Mariamne after
he had become king of Judaea in 30 B.C. The 'man of
Belial' would, in this case, be either Antipater or Mark
Antony.

19. This would be consonant with the fact that Phasael
governed Jerusalem and its vicinity, and Herod the territory of Galilee. The former, the eldest son of
Antipater, committed suicide after falling into the
hands of the Parthian allies of Antigonus, last king of
the Hasmoneans (Josephus, *Ant.,* XIV, 13.10), while
Herod was eventually afflicted by severe disease and
a kind of madness, which Josephus (*Ant.,* XVII, 6.5;
War, I, 38.5) attributes to the vengeance of God.
Thus, the curse of Joshua 6.26 (as our author understood it) may be said to have been fulfilled in their

fate. It is true that Herod was not the *youngest* son of Antipater, as a strict application of the Scriptural text might seem to require, but the Hebrew word rendered 'lastborn' literally means no more than 'younger' and could therefore quite properly be referred to Herod as the junior of Phasael.

III. A 'Messianic' Florilegium

1. The traditional Jewish (Masoretic) text reads in the plural, '*sons of perversity*'.
2. *Literally,* 'a sanctuary of man'. Some scholars have thought that this means a man-made sanctuary (temple), in contrast to that which God's own hands are said to have established. But the true, metaphorical meaning is apparent on comparison with *Manual,* ix.6 (above, p. 63). The same sentiment is to be found in I Cor. 3.16–17 and in Eph. 2.19–22.
3. The 'stumbling blocks' are part of the eschatological picture painted in the Bible itself: cp. Dan. 11.33–34; Mal. 2.4–9.
4. Cp. *Manual,* i.23–24 (above, p. 45); '*Zadokite*' *Document,* iv.13, 15; xii.2 (above, pp. 71, 85); *War, passim.*
5. The traditional (Masoretic) text has 'made', but our reading agrees with that of the Greek (Septuagint) Version; cp. also II Sam. 7.13; Ps. 89.5.
6. The verse is quoted in the same sense in Heb. 1.5.
7. Cp. '*Zadokite*' *Document,* vi.11 (above, p. 73); *Commentary on Habakkuk,* 1.5; 2.2, 4 (above, pp. 318, 321f.). The (priestly) 'Expounder of the Law' and the 'Scion of David' constitute the two future 'messiahs' or 'anointed ones'.
8. In '*Zadokite*' *Document,* vii.16 (above, p. 75), the 'fallen booth of David' is taken to connote the neglected Law (Torah).
9. This meaning is obtained by a different vocalization of the Hebrew word usually rendered, 'instructed me, reproved me'.

10. Note that, in popular speech, 'Israel' denoted the laity, in contradistinction to the priests and levites.
11. Cp. *Manual*, v.2; 'Zadokite' Document, iv.1 (above, pp. 51, 70). This title of the priests derives from Ezek. 40.46; 43.19, etc.
12. These words could also be rendered (but less probably), 'who seek their own counsel', i.e., interests.
13. The future 'Anointed One' (Messiah) is likewise styled 'the Elect' in the Book of Enoch.
14. A standard eschatological epoch in the doctrine of the Scrolls; it is based on Dan. 11.35; 12.10. Cp. also Mal. 3.23.

IV. The Wondrous Child

1. Cp. in this sense: Greek *phakos* (Plutarch, ii.563A; 800B); *phakōdēs* (Hippocr., *Epid.*, iii.1090); *phakōsis* (Hephaest., *Apotel.*, p. 18); Latin *lenticula* (Pliny, *HN*, 20, ii.4, 5); *lentigo* (Pliny, *HN*, 30, ii.5–a term still used in medicine for a kind of rash); Italian *lentigine*.
2. This restoration is suggested by Fitzmyer. It can be supported by the fact that Moses was likewise said to have first displayed his precocity in his third year; cp. Josephus, *Ant.*, iii.9, 6–7; Philo, *Vita Mosis* i.5; L. Ginzberg, *Legends of the Jews*, V. 401, n. 64. The same is said of Jesus in the apocryphal Gospels of Thomas and of Matthew. In Jewish popular tradition, a child was not considered fully weaned until after two years. The successive stages of the Wondrous Child's development are similarly defined in Vergil's Fourth Eclogue, 13f., 17f., 26f., 37f.
3. Cp. Isa. 7.15, 16.
4. Lit., *knows*.
5. The identity of 'the three books' has proved a puzzle. Carmignac suggests that they may be the Book of Study [*Hgw*] mentioned in 'Zadokite' Document, x.6; xiii.2, together with the *Manual of Discipline* and the 'Zadokite' Document. But (a) Did all these documents exist together at the time our text was composed?

(b) Was the Wondrous Child a Qumranite, who had to be reared in what were, after all, manuals for a sect 'preparing the way' for his advent? Fitzmyer thinks the reference is general, not specific, i.e., to apocalyptic books such as the 'books of the living' in Enoch 47.3 or the 'heavenly tablets' mentioned *ib.* 81.1–2; Jubilees 30.22. This, however, I find unconvincing because, as I read the text, the three books are something which the average man has to master in order to be educated, but with which the Wondrous Child will be able to dispense. The books cited by Fitzmyer are, on the other hand, heavenly books to which the average mortal would not have access. Need the number 'three' be taken literally? My rendering presumes that no more is intended than 'two or three textbooks'. (The definite form of the noun would mean simply 'the usual [standard]' textbooks.)

6. Reading *ḥzyn* and *'rkwbt[hwn]*. (I am not assuming that the incomplete verb was *[ytkn]šwn*, because the text has *]šn*, not *]šwn*. My restoration is simply *ad sensum*.)

7. Restoring *ad sensum*, something like: *wbabwhy wbābhtwhy y[tqp w'mhwn 'ark] ḥyn wzqynh*.

8. Borrowed from I Kings 4.29–31 (of Solomon).

9. Heb. *msrt*, which can derive either from *s-r-'/y*, 'be rank, foetid, disgusting', or from *s-w-r*, 'defect, turn aside'.

10. Probably also in the sense of *inspiration*.

11. I take these words to refer to God (an adjectival clause), not to the Wondrous Child; cp. Isa. 11.3.

12. This expression recurs in *'Zadokite' Document*, vi.-15; xiii.14; cp. also Jubilees 10.3; 15.26; John 17.12; II Thess. 2.3; Gospel of Nicodemus 20; *Apoc. Peter*, Akhmim frag., §2. The reference could be either to the rebel 'angels' of Gen. 6.1–4 or—I think more probably—to the generation of the Flood. In favor of the latter is the specific use of the same word, 'corrupt', in Gen. 6.11–12.

13. Cp. Gen. 23.34; Ezek. 4.9. This is the modern Arab *mujedderah*, a compound of lentils, onions, and rice

stewed in olive oil. For the general idea, cp. Isa. 5.6;
7.23–24.

14. Restoring, *ytbyn dy l[hwn]*.

15. Cp. Isa. 3.8.

16. It is not clear whether these words refer to calamities
or to 'angels of destruction' who will come to execute
judgment; cp. *Manual*, iv.12; *'Zadokite' Document*,
ii.6; *War*, xiii.12; xiv.10; Enoch 53.3; 56.1; TB *Shabbath* 88a; etc.

17. A class of celestial beings mentioned in Daniel, Enoch,
etc. and, at Qumran, in the *'Zadokite' Document* and
The Memoirs of the Patriarchs; see T. H. Gaster, in
IDB, s.v. Watcher.

18. This sounds to me like a proverbial tag, 'Deeds, not
words'. (The singular possessive suffix in the following
'his foundation' will be distributive, i.e., we should
restore something like: [*klhwn*] *yswdh 'lwhy ysdwn*.
The suffix in *'lwhy* ['thereupon'] will refer to the
maxim.) A contrasting idiom occurs in Enoch 94.6.

19. E.g., 'will vanish, be purged', cp. Enoch 107.1.

20. E.g., '[they will be like] any holy being or (like) the
Watchers' (see above, n. 17).

VIRTUE

The Wooing of Wisdom

INTRODUCTION

At the end of Ecclesiasticus (or The Wisdom of Jesus the Son of Sirach), in the Apocrypha of the Old Testament, there is a curious poem (51.13ff.) in which the author describes how he pursued and cultivated wisdom and exhorts his readers to do the same. In the Ancient Versions (on which the conventional English translations are based) and likewise in the Hebrew paraphrase discovered, at the close of the nineteenth century, in the Cairo Genizah, the tone of this poem is somewhat solemn and priggish, resembling nothing so much as one of those polite moralistic 'recitations' which Victorian school children were encouraged to inflict on their captive parents and friends at the annual prize-giving ceremonies. Qumran, however, has brought a surprise. Included in what has come to be known as the Psalms Scroll—really, a more extensive liturgical compendium—is a portion of the same poem in its original form, and it there appears as a series of artful *double-entendres*[1] (composed as an alphabetical acrostic) each of which possesses an erotic as well as a moralistic sense. To be sure, the thing is no *Kāma Sutra* or Ovidian *Ars Amatoria* but still an edifying piece of exhortation—else it could never have found place in the liturgical repertoire of a community of ascetics—and the author therefore takes care to point out that, for all his ardor, he did indeed observe the proprieties. Nevertheless, the imagery is far more sexual than has hitherto appeared.

(a) The poet begins by saying that already in his childhood, before he had 'gone a-roving', he went in quest of Wisdom, and whenever he gained access to her, he explored her shapely form 'to the (lit. her) limit'. Here he is referring, on the one hand—with a sly erotic undertone —to a children's game like our own 'blind man's buff',[2] in which the 'catch' is identified by 'feel', and on the other —in a less sensual vein—to searching for Wisdom and studying it, or to praying for it and obtaining it, the words 'seek' (*b-q-sh*) and 'explore' (*d-r-sh*) being also technical terms for these more innocent pursuits. Moreover, the allusion to 'going a-roving' bears the double sense of leaving home and of straying from the path of virtue.

(b) Then, he continues, during his own adolescence, when the comely lass had blossomed into womanhood— 'when the buds became berries and the grapes grew ripe and luscious'—he still kept company with her, but, because he had known her from childhood, he kept to the straight and narrow and did not let himself be swept off his feet. The relationship was strictly platonic; he enjoyed and profited from her companionship and conversation (*dulce loquentem Lalagen amabo, dulce ridentem*). The *double-entendre*, however, again obtrudes itself: what he obtained from her is described by the Hebrew word, *leqah*, which means at once 'learned discourse' and 'captivating charms'.

(c) In the succeeding stage the lady served him virtually as a nursing mother (Heb. *'ālah*): he drank in Wisdom. The fusion of erotic and moralistic nuances is, however, again apparent, and the image is admirably illustrated both by the famous remark of Juliet's nurse, 'Were I not thine only nurse/I would say thou hadst sucked wisdom from thy teat',[3] and by the philological connection of the words 'sapience' and 'sap'.[4]

For this benefit, adds our author, he duly 'rendered his meed of *hôd* to his tutor'. The phrase is derived from Prov. 5.9, which warns, *en revanche*, against forfeiting that quality by consorting with loose women. Normally meaning 'honor, dignity', it here bears the added nuance of 'thanks' (like the post-Biblical *hôda'ah*, which is indeed substituted for it in the Genizah paraphrase), and it is not impossible—seeing that Greek was a second vernacular in Palestine at the time when the Dead Sea Scrolls were composed—that it carries also the nuance of the Greek *timē,* 'honor', in the specific sense of 'remuneration paid to a teacher', i.e., 'honorarium'.

(d) Next comes the awakening of sexual desire. The poet has now 'acquired a zest for pleasure'—a stage expressed by words which bear at the same time the more innocent meaning of 'developing a zeal for goodness'. He plans to 'take his fun without ever turning back' (or, according to a variant reading in the Versions and the Cairo paraphrase, 'unabashedly'). He becomes inwardly 'on fire' for the lady, and pursues her unremittingly. He perseveres in quest of her favors, the Hebrew word which is employed, viz. *tar<aḥ>tî,*[5] denoting at once the assiduous pursuit of his amours and—again more innocently—painstaking absorption in study. He does not 'keep lolling on her heights' —an exquisitely chosen expression suggesting, on the one hand, a supine indolence like that of the amorous goatherds in the *Idylls* of Theocritus or the *Eclogues* of Vergil and, on the other, a lingering on the rarefied heights where Wisdom dwells (cp. Sirach 24.4), i.e., a preoccupation with philosophical abstractions in preference to practical application.

(e) The poet then declares, 'My hand opened [her gates]'.[6] On the literal and erotic level, the reference is, of course, to breaking down her defenses. The metaphor is taken from a military assault on a city, and is pertinently illustrated by the familiar lines of Ovid: *ille (miles) graves urbes, hic (amans) durae limen amicae/ Obsidet; hic portas frangit, at ille fores* (Soldiers lay siege to firm-defended cities; lovers to the thresholds of hard-hearted lady-loves. The one breaks down gates; the other, doors).[7] On the figurative level, however, the words obviously refer to eventual entry into the penetralia of Wisdom, as contrasted with mere superficial dalliance on the periphery.[8]

The phrase is followed by words which describe the poet's intent (see below), viz. 'that I might perceive her hidden secrets'. These words too contain a patent *double-entendre*. Every adult male (except, perhaps, a superannuated theologian) knows what they mean on the literal level. Figuratively, however, the reference is to fathoming Wisdom *au fond,* the same expression recurring in the Hebrew text of Sirach 42.18, where the writer speaks of God's 'perceiving the hidden secrets' of men's hearts.

(f) A strange note is now sounded. After thus describing rather starkly his aggressive pursuit of more intimate intercourse with his beloved, the poet suddenly observes, 'I kept my hands clean'. Apparently, the moralistic intent of his discourse now takes over completely. He loses his erotic nerve, and his frankness deserts him, for from this point on—as the extant sequel in the Versions attests—the piece peters out into a pious exhortation. For this reason it seems to me that the verb should be understood as a pluperfect, i.e., '(Nevertheless) I had kept my hands clean', and that in the preceding clause the correct translation is (as given above), 'that I might perceive her hidden secrets', rather than 'I perceived' them, thus indicating intent rather than performance. As John Donne put it, 'If ever beauty I did see,/which I desired and got, 'twas but a dream of thee'.[9]

As observed above, the Ancient Versions and the Hebrew paraphrase discovered in the Cairo Genizah[10] bowdlerize the erotic nuances of our poem. By less sensual interpretation of the terms used, the allusion to the physical exploration of Lady Wisdom's contours in a childhood game of blind man's buff becomes a reference to seeking and finding her, in early youth, through prayer and intellectual study; while the passage which describes her as suckling her devotee is grotesquely distorted—one might say that the milk runs dry—by interpreting the word for 'nurse', viz. *'ālāh,* as though it were a noun (otherwise unattested) from the root *'-l-h,* 'ascend, advance', bearing the sense (akin to the rabbinic *'illui,* 'advanced student, genius') of making progress in studies! Similarly, instead of planning to 'take his fun' with her, the poet merely longs for the lady in a more innocuous vein, and instead of being 'on fire' for her, he grapples with her intellectually, the relevant verb being twisted into the sense which it bears in the reflexive conjugation. The ardent amorous pursuit and the reference to 'not lolling on her heights'— a phrase which may also possess a sexual connotation— are likewise toned down, as is also the desire to 'contemplate her hidden parts'. In a word, Mrs. Grundy, that obtrusive chaperone, has the situation well in hand.

*   *   *

In the following translation, I have tried especially, even at the risk of paraphrastic license, to bring out the form and flavor, and particularly the sustained *double-entendre* of this basically merry poem. Without the latter, the whole piece falls flat.

NOTES

1. On *double-entendre* as a feature of Old Testament and Arabic poetry see: E. König, *Stilistik, Rhetorik, Poetik* (1900), pp. 10–12; J. Finkel in *Joshua Starr Memorial Volume* (1963), pp. 32ff.
2. On the antiquity of this game see: Alice B. Gomme, *The Traditional Games of England, Scotland and Ireland* (1894–98), ii.37ff.; W. W. Newell, *Games and Songs of American Children* (repr. 1963), No. 108.
3. Wm. Shakespeare, *Romeo and Juliet*, I, iii.71–72.
4. See: R. B. Onians, *The Origins of European Thought About the Body, etc.* (1951), pp. 51ff.
5. For this emendation, see below n. 9 to the translation.
6. The text is incomplete and is here restored from the Genizah paraphrase.
7. Ovid, *Amores*, I.ix, 18–20. A similar imagery underlies John Suckling's well-known poem, *The Siege* (R. Aldington, ed., *The Viking Book of Poetry* [1941], pp. 416f.).
8. See also n. 10 to the translation.
9. *The Good Morrow*, lines 6–7.
10. The Genizah text is not the author's original. It seems to have been based largely on the Syriac Version.

THE WOOING OF WISDOM
(SIRACH 51.13ff.)

1(13)   Already in early childhood,
          ere I had roved astray,
      I used to seek-her-and-find-her
          in games of childish play;
2(14)   But I read her lines to the limit
          whenever she came my way.[1]

3(15)   Came the time when the buds turned to berries,
          when the grapes grew luscious and round;[2]
4   Due to our childhood friendship,
          I kept my feet on the ground.[3]

5(16)   Even when only lightly
          my ear unto her I inclined,
      charm and learning[4] a-plenty
          readily did I find.

6(17)   Feverishly what she gave me
          like mother's milk I drank,[5]
      and never was I unmindful
          my tutor to honor and thank.[6]

7(18)   Gripped by a passion for pleasure
          at last, 'I will take my fun',
      thought I, 'and never turn backward
          when once I have begun!'[7]

8(19)   Heated like fire I became;[8]
          my face never turned away:
9   I grew busy,[9] and on the uplands
          lolled not the livelong day.

10   [Kept shut though they were,] I forced open
                  her gates,[10] having only in mind
              to set my eyes on the treasures
                  which surely lay hidden behind.[11]

11(20)   [Lusty enough was my ardor,]
                  yet clean did I keep my hands;[12]

                        *   *
                            *

              . . . .

23^b(30)   duly get your reward.[18]

NOTES

1. Literally, (*When*) *I was but a child, I used to go looking for her; (when) she came to me in her shapely form, I would search her out to the/her limit.* The primary reference is, I think, to a game of blind man's buff; for the figurative sense, cp. Sirach 4.12. The allusion to 'roving' likewise bears a double sense: in I Kings 3.7, the characteristic of a child is that it does know 'to go out and come in', but for roving in search of wisdom, cp. Sirach 34.11; 39.4. 'Look for' (*b-q-sh*) is also a technical term for 'petition in prayer' (e.g., TB, *Ber.* 16ᵇ) and 'search out' (*d-r-sh*) for 'study'. Not impossibly, the phrasing also carries a *legalistic* connotation, for 'come to' is an expression used of securing a claim: cp. Gen. 43.23; Num. 32.19; and see Y. Muffs, in *Gaster Festschrift* (1973), pp. 287ff. The words, *to her limit*, are a clever variation on the colloquial *to the end*, in the sense of 'utterly', as in Dan. 4.8, 19; 6.27. Cp. similarly Greek *eis telos*, LXX Gen. 46.4; Amos 9.8.

2. The phrasing derives from Gen. 40.10: 'as soon as it (sc. the vine) budded, it blossomed and its clusters ripened into grapes' (NEB). The word here rendered, *turned to berries*, is *g-r-'*, which occurs in this technical sense in Mishnah, *Sheb.* iv. 10. For 'bud' in the figurative sense, cp. Catullus xvii.14: *cum sit viridissimo nupta flore puella* and Ellis' note; *ib.*, lxii.46. Cp. also Song of Songs 7.8 and a modern Palestinian Arab folksong cited in G. Dalman, *Palästinensischer Diwan* (1901), p. 239. Cp. also John Gay's *Acis and Galatea*, where a young girl is described as 'ripe as the melting

cluster'. Note too that in Greek, *omphax*, 'unripe grape', is used of a girl who has not yet reached maturity. (In light of such parallels, it is plain that the words refer to the girl, not to her suitor, as supposed in the *editio princeps!*) For '*luscious*' the Hebrew has, 'that rejoice the heart'—a phrase derived from Ps. 104.15.

3. Literally, *Because I had known her since my childhood, my foot trod on level ground*, i.e., I did not let myself be 'swept off my feet'. In place of $y^e d\hat{i}$'$t\hat{i}h\bar{a}$, 'I had known her', the Versions seem to have read r^e'$\hat{i}t\hat{i}h\bar{a}$, I had cultivated/been friends with her'. The same error appears in the Masoretic text of Hos. 13.5.

4. The Hebrew word, *leqaḥ*, means both 'learning, lesson, discourse' and 'captivating ways'; for the latter, cp. Prov. 7.21; Sirach 26.9 (LXX); and v. D. W. Thomas, in 'Wisdom in Israel and the Ancient Near East' (*Rowley Festschrift*, VTS 3[1955]), p. 284.

5. Literally, 'She was/became a wetnurse unto me'. For a variation on the metaphor cp. Sirach 15.2–3. What is implied in general is a kind of Abélard-and-Héloïse situation, though the lady is here the teacher.

6. The word for 'my tutor' is in the masculine gender, although the specific reference is to Wisdom portrayed as a woman. Hence it is apparent that the poet is quoting a popular tag.

7. Or, according to the Versions and the Cairo Hebrew paraphrase: *Gripped by a passion for pleasure/ 'I will take my pleasure', thought I,/ 'now at long last and no longer/ continue bashful (and shy)!'* The difference rests on reading the Hebrew word, '*a sh ū b*, by transposition of letters, as '*e b ô s h*. A similar variation exists in the texts of Sirach 42.1. (The Masoretic text of Ps. 25.3 is possibly to be corrected in the same way.)

8. Heb. *ḥarîtî*. The Versions gave to the verb the sense which it bears in the reflexive conjugation, viz., 'vie, grapple with'.

9. The manuscript reads *ṭ-r-t-î*, which makes no sense. My emendation, *ṭ-r<h>-t-î*, is based on the antithetical

sh-l-h, 'be at ease, loll', in the succeeding clause and on the fact that in post-Biblical Hebrew *ṭ-r-ḥ b-* is indeed used of assiduous study.

10. Not impossibly, these words also continue the military metaphor, the meaning being that the assailant does not linger on the heights surrounding the city but makes straight for the gates—the Roman *succedere portis*. (The form *bᵉ-rûmêhā*, in place of the more usual *bi-mᵉrômêhā*, would have been chosen as lending itself more readily to the metaphorical nuance.) It may perhaps be suggested that there is also an allusion to the Graeco-Roman custom whereby young blades used to make the rounds ('go *epi kōmon'*) after dinner battering on the doors of their lady-loves. If the latter refused them admission, the ardent suitors would often force entry; see fully Headlam-Knox, *Herodas* (1925), pp. 85f. The Versions squeamishly substitute, *I spread my hands to heaven!*

11. The conventional rendering (RSV), *and lamented my ignorance of her*, rests on a lamentable ignorance of the fact that the Greek Version's *I lamented* (*epenthēsa*) is simply a corruption (and what a corruption!) of a very similar word (viz. *epenoēsa*) meaning *I contemplated*. (This, however, is itself a mistaken rendering of the Hebrew, which really means, *that I might contemplate*.)

12. For the moralizing tone of these lines, cp. Erasmus' description of Thomas More in his celebrated letter to Ulrich Hutten: 'When he was of an age for it, he was not averse to love-affairs with young women, but kept them honorable, preferring the love that was offered to that which he must chase after, and was more drawn by spiritual than by physical intercourse' (tr. Barbara Flower, in J. Huizinga, *Erasmus of Rotterdam* [1952], p. 235).

13. This is the end of the pious exhortation into which our merry poem so dismally peters out.

VICE

The Wiles of the Harlot

INTRODUCTION

This ingenious little sermon (composed in verse and based largely on the seventh chapter of the Biblical Book of Proverbs) is obviously to be understood allegorically, for there would be no point in warning desert ascetics against the ploys of real live urban streetwalkers. The harlot is evidently Apostasy or the like, in line with the Biblical characterization of it as 'whoredom'.

The subtle artistry of the poem should not be missed. Almost every statement is couched in terms of *double-entendre*, the actual characteristics of a prostitute (as frequently portrayed in classical literature) being interpreted in a metaphorical sense. Thus, the raucous banter, coarse jests, and wheedling flattery with which she customarily accosts passers-by become the worthless, blasphemous, and seductive mouthings of apostasy; the earnings which she stashes in the folds or bosom of her dress become the multitude of transgressions which impiety carries with it. Similarly, the bright (usually yellow) garments which ladies of easy virtue commonly affected in ancient times are the shades of night and gloom in which sin is enveloped; the little patches of gold foil with which, in Roman times, loose women concealed defects of complexion are caustically identified as the scabs and blotches of corruption. The harlot's bed is the bed of worms spread in the netherworld; the darkened chamber in which she receives her clients is darkling Hell; the furtiveness which pervades it is the silence of the grave; and the heat of lust is the 'everlasting fire'. The alleys which she frequents are the gates of the netherworld; her smooth blandishments are slippery morasses. And in almost every case the point is made by a deft application of Scriptural phrases or clichés.

Nor is it only the content, but also the structure of the
poem that is cunningly contrived. The poet passes successively from the whore's demeanor and talk (her mouth,
tongue, lips, wiles, blandishments, and badinage) to her
physical traits (the characteristics of her heart, reins,
hands, and feet); then to her dress and ornaments (cloak,
skirts, spangles); then to her abode (bed, darkened chamber, 'pavilion', 'tent', and doorway); and finally to her behavior on her 'beat'.

THE WILES OF THE HARLOT

[Out of] her [mouth] she brings forth emptiness,
  and on [her tongue lie] devious wiles.[1]
Ever importuning,[2] [she] gives sharp edge to [her]
    words;[3]
    with reprobate [lips][4] she plies her blandish-
      ments[5]—
[banter][6] and badinage and mocking jests.[7]
  Her heart contrives wantonness,
and her reins are a well[spring of filth].[8]
  Her hands are stained with wrongdoing,[9]
her feet are close to a pit;[10]
    they run[11] to do wickedness,
and to go about amid transgressions;[12]
    [her steps] are grounded in darkness.[13]
  (Stored) in the lappet of her garments
are a million transgressions.[14]
    [Her skirts][15] are the shades[16] of night,
and her vestments [the shadow of death].[17]

5   Her raiment is the murk of twilight,[18]
and her spangles are squalid blotches.[19]
  Her couch is the mattress of Corruption;[20]
[her bed] the depths of the Pit.[21]
  To pass the night with her
is to lie in darkness,[22]
    and her [   ][23] is the blackness of night.[24]
  She sets her pavilion[25] in the darkling realm,[26]
and dwells in the tents of Silence,[27]
    amid the eternal burnings;[28]
she does not partake at all
  of the lights of the dayspring.[29]

From her start all ways of wrongdoing.[30]
Alas, she has ever brought ruin
　　on all who possessed her,
and destruction on all who laid hold on her;
　　for her ways are the ways of Death,[31]
and her roads are the paths of Sin;
10　　her trails are the twists and turns of wrongdoing,
and [her] byways are lawless transgression.[32]
　　Her gates are the gates of Death;[33]
beside her doorway she strides,[34]
　　<luring men> to Hell.[35]
All that go into her never come back,[36]
　　and all that possess her go down to Corruption.[37]
　　[. . .] She lies in wait in hidden places[38]
[to catch][39] all who [pass by].[40]
　　She goes muffled up[41] through the city squares,
takes her stand at the gates of towns.[42]
　　There is no cal[ming her] cla[mor] (?).[43]
Her eyes peer[44] hither and yon,
　　and wantonly lifts she her lids,
to see [if perchance there be][45]
　　a righteous man to turn back in his course,[46]
or a [blame]less man to trip up,
　　turning the upright from their path,[47]
God's honest and true elect[48]
15　　from keeping the commandments;[49]
converting soothfast men[50] to wantonness (?)[51]
　　and causing those that walk straight
to alter [their course];[52]
inciting the meek to rebel against God,
　　and turning their steps from the paths of right-
　　　　eousness;[53]
bringing intemperance[54] [into their hearts][55]
　　so that they keep not their stance
on straightforward paths;[56]
　　leading men astray
on pit-ridden ways.[57]
　　and seducing the sons of men
into morasses.[58]

NOTES

1. In a literal sense, the Heb. word *to'oth* here means 'fatuities', being taken as the equivalent of *tu'ªtū'îm*, which is similarly juxtaposed with 'emptiness' (*hebel*) in Jer. 10.15; 51.18. It thus characterizes the chatter of whores. Metaphorically, however, it means 'errors', i.e., the false and blasphemous doctrines fostered by apostasy and irreligion. Nicholas Breton (1626) similarly describes the reprobate: 'His breath is the fume of blasphemy, and his tongue a firebrand of hell'.
2. Cp. Prov. 7.15.
3. For the Heb. expression, cp. Palestinian Talmud, *Ber.* iii.6 (though there used in a different sense).
4. Cp. Job 27.4; cp. also Mal. 2.6. The expression recurs in *Hymns* v.24.
5. Cp. Prov. 2.16; 7.5.
6. Restoring [*la'ag*] *wa-qeles*, after Pss. 44.14; 79.4. The expression recurs in *War*, ii.10. In the literal sense, it refers to the banter and persiflage in which streetwalkers customarily indulge; metaphorically, to the taunts which apostasy habitually flings at faith.
7. The Heb. word (*hêlîṣ*) means both 'jest' and 'scoff'. In the literal sense it refers to the ribaldries hurled by more brazen harlots at passers-by. In Greek literature, such gay talk is regarded as a hallmark of loose women: see Headlam-Knox, *Herodas* (1922), pp. 34f. Metaphorically, it refers to the mocking tone of apostasy.
8. I restore: *mᵉ[qôr niddah]*, after *Hymns* i.22; xii.25. The expression derives from Zech. 13.1 (though there used in a different sense). Literally, this refers to the

physical uncleanliness of streetwalkers—possibly even to venereal disease; metaphorically, to moral turpitude and base doctrine.

9. Modelled on Isa. 59.3. Cp. also Ezek. 23.37, 45.

10. Cp. Ps. 17.5.

11. The manuscript is here indistinct. I read *yārūṣū*, after the similar (though not identical) expression in Isa. 59.7; Prov. 1.16.

12. Cp. Ps. 68.21.

13. 'Darkness' is here a popular term for the netherworld; cp. Ps. 143.3; Job 10.21; 17.13; Lam. 3.6. Comparable are the Akkadian expressions, 'Dark House' (*bītu eṭû*) and 'House of Gloom' (*bīt ekleti*); see M. Held, in *Th. Gaster Festschrift* (1973), p. 179, n. 53.

14. In the literal sense, this refers to the practise of stashing money, etc. in the lappet (Latin, *lacinia;* Akkadian, *qannu*) of the robe; it is there that the harlot would carry her earnings. Metaphorically, what wanton apostasy carries around is a load of transgressions. ('A million' is simply a rendering *ad sensum* of the Heb. 'a multitude'.)

15. Restoring [*shūlêhah*]. Cp. the familiar English 'trailing garments of the night'.

16. The Heb. word *tô'ᵃfôth*, which occurs, in quite a different sense, in Num. 23.22; 24.8, and in Ps. 95.4; Job 22.25, is here equated with *ṭ'ūfah*, 'darkness', in Job 11.17; cp. also *ib.* 10.22.

17. Restoring [*ṣalmoaweth*]—a word (properly, *ṣalmûth*) which really means 'darkness', but was popularly interpreted in antiquity as 'shadow of death' (i.e., *ṣel maweth*); cp. Job 10.22.

18. The harlot walks her beat at twilight; cp. Prov. 7.9. On the literal level, these words are a pointed gibe at the bright colors (especially yellow) affected by loose women; see Kirby Smith, on Tibullus, i.7.46; T. H. Gaster, *Myth, Legend, and Custom in the Old Testament* (1969), §266(b).

19. For the ornaments (spangles) worn by harlots, cp. Ezek. 23.40. On the literal level, this phrase satirizes the gold patches (Latin, *splenia;* cp. Martial, ii.29, 9)

which, in Roman times, women wore to conceal bodily blemishes.

20. I.e., the bed of worms spread in the netherworld, cp. Isa. 14.11. ('Corruption' may here be a pure synonym for Sheol; for the sentiment, cp. Ps. 139.8.)

21. For the sentiment, cp. Prov. 7.27; 9.18.

22. Literally, 'her lodgings are darkness', see above, n. 13.

23. The manuscript is here indistinct. Allegro reads [me]mshᵉlôtêhah, 'her realm, bailiwick', but what is required is a closer parallel to 'her lodgements', in the preceding line.

24. Cp. Prov. 7.9—here again a popular term for the netherworld.

25. The Heb. expression is based on Isa. 40.22. Cp. also Gen. 13.18.

26. Cp. Prov. 7.9.

27. I.e., in the netherworld; cp. Pss. 94.17; 115.17.

28. Cp. Isa. 33.14, but here denoting the fires of hell; cp. *Manual*, ii.8; iv.13; *Hymns* xviii.13.

29. Heb. Mᵉ'ôrê nōgah. I interpret the latter word from the specific sense which it bears in Syriac (cp. also Isa. 60.3), because the poet seems to intend a pointed contrast to 'the murk of twilight' previously mentioned. But the expression could mean simply 'bright lights' in general.

30. Modelled on Prov. 8.22.

31. Cp. Prov. 14.12; 16.25; II Esdras 7.48; 8.31. 'Death' here means the netherworld, as in Isa. 26.15; 38.18; Job 28.22. Comparable is the Akkadian 'House of Death' (bīt mūti). For the notion of the road to Death, see T. H. Gaster, in *Iraq* 6 (1939), 130, n. 70; M. Held, in *Th. Gaster Festschrift* (1973), p. 180, n. 56.

32. This expression recurs in *Manual*, ix.4. Cp. also *ib.*, i.23.

33. Cp. Isa. 38.10; Ps. 9.14; Job 38.17; *Hymns* vi.24.

34. Cp. Prov. 9.14. Lurking in doorways is often mentioned in Greek literature as a sign of loose morals, e.g., Theophrastus, *Characters*, xxviii.3; Aristophanes, *Peace*, 978–86; *Thesm.*, 792; Xenophon, *Oec.*, viii.30; Menander, fr. 546 Koch.

35. Cp. Prov. 5.5. Meter and sense alike suggest that two lines have here been accidentally run together.

36. Prov. 2.19; cp. also Job 10.21; 16.22. Comparable is the Akkadian 'Land of No Return' (*erṣet lâ târi*) as a term for the netherworld. Not impossibly, this line is also to be understood *sensu obscoeno*, with a kind of *double-entendre*.

37. Cp. Ps. 30.10; Job 33.24; Ezek. 28.8.

38. Cp. Ps. 10.9; Lam. 3.10.

39. I restore: [*la-ḥᵉtôf*], after Ps. 10.9. For such 'snatching' of wayfarers by lurking harlots, cp. Theophrastus, *Characters*, xxviii.3; Athenaeus, xiii.569C, where an exactly equivalent term (*harpazein*) is used.

40. Restoring, with Allegro: [*'obᵉrê derek*], after Prov. 9.15; but [*'öber ba-shûq*], 'who passes in the street', after Prov. 7.8, would also be possible.

41. Cp. Gen. 38.14 and the traditional (though probably incorrect) interpretation of Song of Songs, 1.7, as read in the Masoretic text.

42. Cp. Prov. 8.3.

43. The text is damaged. Allegro restores: *Wᵉ-ên lᵉ-harg*['iah] *me-ha*[ṭṭo]*t* [*tᵉmîmîm*], 'and there is no stirring (i.e., interrupting) her from leading innocent men astray'. This is certainly possible, but in view of the fact that in Prov. 7.11 and 9.13 the harlot is described expressly as 'boisterous' (*hōmîyah*), the verb may mean 'calm, quieten' (from *r-g-'* II) rather than 'stir' (from *r-g-'* I). An alternative restoration of the following *me-h*[   ] might then be *me'*[*hemyat . . .* (cp. Isa. 14.11)], 'from (her) boisterous [clamor]', the voice contrasting with the eyes.

44. Heb. *yaskîlû* is here used in the post-Biblical sense of 'peer' (*histakel*).

45. I restore: *li-rᵉ'ô*[*th ha-yesh*]; cp. Ps. 14.2.

46. The verb *tśghû* must here be vocalized *tᵉśîgēhū* from *ś-w-g* (=*s-w-g*), 'fall back', rather than *tᵉśśîgēhū*, from *n-ś-g*, 'overtake', in view of the fact that the former is similarly juxtaposed with *k-sh-l*, 'trip, stumble', in *Manual*, ii.12.

47. Cp. Ps. 37.14; Prov. 28.10; 29.27.
48. Literally, 'the elect of righteousness', cp. *Hymns* ii.13.
49. Cp. Pss. 78.7; 119.115; Prov. 6.20.
50. I restore *s^emūḵê* [*yeṣer*], after the expression, *yeṣer sāmūḵ* (taken from Isa. 26.3) in *Manual*, iv.5; viii.3; *Hymns* i.35; ii.9.
51. The manuscript is indistinct. If Allegro's *l^e-h-b-y-l* is correct, the only possible explanation would be to vocalize *l^e-habbîl*, from *n-b-l*, 'be impious, coarse', but the causative (*hif'il*) form of this root occurs nowhere else, so that this reading is suspect. For the sentiment, cp. *Hymns* ii.36.
52. The text is again damaged. Allegro restores: [*ḥôq*], 'the ordinance', but a plausible alternative would be simply *dar*[*kam*] or *der*[*ek*], '(their) way'.
53. Cp. Prov. 16.31. The expression recurs in *Manual*, iv.2.
54. Heb. *zādôn* is usually rendered 'presumption', but it comes from a root which means primarily 'seethe', and 'seething passion, lust, intemperance' seems to be the nuance here intended.
55. Indistinct.
56. Cp. Prov. 4.11.
57. Literally, this means simply 'potholed roads' (cp. analogously Jer. 2.6, 'a land of pits/holes'), but the expression is intended to convey also the notion of 'roads leading to the Pit', i.e., the netherworld.
58. There is here a subtle *double-entendre*, the Heb. *ḥ^alāqôt* meaning both 'smooth talk' and 'slippery places' (cp. Ps. 73.18). Hence the meaning is at once that the harlot seduces men by her blandishments and into a morass!

VISIONS AND TESTAMENTS

The Last Words of Amram

INTRODUCTION

A distinctive genre of Jewish literature in the Graeco-Roman period was the fictitious testament, or deathbed exhortation, of an ancestral worthy or religious leader, usually combined with a prophecy of what was yet in store for his heirs.[1] The parade examples of this genre are *The Testaments of the Twelve Patriarchs* (sons of Jacob), constituent portions of which have indeed turned up at Qumran; and to this category too belongs the curious text presented in the following pages. Composed in Aramaic (the vernacular tongue), all that now remains of it are a few sorry fragments derived from four copies, and even these have not yet been published in their entirety. Any comprehensive interpretation can therefore be but tentative and provisional.

The central theme of the text is a dream-vision seen by Amram, the father of Moses, on the day of his death,[2] and his consequent admonitions to his sons. What Amram sees are two otherworldly beings representing respectively the Prince of Light and the Prince of Darkness—virtual personifications of the good and evil inclinations in man. They are engaged in an altercation about him, and he is invited to choose between them.

The underlying notion that human life is in fact a struggle between these two forces is well attested elsewhere.[3] We have met it already in *The Manual of Discipline* (iii.13–iv.26; above, p. 48), and allusions to it are to be found in *The Testament of Asher* (i–iv), in the *Visions* (v.6) and *Mandates* (ii.12) of Hermes Pastor, in the Slavonic *Book of Enoch* (xix.5), in sundry passages of the Talmud (Ber. 60[b]; Sheb. 119[b]; Ta'an. 11[a]), and—at a far later date—in the apocryphal Apocalypse of Paul (xiv–xvii)[4] and in *The Book of Angels* current among the Falashas of Ethiopia.[5] The Jews, for their part, probably adopted it from Iranian lore, but it is not in fact confined to Judaeo-Christian literature. Censorinus, the Roman scholar of the third century C.E., tells us that it was held by Euclidês of Megara, a disciple of Socrates,[6] and it is the theme of the famous apologue of 'Heracles at the Crossroads' attributed to the Sophist Prodicus and related at length in Xenophon's *Memorabilia* (II, 1.21–34).[7] In our present text, however, a new twist is introduced (as again in the Apocalypse of Paul) in the fact that the two spirits contend over a man's soul on the day of his death and that they invite Amram to choose between them.

In the Epistle of Jude (verse 9) there is a reference to the legend that the angel Michael contended with the Devil for the body of Moses,[8] and this legend is mentioned also in the Slavonic *Life of Moses*,[9] in a statement by Severus, Patriarch of Antioch (542 C.E.), quoted in the *Catena* of Nicephorus (on Deut. ch. 34), in the later rabbinic Midrash known as *The Demise of Moses* (*Peṭirath Môsheh*)[10] and in the apocryphon entitled *The Testament of Abraham* (ch. xvii). At first blush it might seem that what is related in our text is simply a variation of that legend. The comparison, however, is utterly misleading, for what is implied in those works is really something quite different, viz., the resistance offered by a benign angel to the attempt of Death (acting, to be sure, under orders from God) to snatch away the *body* of a preeminently righteous and virtuous man. There is no question of a choice between good and evil offered to the dying.

On the other hand, it would appear that our text was indeed known to Origen (185–254 C.E.), for in his Thirty-fifth Homily, on Luke 12.58–59, as translated by Jerome in 389–90 C.E., he speaks of angels struggling for the soul of Abraham, and J. T. Milik has argued persuasively that Abraham is there, in all probability, a corruption of *Ambram, a frequent distortion of Amram![11]

A word may be added on what might otherwise seem a puzzling feature of our text, namely, that *both* of the angels (or spirits) have the grim face of a reptile. To be sure, for purposes of the story, both would have to look alike; otherwise there could be no real choice between them. In Prodicus' apologue, however, and again in *The Testament of Abraham*, the evil one disguises itself in fair colors, whereas here just the opposite is the case; the good one wears the mien of his sinister opponent, who is indeed described elsewhere as possessing the face of a reptile.[12] The only difference between them is that the good one is light, and the evil one dark. The virtuous Amram, however, is 'tipped off' by the former, and by reason of that information and of his own innate proclivity toward goodness is able, evidently, to make the right choice!

The Admonitions (preserved in a supplementary fragment) play, in a hortatory vein, on the same distinction between the 'light' and the 'dark', matching their ultimate fate with their character. It is perhaps possible to detect in the descriptions the influence of Iranian lore. (The correspondences are pointed out in the notes to the text.)

NOTES

1. On the widespread notion that the dying are prescient, see T. H. Gaster, *Myth, Legend, and Custom in the Old Testament* (1969) §74.
2. The dream-vision in classical literature is familiar especially from Cicero's *Somnium Scipionis*. It became a standard device of medieval writers, as witness Dante's *Divina Commedia*, Langland's *Piers Plowman* and *Pearl*. 'Dream', as Brian Stone has observed (*Medieval English Verse* [Penguin Classics, 1964], p. 138), 'was out of consciousness and therefore an extension of the mind beyond life'.
3. See: S. Schechter, *Aspects of Rabbinic Theology* (1909), pp. 241–63; G. F. Moore, *Judaism in the First Centuries of the Christian Era* (repr. 1971), i.483ff.; F. C. Porter, in *Biblical and Semitic Studies* (Yale Bicentennial Publications, 1902), pp. 98–107; H. L. Strack and P. Billerbeck, *Kommentar zum Neuen Testament aus Talmud und Midrash*, iv (1928), pp. 466–68; W. D. Davies, *Paul and Rabbinic Judaism*[2] (repr. 1967), pp. 21ff. On this doctrine in the Dead Sea Scriptures, see: H. W. Huppenbauer, *Der Mensch zwischen zwei Welten* (1959); J. Licht, in *Scripta Hierosolymitana* 4 (1958), pp. 88–100; O. J. F. Seitz, in *New Testament Studies* 6 (1960), pp. 82–95; P. Wernberg-Møller, in *Revue de Qumran* 3 (1961–62), 413–41; M. Treves, *ibid.*, 449–52.
4. Translated in M. R. James, *The Apocryphal New Testament* (1924), pp. 531ff.
5. J. Halévy, ed., *Taazaze Sanbat* (1902), pp. 173f.; W. Leslau, *Falasha Anthology* (1951), pp. 52f.

6. Censorinus, iii.3.

7. The apologue is said to have formed part of Prodicus' work, *Hôrai*. K. Joel (*Socrates*, iii, i, 125f.), however, attributes it to Antisthenes; see W. C. Greene, *Moira* (1944), pp. 242f. On the idea in general in Classical thought, see: P. Boyané, in *Revue de Philologie 9* (1935), 189ff., R. B. Onians, *The Origins of European Thought About the Body*, etc. (1951), p. 265.

8. Origen and others say that this was taken from the pseudepigraphic Assumption of Moses, but it is not found in the extant, albeit incomplete, Latin version of that work.

9. Edited by R. Bonwetsch in *Göttingen Nachrichten*, 1900, 581f. So too in the Byzantine Palaea; see Vassiliev, in *Anecdota Graeco-Byzantina* (1893), p. 247; M. R. James, *op. cit.*, p. 47.

10. A. Jellinek, *Beth ha-Midrash*, vi (1878), 71f.; J. D. Eisenstein, *Oṣar Midrashîm* (1915), ii.361f. On the later survival of this legend, see M. Asin Palacios, *Islam and the Divine Comedy* (1926), pp. 221f.

11. J. T. Milik, in *Revue Biblique* 79 (1972), 91f.

12. See L. Ginzberg, *Legends of the Jews*, ii.195; v.101, 123; *Testament of Abraham*, xvii; Gabriel too sometimes takes this form: Ginzberg, *op. cit.*, v.423. Possibly, the author was influenced also by the popular notion of the two celestial assessors who present to God the cases for the prosecution and defense of a dying man, for these are commonly portrayed as *both* possessing a grim aspect.

THE LAST WORDS OF AMRAM

*Transcript of the text[1] relating the vision of Am-
ram, son of Kehath, son of Levi—all that he revealed to his sons and that he enjoined upon them
on the day he died in (his) one hundredth and
sixty-sixth year;[2] the year of his death being the
one hundredth and fifty-second since Israel made
its departure into Egypt.*

¶In a dream I had a vision; two beings were disputing
about me and exchanging words and holding a fierce
argument.

'Who are you', I asked them, 'that you should be [argu-
ing and wrangling] in this way over *me?*'

'We', they replied, 'are [the two powers that have been
given r]ule, and indeed wield it, over all mankind'.

'Which of us', they continued, 'do you [choose   ]?'

¶I raised my eyes and looked them over. [The one] of
them had a terrifying mien like an asp.[3] His r[ai]ment was
deep-dyed, and (he himself) very dark.[4]

Then I looked at the other. He was [   ] of mien,
with the face of a viper, and [   ], and all his eyes
were [   ].[5]

¶[I turned to the latter of the two. 'What', I asked, 'is the
matter of your dispute?']

'[Each of us', he replied, 'is out to claim] rule over you
[in this hour of your death]'.[6]

¶'[But] who', [I pursued,] 'is this unearthly being[7] (standing beside you)?'

'This unearth[ly being]', he rejoined, 'is [one who operates under several guises: to wit, as . . . , as . . .] and as the King of Wickedness'.[8]

'Sir', said I, 'what is [his] name?'

'[His name', came the answer, 'is Belial (?).[9] His every thought is dark]ling, and d[ar]kling his every act, and in darkness he [walk]s.[10] [That is why he himself is dark, as] you see. He has been given rule over all that is dark, whereas I [have been given it over all that is light. By the command of Him Who wields sway] alike above and below. I am he that bears rule over all that is light and all that is [   ]. I bear it, to boot, over (every) man [that   ], and (so) I bear it [over all the sons of light]'.

¶(Thereupon) I asked him, '[   ]. [Under what] names do you go?'*

'Of my three names', [he rep]lied, '[the first is . . . , and the second . . . , and the third . . .]'.[11]

* * *

[The Admonitions]

¶'. . . . I hereby make [kn]own [unto you. More]over, I make known [to you] in sooth

[that all the sons of light] will (hereafter) abide† in light,[12] [while all the sons of] darkness will abide in darkness;[13]

[that, because of all the knowledge[14] which is theirs, [the sons of light will be like a robe without tear or spot], while the sons of darkness will be [like soiled patches] cut away;[15]

that, (since) all folly and wicked[ness][16] are things of [darkness], while all [probi]ty and truth [are] things of light, [all the sons of light will go (hereafter)] into light, into joy [everlasting and into] renewal,[17] while all the sons of dark[ness] will go [into darkness, hell (and)] perdition;

[that (hereafter)] enlightenment [will come] to the people,[18] and [God] will reveal [   ].

* * *

---

* Literally, '[What are] your names?'
† Literally, 'be'.

NOTES

1. The initial words of the title correspond to the formula which introduces several of the *Testaments of the Twelve Patriarchs.*
2. This agrees with the Samaritan text of Exod. 6.20—a reading found also in the Codex Alexandrinus of the Greek (Septuagint) Version. The Masoretic text has 'the one hundred and sixty seventh', and other LXX manuscripts 'the one hundred and sixty second'.
3. Perhaps this refers more specifically to their terrifying stare. Compare Euripides' description of serpents as 'gorgon-eyed' (*Hercules Furens,* 1266). In a tablet from Asshur (7th cent. B.C.) describing Prince Kummiya's journey to the netherworld, he sees the demonic 'Death' (*ᵈ Mu-ū-[tu]*) with the head of a dragon (*mushḫushshu*), two human hands, and two serpent-twined feet; E. Ebeling, *Tod und Leben,* I (1931), p. 5; A. Heidel, *The Gilgamesh Epic and Old Testament Parallels*[3] (1949), p. 133; E. A. Speiser, in *ANET,* 109ᵃ—110ᵇ.
4. The idea that the Evil One is dark or black recurs elsewhere, e.g., *Epistle of Barnabas,* 4.9; *Apocryphal Acts of Thomas,* ch. 33; *of Andrew,* ch. 22; *Pistis Sophia,* Coptic text, 637; Paris *Magical Papyrus,* 1238–39. So too in German folklore: J. Grimm, *Teutonic Mythology,* tr. F. Stallybrass (repr. 1966), 993. In Gaelic he is known as 'Black Donald', and in English proverbs is likened to a collier: Samuel Butler, *Hudibras,* ii.350; *Notes and Queries,* III.v (1864), 282, 389.
5. In view of the defective state of the text it is impossible to determine whether these words refer to only one of

the two spirits or (as Milik thinks) to both. In Talmud, 'Abodah Zarah 20ᵇ, Death is said to have several eyes; while in Revelation 4.6 the four 'Creatures' who surround the heavenly throne are 'covered with eyes'.

6. The supplements in this paragraph are purely conjectural, based on the fact that it is the Prince of Lights that describes his adversary, rather than the latter speaking for himself. Perhaps in the intervening gap Amram actually made his choice.

7. The Aramaic word is *'îr*, the name of a class of celestial beings both in Daniel and in the Qumran *Memoirs of the Patriarchs*. Whatever the word may originally have meant (v. T. H. Gaster, in IDB, s.v. Watcher), it was popularly taken to denote 'Watcher' (as though from the root *'-w-r*, 'be awake'), and is so understood in Enoch, where it is paraphrased (61.12), 'sleepless ones'.

8. The opposite of Melchizedek, i.e., 'King of Righteousness'. Milik says (in *Journal of Jewish Studies* 23 [1972], 127f.) that in the yet unpublished Qumran text, 4Q 280.2, the name occurs in a commination-formula parallel to that in *Manual*, col. ii, where it is applied to Belial.

9. Restored *ad sensum* from *Manual*, col. ii.

10. Cp. *Manual, ibid.*

11. In Talmud, Babâ Bathrâ 16ª, R. Simon ben Lakish (c. 200–75 C.E.) is reported as saying that the Evil Inclination (*Yeṣer Ra'*) has two other names, viz. Satan and the Angel of Death. (This view is included also in the rabbinic florilegium, *Pirqê Rabbēnū ha-Qadôsh* = J. D. Eisenstein, ed., *Oṣar he-Midrashîm* [1915], ii.510a 1.) Cp. the similar statement in King James the First's *Demonologie* (1597), 76: '[That same devil] illudes the necromancers with innumerable feigned names for him and his angels, as in special, making Satan, Beelzebub and Lucifer to be three sundry spirits, where we find the two former, but diverse names given to the Prince of all the rebelling angels by the Scripture. . . . Even so, I say, he deceives the witches by attributing to himself diverse names; as if

every diverse shape that he transforms himself in were a diverse kind of spirit'. Cp. also Shakespeare, *Macbeth*, II.iii, 'Who's there, i' the name of Beelzebub? . . . Who's there, in the other devil's name'—which some commentators take to mean, in the Devil's other name.

12. See Analytical Index, E. 3 (*c*). The notion may reflect the influence of Iranian lore, for the expression corresponds to the 'endless light' (*anaghra raochah*) mentioned in Yasht xxii.15; xxiv.61 as the future destination of the righteous.

13. Cp. *Manual*, ii.8. This too has an Iranian ring, for it corresponds to the 'endless darkness' (*anaghra temah*) mentioned in Yasht xxii.33, etc., as the future destination of the wicked.

14. I.e., inner knowledge, gnosis—in contrast to the 'folly' of the wicked.

15. Reading, with Milik, *ytqdn*, which means, however, 'cut away', rather than 'cut down'. The word is used in the Syriac Bible (Lev. 13.56) to denote the cutting out of a stained patch from the garment of a man not yet completely recovered from skin disease. The picture intended by our author may thus have been that the righteous will be like a clean garment, white and unstained (cp. Dan. 12.10), whereas the wicked, themselves 'sons of darkness', will be like the dark patch, symbolic of lingering impurity, which had then to be cut out; the implication being, of course, that they will be severed from the community of Israel.

16. Cp. Eccles. 7.25.

17. See Analytical Index, E. 3 (*e*). This suggests the Iranian *frashokereti*.

18. See above, n. 12. Cp. also Isa. 9.1; 58.8; 60.1, 19–20; *Manual*, iv.8.

DESTINY

The Epochs of Time

INTRODUCTION

Josephus tells us (*Ant.*, xiii.5, 9) that the Essenes—with whom the Qumran Brotherhood may be identical—believed that all things were predetermined. Interesting light is shed on this by a fragmentary text recovered from Cave Four.[1] Reconstructed from scraps of two mutually complementary copies, the contents present an intriguing combination of two doctrines, viz., (a) that the history of mankind is disposed by God in a series of preordained epochs,[2] and (b) that the cardinal events of each epoch are brought about by angels whose activities were determined by God before He created them.[3] The former of these doctrines probably reflects, in a religious vein, a preoccupation with systematic chronology which was a notable feature of Hellenistic literature, attested especially by quotations from the lost work of the historiographer Demetrius (*ca.* 215 B.C.) and by the *Book of Jubilees.*

The text opens with a summary statement of these two doctrines. In proof of the former it is then pointed out that the sequence of the ages seems indeed to follow a systematic scheme, since exactly ten generations elapsed from Adam to Noah and from Noah to Abraham's begetting of Isaac.[4] The latter doctrine is in turn validated by the observation that all the crucial events in the career of Abraham, viz., the promise of the land to his descendants (Gen. 17.1–8), the apparition beside the oaks of Mamre and the rescue of Lot (*ib.*, 18.2, 29; 19.1, 15), the incident on Mount Moriah (*ib.*, 22.11, 15), and the plaguing of Pharaoh for molesting Sarai (*ib.*, 12.17), involved the intervention of angels.

There is, however, one obvious objection which has to

be offset: in at least one notorious instance, namely, that of the commerce between the 'sons of God' and the daughters of men, recounted in Gen. 6.1–4, the angels in fact flouted God.[5] Identifying the ringleader (as in the Book of Enoch) with Azazel, the author surmounts this difficulty by the argument that, after all, the rebels received condign punishment, while those who did not join them enjoyed divine favor,[6] so that, in the long run, what the incident really demonstrated was that God will not brook any interference with His plan and that His rule is essentially benevolent.

Then, too, in the case both of the promise about the land and of the plaguing of Pharaoh the author has to stretch a point in order to find evidence of intervention *by angels,* for the Scriptural text describes them as actions performed directly by God Himself. Such pious substitution has, however, good precedent and parallel. Thus—to cite but a few examples—the strange being with whom Jacob wrestles at the Ford of Jabbok (Gen. 32.23ff.) and who is indeed subsequently identified as a *god* (verses 29, 31), is described in Hos. 14.5 as an *angel.* Similarly, in Exod. 4.24, where the traditional Hebrew text states that 'the LORD met Moses at the inn, meaning to kill him', the Greek (Septuagint) Version and the Aramaic Targum substitute '*an angel* of the LORD'; and in the case of the disease inflicted on Pharaoh, the Qumran *Memoirs of the Patriarchs* says that the LORD sent 'a noisome spirit' to do so,[7] and the same statement is made also in the Ethiopic *Kebra Nagast* (ch. 82, ed. Bezold).

NOTES

1. The texts were first published in full by J. M. Allegro in *Discoveries in the Judaean Desert,* V (1968), nos. 180–81, and were then combined and interpreted by J. T. Milik in a brilliant study which appeared in *Journal of Jewish Studies* 23 (1972), pp. 109ff. Valuable corrections of Allegro's readings were supplied by J. Strugnell in *Revue de Qumran,* 1970, pp. 252–55.
2. On this doctrine, see Analytical Index, E. 1–2; *II Baruch,* chs. 56–71; *IV Ezra,* 14.11–12. As applied eschatologically, cp. Dan. 9.24–27; *Testament of Levi,* 16.1; Enoch, 93.1–10; 91.12–17 ('The Apocalypse of Weeks').
3. On the predetermined roles of angels, cp. *HI* 7, 20, 28; *Hymns* viii.8; xi.34; xv.14, 22; xx.14.
4. Cp. Gen. 5.1–31; 11.10–26. This is pointed out specifically in Mishnah, *Abôth,* v.1–2.
5. On this legend in post-Biblical literature, cp. Enoch, chs. 6–10; 15–16; *Jubilees,* 5.1, 10; 10.5, 11; 11.4; *Testament of Reuben,* ch. 5; *Testament of Judah,* 25.3; *Syr. Baruch,* 56.10–13; Josephus, *Ant.,* i, 3, 1; Philo, *De Gigantibus,* i.2; TB, *Yômâ,* 67b; *Midrash Akbîr,* quoted in *Yalqûṭ,* Gen. §44; L. Ginzberg, *Legends of the Jews,* vol. v, pp. 150ff.
6. For my interpretation of this passage, which differs from that proposed by Milik, see below, Notes to the Text, n. 5.
7. See above, p. 366.

THE EPOCHS OF TIME

CLARIFICATION[1] (OF THE DOCTRINE) CONCERNING THE
FIXED EPOCHS (OF HISTORY):

As regards ᴳᴼᴰ's* having set a fixed epoch for the [oc-
currence of everything past] and future, (the fact is that)
before He created [the angels] He determined what [they]
were to do [in their several epochs], epoch by epoch.
Moreover, this was engraved on (heavenly) tablets[2] [and
duly prescribed] for the respective epochs in which they
were to bear rule.

Here is the ordered scheme: [from Adam to Noah, and
again from Noah] until [Abraham] begat Isaac [He ap-
pointed] ten [generations].

CLARIFICATION (OF THE STORY) CONCERNING AZAZEL AND
THE ANGELS WHO [HAD INTERCOURSE WITH THE DAUGHTERS
OF MEN], SO THAT THE LATTER BORE GIANTS TO THEM, AND
CONCERNING HOW AZAZEL [LED MEN ASTRAY ALONG WAYS
OF] INIQUITY AND (THEREBY) LEFT ISRAEL A LEGACY OF
WICKEDNESS (WHICH IS TO LAST) THROUGH AN EPOCH OF
SEVENTY WEEKS (OF YEARS):[3]

[(The fact is that) ᴳᴼᴰ eventually sent these rebels to
perdition][4] for [ever, so as to execu]te (condign) judgments (upon them), [and He also brought] judgment on
all who had associated themselves with them in their filth.[5]
These were [   ], lovers of iniquity and such as leave
a legacy of guilt. [At the same time, however, God showed
mercy and displayed His glory] in the sight of all that indeed acknowledged (*lit.* knew) Him and mini[stered to His
holiness. To those who serve Him His love is endless (?)],

* Written in archaic script.

and His goodness knows no bounds. [   ]. Such men
have (ever) been singled out through [their] knowledge
(of Him)[6], [   ]; through His truth has He given
them ordered mode of life [   ] throughout their various epochs [   ], whenso [they] are brought into
being.

(ii)

*(The next passage seems to allegorize the Story
of the Fallen Angels, taking them to typify the
reprobate among men, who are destined, on account of their impurity, to suffer 'great judgments
and grievous diseases'. The text is too imperfect
and obscure to permit reliable translation. One
recognizes such significant words as* 'guilt', 'the
communion of unch[astity]',[7] 'wallowing(?) in
human sinfulness', *and* '(destined) for great
judgments and grievous diseases of the flesh in
conformity with God's acts of power and in face
of their wickedness'.

   *This is followed by a much clearer passage in
which, conversely, those who did* not *join the
rebels are taken to typify the godly and pure
among men. Here too, however, the restoration
of several phrases can be little more than guess-
work:)*

(Howbeit), in accordance with the tender mercy of 𝕲𝖔𝖉,
in accordance with His goodness and with the wondrous
manifestation of His glory, He has (always) granted it to
some of the earth-born to gain admittance[8] to the Congregation of the Holy, to be reckoned among the community
of angelic beings who are with Him, to have station there
for life everlasting and to be in one lot with His (celestial)
Holy Ones.[9] A[ll men are punished(?) or mar]ked out for
distinction[10] according to the lot which [𝕲𝖔𝖉] has assigned to each, [some for eternal shame and contempt, and
some] for life everlasting.[11]

(iii)

*(The ensuing fragment begins with a reference
to the promise to Abraham that his offspring
would inherit 'the land of his sojournings' [Gen.
17.8]—evidently regarded as another instance of
the intervention of angels. The promise appears
to be interpreted allegorically, possibly as a reference to '[Mount Zi]on, where God dwells',[11]
but the text is too imperfect for confident restoration:)*

.   .   .   .

[CLARIFICATION OF (THE INCIDENT CONCERNING)] THE
THREE MEN [WHO] APPEAR[ED] TO [ABRAH]AM BESIDE THE
OAKS OF MAMRE:

They were angels. [As regards the (subsequent) statement: 'Because the out]cry from Sodom and Gomorrah
is gr[eat] and because their sin is very grave, I will go
down to see whether they have been doing as the outcry
which has reached [Me] from them suggests, and if not,
I will know' [Gen. 18.20–21], the clarification of the matter is that it refers to (human) flesh, the evil of which
is indeed great, and to all who [   ], and to every
[mouth] that utters [infamy]. And as to the statement, '(I
will go down) to *see*', this means that I will see that everything [is in accord with what has been duly pre-
scribed(?)].[12] Before He created them, He knew [their]
designs.

(iv)

*(A further fragment, likewise little more than a
sorry scrap, refers to a place 'two days' journey
away.' This evidently refers to the incident on
Mount Moriah, for Scripture says explicitly [Gen.
22.4] that 'on the third day (after he had set
out) Abraham lifted up his eyes and saw the
place afar off'. The mountain appears to be identified figuratively with Zion.*

This is followed in turn by an allusion to 'what Scripture says about Pharaoh'. *Since both incidents are cited in proof of the contention that events are controlled by angels, and since the* Memoirs of the Patriarchs *say clearly that a 'spirit' afflicted Pharaoh when he molested Sarai, it is plain that this is the incident to which the text refers. Moreover, this would chime neatly with the preceding statement about the diseases of the flesh which are visited on the reprobate.)*

NOTES

1. Heb. *pesher,* the technical term used in the Qumran commentaries on Scripture.
2. For this notion, cp. *HI* 24; *War,* xii,3; Enoch, 81.1–2; 103.2; 106.19; 107.1; 108.7. See T. H. Gaster, *Thespis*[2] (1961), pp. 288f.
3. Cp. Enoch, ch. 10; 21.7–10; 67.7.
4. Restored after Enoch, 10.4ff.
5. Milik restores this entire sentence to refer to Azazel and renders: '[making them forget] the commandments and the commandment concerning the mystery of [their] (law of) impurity'. But (*a*) the restoration, 'forget', introduced an unparalleled form of the Hebrew verb; (*b*) the word *mishpaṭîm,* which he renders 'commandments', is usually employed in the Qumran texts in the sense of 'judgments, punishments' (cp. *Hymns* iii.24; iv.26; v.4, 8; vi.29; ix.29; *War,* iv,6; vi,5), 'commandments' being expressed by *miṣwôth,* and it is precisely this condign punishment that is the *raison d'être* for the author's mentioning the incident; (*c*) the words *sôd nidda[tham],* rendered 'the mystery of (their law) of impurity', more naturally mean 'their associates/company in filth', for cp. an analogous expression in *HI* 22. Cp. also Enoch, 10.11.
6. Milik, reading *'elleh niflā'ê madda'[ô]*, renders, 'these are the marvels of [His] knowledge'. This, however, would require *pᵉla'ê,* not *nifla'ê.* I therefore restore: *'elleh niflᵉ'û mi-da'[tham].* There may even be a subtle point in the choice of the verb. The Scriptural text (Gen. 6.4) associates the fall of the angels with the presence on earth of certain beings termed Nephilim.

Although the name was usually explained from the root *n-ph-l*, 'fall', in the sense of 'fallen angels', there was an alternative interpretation which derived it from *p-l-'*, 'be extraordinary'; cp. *Aggadath Bᵉreshîth*, Introd., §39; L. Ginzberg, *Legends of the Jews*, vol. v, p. 154. Hence, what our author may have had in mind was that, just as the rebels were distinguished for their impiety, so are the pure for their knowledge of God.

7. 1, lines 1–2. In line 1 I restore tentatively, *sôd 'er[wah]*, after *HI* 22.

8. Heb. *higgîsh*. This is a technical term for admission to the Qumran Brotherhood; cp. *Manual*, vi.19; *Hymns* xii.23; xiv.13, 18; xvi.12.

9. For the terms here used for the angelic hosts, see Analytical Index, F. 1 (*a, b*). For the general notion, see Analytical Index, A. 12.

10. Restoring, *[nif]lᵉ'û;* see above, n. 6.

11. Tentatively restored after Dan. 12.2.

12. This follows Milik's restoration.

APPENDIX

The Copper Scroll
The 'Prayer of Nabonidus'

APPENDIX

While the major Scrolls—apart from such as may still be in the hands of the Bedouin—have now been made available, there are still thousands of fragments from the Dead Sea caves which await publication.* The small band of devoted scholars who have been working on the documents in Jordan deserve all of our admiration for the skill and patience with which, over the years, they have endeavored to piece together these sorry scraps, and for their unremitting perseverance in the face of difficulties, political and other. At the same time, it is perhaps permissible to say that the extremely slow rate at which the documents are being made available and the tendency to publish 'snippets' and excerpts in piecemeal fashion, together place a severe strain on the patience of their colleagues in many lands. It is perhaps permissible also to suggest that the interests of scholarship might be better served at this juncture if these scholars were to conceive of their charge as that of sorting, assembling and classifying the documents and then promptly publishing grouped photographs of them rather than of providing full-fledged first editions. Meanwhile, even among the documents which *have* been published

* A long, but incomplete, scroll presents, in the form of direct instructions by God, rules concerning clean and unclean, festivals, the structure and service of the Temple, and the role of the king. A preliminary description has been published by Yigal Yadin in *The Biblical Archaeologist*, 36 (1967), 135–39, but his edition of the text was not yet available at the time this book went to press. It is my hunch that the scroll may turn out to be a copy of the comprehensive *Book of Study* [Hgû] mentioned in the 'Zadokite' *Document* (x.6; xiii.2) and in the *Manual of Discipline for the Future Congregation of Israel* (i.7).

there are two which, though of considerable interest, do not yet admit of reliable translation, either because no photographs have been published, or else because they are too fragmentary. For the sake of completeness, these are summarized in the following pages.

THE COPPER SCROLL

In 1952 there was discovered in Cave III at Qumran three tightly rolled sheets of copper, engraved with writing. Unfortunately, the copper had become so seriously corroded that unrolling proved impossible. Eventually, however, by a remarkable feat of resourcefulness and skill, Professor H. Wright Baker, of the College of Technology at Manchester, England, succeeded in cutting the sheets into strips, so that the inscription could be read. It then became apparent that the three sheets belonged to a single document, prepared in the manner of a leather scroll, with rivets doing duty for sutures.

The document has turned out to be a register of buried treasure, purportedly hidden in various spots in and near Jerusalem and in an area extending from Hebron to Mount Gerizim and including the Valley of Qumran. No less than sixty-four deposits are listed, and in each case minute details are given of location and depth. The objects in question include: a silver chest, ingots of gold and silver, jars of all shapes and sizes, bowls, perfumes and—if the decipherment be correct—even vestments. In each case, the amount and value of the objects are explicitly recorded, and sometimes the entry is followed by a curious and enigmatic notation in *Greek* characters. It has been calculated that, by Old Testament standards, the total value of the treasure would have amounted to some 138 tons of precious metal!

The purpose of the Scroll remains a puzzle. There are three main theories. The first is that it is a record of the Qumran community's possessions which were cached in various places just before the Romans advanced upon their 'monastery' in 68 A.D. Against this, however, it has been objected that the amount of the treasure listed is prodigiously disproportionate to the probable resources of an ascetic brotherhood!

The second theory is that the treasure is that of the Second Temple, committed for safekeeping to the desert community when the sacred edifice fell, or was about to fall, to the Roman forces. But this too is not without its difficulties. According to Josephus, (*War*, vi.5, §2) the main treasure of the Temple was still in the building when it fell, and this happened in 70 A.D., whereas, according to the archaeological evidence, the Qumran monastery had already been abandoned two years earlier. Moreover, if the censorious references to the Jerusalemitan priesthood which we find in the Scrolls really represent a contemporary attitude, it is not very likely that those officials would have turned to the Qumran brotherhood for the safekeeping of their sacred vessels!

A third hypothesis is that the Scroll registers the treasure not of the Second but of the First (Solomonic) Temple, removed from Jerusalem when it fell to Nebuchadnezzar in 586 B.C. Opinion is divided, however, as to whether the list is factual or fictitious, seeing that accounts of somewhat similar character indeed appear in later Jewish legend.

Perhaps there is room for a fourth theory. May not the Scroll represent an unconscionable fraud (or even a cruel practical joke) perpetrated by some cynical outsider upon the naive and innocent minds of the ascetics of Qumran? The fraud (or joke) would have been founded upon time-honored legends about the buried treasure of the First Temple and have been calculated especially to appeal to the hearts and minds of men who were looking to an imminent restoration of the past glories of Israel. In support of this theory two significant points may be mentioned:

(*a*) In a Jewish legend concerning the concealment of the sacred vessels at various places in Babylonia,* it is stated expressly that a certain Shimmur the Levite and his

---

* *Masseketh Kelîm*, reprinted in J. D. Eisenstein's *Oṣar Midrashîm* (1915), pp. 260ff.

colleagues, who were responsible for the operation, 'listed on a copper tablet the vessels of the First Temple which were in Jerusalem or in any other holy place'. Fictitious as this account may be, it yet establishes what the popular tradition was, and it is that tradition that a pretender (or practical joker) would have had to follow.

(b) Josephus tells us (*Ant.*, XVIII.4, §§1–2) that during the administration of Pontius Pilate (26–36 A.D.), someone did indeed perpetrate such a hoax on the Samaritans, whose independent temple on Mount Gerizim had been razed by John Hyrcanus in 128 B.C. Samaritan legend said likewise that the sacred vessels had then been cached against the day when the promised Restorer would arise and mend their fortunes.† The hoaxer professed to be that deliverer, and rallied a large crowd of the credulous under promise of revealing where the buried treasure lay. Surely it is not farfetched to imagine that such a pretender may have made the rounds of credulous communities, armed, by way of 'credentials', with a document comprehensively listing hidden troves within their respective vicinities. Such a comprehensive document, covering 'at one swoop' the diverse enclaves of the faithful, and inscribed—in accordance with tradition—on copper, may well be what we have before us in our mysterious Scroll.

That the document was intended to be taken seriously and not simply as a piece of fiction is obvious from two considerations. First, it is incredible that anyone would have taken the trouble to punch out the text on copper if he had desired merely to tell a tale. Moreover, the document says distinctly that another copy was buried elsewhere in the country, and this shows clearly that it purported to be a genuine list. Second—and this point seems strangely to have been overlooked—the curious notations in Greek characters are inexplicable on the assumption that the whole document was just a product of storytelling romance. Patently, they were some kind of identification mark, and

† See: T. Juynboll, ed., *Chronicon Samaritanum cui titulus est Liber Josuae* (1843), pp. 303–4; M. Gaster, *Samaritan Eschatology* (1932), pp. 251, 271.

the only reason for introducing them could have been either that the document was indeed a genuine list of treasure, the ownership of each deposit being clearly indicated against future recovery, or that this was an extra touch designed to lend verisimilitude to a fraud.

Two transcriptions of the Copper Scroll have thus far been published, by J. T. Milik‡ and John Allegro§ respectively. But they differ so radically in almost every line that we must simply await photographs before any translation can be safely attempted.

‡ *Revue Biblique*, 66 (1959), 321–57; 550–75. Revised in *Discoveries in the Judaean Desert*, III (1963).

§ J. M. Allegro, *The Treasure of the Copper Scroll*. London–New York, 1960.

THE 'PRAYER OF NABONIDUS'

The collection of Scroll fragments in the possession of the Government of Jordan has yielded three small scraps of a legendary narrative, written in Aramaic, relating how Nabonidus (called N-b-n-y), the last king of the Neo-Babylonian empire (556–39 B.C.), while residing at Teima, was afflicted with a grievous disease by the God of Israel. A Jewish adviser counselled him to 'render honor . . . to the name of God Most High' and admonished him that 'Thou hast been smitten with this noisome fever . . . for seven years because thou hast been praying to gods of silver and gold, which gods are but stock and stone, mere clay' . . . The fragments, published with remarkable skill by J. T. Milik,* are, unfortunately, in too sorry a condition for much to be made of them.

* Revue Biblique, 63 (1956), 407ff.

SOURCES

THE SERVICE OF GOD

1. THE MANUAL OF DISCIPLINE

Cross, F. M., et al., *Scrolls from Qumran Cave I*. American Schools of Oriental Research and Shrine of the Book, 1972.

Licht, J., *Megillath ha-Serachim*. Jerusalem, 1965.

2. THE 'ZADOKITE' DOCUMENT

Zeitlin, S., ed., *The Zadokite Fragments*. (Jewish Quarterly Review Monograph Series, no. 1.) Philadelphia: The Dropsie College, 1952. (Photographs of the Cairo Genizah manuscripts.)

Rost, L., ed., *Die Damaskusschrift*. (*Kleine Texte für Vorlesungen und Übungen*, ed. H. Lietzmann, No. 167.) Berlin, 1933.

Rabin, Ch., ed., *The 'Zadokite' Documents*.[2] Oxford, 1954.

3. THE LETTER OF THE LAW: ORDINANCES

Allegro, J., ed., *Discoveries in the Judaean Desert*, V. Oxford, 1968; no. 157, pp. 6–7, plate ii.

4. A FORMULARY OF BLESSINGS

Barthélemy, D., and Milik, J. T., eds., *Discoveries in the Judaean Desert*, I. Oxford, 1955; no. 28*b*, pp. 118–29, plates xxv–xxix.

THE PRAISE OF GOD

5. THE HYMN OF THE INITIANTS

Manual of Discipline, cols. x–xi.

6. THE BOOK OF HYMNS

Sukenik, E. L., ed., *The Dead Sea Scrolls of the Hebrew University*. Jerusalem, 1955; plates xxv–lvii.

Licht, J., ed., *Megillath ha-Hodayoth*. Jerusalem, 1957.

POEMS FROM A QUMRAN HYMNAL

7. DAVID: PSALM 151

Sanders, J. A., ed., *DSD* IV (1965), pp. 54–64, plate xvii.

8. INVITATION

ibid., pp. 64–70, plate xii.

9. PLEA FOR GRACE

ibid., pp. 70–76, plate xv.

10. SUPPLICATION

ibid., col. xix, pp. 76–79, plate xii.

11. THE CITY OF GOD

ibid., col. xvii, pp. 85–89, plate xiv.

12. MORNING HYMN

ibid., pp. 80–91, plate xvi.

13. LAMENT FOR ZION

Allegro, *op. cit.*, no. 179; pp. 75–77, plate xxvi.

14. HYMNS OF TRIUMPH

J. Starcky, in *Revue Biblique* 73 (1966), 356–57.

THE MERCY OF GOD

15. PRAYER FOR INTERCESSION

Baillet, M., in *Revue Biblique* 69 (1961), 195–250.

GLORY TO GOD IN THE HIGHEST

16. THE LITANY OF THE ANGELS

(a) Strugnell, J., in *Vetus Testamentum*, Suppl. 7 (1960), 336ff.

(b) *ibid.*, 318ff.

THE WORD OF GOD

I. Expositions of Scripture

17. ISAIAH

(a) 5.5-6, 11-14, 24-25, 29-30
DJD V, no. 162, cols. i-iii; plate vi.
(b) 6.9
ibid., col. iii.
(c) 10.12-13, 20-24
ibid., no. 163, col. ii; plates vii-viii.
(d) 10.21-22, 24-27, 28-32
ibid., no. 161, frags. 1-6; plates iv-v.
(e) 14.8, 26-30
ibid., no. 163, frags. 8-10; plate viii.
(f) 30.15-18
ibid., frag. 23, col. ii; plate viii.
(g) 52.1-3
ibid., no. 176, frags. 8-11; plates xxii-xxiii.
(h) 54.11-12
ibid., no. 164, frag. 1; plate ix.

18. HOSEA

ibid., nos. 166-67, plate x.

19. MICAH

DJD I, plate xv, lines 8-19.

20. NAHUM

DJD V, no. 169, plates xi, xiv.

21. HABAKKUK

Cross et al., *op. cit.*
Habermann, A. H., *'Edah we-'Edûth.* Jerusalem, 1958; pp. 39-56.

22. PSALM 37

DJD V, no. 171, plates xiv, xvii.

23. PSALM 45

ibid., no. 170, iii.23-27; plate xvii, 5, 10.

II. Everyman's Bible

24. MEMOIRS OF THE PATRIARCHS

Avigad, N., and Yadin, Y., eds., *A Genesis Apocryphon.* Jerusalem, 1956.

Fitzmyer, J. A., *The Genesis Apocryphon of Qumran Cave 1.*[2] Rome, 1971.

25. THE ORATION OF MOSES

DJD I, no. 22, plates xviii–xix.

THE TRIUMPH OF GOD

26. THE WAR OF THE SONS OF LIGHT AND THE SONS OF DARKNESS

Sukenik, *op. cit.,* plates xvi–xxiv.

Yadin, Y., *Milḥamath Benê 'Or bi-benê Ḥoshech.* Jerusalem, 1957.

27. THE ROUT OF BELIAL [CATENA]

DJD V, no. 177, frags. 1–14, plates xxiv–xxv.

28. THE COMING DOOM

DJD I, no. 27, col. i, plates cii–cv.

29. WEAL AND WOE: AN EXHORTATION

DJD V, no. 185, plates xxix–xxx.

30. THE LAST JUBILEE: A SERMON. [MELCHIZEDEK]

Milik, J. T., in *Journal of Jewish Studies* 23 (1972), 96–126.

Van der Woude, A., in *New Testament Studies* 12 (1966), 301–26.

Fitzmyer, J. A., in *Journal of Biblical Literature* 86 (1967), 23–41.

Carmignac, J., in *Revue de Qumran* 27 (1971), 343–78.

Sanders, J. A., in *The Gaster Festschrift* (New York, 1973), pp. 373–82.

31. THE NEW COVENANT

DJD I, no. 34, ii.

32. MANUAL OF DISCIPLINE FOR THE FUTURE CONGREGATION OF ISRAEL

ibid., no. 28a, plates xxii–xxiv.

'THY KINGDOM COME':

33. THE MESSIANIC KING

Allegro, J., in *Journal of Biblical Literature* 75 (1956), 174–76.

34. TESTIMONIA: PROOF-TEXTS OF THE MESSIANIC ERA

DJD V, no. 175, plate xxi.

35. A 'MESSIANIC' FLORILEGIUM

ibid., no. 174, plates xiv–xx.

36. THE WONDROUS CHILD

Starcky, J., in *Mémorial du cinquantenaire de l'École des langues orientales anciennes de l'Institut Catholique de Paris* (1964), 51–66.

Carmignac, J., in *Revue Biblique* 18 (1965), 199–217.

Fitzmyer, J. A., in *The Catholic Biblical Quarterly* 27 (1965), 348–72 (reprinted in his *Essays on the Semitic Background of the New Testament* [1974], pp. 127–60).

VIRTUE

37. THE WOOING OF WISDOM [Sirach 51.13ff.]

Sanders, J. A., ed., *The Dead Sea Psalms Scroll* [*DJD* IV], cols. xxi, 11–17; xxii, 1; plates xiii–xiv.

[For a convenient text of the paraphrase from the Cairo Genizah, see H. L. Strack, ed., *Die Sprüche Jesus' des Sohnes Sirachs* (Leipzig, 1903), pp. 56–57.]

VICE

38. THE WILES OF THE HARLOT

DJD V, no. 184, plate xxviii.

VISIONS AND TESTAMENTS

39. THE LAST WORDS OF AMRAM

Milik, J. T., in *Revue Biblique* 79 (1972), 76–97.

DESTINY

40. THE EPOCHS OF TIME
   DJD V, nos. 180–81.
   Milik, J. T., in *Journal of Jewish Studies* 23 (1972), 109–26.

ANALYTICAL INDEX

This index consists of a list of the major themes and concepts which appear in *The Dead Sea Scriptures*. They are arranged in the following categories:

A. THE COMMUNITY
B. GOVERNMENT OF THE COMMUNITY
C. LAWS AND PRACTICES
D. OPPONENTS OF THE BROTHERHOOD
E. THE LAST THINGS (Eschatological Doctrines)
F. ANGELOLOGY

Within each category the reader will find listed the topics relevant to it and where references to these topics occur in the scrolls themselves and elsewhere in ancient literature. The abbreviations used are as follows. These same abbreviations are used as well in the following index entitled BIBLICAL QUOTA-TIONS AND PARALLELS.

AL	The Litany of the Angels
Am	The Last Words of Amram
Blessings	A Formulary of Blessings
C	The City of God
CD	The Coming Doom
D	David (Psalm 151)
ET	Epochs of Time
Ex	[Exhortation.] Weal and Woe
F	A 'Messianic' Florilegium
H	The Book of Hymns
HabC	The Commentary on Habakkuk
Hfr.	Fragments from the Book of Hymns
HI	The Hymn of the Initiants (=Manual, x–xi)
HosC	The Commentary on Hosea
HT	Hymns of Triumph
Inv.	Invitation to Grace After Meals
IsaC	The Commentary on Isaiah

L	Lamentation for Zion
LJ	The Last Jubilee [The 'Melchizedek Texts']
M	The Manual of Discipline
MFC	Manual of Discipline for the Future Congregation of Israel
MH	Morning Hymn
MiC	The Commentary on Micah
MP	Memoirs of the Patriarchs
NC	The New Covenant
O	[Ordinances.] The Letter of the Law
Oration	The Oration of Moses
PG	Plea for Grace
PI	Prayer for Intercession
Ps 37C	The Commentary on Psalm 37
Ps 45C	The Commentary on Psalm 45
RB	The Rout of Belial
Sp	Supplication
W	The War of the Sons of Light and the Sons of Darkness
WC	The Wondrous Child
WH	The Wiles of the Harlot
WW	The Wooing of Wisdom (Sirach 51.13ff.)
Z	The 'Zadokite' Document

A. THE COMMUNITY

1. *The Community as a whole is called 'the Congregation',
i.e., of Israel, of God (cf. Num. 27.12; 31.16, etc.)*

M v.20; Z ix.15, 42; xi.1–2; xv.7; xvii.7; W ii.1, 3, 7; iii.4,
11, etc.

The Heb. term is *'edah*. This is usually rendered 'synagogue'
by the Septuagint. The cognate Syriac word was the technical
term for 'the Church'; see Nestle, ZNTW, 1901: 263.

2. *The Community is distributed over several 'encampments'.*

Z vii.6; xii.22; xiii.4, 7, 13, 20; xiv. 3, 8–9; xix.2–3

As applied to the brotherhood at Qumran, the term not only
described their actual situation in the Desert of Judah, but also
defined them as the 'army of God' about to fight the apocalyptic
war against the forces of evil.

The building at Qumran is best regarded as the headquarters of the entire Brotherhood, possibly the place where it met for those annual conventions described in *The Manual of Discipline*. Its library would thus have comprised the literature of the entire movement, and not simply of a local 'chapter'.

3. *The several 'chapters' are called 'communes' or 'cenobies'* (*Heb.* yaḥad).

M i.12, 16; ii.22, 24; vi.15, 24, 26; vii.6, 17, 18, 20, 23; viii.10, 11, 12, 16–17, 19, 22; ix.2, 5–6, 7, 10, 18–19; Z ix.39–40, 52–53, 70–71.

R. Marcus has pointed out (JBL 71 [1952], 207ff.) that Philo and Josephus use the comparable Greek term *koinonia* in speaking of the Essenes.

4. *Another term is 'the corporation'* (*Heb.* ḥibbur).

Z xii.8

Such corporations (Heb. *haburôth*) of Pharisees are often mentioned in Talmudic literature.

5. *The Community constitute 'the Elect'.*

M viii.6 ('elect of favor'); H ii.13 ('elect of righteousness')

The title expressed the fact that they were indeed the 'chosen' of God, pledged to the Covenant (cp. Isa. 65.9; Ps. 105.43, etc.). The title was adopted also by the early Christians: Mat. 24.22, 24; Mark 13.20, 22, 27; II Tim. 2.10; I Peter 1.1. Cp. also 'the elect of God', Luke 18.7; Rom. 8.33; Col. 3.12; Titus 1.1.

The Mandaeans likewise call themselves 'the Elect': Lidzbarski, *Mandäische Liturgien*, 75, 106f.; id., *Johannesbuch*, ii, 69, 102, 221. So, too, among the Manichaeans, the true followers of Mani are termed 'the Elect' (*vičidagan*).

6. *They are 'those in the lot (portion) of God'.*

M ii.2; W i.5; xiii.5; xvii.7

Cp. Ignatius, *Ad Eph.*, 3.8: 'that I may be found in the lot of the Christians at Ephesus'.

The opposite was 'those in the lot (portion) of Belial'.

7. *They enjoy special 'illumination' and are designated 'Sons of Light'.*

M i.9; iii.13, 24; W i.3, etc.; Z xiii.12 ('the portion of light'),
LJ 8; RB i–iv.8; xii–xiii.7, 11.

The title was adopted also by the early Christians: Luke 16.8;
John 12.36; I Thess. 5.5. Cp. also Enoch 108.11.

Among the Mandaeans, 'sons of light' meant 'angels', with
whom, indeed, the *illuminati* claimed association: Lidzbarski,
Mand. Lit., 18.24, 36. Cp. also Montgomery, *Aram. Incantation
Texts from Nippur* (1913), i.9. Men predestined to eternal life
were called likewise: Brandt, *Mand. Schriften*, 13.9.

'Light' is a common designation of the Torah in Biblical and
later literature: cp. Pss. 19.9; 119.105; Prov. 6.23; Test. Levi
19; TB Berachoth 17a; Ex. Rabbah §36, etc.

   (a) *The illumination is an 'enlightenment of the countenance'*

    H iii.3; iv.5, 27; ix.26–27; Blessings iv.27

Cp. Odes of Solomon 41.6, 'Let our faces shine in His light'.
(cp. also *ib.*, 36.3)

   (b) *It is called 'Light-Perfection'* (*Heb.* Ôr-Tôm).

    H iv.6, 23; xviii.29

An imitation of the Biblical Urim and Thummim, interpreted
as 'lights and perfections'.

The idea may have originated with the Assidaeans (*Hasidim,*
'pious ones') of the Maccabean age, and have been based
on Deut. 33.8–9.

On the concept of divine illumination, cp. John 1.19; Eph. 1.18;
3.9; Heb. 6.4; 10.22; II Cor. 3.4, 6.

For the idea in mysticism, cp. Jacopone da Todi, *Lauda* xci:
'Lume fuor di mesura Resplende nel mio core' (A light immeas-
urable Shines in my heart); see Underhill, *Mysticism*, 249–50.

  8. *Members of the Community are 'Sons of Truth'.*

    M iv.5–6; H vi.29; vii.30; ix.35; x.27; xi.11; W vii.8

  8a. *It is described as 'the House of Truth'.*

    M v.6; viii.9

  9. *Forms of Revelation:*
   (a) *The Community is the recipient of God's 'truth'.*

    H i.27; ii.10; v.9, 26; vii.24; ix.4, 9, 10; W xiii.9–10, 12

In Jewish tradition, this 'truth' is often identified directly with the Torah (Law). So, too, in Mandaean thought, 'truth' (Kushta) is, virtually, mystic revelation; see W. Sundberg, *Kushta* (1953). In Samaritan, 'the Verity' (Qushtah) is a common term for the Law.

See also: Rom. 15.8; Gal. 2.5.

(b) *this 'truth' is an esoteric doctrine.*

H v.11, 25; ix.24; cp. M iv.6

Cp. Odes of Solomon 8.11: 'Keep My secret, ye who are kept by it'.

For a similar concept among the Mandaeans, cp. *Right Ginza*, iii.13; Brandt, *Mand. Religion*, 168.

(c) *God has 'opened the ears' of the faithful.*

H i.21; vi.4

(d) *God has engraved the 'truth' on their hearts.*

H xviii.27

(e) *they are especially 'schooled' by God.*

H ii.39; vii.14

Derived from Isa. 54.13. Cp. John 6.45; I Thess. 4.9.

(f) *they possess the 'vision' of knowledge (or understanding).*

H iv.18

On vision in mystic experience, see Underhill, *op. cit.*, 279ff.

(g) *they drank from the fountain of knowledge.*

H ii.18; iv.11; v.26; 'fount of light', H vi.17

Derived from Ps. 36.10. Cp. Odes of Solomon 6.7f.; 30.1–2; II Baruch 59.7; IV Ezra 14.47; Enoch 48.1. St. Francis of Assisi gives the mystic chalice to John of Parma and other brethren: *Fioretti*, cap. 48. Mechthild of Magdeburg speaks of 'drinking for a space of the unmingled wine': *Flieszende Licht der Gottheit*, pt. i, ch. 43. Blake declares, 'I am drunk with intellectual vision': *Letters*, ed. Brussel (1906), 171. See Underhill, *op. cit.*, 235.

(h) *they share the transcendental knowledge of God and angels.*

M iv.22 ('knowledge of the Most High'); cp. H ii.3

Cp. Odes of Solomon 23.4: 'Walk ye in the knowledge of the Most High'.

(i) *they have direct access to God, need no intermediary.*

H vi.13

(k) *they ascend to the 'height of eternity'.*

H iii.20; Blessings v.23

Cp. the familiar mystic symbol of the 'ascent'; W. R. Inge, *Mysticism in Religion* (1948), 80–82.

(l) *God's 'power' is manifested in them (Heb.* higbir).

H i.34; ii.24; iv.8, 23, 27, 28; v.15; W xvi.1

'Power' (Heb. *geburah*) is a common synonym for God in Rabbinic literature.

10. *The members of the Community are styled 'volunteers'* (*Heb.* mithnadebim).

M v.1, 6, 8, 10, 21, 22; vi.13; MiC x.5

The term has a military connotation (cp. Ju. 5.9) and thus suggests the idea of an 'army of God'—the 'Onward, Christian soldiers' concept.
Cp. I Macc. 2.42 (of the Hasidim); *Didascalia Apostolorum*, init.
In the mystery religions, the brotherhood of the initiants often regarded itself as a militia: F. Cumont, *Oriental Religions in Roman Paganism* (1911), 213, n. 6.

11. *The Community is called 'God's (eternal) plantation'.*

H vi.15; viii.6, 10

Based on Isa. 60.21. Cp. Mishnah, Sanhedrin 1; *Psalms of Solomon*, 14.3–4; Enoch 93.2, 5, 10; Odes of Solomon 38.18–21. Mandaean: *Right Ginza*, II.iv. init.; *Mand. Liturg.*, 149.190, 179ff., *Apostolic Constitutions*, init. Analogous is 'neophyte' (KJV 'novice'; RSV 'recent convert') in I Tim. 3.6.

12. *The Community forms one congregation with the celestial hosts ('communion of the saints').*

M ii.25; xi.7–8; H iii.21; vi.14; xi.11–12; frag. ii.10

Cp. Enoch 43.104; Eph. 2.19.

13. *Its members are driven from their native haunts.*

H iv.8–9 ('like a sparrow from its nest')

Cp. *Psalms of Solomon* 17.15–16.

For an Iranian parallel, cp. Yasna 46.1: 'From nobles and from my peers they sever me, nor are the people pleased with me, nor the rulers of the land who follow the lie (Druj)'.

14. *They are dwelling in a desert, or in 'the land of Damascus'.*

Z vi.15, 19; vii.19; viii.21a; xx.12; W i.2–3

Based on Amos 5.25–27; not to be taken literally. It is not necessary to suppose that there was an actual migration from Qumran to Damascus, because this entire text may refer to an *ideal* community, rather than to the specific brotherhood beside the Dead Sea!

Like all mystics, the Covenanters oscillate between a keen sense of God's nearness and a despair at His seeming remoteness. Cp. John of the Cross, *The Dark Night of the Soul*, I ii, ch. 6: 'That which this anguished soul feels most deeply is the conviction that God has abandoned it . . . cast it away into darkness . . . It has also the same sense of abandonment with respect to all creatures, and that it is an object of contempt to all, especially to its friends' (cp. H v.25f.).

15. *They are being tested and proven.*

M viii.4; H v.16f.; W xvii.1, 9; Ps 37C, b4; F ii.1

They are exposed to 'snares of wickedness', H v.8; to 'snares of corruption', H iii.26.

Cp. Underhill, *op. cit.*, 385: 'Trials, taken *en bloc*, mean a disharmony between the self and the world with which it has to deal'.

B. GOVERNMENT OF THE COMMUNITY

1. *The formal Deliberative Council (Heb. 'eṣah).*

M i.8, 10; ii.25; v.7; vi.12; vii.22; viii.5, 22; Z xx.24; MFC i.26, 27; ii.2, 9, 11

In the Syriac dialect of the early Christians of Palestine, the cognate term serves as the equivalent of Greek *synhedrion;* cp. F. Schwally, *Idioticon* (1893), 41f. A. Dupont-Sommer (*The Jewish Sect of Qumran and the Essenes*, 63) thinks that '*eṣah* denoted the sect as a whole and that it may be the origin of the name Essenes!

2. *Officers:*
(a) *'Leader (Prince) of the Entire Congregation'.*

  Z viii.7, 20; Blessings; MFC; W v.1

Cp. I Macc. 14.27 (of Simon). Yadin thinks this is the equivalent of the term *ethnarch*.
(b) *'Overseer of All the Camps'.*

  Z xiv.8–9

Virtually, 'archbishop'—albeit in a primitive sense.
The 'leader of the entire congregation' and 'the overseer of all the camps' would have been officers of the entire fraternity.
(c) *high priest*
It is noteworthy that the high priest is mentioned only in texts concerned with the eventual state of the Restored Community, e.g., in the *War of the Sons of Light and the Sons of Darkness* and in *The Manual of Discipline for the Future Congregation.* This would suggest that the Brotherhood, while it condemned the venality of the hierarchy at Jerusalem, did not appoint its own 'antipope'. In Z xiv.7 there is, to be sure, mention of a 'priest who supervises the general membership', but this is not a high priest in the accepted sense, and it is significant that in M vi.14 the same officer is described simply as 'the supervisor' without reference to priestly status.
(d) *priests*

  M i.18, 21; ii.1, 19; v.2; vi.3–4, 5, 8, 19; vii.2; viii.1; Z iii.21; iv.2; vii.1; ix.13, 15; xiii.2, 5, 7; xiv.3; xvi.44; W *passim*

(e) *priests are called 'sons of Zadok'*

  M v.2; ix.14; Z iv.1; Blessings iii.22, etc.

It is not the community as a whole but solely its priests that are described in the Scrolls as 'sons of Zadok'. It derives directly from Ezek. 40.46; 43.19; 44.15; 48.11, and there is no need to look for a 'righteous teacher' named Zadok as the 'founding father' of the Brotherhood of Qumran in the days of the Second Commonwealth.
(f) *courses of priests*

  W ii.4

(g) *'the priest anointed for war'*

  W xv.16

Cp. Mishnah, Soṭah VIII, 2.

(h) *the 'teacher of righteousness'* (*Heb.* môreh zedeq).

Z i.11; vi.11; xx.1, 28, 32; MC ii.5 (on 1.5); Comm. on Ps. 37.24; HC i.13 (on 1.4); ii.2 (on 1.4–5); v.10 (on 1.13); vii.4 (on 2.2); viii.3 (on 2.4); ix.10 (on 2.8); xi.5 (on 2.15); Ps 45C, 5.

The term means really 'the right guide', i.e., the true expounder of the Law; see General Introduction, pp. 6, 29f.

There is no need to assume that all references refer consistently to a single historical figure.

The title was later adopted by the Karaites.

In Jewish usage, it is a common designation for a rabbi. Indeed, it is related that when Isaac Bernays was appointed to the chief rabbinate of Hamburg in 1821, he expressly rejected the title as having fallen into disrepute through repeated misuse!

(i) *teacher acts as 'father' to the brethren*

Z xiii.9; H vii.20

Cp. *Apostolic Constitutions* ii.6, 7.

(k) *three priests at head of community*

M viii.1ff.

Modelled on the organization of Israel in the wilderness; cp. General Introduction, p. 11.

(l) *presbyters; the 'twelve perfect men'*

M viii.1; Z [vii.5]; xx.25, 7

Modelled on the twelve tribal leaders during Israel's sojourn in the wilderness.

Cp. the Mandaean *shalmana*, Brandt, *Mand. Religion*, 74; *Right Ginza*, 3, etc. (*Teleios* in pagan mystery cults probably had a different meaning; see O. Gruppe, *Griech. Mythologie*, 1616, n. 1.)

Note also that among the Waldenses, advanced members of the brotherhood were called 'the perfect'.

(m) *judges*

Z x.1, 4; xiv.13; xv.4, 16; xvi.19

Ten in number (Z x.4). Hence, cp. the courts of ten in Temple law: Mishnah, Sanhedrin I, 3.

(n) *levites*

M i.19, 22; ii.4, 11; Z iii.21; iv.3; x.5; xiii.3; xiv.4; W *passim*

(o) *'messiahs'* (*anointed*)

M ix.11; Z vii.21a; xii.23; xiii.20; xiv.19; MFC

The usual expression is 'messiahs (or, messiah) of Aaron and Israel'. This has led to all kinds of wild speculation. But all it means is simply 'the anointed high priest and the anointed king'. (For 'messiah' as applied to the high priest, cp. Lev. 4.3; Mishnah, Shebu'oth i.7; Horayoth ii.1, etc. As the title of the king, cp. Ps. 18.51, etc.).

(p) *'overseer, inspector'*

M vi.19–20; Z ix.18, 22; xiii.16, 17; xiv.11, 13; xv.14

Such 'overseers' served as executives of religious brotherhoods in Hellenistic times: cp. Inscr. Agora 63 IG, ii², 917 (181 B.C.); J. H. Oliver, in *Amer. Journal of Philology* 68 (1947), 148. Josephus mentions a similar officer among the Essenes.

(q) *'overseer of the camp'*

Z xiii.7, 13

(r) *'overseer of the general membership* (lit. *the many*)'

M vi.12; Z xv.8

(s) *'inspector'* (*Heb.* paqid)

Z xiii.11; xiv.6

It is not quite clear whether the 'overseer' (*mebaqqer*) or the 'inspector' (*paqid*) more closely answers to the *episkopos* or 'bishop' of the early Church, for the Septuagint uses the Greek term to translate both of the Hebrew words.

For *episkopoi* in the mystery cults, see A. Thieme, *Inschriften*, 17f., 32f.

(t) *'interpreter'*

H ii.13; H fr.ii.6.

Cp. I Cor. 14.28.

(u) *'expositor'* (*Heb.* doresh)

M vi.6; Z vi.7; vii.18; F i.11

Cp. Mishnah, Yomâ i.6; Josephus, *BJ* II, viii.6, 19; *Ant.*, XIII, v.9, on 'expositors' among the Essenes.

(v) *'instructor'* (*Heb.* maskîl)

M iii.13; ix.12, 21; Blessings i.1; iii.22; v.20; Z xii.21; xiii.22
Cp. Dan. 12.3, 10.
Literally, 'one who imparts insight, intelligence'. (It is probable that in the Scrolls the word has a causative sense, but it can also mean simply 'one who possesses insight'.)

C. LAWS AND PRACTICES

ablutions	M iii.4f., 9; iv.21; v.13; Z x.10–13
atonement	M viii.6–9; ix.4–14; H col. iv.
blasphemy	M v.19; Z xv.1–5
calendar	HI (=M x) 1–7
contamination	Z xii.15–18
demoniacal possession	Z xii.2–3
dietary laws	Z xii.11–15
fraud	M vii.6f.
lost property	Z ix.11ff.
marriage	Z iv.21–v.6
name of God	M ii.6–7; Z xv.1–5
oath	M v.8; Z ix.9–16
oath, abrogation of	Z xv.6ff.
purity	M vi.16–22, 25; vii.3–16; viii.24
revenge	M i.11; ii.6–9; iv.11; v.2–25; Z ix.2–8
sabbath	Z x.14–xi.18
sacrifices	M ix.4–5
sanctuary, defilement of	Z xi.18–xii.2
slaves (servants)	Z xii.11
testimony	Z ix.17–x.3
vows	M v.8; Z xvi.13

D. OPPONENTS OF THE BROTHERHOOD

1. *Belial and his forces*

   M i.18, 23–24; Z iv.13, 15; v.18; viii.2; xii.2; W *passim;* RB *passim.*

Cp. Or. Sib., ii.165f.; Jubilees i.20; Testament of Reuben ii, of Levi, iii; of Zebulun, ix; of Naphtali, ii; of Benjamin, vi; Called 'spirit of darkness': Test. Levi xix; Joseph vii, xx. Cp. also Mat. 24.5–12; II Tim. 3.1f.; II Cor. 5.15; *Didache* 21.3.

2. *'Children of Corruption'*

Z vi.15; xiii.14

Cp. Jub. 10.3; 15.26; John 17.12; II Thess. 2.3; *Gospel of Nicodemus* 20.
The expression may have been derived from Deut. 32.5. (Cp. also Isa. 1.4.)

2a. *'Men of Corruption'*

M ix.16, 22; x.19

3. *'Sons of Darkness'*

M i.10; W i.1, 7, 10, 16; iii.6, 9; xiii.16; xiv.17, etc.

Cp. Montgomery, *Aram. Incantation Texts from Nippur* (1913), 16.7, where the epithet characterizes *demons* (like Arabic *jinn*).

4. *'Builders of a rickety wall'*

Z iv.19; viii.12, 18

Derived from Ezek. 13.10.

5. *'Prophets of deceit (delusion)'*

H iv.10, 20

Cp. in Mandaean, *Right Ginza* II, i.107 (tr. Lidzbarski, p. 43).

6. *'False prophets'*

H iv.16

Cp. Mat. 7.15; 24.11, 24; Mark 13.22; Luke 6.26; Acts 13.6; II Peter 2.1; I John 4.1. Mandaean, *Right Ginza* II, i.107.
H v.26: 'They that alter the works of God by propounding sinful mysteries'.
By 'prophets' the writers meant simply 'teachers', as in I Cor. 12.28; 14.29.

7. *'Lying (deceitful) interpreters'*

H ii.31; iv.9–10. Cp. also H ii.14

8. *'Seekers after smooth things'*

H ii.15, 32; Z i.18; NaC 2, 7

9. *'The froward'* (*Heb.* ḥelka'im).

H iii.25–26; iv.25, 35

Derived from Ps. 10.10 (where, however, the meaning is uncertain).

10. *'Furtive men, dissemblers'* (*Heb.* na'alamim).

H iii.28; iv.13; vii.34

Derived from Ps. 26.4.

11. *Specific Opponents:*
  (*a*) *'Man of lies'*

   Z xx.15; HabC ii.2; v.11

  Rabin cps. II Thess. 2.3.
  (*b*) *'Preacher of Lies'*

   Z viii.13

The Heb. means properly, 'Dribbler of lies', in reference to Mic. 2.6, 11.
  (*c*) *'Man of Scoffing'*

   Z i.14; xx.11 (pl.)

Cp. Isa. 28.14; Prov. 29.8.
  (*d*) *'Men of Scoffing who are in Jerusalem'*

   IsaC, *b* ii.6, 10; cp. Z xx.11

  (*e*) *'House of Absalom'*

   HC v.9

For the interpretation, see above, p. 29.
  (*f*) *'House of Peleg'*

   Z xx.22

A concocted name. Heb. *p-l-g* means 'divide'. Hence, the meaning is, 'devisive elements'.
  (*g*) *'The Wicked Priest'*

   HabC viii.3; ix.9; xi.4

  (*h*) *'The Lion of Wrath'*

   NaC 5, 6

Perhaps intended to convey the idea of 'the Lion *of the Era of Wrath'*; see below, E. 1.
Cp. Slavonic Enoch 56.5: 'They (the heathen kings) will break forth as lions from their lairs . . . and go up and tread under the land of the elect'.

E. PAST AND FUTURE
(Theory of History and Eschatological Doctrines)

1. *History divided into 'Era of Wrath (Sin, Wickedness)' and 'Era of Favor'*
   (a) *'Era of Wrath'*

   Z i.5; H iii.28; frag. i.5; HosC, *b* i.12

   Cp. Zeph. 1.5 ('Day of Wrath'), and cp. Talmud, B.B. 10a, Shab. 11a; Ab.Zar. 18b, for 'Wrath' as an eschatological term. Cp. also Ecclus. 48.10.
   (b) *'Era of Wickedness'*

   Z vi.10, 14; xii.23; xiv.19; xv.7, 10; xx.23 ('Era of Perfidy')

   Cp. Enoch 22.12; 80.2.
   (c) *'Era of Favor'*

   H xv.15; frag. ix.8; NC

   Cp. Isa. 61.2 ('Year of favor'). The Samaritans likewise divide history into the 'Era of God's Turning Away' (*Fanutah*) and that of His 'Favor' (*Raḥutah*).

2. *Requital:*
   (a) *'The Final Era'* (*Heb.* qeṣ).

   M iii.23; iv.18, 25; Z iv.9, 10; xix.10; xx.15; HC vii.2

   (b) *'Time of Visitation Inquisition'* (*Heb.* pequdah)

   M iii.18; iv.18–19, 26

   (c) *Final Judgment*

   M iv.20

   (d) *'Day of Requital'*

   M ix.23

   Based on Deut. 32.35, read as in LXX and Samaritan text.
   (e) *Spirits and angels also will be judged*

   H vii.29

   (f) *'Messianic Travail'*

Hymn No. 5, *passim*

For the expression 'pangs of the Messiah', cp. Talmud, Shab. 118a; Sanh. 98b; Mat. 24.8; Mark 13.8–9; I Thess. 5.3. Cp. also Enoch 62.4.

Described: Jubilees 20.11–25; Or. Sib. ii.154f.; II Esdras v–vi; Mat. 24.6–29; Rev. chs. 6–9; Talmud, Sanh. 96b–97a.

(g) *Conflagration (Ekpyrosis)*

H iii.29ff.; W xiv.17. Cp. also M ii.8

Cp. Mal. 3.19 (4.1); Dan. 7.10f.; Psalms of Solomon 15.14f.; Enoch 67.6; 98.3; 108.3; Test. Zebulun 2.38; Or. Sib., ii.253f., 296; iii.542, 689; iv.176; Luke 17.28; II Peter 3.6ff.; II Thess. 1.7f.; Rev. 19.20; 20.10, 14f.; 21.8. Berosus (quoted in Seneca, *Nat Qu.* ii.29, 1) predicted a final conflagration.

On non-Semitic parallels, cp. C. Clemen, *Primitive Christianity and Its Non-Jewish Sources* (1912), 161f.; M. Eliade, *The Myth of the Eternal Return* (1954), 87–88; R. Mayer, *Ist die biblische Vorstellung vom Weltenbrand eine Entlehnung aus dem Parsismus?* (1947).

(h) *Messianic Era of Forty Years*

Ps 37C, a7

Cp. Apoc. Esdras xiii.23–25; Talmud, Sanh. 99a; Midrash Tehillim xc, §393. Possibly based on Ps. 95.10 (cp. Yalqut Shime'oni *in loc.*).

(i) *War against Belial, Gog, etc.*

H iii.35f.; vi.29ff.; x.34–35; W *passim* (especially, i.10, 13–14)

Cp. Test. Levi, v.27; of Dan. ii.10–11; John 12.31; II Cor. 6.15.

Gog and Magog: Isa. 25.6; Zech. 14.2. Cp. Or. Sib. iii.319, 519, 632f.; v.101; Syriac Apoc. Baruch 70.7–10; Pal. Targum to Num. 9.6; 24.17; Enoch 56; 90.16; Assum. Mosis 8.1ff.; II Esdras 5.6; 13.33f.; Mishnah, 'Eduyoth ii.10. The basic notion occurs already in Theopompus quoted by Plutarch, *De Is.*, 47.

ablution after victory	W xiv.3
cavalry	W vi.8–17
exhortation before battle	W xv.6ff.
prayer before battle	W x.2–xiv.2
prayer, high priest's, before battle	W xv.4–6
priests, role of	W vii.9ff.

song of return	W xiv.2
song of victory	W xiv.2–18
standards, military	W iii.12–v.2
testudo ('tower')	W ix.10ff.
troops, age of	W vii.1–9
trumpets	W col.iii.
trumpet signals	W vii.9–ix.9
weapons, described	W v.2–vi.6

(*k*) *Other Disasters:*

(i)	shafts of perdition loosed	H iii.16, 27
(ii)	doors of perdition opened	H iii.18; vi.24
(iii)	traps of perdition sprung	H iii.24
(iv)	dispersal of wicked	H iv.26

3. *Rewards:*

(a) *Renewal (Rebirth) of the World*

M iv.25; H xi.13–14; xiii.11–13

Cp. Test. Abraham; Jubilees i.29; Enoch 72.1; IV E--
5.45; Mat. 19.28; Jewish 'Burial Kaddish'; *Manichaean:*
F. W. K. Müller, *Handschriftenreste,* ii.15 (employing the
Iranian term *frasagard*).
Renewal (rebirth) is also an element of mystical experi-
ence; cp. George Fox, *Journal,* ed. N. Penny (1911), I, ch.
ii. 'Now was I come up in spirit through the Flaming
Sword into the Paradise of God. *All things were new'.*

(b) *Eternal Peace*

M ii.4; H xi.27; xv.16; xviii.30; Blessings iii.5, 21

(c) *Sevenfold Light*

H vii.24–25

Cp. Talmud, Sanhedrin 91b (sevenfold Messianic sun);
Midrash Konen 24–25 (based on Isa. 30.26). Cp. also Isa.
60.19; Rev. 21.23, 25; 22.6; *Odes of Solomon,* 21.5; Slav.
Enoch 66.8.

(d) *Prophetic Forerunner of Messianic Age*

M ix.11; RB, *passim;* WC, *passim.*

Based on Deut. 18.18 and Mal. 3.23ff. (Cp. Ecclesiasticus
48.10.) Samaritans identify him with Moses Redivivus;
Jews, with Elijah (Talmud, Menaḥoth 45a; B.M. 3a;
Aboth de Rabbi Nathan 24.4).
Cp. I Macc. 14.41; 4.46; Mat. 11.14; 17.10ff.; Mark 9.11f.;
John 1.45; 5.46; 6.14; 7.40; Acts 7.37; Rev. 11.3ff.
Often alternates with *priestly* forerunner. (Note that both

Moses and Elijah were priests.) Cp. Test. Levi, v.13–20; Heb. 3.1; 4.15ff.; 5.4, 10; 6.20.

(e) *Messianic 'Star'*

Z vii.18

Based on Num. 24.17. Cp. Test. Levi, v.15; Judah, iv.20; Samaritan Liturgy, ed. Cowley, ii.88; Heh 10; 92.17; 96.32 (all by Abisha b. Pinehas, d. 1376).

(f) *'Faithful Shepherd' will arise*

NC 3, 2, 8

Based on Isa. 63.11. Cp. Heb. 13.20. 'Shepherd of souls': I Peter 2.25. Cp. also John 10.11, 14; I Peter 5.4.
Enoch 90.17–27 speaks of God as the Master Shepherd who will deliver his flock from the seventy evil shepherds.

(g) *New Covenant will be concluded*

NC 2, 6

Based on Jer. 31.32–33. For the true meaning, see above, pp. 4, 23. The Covenant will be inscribed on human hearts: H xviii.27. Cp. Jer. 31.33; Rom. 2.14f. (Stoic parallel adduced in Feine, *Der Römerbrief* [1903], 95ff.)

(h) *God records deeds of men for reward or punishment*

H i.23–24; xvi.10; RB v–vi.11.

Cp. Dan. 7.10; II Esdras 6.20; Rev. 20.12; Slavonic Enoch 50.1; Odes of Solomon 9.12; Apoc. Baruch 24.1. Rabbinic parallels in L. Ginzberg, *Legends of the Jews*, v.128, n. 141.
Iranian parallel: Yasna 31.13–14; 32.6 (record kept by Ahura Mazda).

(i) *Righteous will acquire crown of glory*

M iv.7; H ix.24

Odes of Solomon 9.11; I Peter 5.4; *Mandaean:* Lidzbarski, *Mand. Lit.*, 4f., 29, 108, 177, 243, 267.
Initiants in mystery cults sometimes received a crown: Apuleius, *Met.* xi.24; Tertullian, *Cor.* 15a; *Praescr. haer.* 40. Was this a prefiguration of the heavenly crown which awaited them?

(j) *Righteous will acquire robe of majesty*

M iv.8

Cp. Enoch 62.16; Slavonic Enoch 22.8.

(k) *Righteous will unite in triumphant song*

H xi.5, 14, 26

Cp. TB Sanhedrin 19b: 'All the prophets will then intone a song in concert'; Yalqut, Isa. 296.
Iranian parallel: Bundahesh 31.
(1) *Future Community will be the true temple of God*

M viii.5f.; F i.6

Cp. I Cor. 3.16–17; Eph. 2.20–22. Cp. also Heb. 8.2; Barnabas, 3.12.

F. ANGELOLOGY

See in general the writer's article, 'Angel' in *The Interpreter's Dictionary of the Bible.*

1. *General names for angels:*
    (a) *'divine beings'*

    Heb. *elim:* H x.8; frag. ii.3, 10; W i.10, 11; xiv.15, 16; xv.14; xvii.7; Oration iv.1; AL *(a)* 2, 5, 10

    Heb. *elohim:* AL *(b)* 5, 7
    (b) *'holy ones'*

    Z xx.8; H iii.22; iv.25; x.35; xi.12; W xii.4, 7, 8; xviii.2; Oration iv.1, etc.

    Cp. Enoch, *passim.*
    (c) *'host of heaven'*

    H iii.35; W vii.6; xii.1, 8, 9

    (d) *'host of the holy ones'*

    H iii.22; x.34–35. Cp. 'host of angels', W xii.8

    (e) *'eternal host'*

    H xi.13

    (f) *'communion of the holy ones'*

    H iv.25; frag. lxiii.2

    Derived from Ps. 89.8(7).
    (g) *'sons of heaven'*

    H iii.22; frag. ii.10; W iv.22; xi.8

    Cp. Enoch 6.2; 13.8; 14.3.
    (h) *'stalwarts'* (Heb. *gibbôrê kôᵃḥ*)

H viii.11; x.34–35. (Cp. W v.21; iii.35–36; AL (*a*) 5)

Derived from Ps. 103.20.

(i) *'glorious ones'*

H x.8

Cp. Enoch 24.6 (Charles); Slavonic Enoch 21.3; 22.9.

2. *Classes of angels:*

(a) *seven archangels*

AL (*a*). Called 'arch-princes'; cp. Ezek. 38.2; 39.1.

Cp. Tobit 12.15; Enoch 20.1–8; 21; 81.5; 90.21–22; Test. Levi 8.1; Luke 1.19, 26; Rev. 1.4; 8.2; Hermas, Sim. 9.31; Hechaloth, c.iv.

(b) *'angels of the presence'*

H vi.13; Blessings iv.25–26; AL (*b*) 1

Cp. Enoch 104.1; Slavonic Enoch 21.1; Jubilees 1.27, 29; Test. Levi 3.5, 7, and very frequently in rabbinic literature.

(c) *'ministering angels'*

H v.21; xii.23; xv.24; frag. ii.14; AL (*a*) 1

Cp. Heb. 1.14. The morning *Yoser*-prayer in the Jewish liturgy mentions the 'holy ones' and the 'ministering angels' as standing 'at the crest of the world', singing praises and 'receiving each from each the yoke of the kingdom of heaven' (Singer, p. 38).

(d) *'angels of sanctification'*

M vii.6; x.11; H i.11; Oration ii.8; Blessings iii.6; AL (*a*)

(e) *Cherubim*

AL (*a*)

Derived directly from Ezek. 10. Cp. also Enoch 14.16–17; 71.7; Slavonic Enoch 21.1.

3. *Particular angels:*

(a) Prince of Lights   M iii.20
(b) Angel of Darkness   M iii.20–21
(c) Angel of Truth   M iii.24
(d) Maṣṭemah   Z iv. 13; v. 18; vii.2; xvi.5

Cp. Jubilees 49.2. The name is related to Satan.

4. *Protective angels:*

   (a) Gabriel   W ix.16

   Cp. Ginzberg, *Legends*, v.21. Origen. *De princip.*, i.81, says
   that Gabriel is the angel of war.

   (b) Michael   M ix.15, 16; xvii.6, 7

   Cp. Dan. 10.21; Rev. 12.7; Jude 9; Ginzberg, *op. cit.*, v.4.

   (c) Raphael   M ix.15

   (d) Sariel (or Uriel)   W ix.15

   Gabriel and Michael are mentioned also in a fragmentary
   text from Qumran provisionally entitled *The Book of
   Noah;* D. Barthélemy and J. T. Milik, *Discoveries in the
   Judean Desert,* I (1955), 84–86.

5. *Angels possess transcendental knowledge*

   M iv.22; H iii.23; frag. xiii.23; AL (*a*) 1

   Cp. Slavonic Enoch 22.11; TB Ḥagîgah 16a.
   Michael, Uriel and Raguel initiate Enoch into the 'mys-
   teries of the world': Jubilees 4.21; Enoch 40.4–5.
   Michael tells Adam and Eve the mysteries of creation:
   Apoc. Mosis 3.13.

6. *Angels sing praises in heaven*

   H ix.13; AL (*a*) *passim*

   They sing the Trisagion: Isa. 6.2–3; cp. Enoch 39.12f.;
   Slavonic Enoch 8.8; 17.1; 19.6; 20.3; 21.1; 22.3; 31.1f.;
   42.4; TB Ḥullin 14a. See also S. Baer, *Abodath Israel,*
   120; Apoc. Paul, 10.
   On the liturgy of the angels, cp. Apoc. Mosis 17; Test.
   Abraham B, iv; Pal. Targum, Gen. 32.27; Ex. 14.24;
   S. Singer, *Authorized Daily Prayerbook,* 38, 45, 160.

7. *Angels participate in the eschatological war*

   H iii.35f.; vi.29f.; x.34–35; W xv.14

   Based on Zech. 14.3, 5. Cp. also Test. Levi 1.19

8. *Evil Spirits:*
   (a) *'angels of destruction'*

   M iv.12; Z ii.6; W xiii.12; xiv.10

   Cp. Enoch 53.3; 56.1; TB Shabbath 88a, and often. The
   Samaritans speak similarly of 'angels of perturbation'
   (*mala'che rigzah*).
   (b) *'satans'*

H frags. iv.6; xlv.3; Blessings i.8

(c) *'ruinous spirit'* (Heb. *mashḥîth*)

H frags. iv.6; xlv.3

Derived from Ex. 12.13, as popularly interpreted.

BIBLICAL QUOTATIONS AND PARALLELS

This index is intended to serve as a tool for those who may wish to trace the main Biblical parallels to the Scrolls. It is therefore geared to the columns and lines of the original texts, even though these have been indicated in the translations only *by sections.*

In the case of the Old Testament, the parallels are *verbal,* representing direct quotations woven into the texts. In that of the New Testament, however, what is usually involved is a correspondence of *ideas and concepts,* though in certain instances verbal identity is also to be found.

An interesting feature of the Old Testament parallels is that there is no quotation from the Book of Esther, the one book of Scripture that has not yet turned up among the Qumran fragments.

Parallels which depend on restoration of the text are indicated by asterisks.

19.18	H ix.5
20.13, 16, 19	RB i–iv, 14
21.8	H v.5
23.7	M v.15
33.7	Inv. 20
34.6	H i.16; xvi.6

LEVITICUS

12.8	H fr. ii.13
13.6, 17	PG 13
13.51	H v.28
14.43	PG 13
14.48	PG
16.30	H fr. ii.13
17.7	M i.6
18.13	Z v.9
19.17	Z vii.2
19.18	Z vi.20; vii.5
23.28	Z xi.18
26.4	HT I.4
26.5	PI vi.7
26.15	PI vi.7
26.21, 23	M i.25–26
26.24, 27, 40, 41	PI vi.6
26.40	PI vi.5–6
26.41	PI vi.5
26.44	PI v.7
26.45	Z i.4; PI v.9–10

NUMBERS

4.13	Inv. 11
4.32	W ii.5
5.14, 30	H ii.15
6.9	C 1
6.24–26	M ii.2–4
8.21	H fr. ii.13
10.9	W x.6–8
10.35	C 13
	(Targ. Onqelos)
11.4	RB x–xi.5
14.9	Sp. 13–14
14.17	PI ii.7

14.19–20	PI ii.7
14.22	RB i.7
21.18	Z vi.23
24.8	W xii.11
24.17	W vii.19–20; xi.6–7
24.18	W xi.6–7
30.17	Z vii.9; viii.2

DEUTERONOMY

1.43	PI ii.18
4.29	PI ii.13
5.12	Z x.16
5.29	M i.15
6.5	M v.9; C 1
6.6–7	H iv.9
6.18	M i.2
7.12	Blessings
7.21–22	W x.1
8.5	PI iii.6–7
8.10	Inv. 13
9.5	Z viii.14
9.8	PI ii.18
9.19	PI ii.8
9.23	Z iii.7
10.12	PI ii.13
11.13	PI ii.13
11.17	HT I.4
12.28	M i.2
14.1	PI iii.4–5
14.2	PI iii.9
15.2	LJ 3
17.11	M i.15
17.17	Z v.2
17.20	M i.15
20.3	W x.2–5; xv.8
20.4	W x.2–5
23.24	Z xvi.6
26.7	PI vi.11–12
26.15	W xii.2
28.12	Blessings
28.15	M i.15
28.20	L I, i.2

28.28	PI ii.14	**II SAMUEL**	
29.17(18)	H iv.14	1.19, 25	W xii.11
29.18(19)	M ii.13–14	7.8	PI iv.7
30.2, 8	PI v.13	17.20	Ex I–II, i.12
30.3–4	PI v.11–12	22.5	H ix.3–4
*30.19	L I, i.2	22.6	H iii.19
*31.14	L I, i.2		
31.21	PI iii.12	**I KINGS**	
*31.26	cp. L I, i.2	5.18	PI iv.12–13
*31.28	cp. L I, i.2	8.38–39	PG 2
31.29	PI iii.13, 17		
32.22	H iii.31; xvii.13	**II KINGS**	
32.24	H v.27	19.3	H iii.8
32.33	Z viii.9; H v.10, 27	24.2	W i.1
32.35 (Sam., LXX)			
	HI 19 (=M x.19);	**I CHRONICLES**	
	W vii.22; LJ 15	16.27	MH 2
33.28	HT I.3	28.18	AL *a* 12
34.42	W xii.11–12; xix.4	29.15	RB i.8, 12, 13
		II CHRONICLES	
JOSHUA		6.29	PG 2
1.7	M i.15	11.2	PI iv.7
23.6	M i.15	14.1	M i.2
		*20.6	H fr. iii.12
JUDGES		*29.15	Ex I–II, i.13
5.12	W xii.10	30.7	PG 2
13.8	H fr. i.2	30.27	W xii.2
		31.20	M i.2
RUTH			
2.20	Sp 6	**EZRA**	
		9.8	H vi.8; W xiii.8
I SAMUEL		9.9	H vi.8
1.27	PG 3	10.2	H iii.20
2.3	M iii.15; H i.26;		
	*H fr. iii.12; iv.15	**NEHEMIAH**	
4.19	H iii.7	2.11	RB xiv.3
6.18	H iii.7	4.6	RB i.7
6.21	RB i.12	5.5	L I, i.1
9.6	D 7		
13.14	D 7	**JOB**	
16.7–12	D 1–7	1.10	H ii.21
16.21	Ex I–II, i.12	3.3	H iii.19
25.29	H ii.20		

3.5	H v.34	9.6	H ii.29
3.10	H xi.1, 19	9.9	C 10
4.7	C 22	*10.9	WH 11
*8.7	Ex I–II, i.13	10.10	H iii.25
8.9	Ex I–II, i.13	11.1–2	RB v–vi.7–8
8.12	Ex I–II, i.10	11.6	H v.30
8.13	C 10	12.7	H v.16; RB x–xi.1
9.16	PG 17	13.2–3	RB ix–x.10
9.18	H xi.19	16.3	RB xiv.2
10.21	WH 11	17.5	WH 3
12.10	Sp 3	17.6	PG 3
14.19	C 10	*18.4	H v.38–39
*15.8	H x.4–5	18.5	H iii.28, 29
16.22	WH 11	18.6	H iii.8
18.9	H fr. iii.8;	18.40	W i.3
	*RB v–vi.6	19.14	H iii.21
19.3	RB i.7	20.4	Inv. 11
25.6	H vi.34	20.9(8)	H iv.22, 36
27.4	WH 2	22.15(14)	H vii.4
29.10	H v.31	22.27	HT I.5
30.3	H v.30; ix.6	24.8	W xii.9
30.9	H ii.11	25.5	Sp 17
31.22	H vii.2; viii.33	25.7	PG 12
33.6	HI 48 (=M xi.22)	25.20	PG 20
33.24	WH 11	26.7	H iii.23
33.30	M iii.7	26.11	H ii.30
34.22	Ex II.6–7	27.14	Sp 12 (cp. Targum)
38.7	MH 5	28.4	L I, i.4
38.17	WH 10	29.5	H fr. iii
38.27	H v.30; ix.6	30.10	WH 11
39.23	H ii.26	31.3	PG 3
41.23(31)	H iii.15	31.10(9)	H v.34
		31.13(12)	H iv.9
PSALMS		31.22	H fr. v.8–9
1.4	H vii.23	35.5	H vii.23
3.5–6	PG 17	35.7	PI vii.7–8;
3.17	H fr. iii		H fr. iii.4
5.12	Sp 5	35.7–8	H ii.29
6.2–3	RB xii–xiii.2–3	36.7	PI vii.7–8
6.8	H v.34	36.8	Sp 12
*7.3	L I, i.9	37.2	W xv.11
7.7	W xiv.16	37.14	WH ˙˙
9.2	H iii.23	37.23	H xv

37.39	Inv. 17	82.3	H ii.24
40.3	H v.20; vii.8	84.11	Ex II.4–5
40.18	PG 19	86.1	PG 3
41.10(9)	H v.23	86.14	H ii.21
42.5	AL *a* 2	88.4	H viii.29
42.6, 12(11)	H viii.29	88.6	cp. H viii.29
42.7	H viii.32	89.8(7)	H iv.25
43.5	H viii.32	89.14	HT II.4
44.14	WH 1–2	89.15	MH 3
46.7	H vi.7	91.3	Ex II.5
48.12	W xii.13; xix.5	92.3	Sp 9
*50.22	L I, i.9	92.10	HT II.5
51.4	Sp 13	92.11	H vii.22
51.10	H ii.5	94.17	WH 7
51.19(17)	M viii.3	96.6	MH 2
54.5	H ii.21	97.2	MH 3
55.9	H fr. iii.6	102.5	PG 17
55.16	H vi.28	102.6	H ix.4
56.14(13)	M iii.7	102.10(9)	H v.34
57.2(1)	Sp 12	103.4	Sp 8
57.3	H v.10	103.6	Sp 7
57.5	H v.6–7, 10	103.15	RB i.11
57.6, 12	W xii.18	104.35	cp. HT I.2
58.6(5)	H v.27–28	105.27	Ex I–II, i.15
59.4	H fr. iii.15	105.28	Ex II.3
59.8	H v.10	106.15	PG 3
64.4	H v.13	106.22	Ex I–II, i.15
65.12	MH 6	106.43	C 15
67.4	Inv. 19	107.11	Ex II.3
67.7	HT I.4	107.16	H v.37
68.6	W xii.2	107.25	H fr. iii.6
68.21	WH 3	107.27	H iii.14–15
69.15	H v.20	107.29	H v.18
69.22	H iv.11	108.6	W xii.18
69.35	HT II.1	112.6	C 1
69.37	Sp 5	115.17	WH 7
70.16	PG 19	116.3	H iii.28
*74.21	RB xii–xiii.3	*116.16	H xi.32
78.7	WH 15	118.15	H xii.3
78.21	L I, ii.1	119.1	M iv.22; AL *b* 6
78.70–71	D 7	119.7	PG 9
79.4	WH 1–2	119.34	PG 9
82.1	LJ 9	119.50	RB v–vi.5–6

119.115	WH 15
119.132	Sp 5
120.1	PG 17
120.4	H v.13
122.3	Inv. 4, 13
137.6	H v.31
138.3	H xii.1
139.6	H vii.8
139.12f.	Ex II.6–7
140.4	H v.13
142.4	H fr. iii.4
142.5	L I, i.13–14
143.2	PG 8
144.8	PG 9
145.5	PG 10
148.8	H fr. iii.6
148.13	HT I.1

PROVERBS

1.16	WH 3
2.16	H iv.7; WH 2
2.19	WH 2
3.17	H fr. iii.3
3.20	HT I.3
4.11	WH 17
4.24	H v.24
4.26	H vii.31
*5.5	WH 10
6.19	H v.23–24
6.20	WH 15
7.5	H iv.7; WH 2
7.9	WH 2
7.15	WH 1
7.27	H x.34
8.3	WH 12
8.22	WH 8
9.14	WH 10
10.7	C 1
10.28	C 10
11.7	C 10
12.1	H ii.14
14.22	WH 9
15.8	Z xi.20

15.11	H iii.19
16.1	H ii.7
16.9	HI 36 (=M xi.10)
16.31	WH 15
20.24	H xv.13
20.27	Ex III.12
21.10	H iv.13
28.10	WH 14
29.5	H fr. iii.4
29.27	WH 15

ECCLESIASTES

7.22	C 15
10.18	M iv.9

ISAIAH

*1.26	
2.3	Inv. 19
2.19, 21	Ex I–II, i.15
2.22	M v.17
5.2	H viii.22
5.6	H viii.25
*5.29	L I, i.9
*6.3	H xvi.3
6.10	H vii.2
6.13	RB xii–xiii.5
7.17	Z vii.11; xiv.1
8.11	LJ 24
9.5	H iii.10
*10.3	Ex II.8
11.12	RB xii–xiii.11
13.4	H vi.7
14.1	C 8
14.4	H iii.25
14.11	WH 5
*16.7	L II.10
17.11	H v.28; viii.9
17.13	H vii.23
19.8	H iii.26; v.8
19.14	H vi.23
24.17	Z iv.14
24.21	H fr. v.12

26.1	H iii.27
26.3	M iv.5
26.6	H vii.8
26.16	PI v.16–17
27.11	H ii.19
28.11	H iii.18–19; iv.16
28.15, 18	H vi.35
28.16	M viii.7; H vi.26
28.17	H iii.27; viii.22
29.24	HI 27 (=M x.1)
30.2	Sp 12
30.7	W i.11–12
30.7–8	Ex II.4
30.10	H ii.15
30.17	H vi.34
30.18	AL *a* 7
30.30	H ii.27
31.8	W xi.11–12
32.2	Inv. 17
32.14	H vii.9
33.14	WH 7
34.9	H iii.31
35.4	H ii.9; v.21–22
35.6 (adapted)	W xiv.6
35.7	H viii.4
37.5	H iii.8
37.17	PG 3
37.30	RB v–vi.2
38.10	WH 10
38.17	H iii.19
38.18–19	Sp 1–2
40.3	M viii.14; ix.19
40.6–7	Ex I–II, i.10
40.17	PI iii.3; H fr. iii.10
40.22	WH 7
40.24	H viii.23
41.12	Ex I–II, i.12
41.14	H xi.12
41.19	H viii.5
41.24	H ii.28
42.1	M viii.6
42.13	H ix.3

42.14 (adapted)	H iii.12
43.3	NC i.5
43.23–24	PI v.19
44.3	PI v.15
44.18	H iv.23
45.2	H v.37
*45.17	H i.10; *Ex II.12
48.17	PI v.20–21
49.10	H viii.4
49.18	H ix.36
49.23	W xii.14–15
50.1–2	PI ii.15; Sp 10
50.3	H v.31
50.4	H vii.10; viii.36
50.5	C 8
51.6	W xv.10
51.7	Z i.1; PI ii.13
51.12	RB i.11
51.13	PI v.18
52.7	LJ 16
54.6	L II.6
54.16	Z vi.8
55.4	D 7
56.1	H v.12; C 2
56.3	C 8
56.8	RB xii–xiii.11
57.20	H ii.12–13; iii.32; viii.15
58.9	HI 27 (=M xi.1)
58.11	H viii.16
59.7	WH 7
59.8	H ii.27–28
*59.12	L I, i.15
59.20	HI 20 (=M x.20)
60.7	PI iv.12
60.11	W xii.13–14; xiv.6
60.20	H vii.25
60.21	H xviii.14
61.1	H xviii.14; LJ 1
61.2	*H xviii.15; LJ 9
61.13	LJ 19
*63.2, 3, 6	RB i–iv.15

63.15	HI 3 (=M x.3);
	H iii.34; W xii.1
64.10	PI iv.12
66.7	H iii.9
66.10	C 9
66.11	C 5
66.24	H xiii.16

JEREMIAH

3.17	M i.6
4.19	H fr. iv.13
4.31	H iii.7
6.8	L I, i.12–13
*9.10	L I, i.11–12
10.12–13	MH 7–9
*10.22	L I, i.11–12
10.23	HI 36 (=M xi.10)
*14.7	L I, i.15
14.8	Inv. 17
14.22	PI vi.14
15.4	M ii.6
15.11	Inv. 17
*16.9	H ii.2
17.3	PI viii.24
*17.18	H viii.17; x.25–26
18.18	RB xii–xiii.1
18.22	H fr. iii.4
*20.9	H viii.30
21.8	Ex II.1–2
23.22	RB i–iv.7
25.31	Z i.14
30.7	Inv. 17
31.11	H ii.35
31.22	H xiii.11–12
32.19	H i.5; xvi.8
33.6	RB x–xi.4
33.8	Sp 13
*34.22	L I, i.11–12
34.23	NC ii.8
42.18	H iii.28
47.2	H viii.17
47.6	H v.14–15

*48.6	H viii.24
48.26	H fr. iv.13
*48.31	L II.10
49.32	W xii.12
51.15–16	MH 7–9

LAMENTATIONS

1.1	L II.4, 5
*1.2	L II.9
1.3	H fr. iii.4
1.4	L I, i.11
1.7	W i.6
*1.15	L I, i.14–15
*2.18	H xi.19
3.9	H v.25
3.10	WH 11
3.22	C 2
3.40	Ex II.1
*4.2	H iii.6
4.3	L I, ii.4
*4.5	L I, ii.6–7

EZEKIEL

1.27	AL a 4
4.5	Z i.6
7.17	H iv.33–34
10.1	AL a 2
10.9, 11	AL a 3
11.17	RB xii–xiii.11
11.19	H xviii.26
14.3, 4, 7	M ii.12; H iv.5
16.10–13	L I, ii.12
18.31	PI vi.2
19.5	C 10
20.28	RB ix.3
20.34–36	RB v–vi.4
20.35	W i.3
21.3 (20.47)	H iii.29–30
21.8	RB ix.8
21.8, 9, 13	RB i–iv.16
21.12(7)	H iv.33–34
22.4–5	PI vi.13
23.46	M ii.6

26.21	Ex I–II, i.12	6.3	H iv.5
28.23	MH 1	*9.11	RB v–vi.11
31.6	cp. H viii.8	9.16	PG 14
31.14	H viii.5–6	10.8	H viii.25
34.27	HT I.4	12.15	H xi.19
35.8	W xv.1	14.2	Sp 14
36.3	H ii.1; Sp 14	14.3 (LXX)	H i.28
36.26	H xviii.26	14.5	H xiv.26; xv.10
37.11	C 10		
38.10 (39.1)		**JOEL**	
	AL *b* 1, 3, 5, 7, 10	2.6	H fr. iii
38.16	W xii.9	2.20	RB xii–xiii.8
38.23	W xi.15		
39.10	W xii.10	**AMOS**	
44.15	Z iii.21–iv.2	2.14	W xix.11
		3.9	H iii.25
DANIEL		5.11	C 4
4.9	cp. H viii.8	5.16 (adapted)	H xi.14
4.13, 17, 23	MP ii.1	5.26–27	Z vii.14
7.15	MP ii.10	7.4	PI vii.7–8
9.7	H xvi.9; PI vi.3	9.11	Z vii.16
9.24	C 16		
9.26	LJ 18(?)	**OBADIAH**	
9.27	H iii.36	21	W vi.16
10.5(6)	H iii.7		
11.15	Ex I–II, i.8	**JONAH**	
11.34	RB i–iv.16	2.6	H iii.18
11.35	RB v–vi.3; ix.3;	2.8	H viii.29
	x–xi.10	4.8	H vii.5
12.1	PI vi.14		
*12.2	ET ii.5–6	**MICAH**	
12.10	RB v–vi.3; ix.3;	1.4	H iv.34
	x–xii.10	2.10	H iii.8
		2.12	RB xii–xiii.8
HOSEA		6.8	M iv.5; v.4; viii.2
2.17	W x.9	7.2	Z xvi.15
3.4	Z xx.16	7.19	H xvii.15
4.14	H ii.19; iv.7		
4.16	Z i.13	**NAHUM**	
5.5 (Targum)	Sp 14	1.2	Z ix.15
5.8	RB i–iv.13	1.6	H iii.28
5.10	Z v.20; viii.3	1.11	H vi.21

2.1	HT II.3
2.2	H ii.6

HABAKKUK

1.4	H iv.25
2.1	H vii.29; H fr. iv.5
2.3 (LXX)	H v.27
2.15	H iv.10–11

ZEPHANIAH

1.15	H v.30; ix.6
2.15	LJ i.9; C 8
3.4	RB i–iv.7

ZECHARIAH

2.15	C 8
2.17	W xii.2; PG 2
3.2	H fr. iv.6
3.8	H vii.21
7.14; 9.8	PI v.6
12.6	W xi.10
*13.1	WH 2

MALACHI

1.4	H ii.7; iii.24
1.10	Z vi.13

MATTHEW

3.3	M viii.14
3.11	M iii.7–8
5.33–37	cp. M v.8
7.13	M iii.18
10.1	Sp 15
11.14	M ix.11
12.43	Sp 15
17.10	M ix.11
18.8	M ii.7
19.28	M iv.25
24.8	H v, *passim*
24.22, 24	M viii.6; H ii.13

MARK

1.8	M iii.7–8

1.23	Sp 15
3.11, 30	Sp 15
5.2, 8, 13	Sp 15
6.7	Sp 15
9.11ff.	M ix.11
9.25	Sp 15
9.43	M ii.7
13.8	H v, *passim*
13.20, 22, 27	M viii.6; H ii.13

LUKE

3.16	M iii.7–8
4.35–36	Sp 15
6.18	Sp 15
8.29	Sp 15
9.42	Sp 15
11.24	Sp 15
16.8	M i.10
17.28	H iii.29f.
18.7	M viii.6; H ii.13

JOHN

1.3	HI 20 (=M xi.1–2)
1.9	H iv.6; xviii.29
1.21	M ix.11
1.23	M viii.14
1.33	M iii.7–8
3.21	M i.5; v.3
4.4	H ii.18; v.26; viii.4, 7
5.46	M ix.11
6.14	M ix.11
7.40	M ix.11
8.23	HI 27–28 (=M xi.5–6)
8.31	M i.10; v.10
8.42	M iv.9
10.11, 14	NC
12.31	W i.5; xiii.1–2; xv.10–12; xvii.5; xviii.3
12.36	M i.10
12.43	M iv.23; H xviii.15
14.7	Z xx.10

17.22	WC 3; Z iv.15
20.22	M iv.20f.

ACTS

1.5	M iii.7–8
2.17	M iv.21
2.42	M vi.3
4.32	M vi.2
4.34	M i.11f.
5.16	Sp 15
7.37	M ix.11
7.42–43	Z vii.14
10.45	M iii.6–7

ROMANS

1.24	H ii.16–19; v.36
1.29	M ix.11
2.7	M iv.6–7
2.14f.	H xviii.27
2.19	M i.10
8.17	M ii.2
8.33	M viii.6; H ii.13
11.4–5	Z i.4; ii.11

I CORINTHIANS

2.6	M viii.1
2.7	M i.20f.
2.9–10	
	HI 31–34 (=M xi.5–8)
3.9	H vi.15; viii.6, 10
3.13, 15	H iii.29f.
3.16–17	M ix.6;
	HI 34 (=M xi.8)
6.3	H x.34–35
6.9	M iv.11
10.16–17	MFC 17–21
14.15	HI 9 (=M x.9)
14.21	H iv.16
14.28	M vi.6
15.24	M iv.16–17, 25;
	Z vi.9; vii.8
	HabC vii.2, 12

II CORINTHIANS

3.2	H xviii.27
5.1	M ii.25
6.14	M iii.19ff.; H vi.19
6.17	M iv.15
11.14	Z v.18; M iii.20

GALATIANS

3.29	M iv.11
5.19	M ii.2
6.1	M iii.23

EPHESIANS

1.3	HI 29 (=M xi.7)
1.11	M ii.2
1.18	H iv.6, 27; v.3; xi.26
2.18	M ix.15–16
2.18–22	M viii.7–8
2.20–22	M viii.7–8
4.29	M vii.9;
	HI 22 (=M x.22)
4.31–32	M v.24–26
5.4	M vii.14
5.8–9	M i.10
5.16–17	CD
6.12	W, *passim*
6.16	H v.16

PHILIPPIANS

4.2	H vi.19

COLOSSIANS

1.12	H iii.21–22; vi.13;
	xi.11–12
3.5ff.	M v.23ff.
3.12	M viii.6; H ii.13

I THESSALONIANS

2.6	M iv.23; Z v.29
5.3	H v, *passim*
5.5	M i.9; ii.16;
	iii.13, 24f.;
	W, *passim*

II THESSALONIANS	
1.5	HI 29 (=M xi.7)
1.7f.	H iii.29f.
2.3	WC ii.1
2.13	M viii.6; H ii.13

I TIMOTHY	
3.6	H vi.15f.; viii.6, 10

II TIMOTHY	
2.10	M viii.6; H ii.13
3.8	Z v.19

TITUS	
3.5–6	M iv.21

HEBREWS	
8.2	M viii.7–8
10.22	M iv.21
13.20	NC

JAMES	
2.7	M vi.27

I PETER	
1.1	M viii.6; H ii.13
1.5	W i.5; xv.10–12
1.6	M viii.4; Z ix.66
1.7	M viii.4; Z ix.66
1.20	M iv.16–17; HabC vii.2, 7, 12
2.5	M viii.7–8
2.6	M viii.6
2.9	M viii.6
2.12	M iv.26
2.25	NC
3.6	M i.17
4.7	H i.35; cp. M iv.5; viii.3
5.4	M iv.7; NC

5.5	M v.23; vi.2
5.10	H xi.29

II PETER	
2.1	H ii.14, 31; iv.7, 9, 10, 16, 20
2.4	H x.34–35
2.4ff.	Z ii–iii
3.6f.	M ii.8; H iii.29f.
3.7, 10f.	H iii.29f.; vi.25f.

I JOHN	
1.5–7	M iii.19f.
2.1, 18, 28	Z ii.14
2.16	M i.6
3.19	H xi.11
4.6	M iii.5–6

II JOHN	
1	M viii.6
5	M v.25; Z viii.9

JUDE	
5ff.	Z ii–iii
6	Z ii.18
7	H iii.29f.; x.4
9	W ix.16; xvii. 6–7

REVELATION	
6.11 (7.9)	M iv.8
7.14	M viii.6
11.3ff.	M ix.11
12.7–9	W ix.16; xvii.6–7
16.8	H iii.29f.
17.14	M viii.6
19.20 (20.10, 14; 21.8)	H vi.25f.
20.8	W ix.16
21.23, 25 (22.6)	H vii.24
22.16	Z vii.19